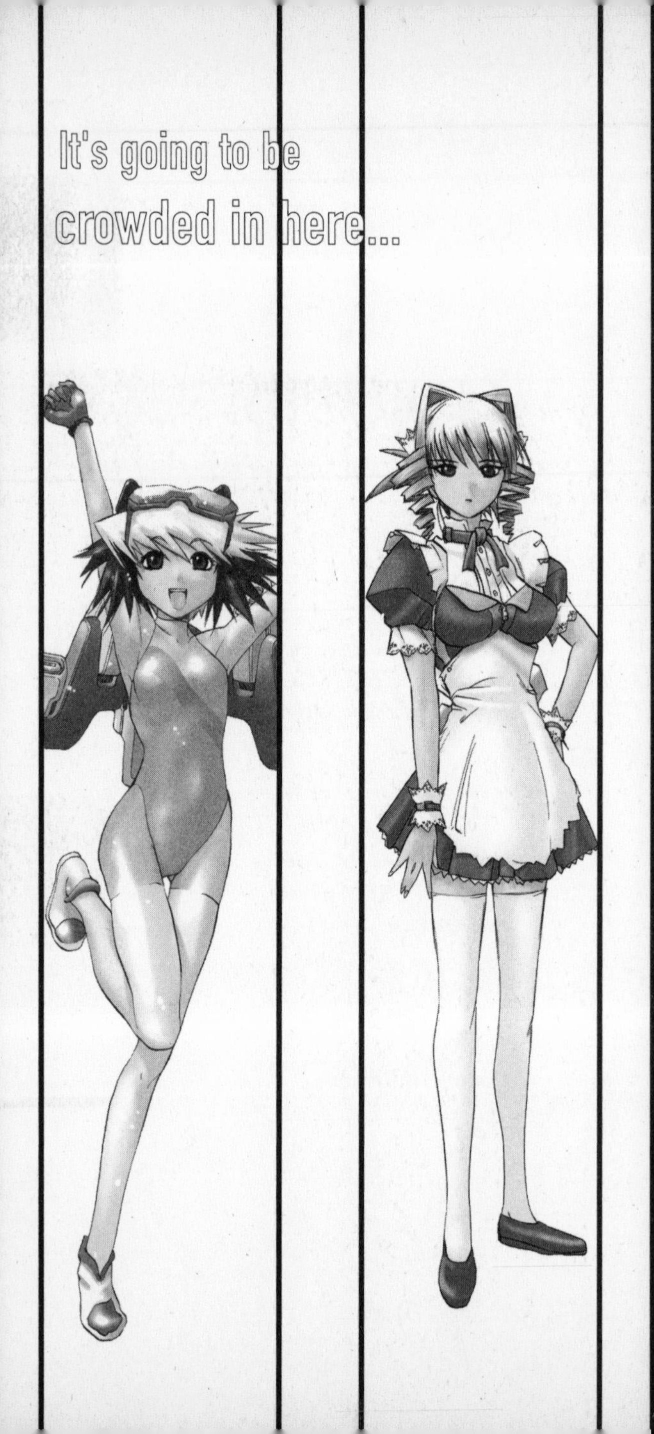
It's going to be
crowded in here...

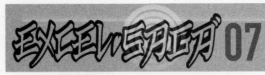

STORY AND ART BY
RIKDO KOSHI

EXCEL SAGA 07

**STORY AND ART BY
RIKDO KOSHI**

**ENGLISH ADAPTATION BY
POOKIE ROLF & CARL GUSTAV HORN**

**TRANSLATION
POOKIE ROLF**

**LETTERING & TOUCH-UP BY
AVRIL DASTRADA**

**COVER DESIGN
BRUCE LEWIS**

**GRAPHIC DESIGNER
NOZOMI AKASHI**

**EDITORS
MEGAN BATES & CARL GUSTAV HORN**

**MANAGING EDITOR
ANNETTE ROMAN**

**EDITOR IN CHIEF
ALVIN LU**

**PRODUCTION MANAGER
NOBORU WATANABE**

**SR. DIRECTOR OF LICENSING & ACQUISITIONS
RIKA INOUYE**

**VP OF MARKETING
LIZA COPPOLA**

**EXECUTIVE VICE PRESIDENT
HYOE NARITA**

**PUBLISHER
SEIJI HORIBUCHI**

EXCEL SAGA © 1997 Rikdo Koshi. Originally published in Japan in 1997 by SHONENGA-HOSHA CO., LTD. Tokyo. English translation rights arranged with SHONENGAHOSHA CO., LTD.

New and adapted artwork © 2004 VIZ, LLC
All rights reserved.

Printed in U.S.A.

Published by VIZ, LLC
P.O. Box 77064
San Francisco, CA 94107

Action Edition
10 9 8 7 6 5 4 3 2 1
First printing, June 2004

For advertising rates or media
kit, e-mail advertising@viz.com

5.   MISSION 1
A FOUL DEED IN SPRINGTIME
27.   MISSION 2
IN THE MIDST OF DRAMA
35.   MISSION 3
SCARS UPON A DREAM
59.   MISSION 4
WINGS TO ETERNITY (T-MINUS)
83.   MISSION 5
WINGS TO ETERNITY (T-PLUS)
109.   MISSION 6
THEY SAW IT
133.   MISSION 7
MY YOUTH IN _____
161.   MISSION 8
WHEN JAA, NE COMES MARCHING HOME
189.   OUBLIETTE
(EXCEL SAGA BONUS SECTION)

www.viz.com

www.animerica-mag.com

store.viz.com

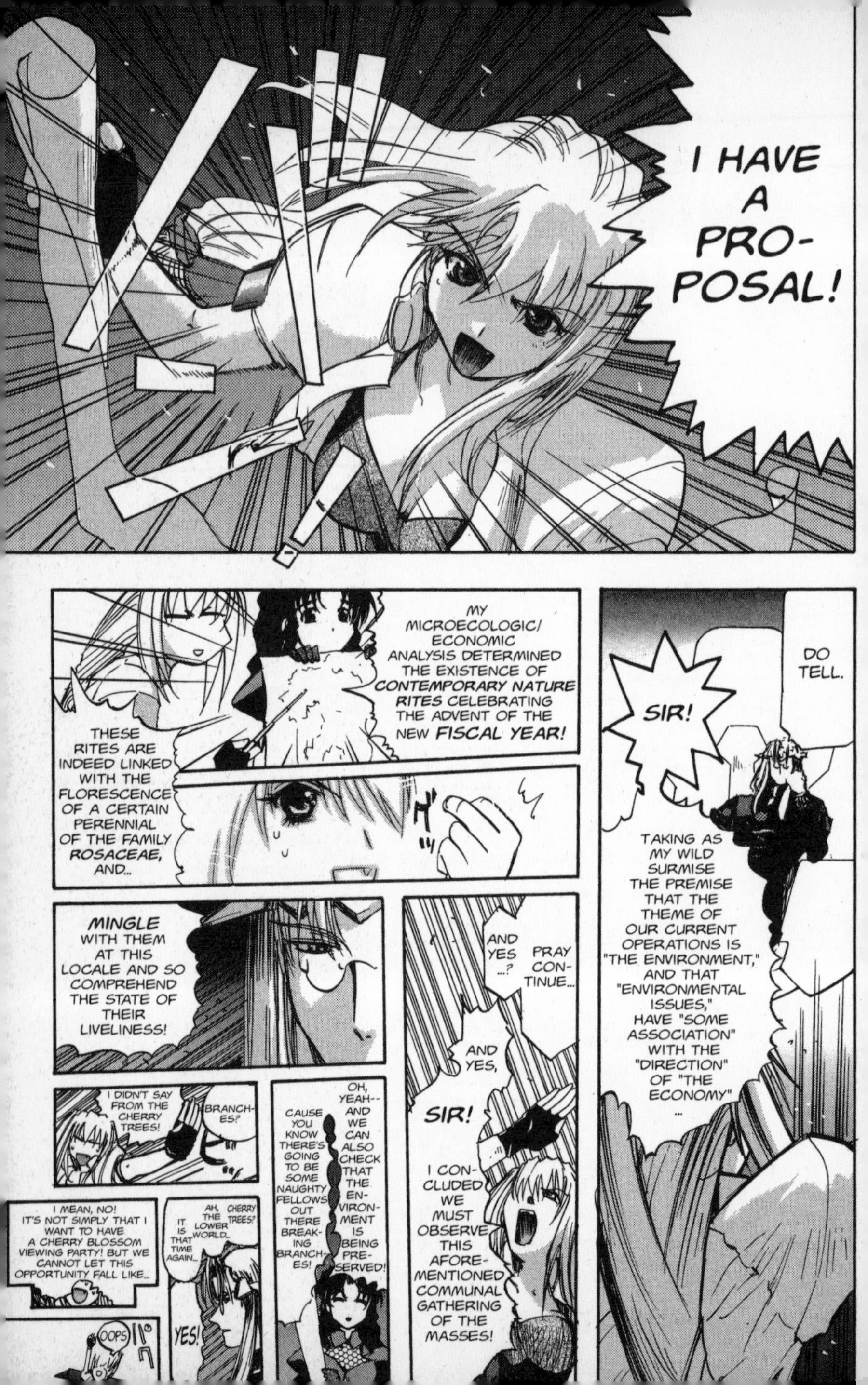

I HAVE A PRO-POSAL!
DO TELL.
SIR!
TAKING AS MY WILD SURMISE THE PREMISE THAT THE THEME OF OUR CURRENT OPERATIONS IS "THE ENVIRONMENT," AND THAT "ENVIRONMENTAL ISSUES," HAVE "SOME ASSOCIATION" WITH THE "DIRECTION" OF "THE ECONOMY"...
MY MICROECOLOGIC/ ECONOMIC ANALYSIS DETERMINED THE EXISTENCE OF CONTEMPORARY NATURE RITES CELEBRATING THE ADVENT OF THE NEW FISCAL YEAR!
THESE RITES ARE INDEED LINKED WITH THE FLORESCENCE OF A CERTAIN PERENNIAL OF THE FAMILY ROSACEAE, AND...
PRAY CONTINUE...
AND YES ...?
AND YES, SIR!
I CONCLUDED WE MUST OBSERVE THIS AFORE-MENTIONED COMMUNAL GATHERING OF THE MASSES!
MINGLE WITH THEM AT THIS LOCALE AND SO COMPREHEND THE STATE OF THEIR LIVELINESS!
OH, YEAH-- AND WE CAN ALSO CHECK THAT THE EN-VIRON-MENT IS BEING PRE-SERVED!
CAUSE YOU KNOW THERE'S GOING TO BE SOME NAUGHTY FELLOWS OUT THERE BREAK-ING BRANCH-ES!
BRANCH-ES?
I DIDN'T SAY FROM THE CHERRY TREES!
CHERRY TREES?
AH, THE LOWER WORLD...
IT IS THAT TIME AGAIN...
YES!
I MEAN, NO! IT'S NOT SIMPLY THAT I WANT TO HAVE A CHERRY BLOSSOM VIEWING PARTY! BUT WE CANNOT LET THIS OPPORTUNITY FALL LIKE...
OOPS

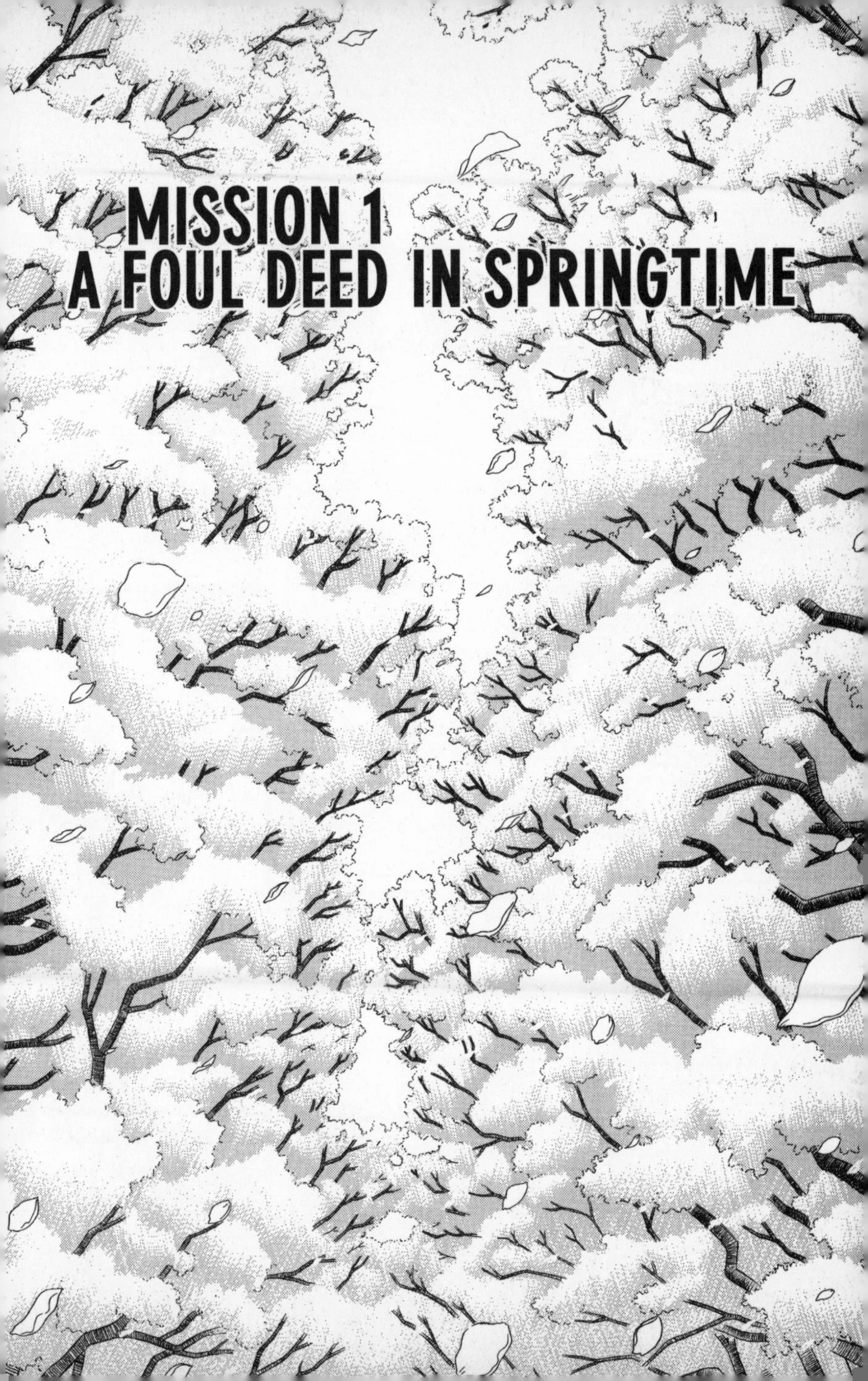
MISSION 1
A FOUL DEED IN SPRINGTIME

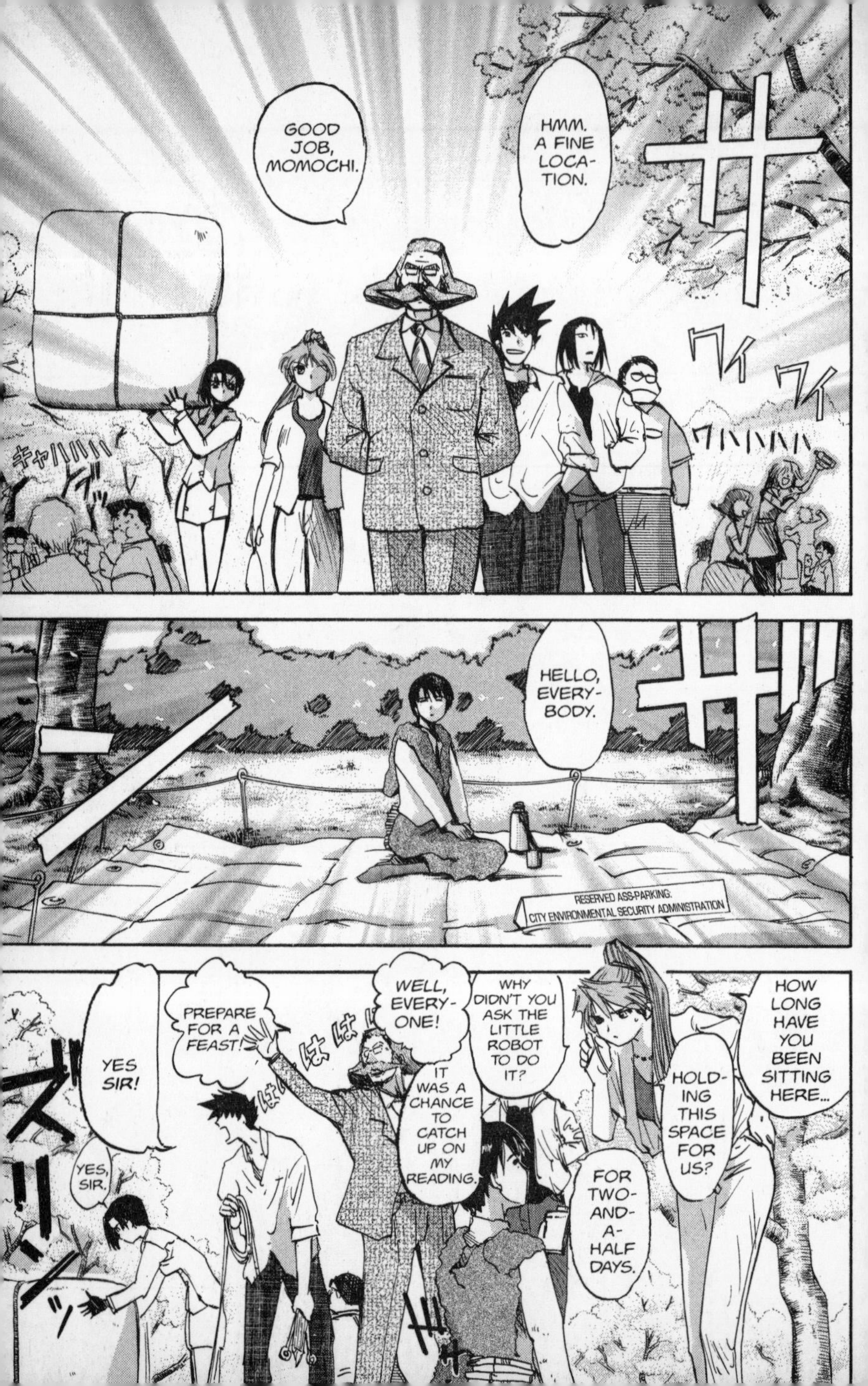
HMM. A FINE LOCATION.
GOOD JOB, MOMOCHI.
ワイ ワイ
HELLO, EVERYBODY.
RESERVED ASS-PARKING: CITY ENVIRONMENTAL SECURITY ADMINISTRATION
HOW LONG HAVE YOU BEEN SITTING HERE...
HOLDING THIS SPACE FOR US?
FOR TWO-AND-A-HALF DAYS.
WHY DIDN'T YOU ASK THE LITTLE ROBOT TO DO IT?
IT WAS A CHANCE TO CATCH UP ON MY READING.
WELL, EVERYONE!
PREPARE FOR A FEAST!
YES SIR!
YES, SIR.

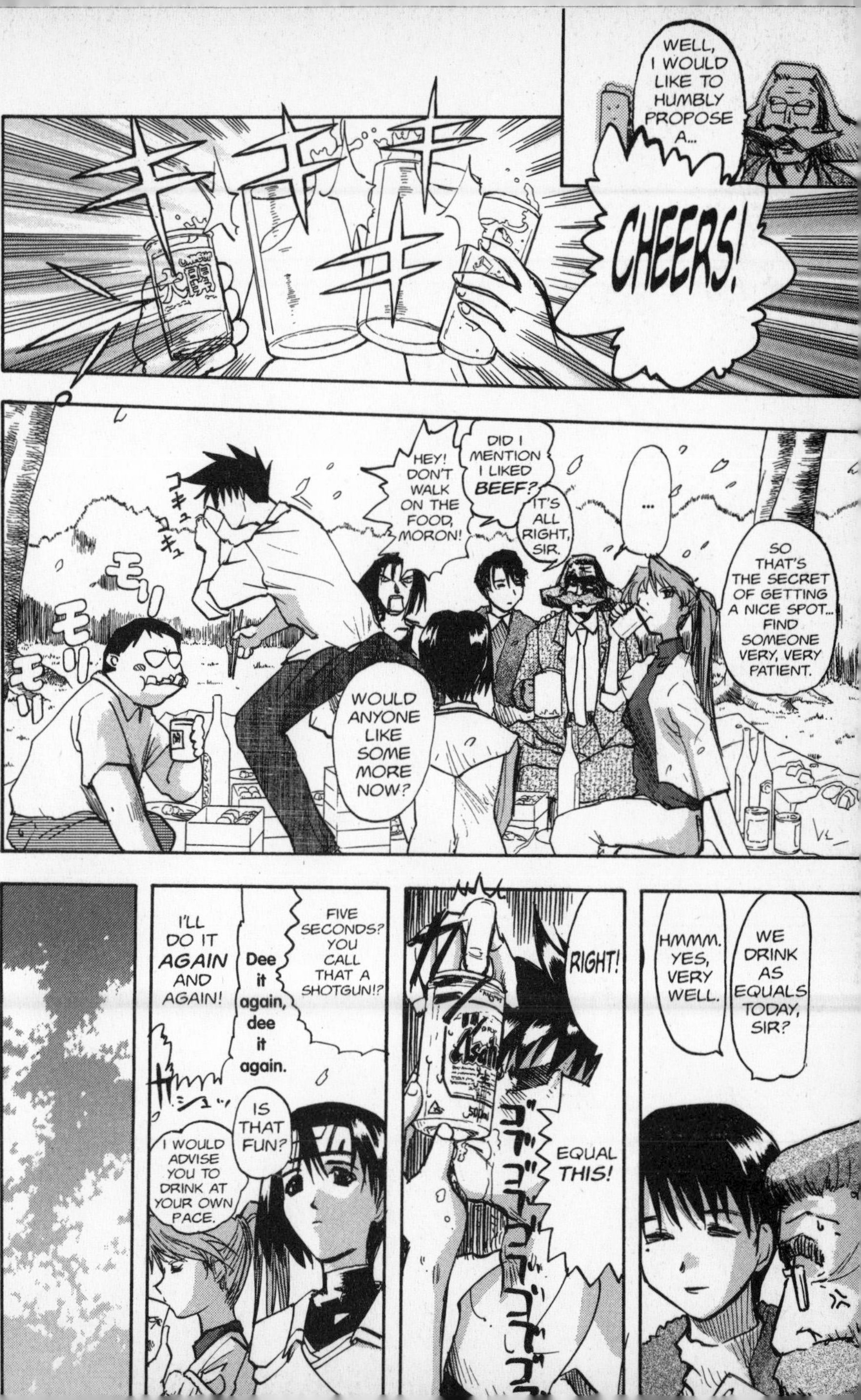
WELL, I WOULD LIKE TO HUMBLY PROPOSE A...
CHEERS!
SO THAT'S THE SECRET OF GETTING A NICE SPOT... FIND SOMEONE VERY, VERY PATIENT.
...
IT'S ALL RIGHT, SIR.
DID I MENTION I LIKED BEEF?
HEY! DON'T WALK ON THE FOOD, MORON!
WOULD ANYONE LIKE SOME MORE NOW?
WE DRINK AS EQUALS TODAY, SIR?
HMMM. YES, VERY WELL.
RIGHT!
EQUAL THIS!
FIVE SECONDS? YOU CALL THAT A SHOTGUN!?
I'LL DO IT AGAIN AND AGAIN!
Dee it again, dee it again.
IS THAT FUN?
I WOULD ADVISE YOU TO DRINK AT YOUR OWN PACE.

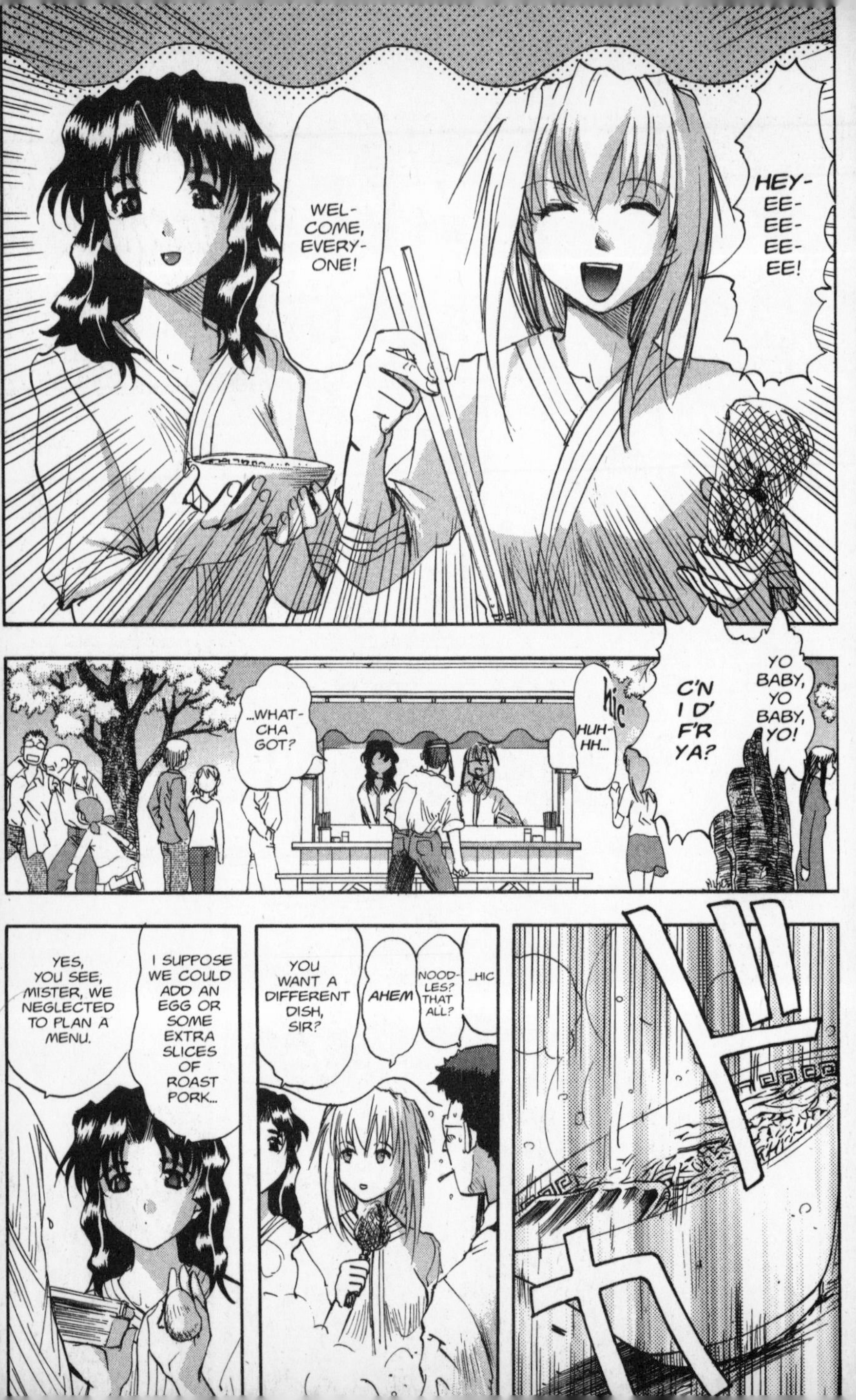
HEY-EE-EE-EE-EE!
WEL-COME, EVERY-ONE!
YO BABY, YO BABY, YO!
C'N I D' F'R YA?
HIC
HUH-HH...
...WHAT-CHA GOT?
...HIC
NOOD-LES? THAT ALL?
AHEM
YOU WANT A DIFFERENT DISH, SIR?
I SUPPOSE WE COULD ADD AN EGG OR SOME EXTRA SLICES OF ROAST PORK...
YES, YOU SEE, MISTER, WE NEGLECTED TO PLAN A MENU.

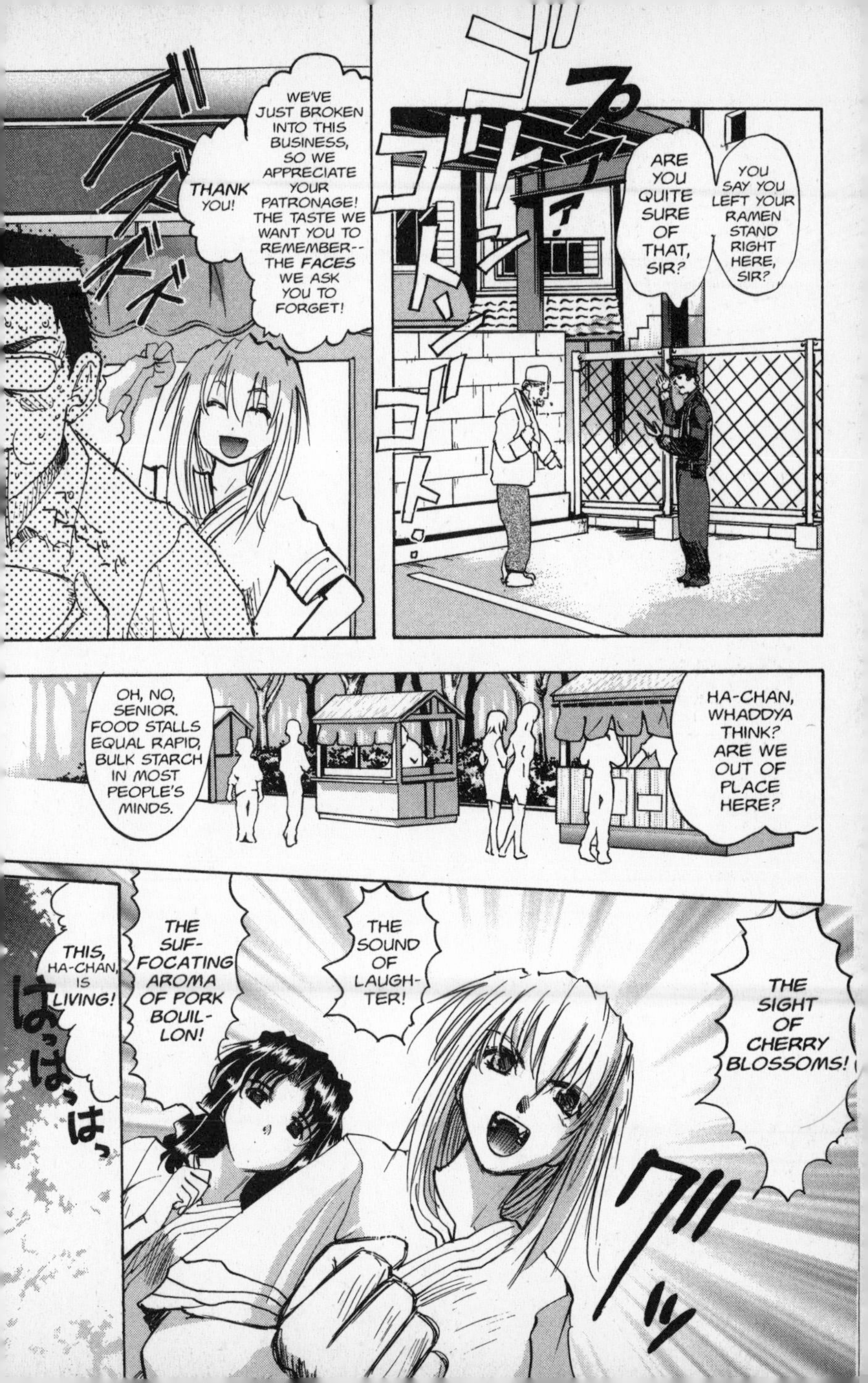
YOU SAY YOU LEFT YOUR RAMEN STAND RIGHT HERE, SIR?
ARE YOU QUITE SURE OF THAT, SIR?
WE'VE JUST BROKEN INTO THIS BUSINESS, SO WE APPRECIATE YOUR PATRONAGE! THE TASTE WE WANT YOU TO REMEMBER-- THE *FACES* WE ASK YOU TO FORGET!
THANK YOU!
HA-CHAN, WHADDYA THINK? ARE WE OUT OF PLACE HERE?
OH, NO, SENIOR. FOOD STALLS EQUAL RAPID, BULK STARCH IN MOST PEOPLE'S MINDS.
THE SIGHT OF CHERRY BLOSSOMS!
THE SOUND OF LAUGHTER!
THE SUF-FOCATING AROMA OF PORK BOUIL-LON!
THIS, HA-CHAN, IS LIVING!

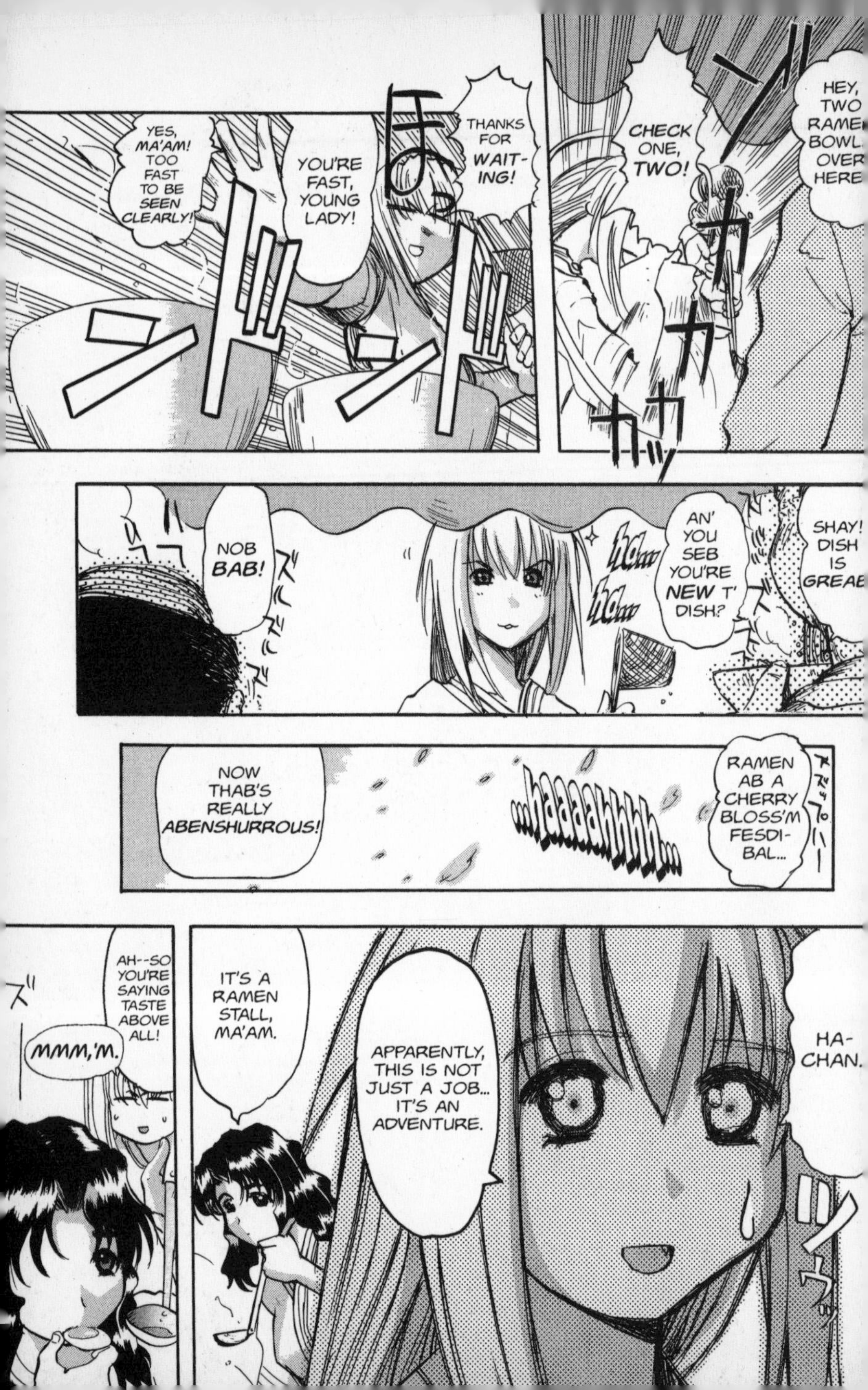
HEY, TWO RAME BOWL OVER HERE
CHECK ONE, TWO!
THANKS FOR WAIT-ING!
YOU'RE FAST, YOUNG LADY!
YES, MA'AM! TOO FAST TO BE SEEN CLEARLY!
SHAY! DISH IS GREAB
AN' YOU SEB YOU'RE NEW T' DISH?
ha... ha...
NOB BAB!
RAMEN AB A CHERRY BLOSS'M FESDI-BAL...
...haaaaahhhh...
NOW THAB'S REALLY ABENSHURROUS!
HA-CHAN.
APPARENTLY, THIS IS NOT JUST A JOB... IT'S AN ADVENTURE.
IT'S A RAMEN STALL, MA'AM.
AH--SO YOU'RE SAYING TASTE ABOVE ALL!
MMM,'M.

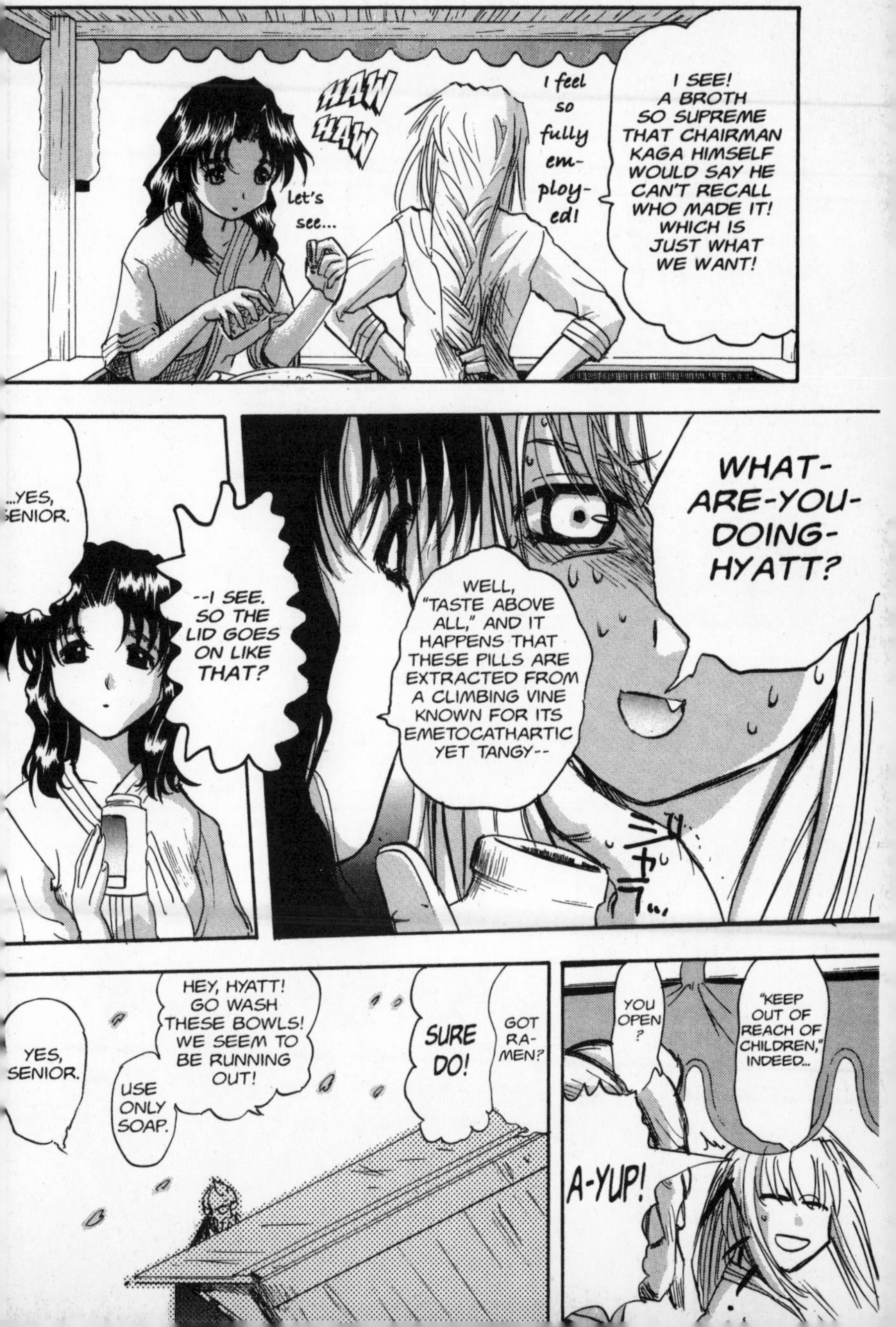
I SEE! A BROTH SO SUPREME THAT CHAIRMAN KAGA HIMSELF WOULD SAY HE CAN'T RECALL WHO MADE IT! WHICH IS JUST WHAT WE WANT!
I feel so fully em-ploy-ed!
HAW HAW
let's see...
WHAT-ARE-YOU-DOING-HYATT?
WELL, "TASTE ABOVE ALL," AND IT HAPPENS THAT THESE PILLS ARE EXTRACTED FROM A CLIMBING VINE KNOWN FOR ITS EMETOCATHARTIC YET TANGY--
...YES, SENIOR.
--I SEE. SO THE LID GOES ON LIKE THAT?
"KEEP OUT OF REACH OF CHILDREN," INDEED...
YOU OPEN?
A-YUP!
GOT RA-MEN?
SURE DO!
HEY, HYATT! GO WASH THESE BOWLS! WE SEEM TO BE RUNNING OUT!
USE ONLY SOAP.
YES, SENIOR.

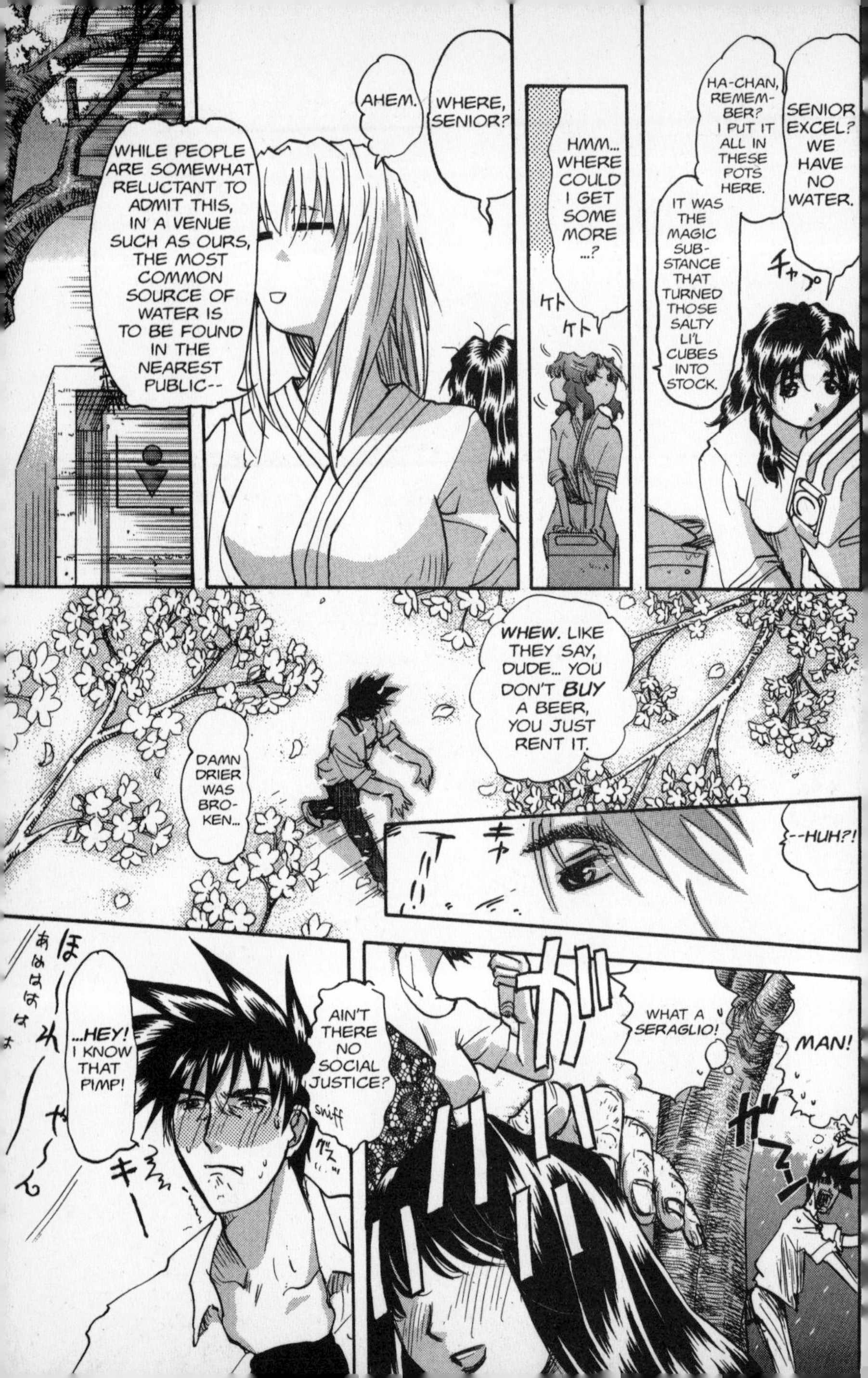
SENIOR EXCEL? WE HAVE NO WATER.
HA-CHAN, REMEMBER? I PUT IT ALL IN THESE POTS HERE.
IT WAS THE MAGIC SUBSTANCE THAT TURNED THOSE SALTY LI'L CUBES INTO STOCK.
チャプ
HMM... WHERE COULD I GET SOME MORE ...?
ケト ケト
WHERE, SENIOR?
AHEM.
WHILE PEOPLE ARE SOMEWHAT RELUCTANT TO ADMIT THIS, IN A VENUE SUCH AS OURS, THE MOST COMMON SOURCE OF WATER IS TO BE FOUND IN THE NEAREST PUBLIC--
WHEW. LIKE THEY SAY, DUDE... YOU DON'T BUY A BEER, YOU JUST RENT IT.
DAMN DRIER WAS BROKEN...
--HUH?!
キャ
MAN!
WHAT A SERAGLIO!
AIN'T THERE NO SOCIAL JUSTICE?
sniff
グス
...HEY! I KNOW THAT PIMP!
キー

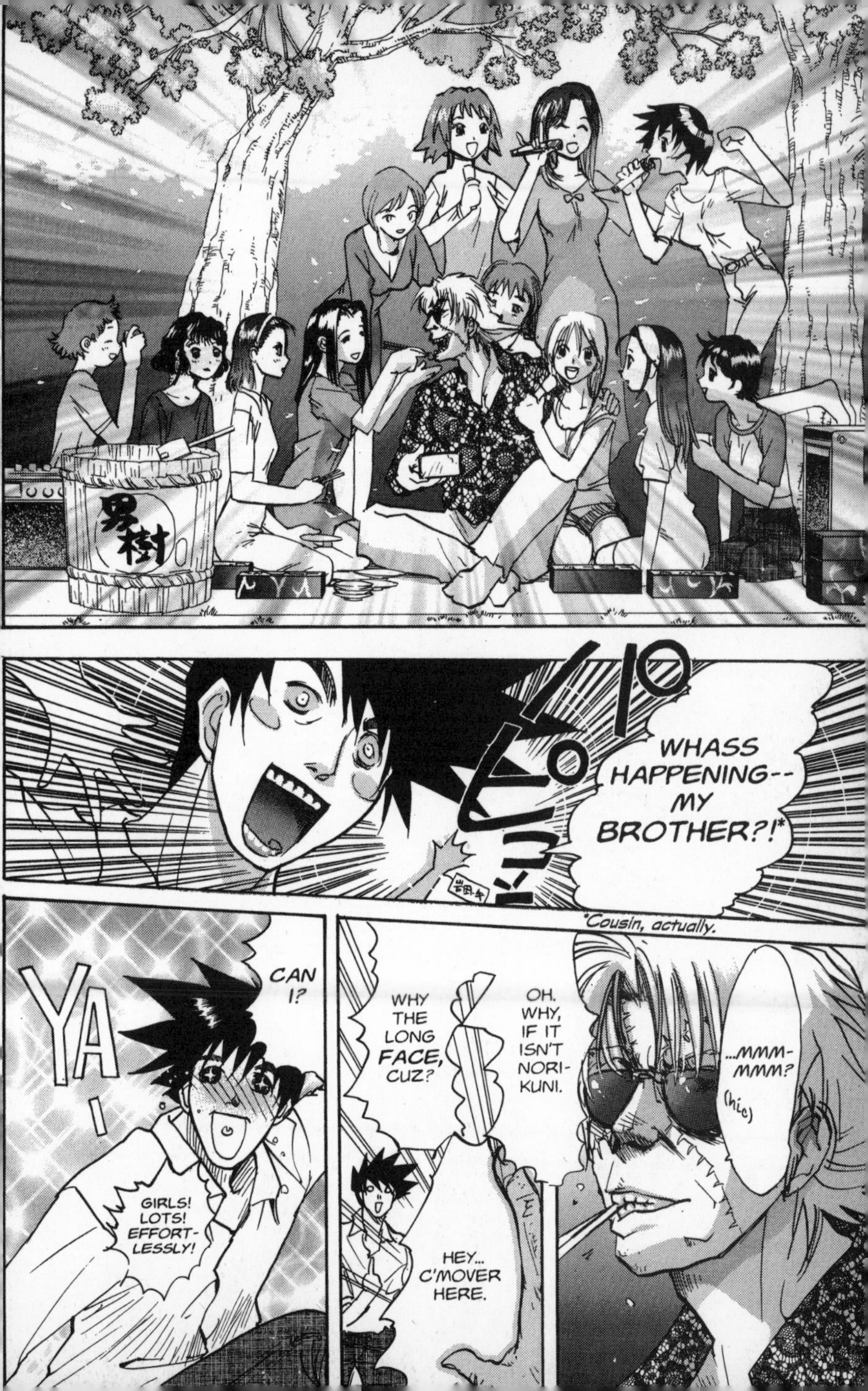
男樹
WHASS HAPPENING-- MY BROTHER?!*
*Cousin, actually.
...MMM-MMM?
(hic)
OH. WHY, IF IT ISN'T NORI-KUNI.
WHY THE LONG FACE, CUZ?
HEY... C'MOVER HERE.
CAN I?
YA
I
GIRLS! LOTS! EFFORTLESSLY!

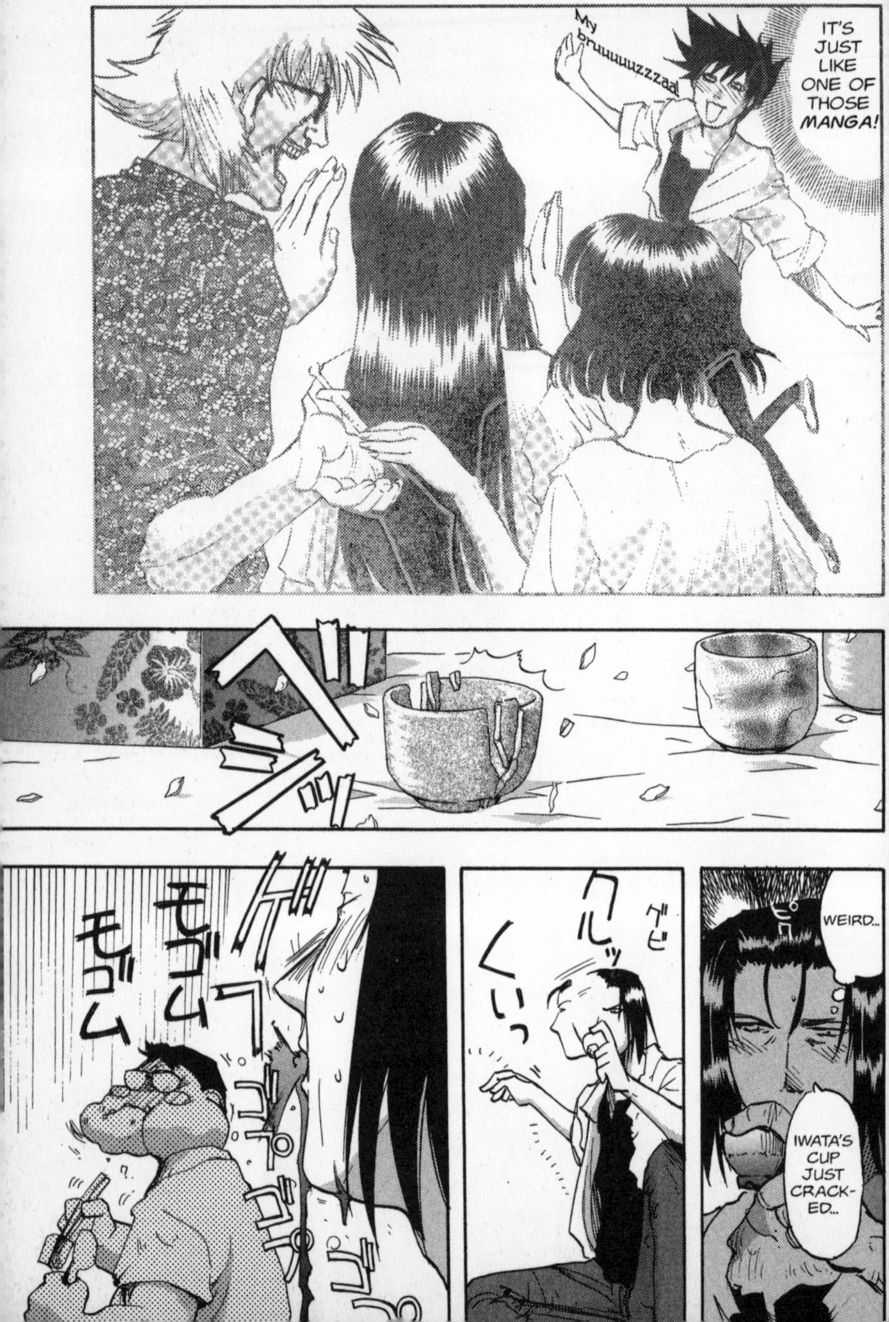
IT'S JUST LIKE ONE OF THOSE MANGA!
My bruuuuuuzzzaa!
WEIRD...
IWATA'S CUP JUST CRACK-ED...
クルッ
ゲビ
くいっ
モゴム
モゴム

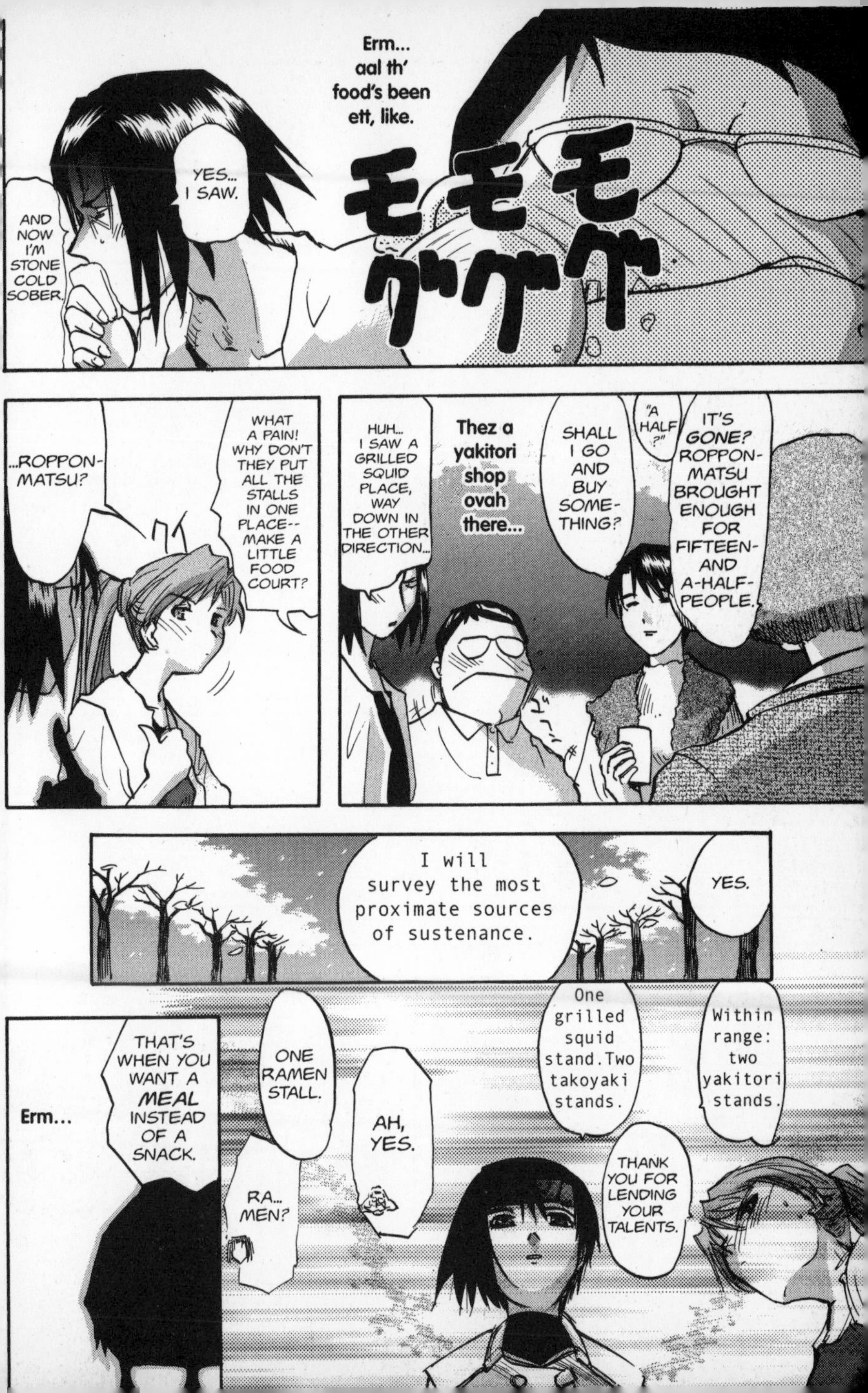

Erm... aal th' food's been ett, like.
モグモグモグ
YES... I SAW.
AND NOW I'M STONE COLD SOBER.
IT'S GONE? ROPPONMATSU BROUGHT ENOUGH FOR FIFTEEN-AND A-HALF-PEOPLE.
"A HALF?"
SHALL I GO AND BUY SOMETHING?
Thez a yakitori shop ovah there...
HUH... I SAW A GRILLED SQUID PLACE, WAY DOWN IN THE OTHER DIRECTION...
WHAT A PAIN! WHY DON'T THEY PUT ALL THE STALLS IN ONE PLACE-- MAKE A LITTLE FOOD COURT?
...ROPPONMATSU?
YES.
I will survey the most proximate sources of sustenance.
Within range: two yakitori stands.
One grilled squid stand. Two takoyaki stands.
THANK YOU FOR LENDING YOUR TALENTS.
AH, YES.
ONE RAMEN STALL.
RA... MEN?
THAT'S WHEN YOU WANT A MEAL INSTEAD OF A SNACK.
Erm...

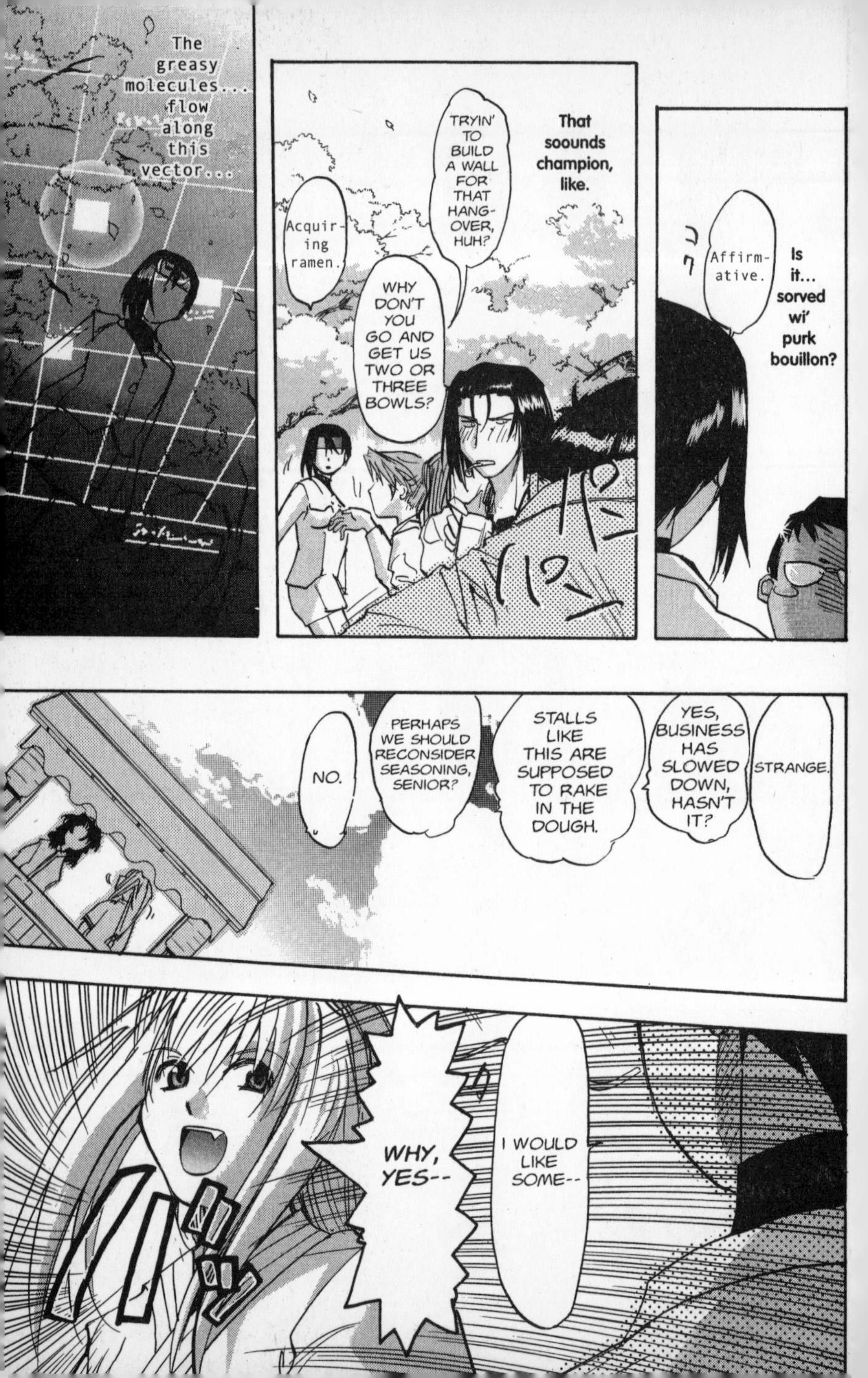
Is it... sorved wi' purk bouillon?
コク
Affirm-ative.
That soounds champion, like.
TRYIN' TO BUILD A WALL FOR THAT HANG-OVER, HUH?
WHY DON'T YOU GO AND GET US TWO OR THREE BOWLS?
Acquir-ing ramen.
The greasy molecules... flow along this vector...
STRANGE.
YES, BUSINESS HAS SLOWED DOWN, HASN'T IT?
STALLS LIKE THIS ARE SUPPOSED TO RAKE IN THE DOUGH.
PERHAPS WE SHOULD RECONSIDER SEASONING, SENIOR?
NO.
I WOULD LIKE SOME--
WHY, YES--

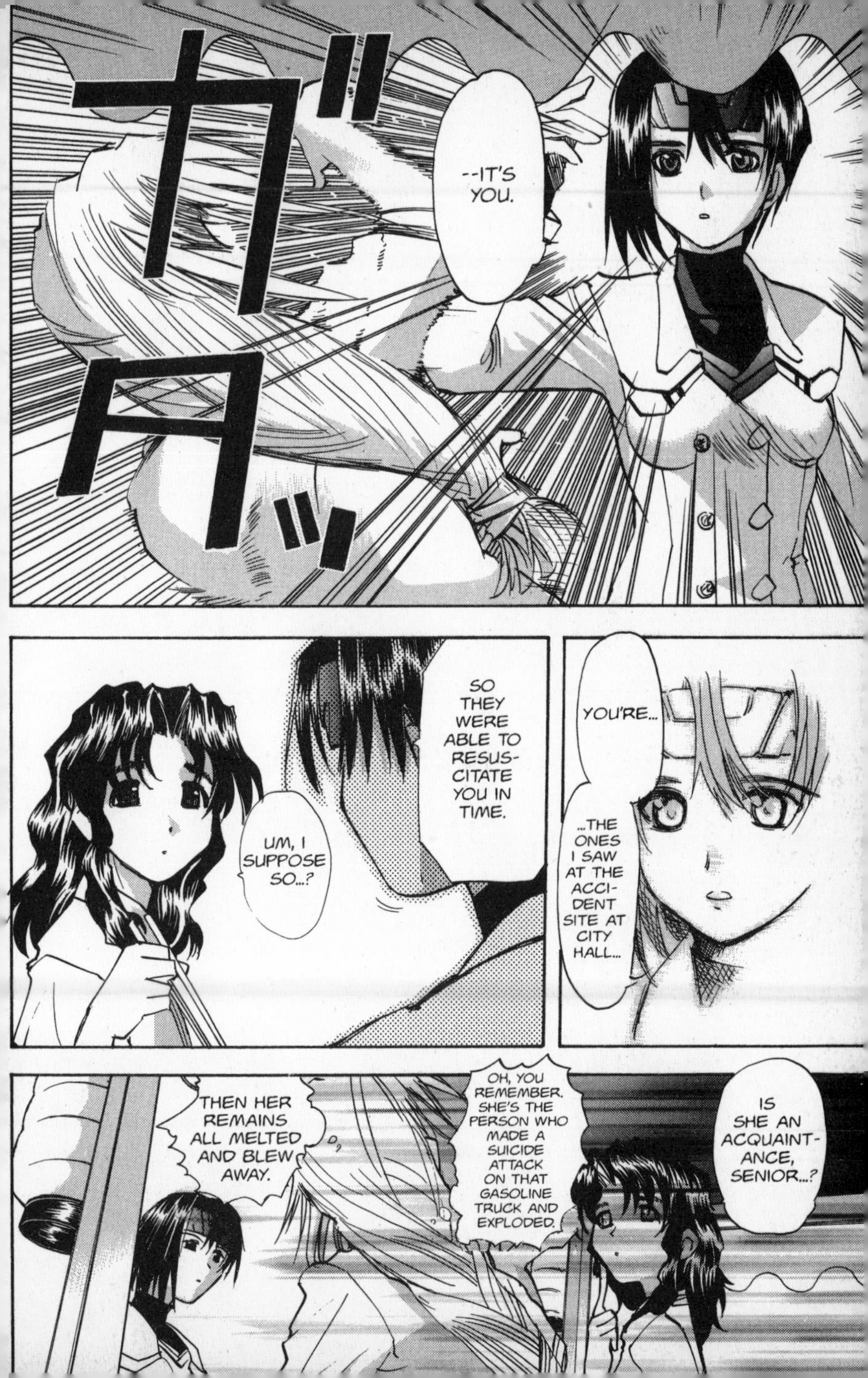
--IT'S YOU.
ガタッ
YOU'RE...
...THE ONES I SAW AT THE ACCIDENT SITE AT CITY HALL...
SO THEY WERE ABLE TO RESUSCITATE YOU IN TIME.
UM, I SUPPOSE SO...?
IS SHE AN ACQUAINTANCE, SENIOR...?
OH, YOU REMEMBER. SHE'S THE PERSON WHO MADE A SUICIDE ATTACK ON THAT GASOLINE TRUCK AND EXPLODED.
THEN HER REMAINS ALL MELTED AND BLEW AWAY.

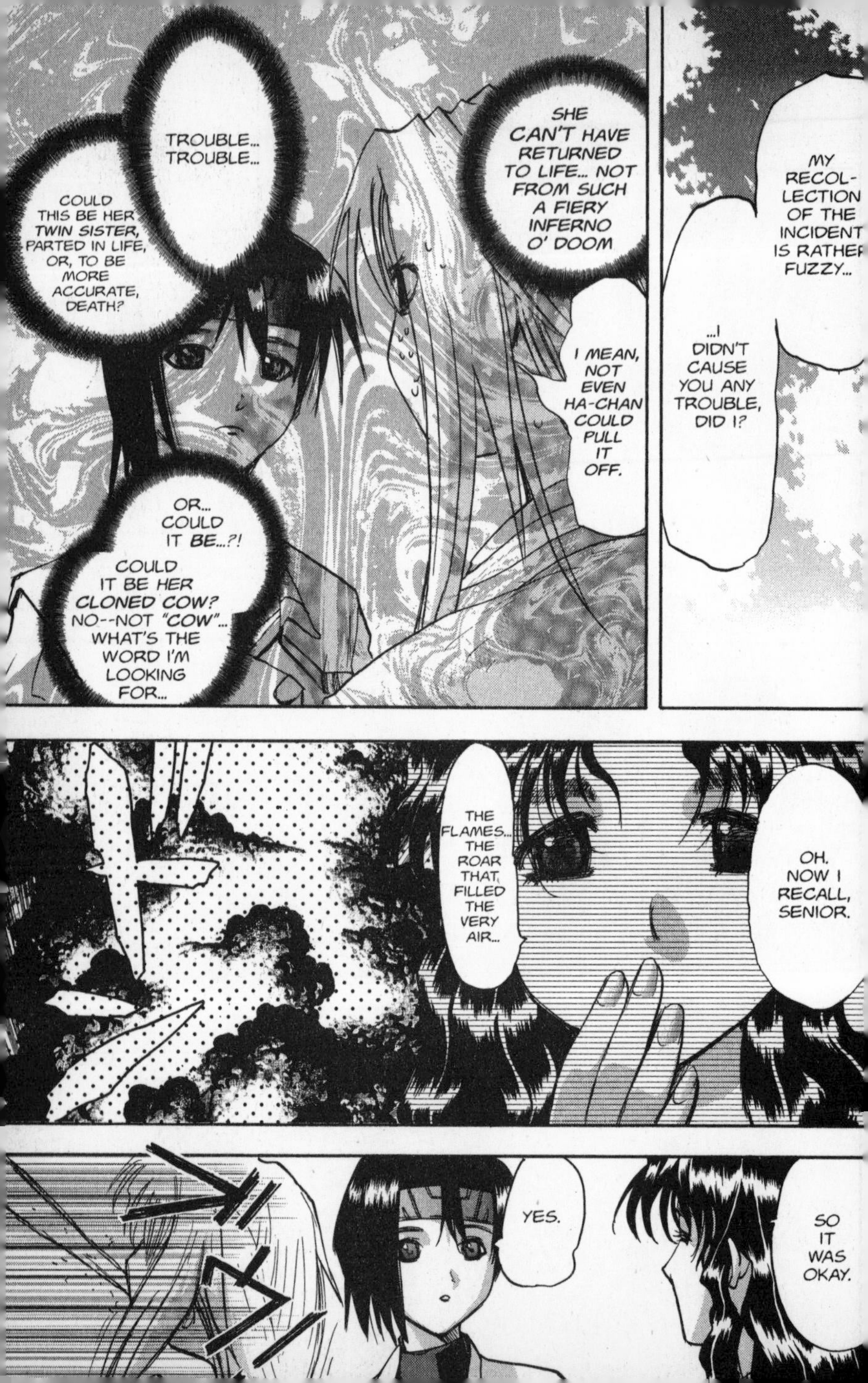
MY RECOLLECTION OF THE INCIDENT IS RATHER FUZZY...
...I DIDN'T CAUSE YOU ANY TROUBLE, DID I?
SHE CAN'T HAVE RETURNED TO LIFE... NOT FROM SUCH A FIERY INFERNO O' DOOM
I MEAN, NOT EVEN HA-CHAN COULD PULL IT OFF.
TROUBLE... TROUBLE...
COULD THIS BE HER TWIN SISTER, PARTED IN LIFE, OR, TO BE MORE ACCURATE, DEATH?
OR... COULD IT BE...?! COULD IT BE HER CLONED COW? NO--NOT "COW"... WHAT'S THE WORD I'M LOOKING FOR...
OH. NOW I RECALL, SENIOR.
THE FLAMES... THE ROAR THAT FILLED THE VERY AIR...
SO IT WAS OKAY.
YES.

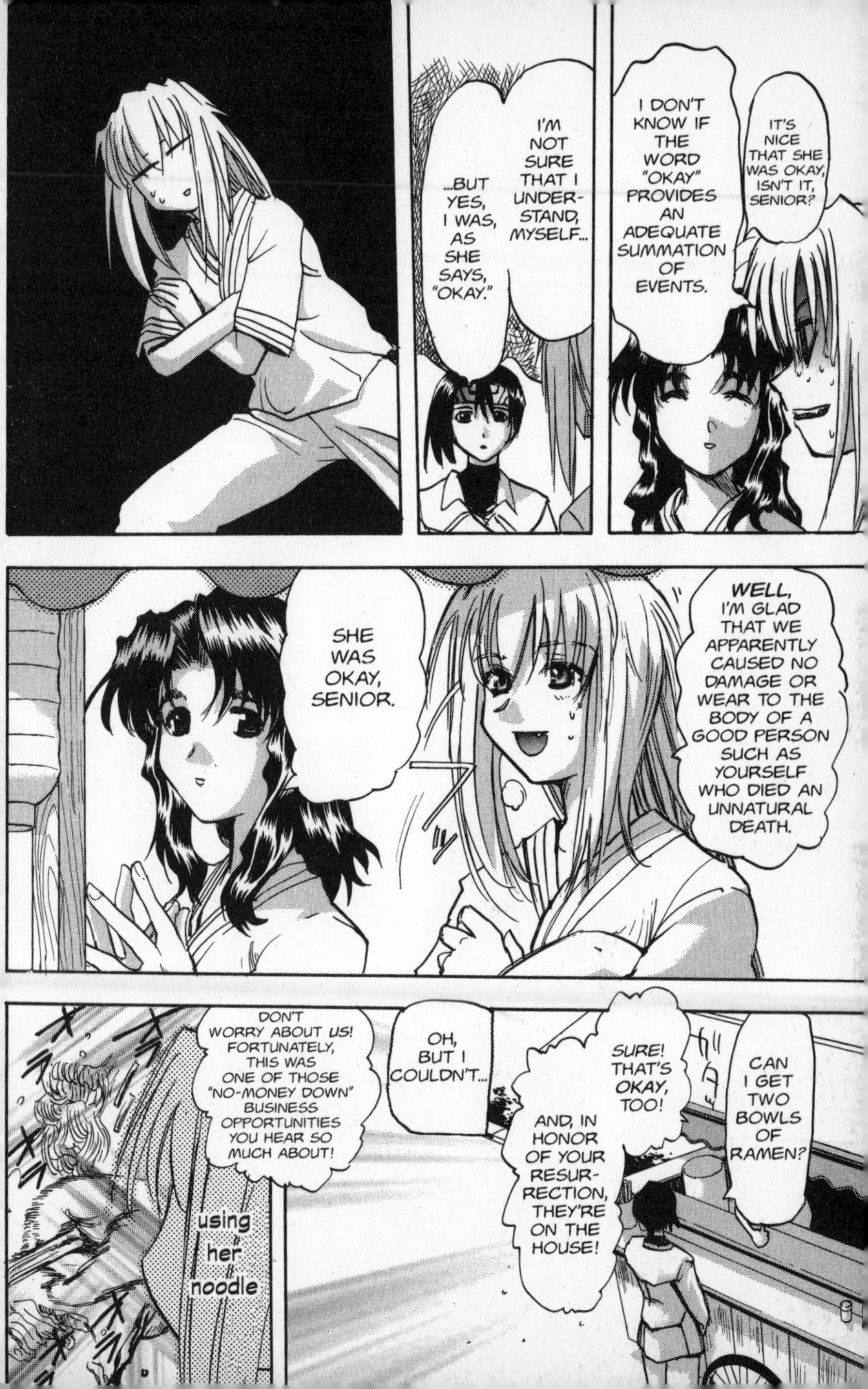
IT'S NICE THAT SHE WAS OKAY, ISN'T IT, SENIOR?
I DON'T KNOW IF THE WORD "OKAY" PROVIDES AN ADEQUATE SUMMATION OF EVENTS.
I'M NOT SURE THAT I UNDERSTAND, MYSELF...
...BUT YES, I WAS, AS SHE SAYS, "OKAY."
WELL, I'M GLAD THAT WE APPARENTLY CAUSED NO DAMAGE OR WEAR TO THE BODY OF A GOOD PERSON SUCH AS YOURSELF WHO DIED AN UNNATURAL DEATH.
SHE WAS OKAY, SENIOR.
CAN I GET TWO BOWLS OF RAMEN?
SURE! THAT'S OKAY, TOO!
AND, IN HONOR OF YOUR RESURRECTION, THEY'RE ON THE HOUSE!
OH, BUT I COULDN'T...
DON'T WORRY ABOUT US! FORTUNATELY, THIS WAS ONE OF THOSE "NO-MONEY DOWN" BUSINESS OPPORTUNITIES YOU HEAR SO MUCH ABOUT!
using her noodle

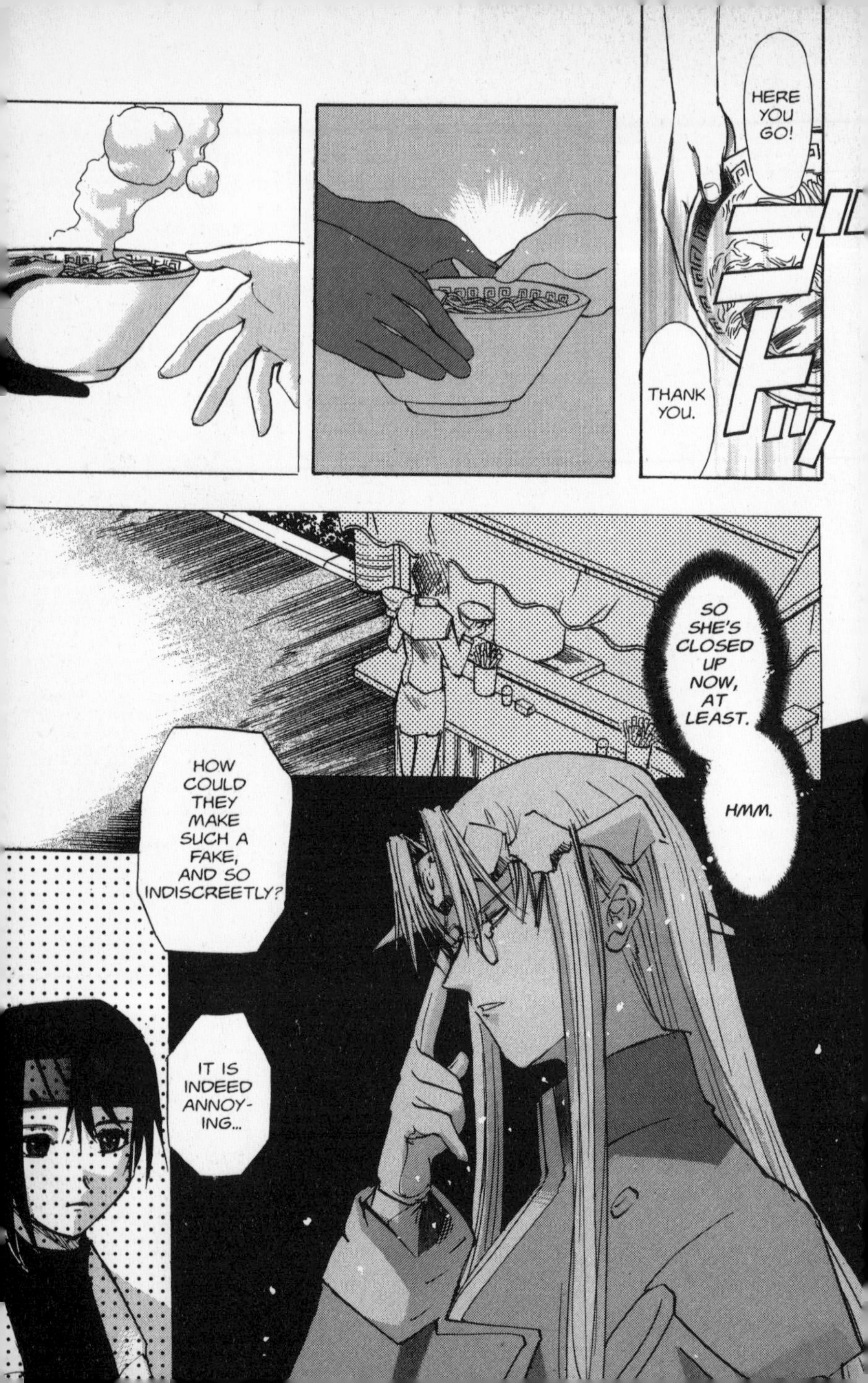
HERE YOU GO!
ゴトッ
THANK YOU.
SO SHE'S CLOSED UP NOW, AT LEAST.
HMM.
HOW COULD THEY MAKE SUCH A FAKE, AND SO INDISCREETLY?
IT IS INDEED ANNOYING...

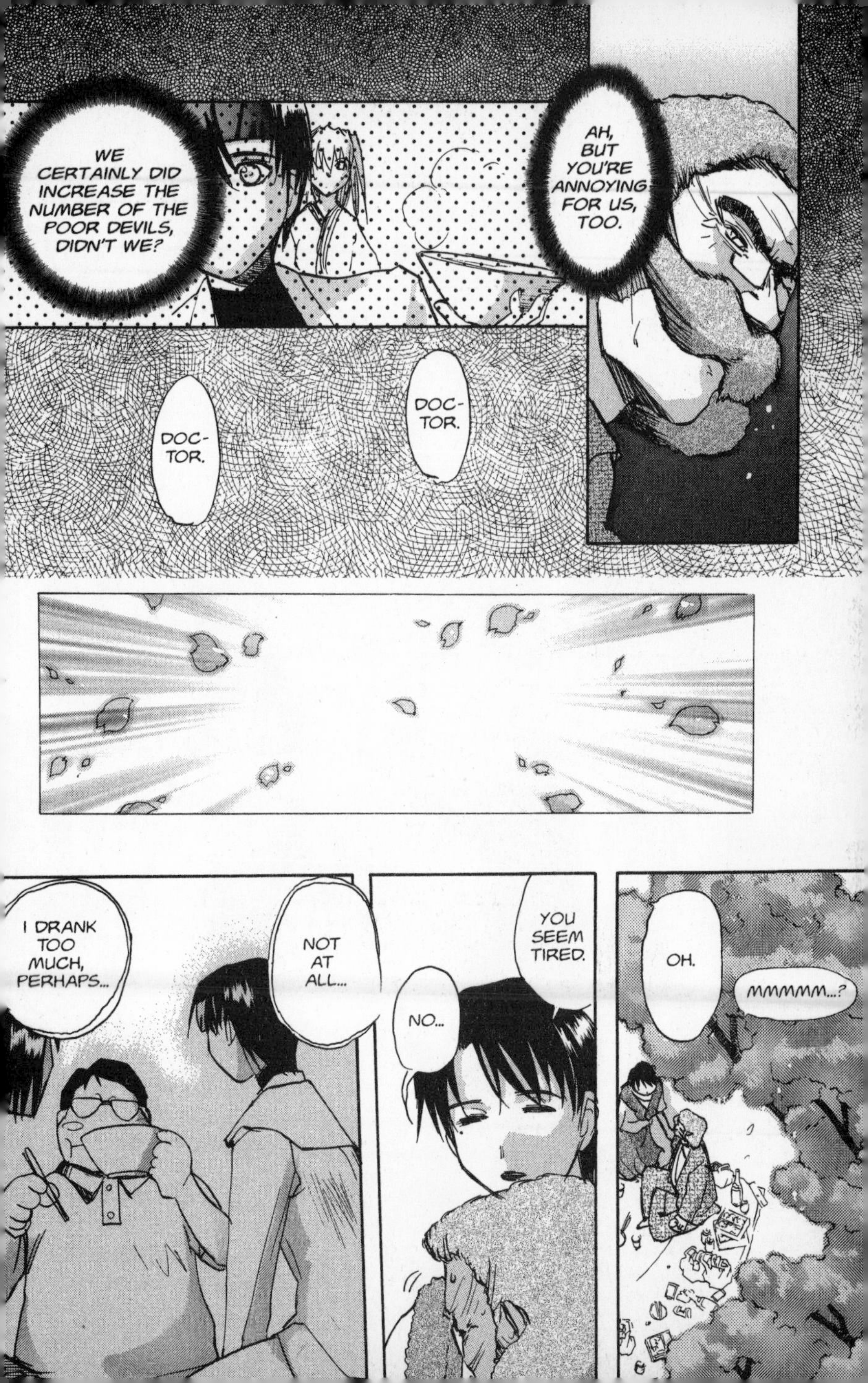
AH, BUT YOU'RE ANNOYING FOR US, TOO.
WE CERTAINLY DID INCREASE THE NUMBER OF THE POOR DEVILS, DIDN'T WE?
DOC-TOR.
DOC-TOR.
OH.
MMMMM...?
YOU SEEM TIRED.
NO...
NOT AT ALL...
I DRANK TOO MUCH, PERHAPS...

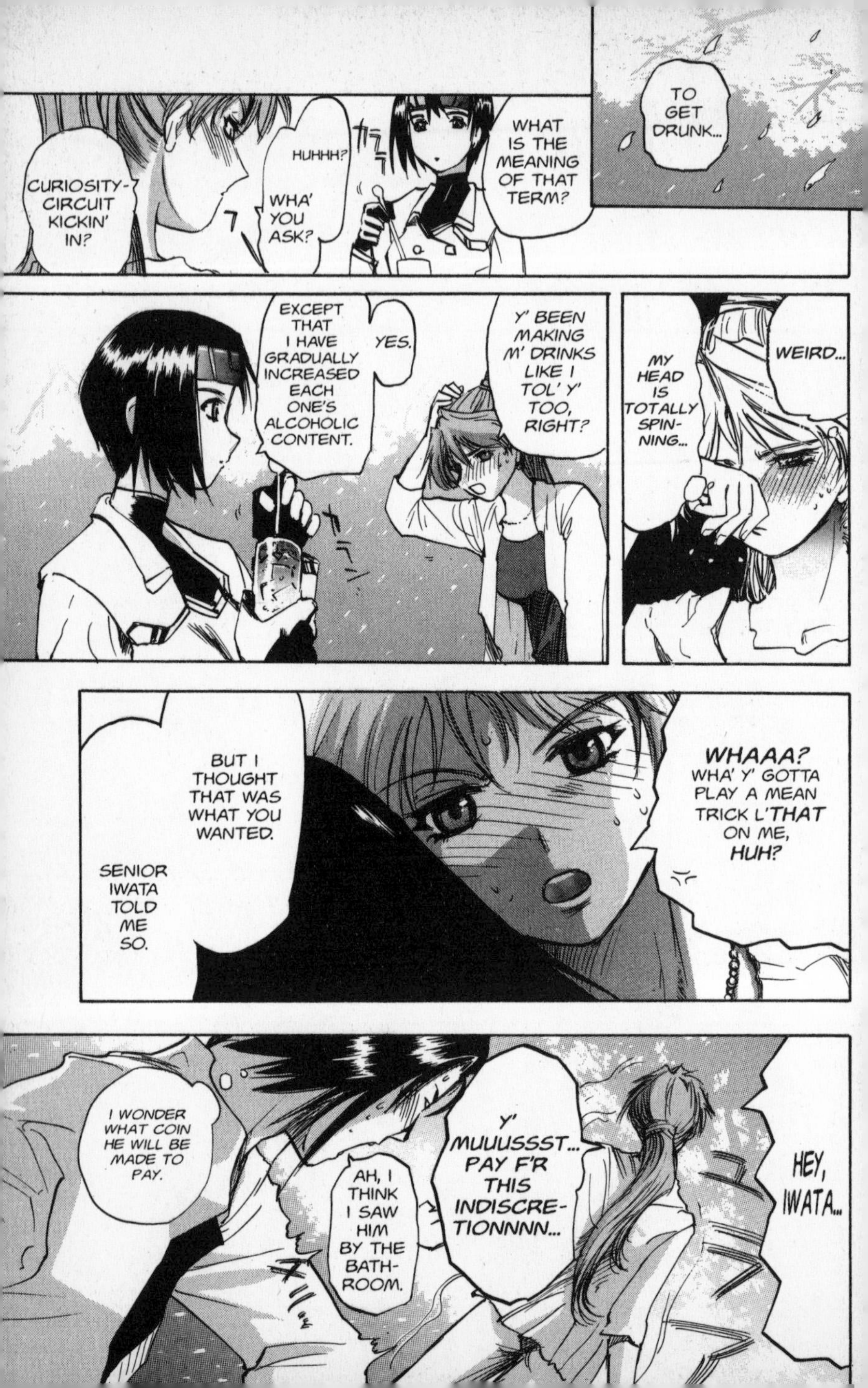
TO GET DRUNK...
WHAT IS THE MEANING OF THAT TERM?
HUHHH?
WHA' YOU ASK?
CURIOSITY-CIRCUIT KICKIN' IN?
WEIRD...
MY HEAD IS TOTALLY SPIN-NING...
Y' BEEN MAKING M' DRINKS LIKE I TOL' Y' TOO, RIGHT?
YES.
EXCEPT THAT I HAVE GRADUALLY INCREASED EACH ONE'S ALCOHOLIC CONTENT.
WHAAA? WHA' Y' GOTTA PLAY A MEAN TRICK L'THAT ON ME, HUH?
BUT I THOUGHT THAT WAS WHAT YOU WANTED.
SENIOR IWATA TOLD ME SO.
HEY, IWATA...
Y' MUUUSSST... PAY F'R THIS INDISCRE-TIONNNN...
AH, I THINK I SAW HIM BY THE BATH-ROOM.
I WONDER WHAT COIN HE WILL BE MADE TO PAY.

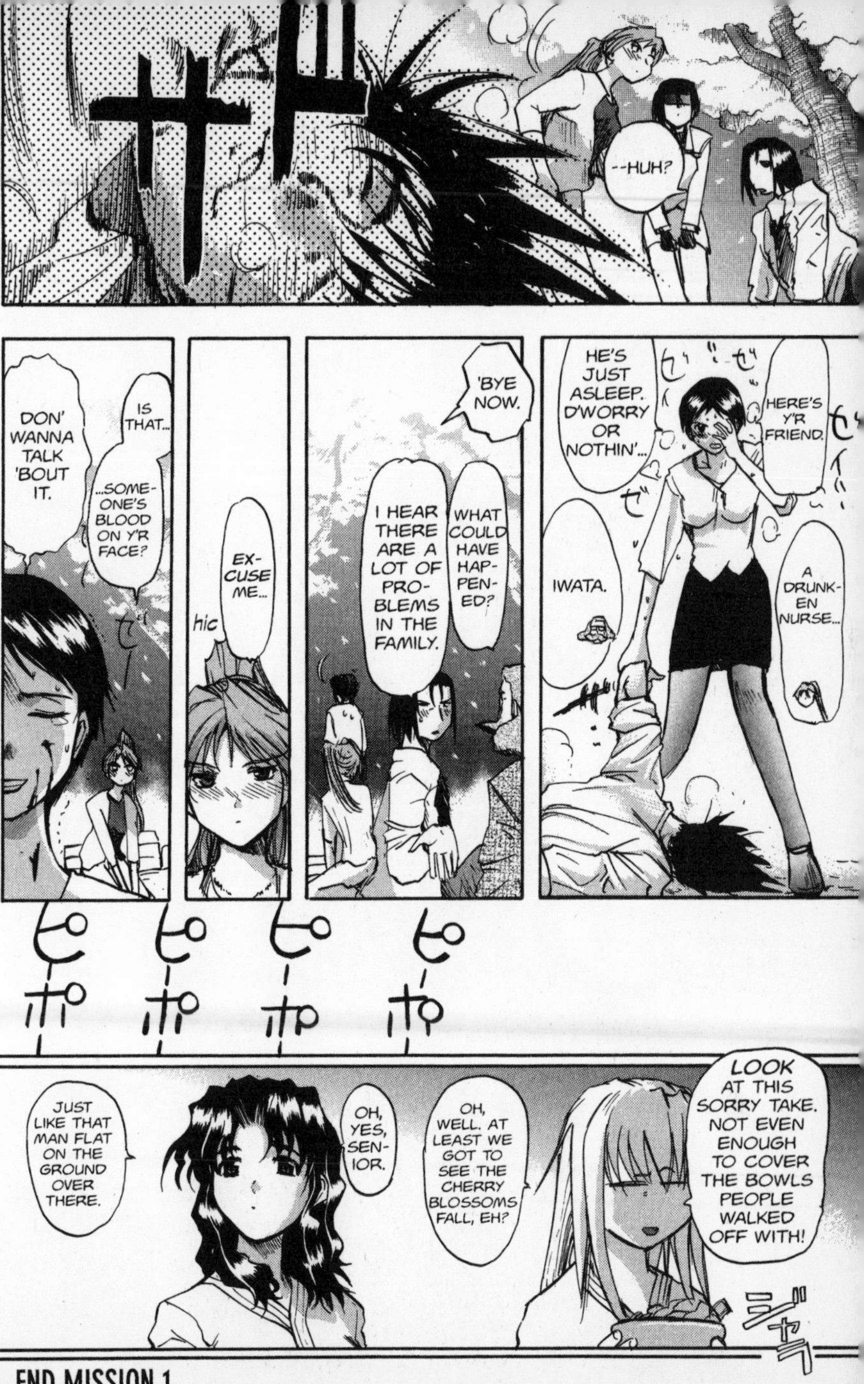
--HUH?
HERE'S Y'R FRIEND.
HE'S JUST ASLEEP. D'WORRY OR NOTHIN'...
A DRUNKEN NURSE...
IWATA.
'BYE NOW.
WHAT COULD HAVE HAPPENED?
I HEAR THERE ARE A LOT OF PROBLEMS IN THE FAMILY.
EXCUSE ME...
hic
IS THAT...
...SOMEONE'S BLOOD ON Y'R FACE?
DON' WANNA TALK 'BOUT IT.
LOOK AT THIS SORRY TAKE. NOT EVEN ENOUGH TO COVER THE BOWLS PEOPLE WALKED OFF WITH!
OH, WELL. AT LEAST WE GOT TO SEE THE CHERRY BLOSSOMS FALL, EH?
OH, YES, SENIOR.
JUST LIKE THAT MAN FLAT ON THE GROUND OVER THERE.

END MISSION 1

EXCEL SAGA

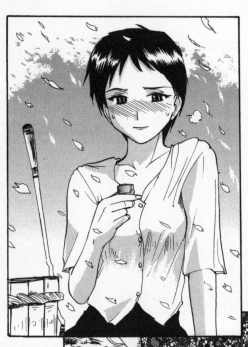

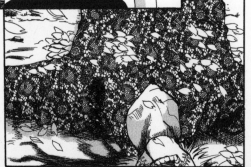

エクセル・サーガ

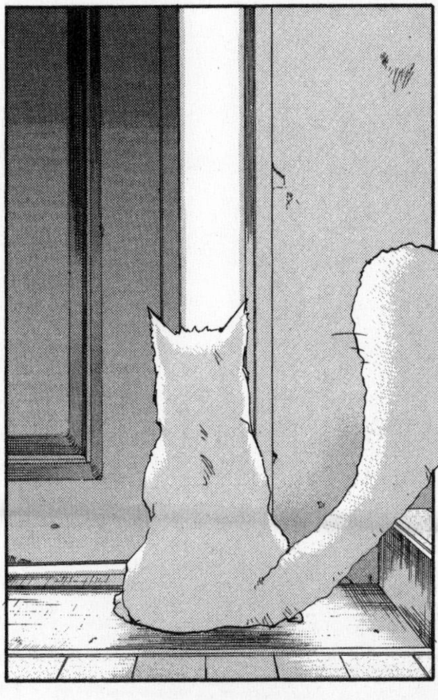

MISSION 2
IN THE MIDST OF DRAMA

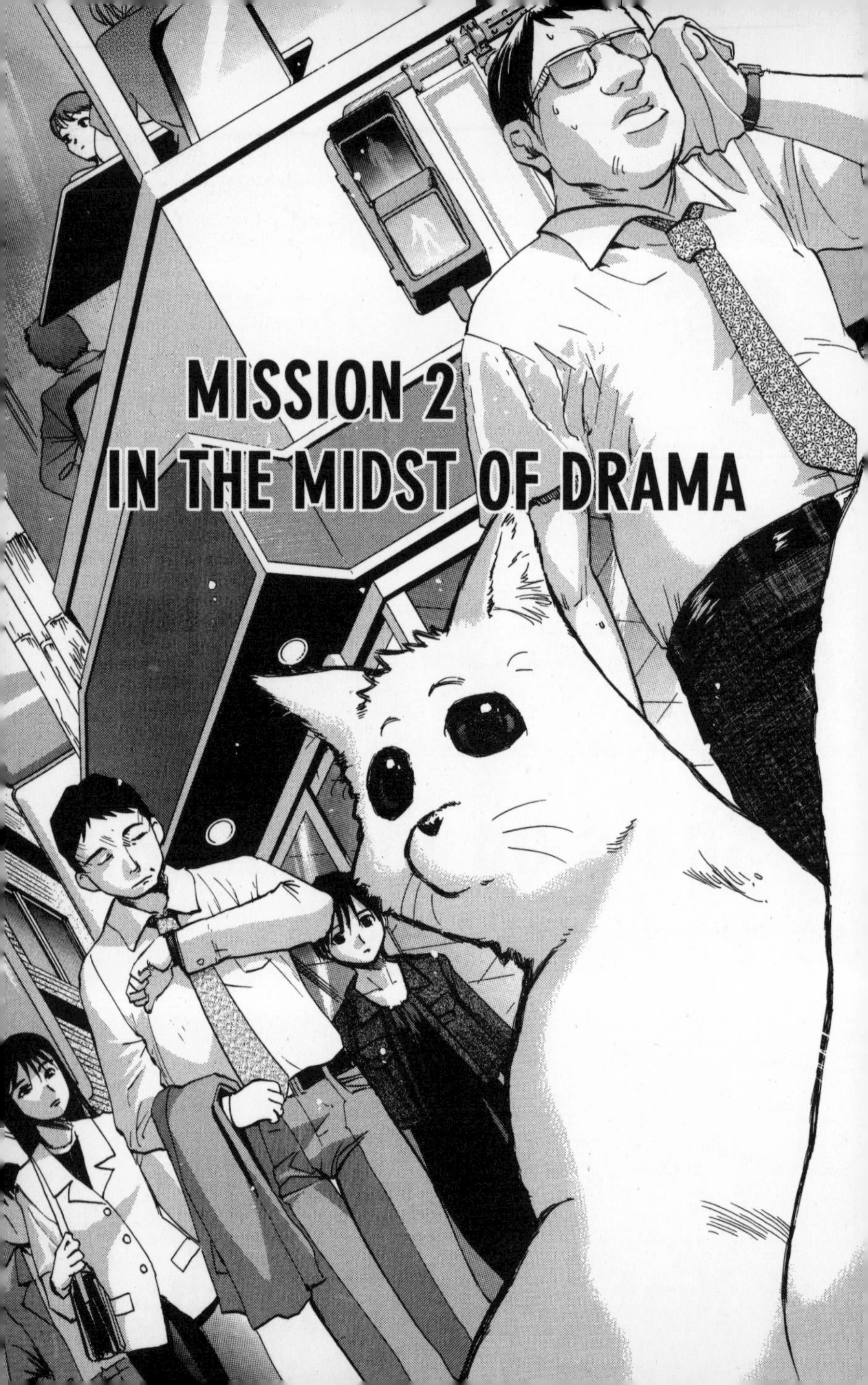

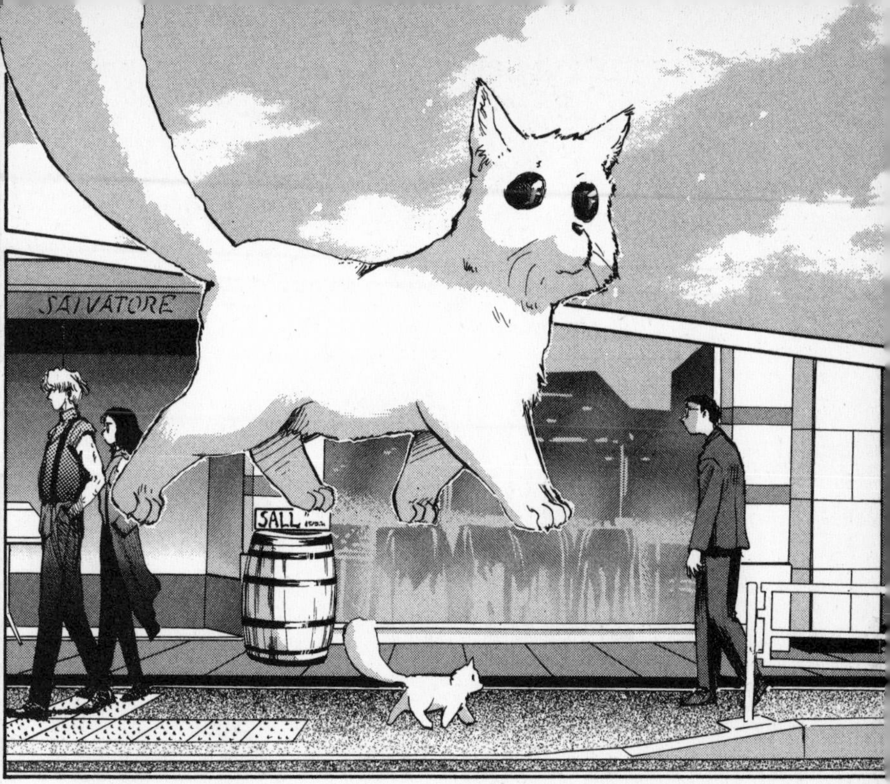

She's on the loose.

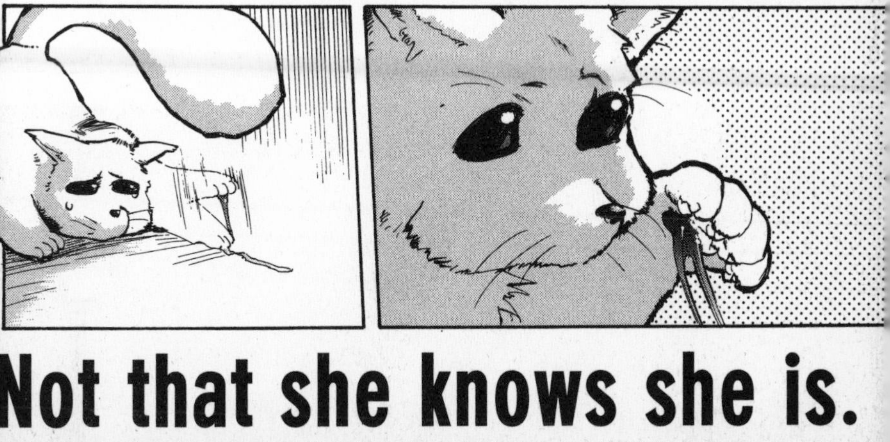

Not that she knows she is.

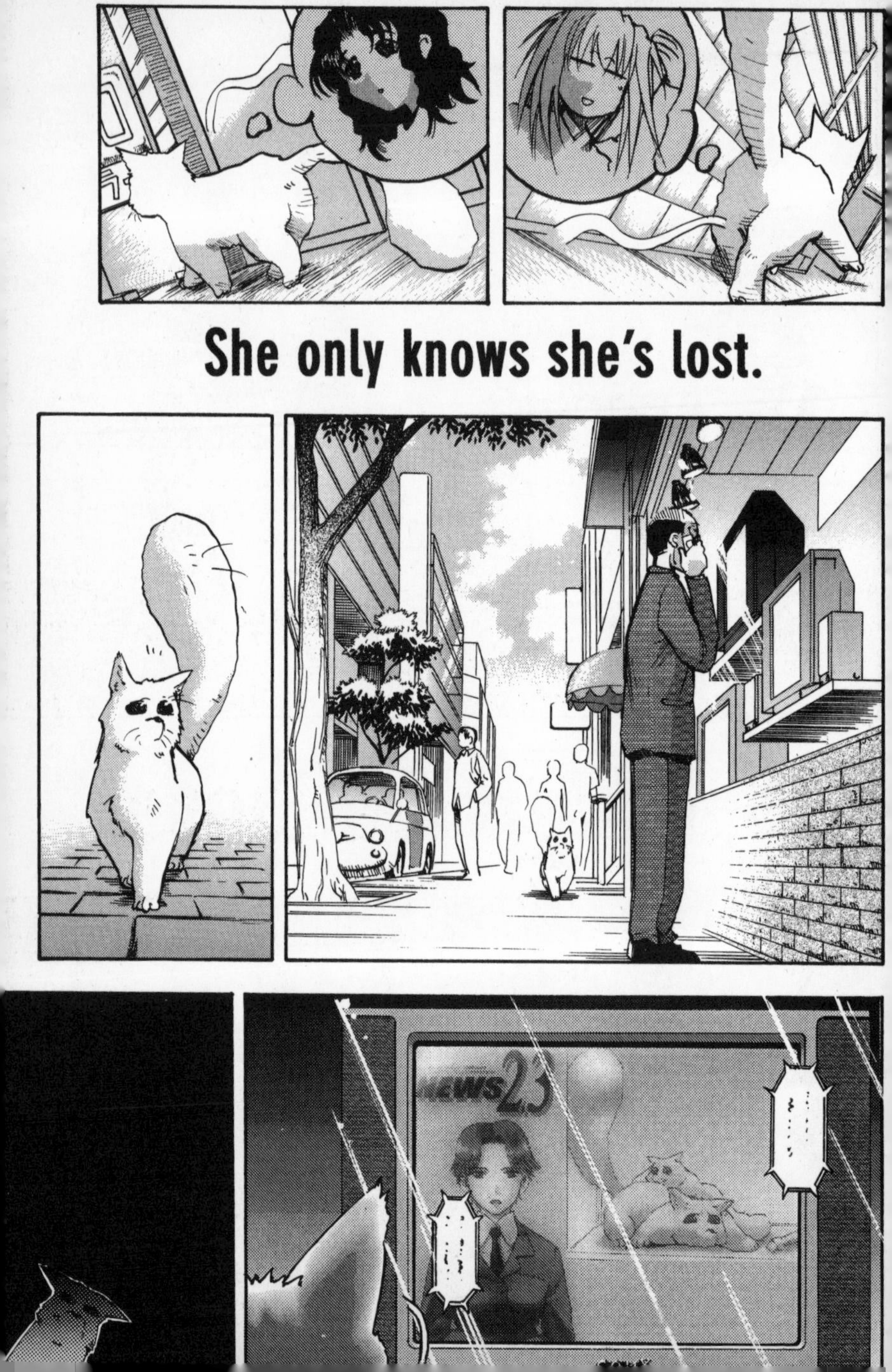
She only knows she's lost.

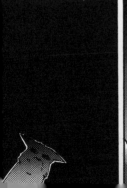

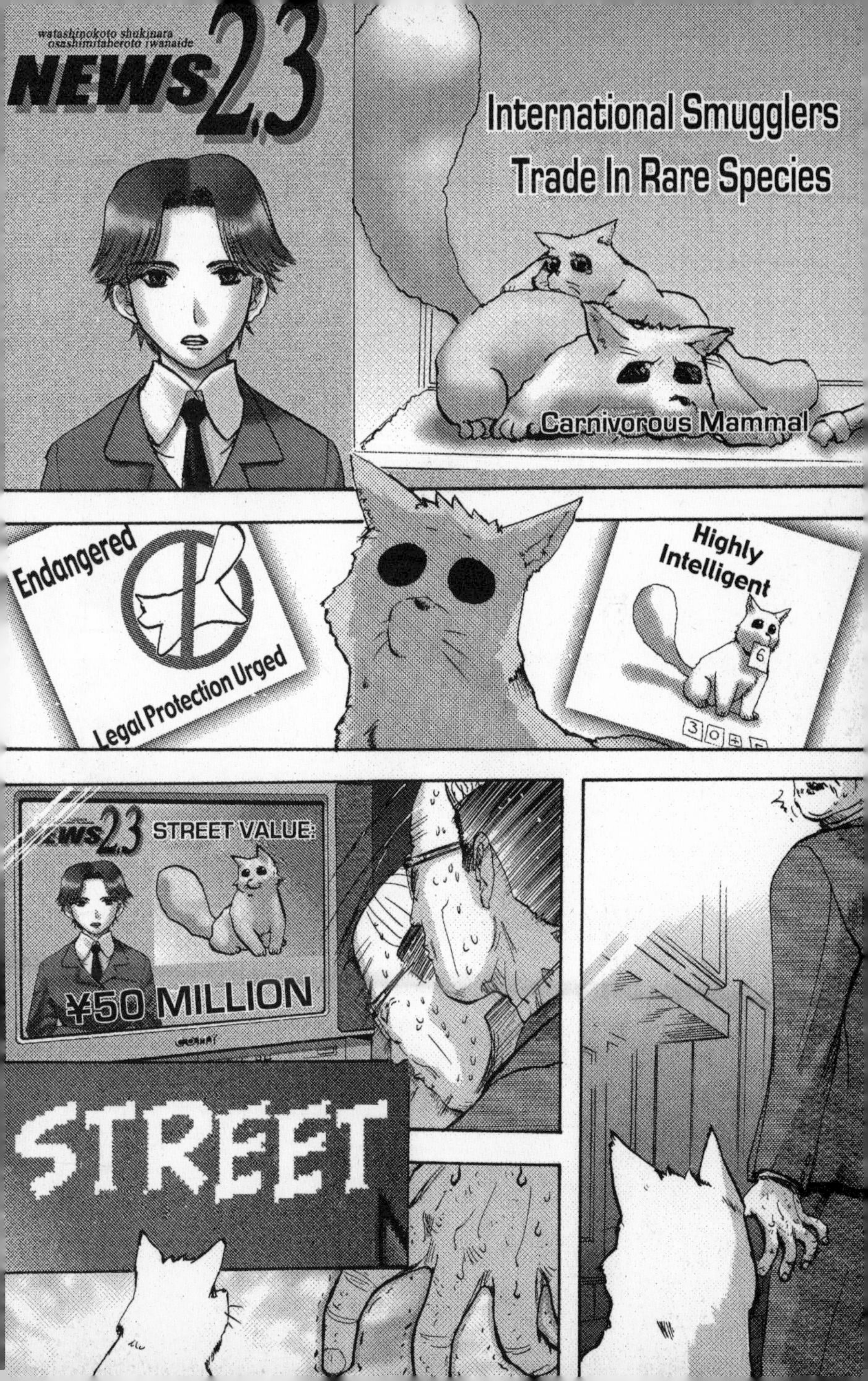
International Smugglers Trade In Rare Species
Carnivorous Mammal
watashinokoto shukinara osashimitaberoto iwanaide
NEWS 2.3
Highly Intelligent
6
Endangered
Legal Protection Urged
NEWS 2.3
STREET VALUE:
¥50 MILLION
STREET

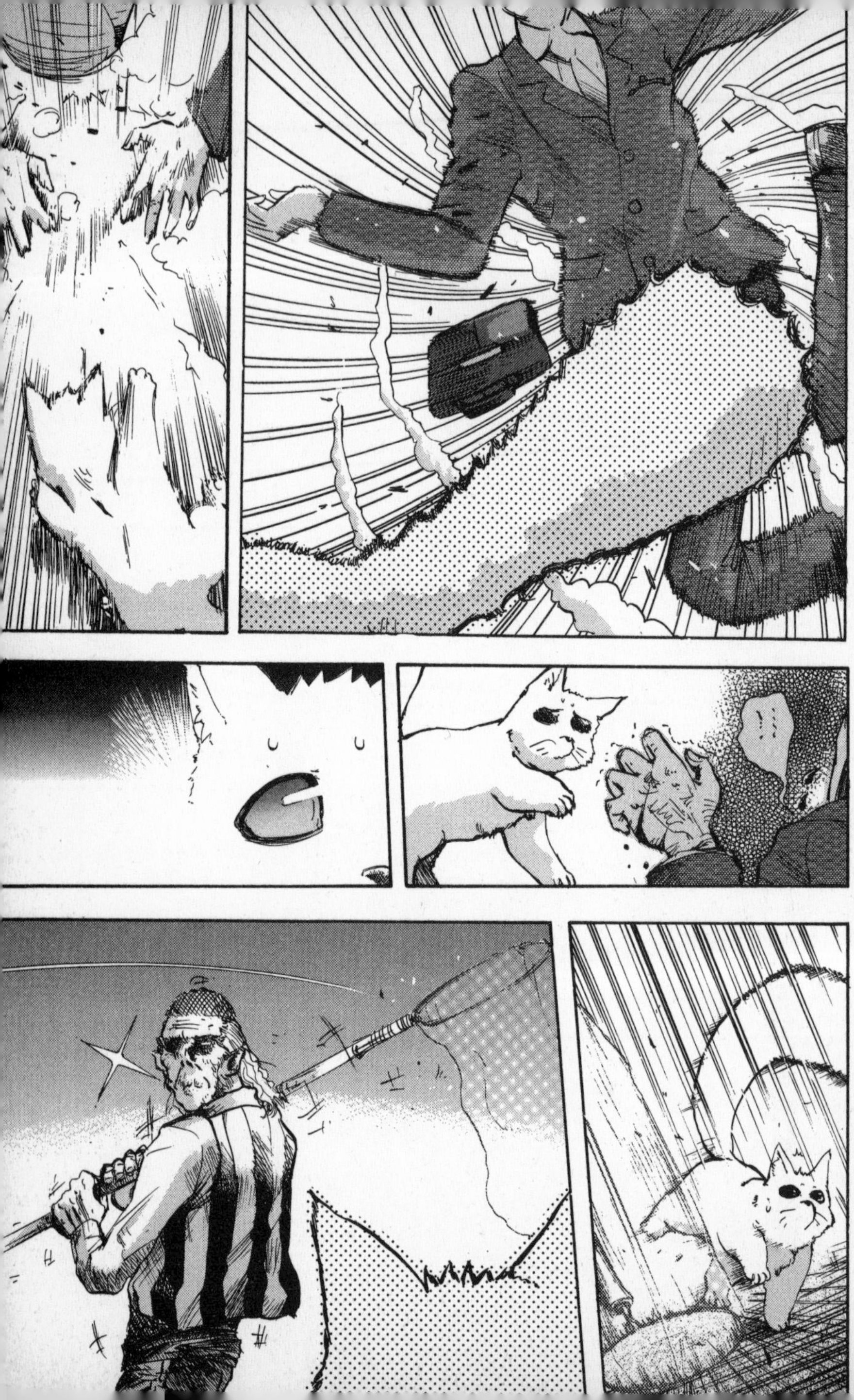

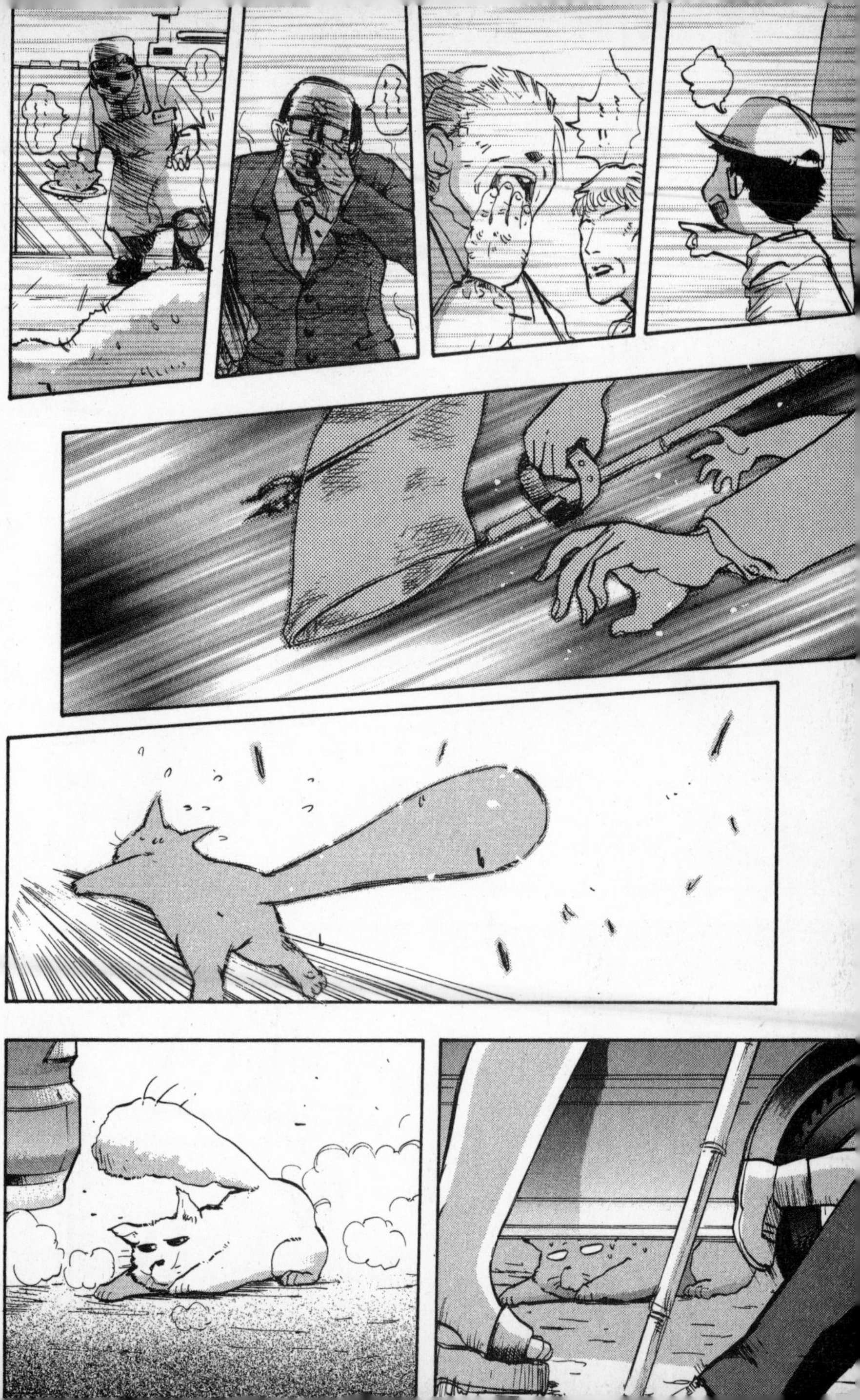

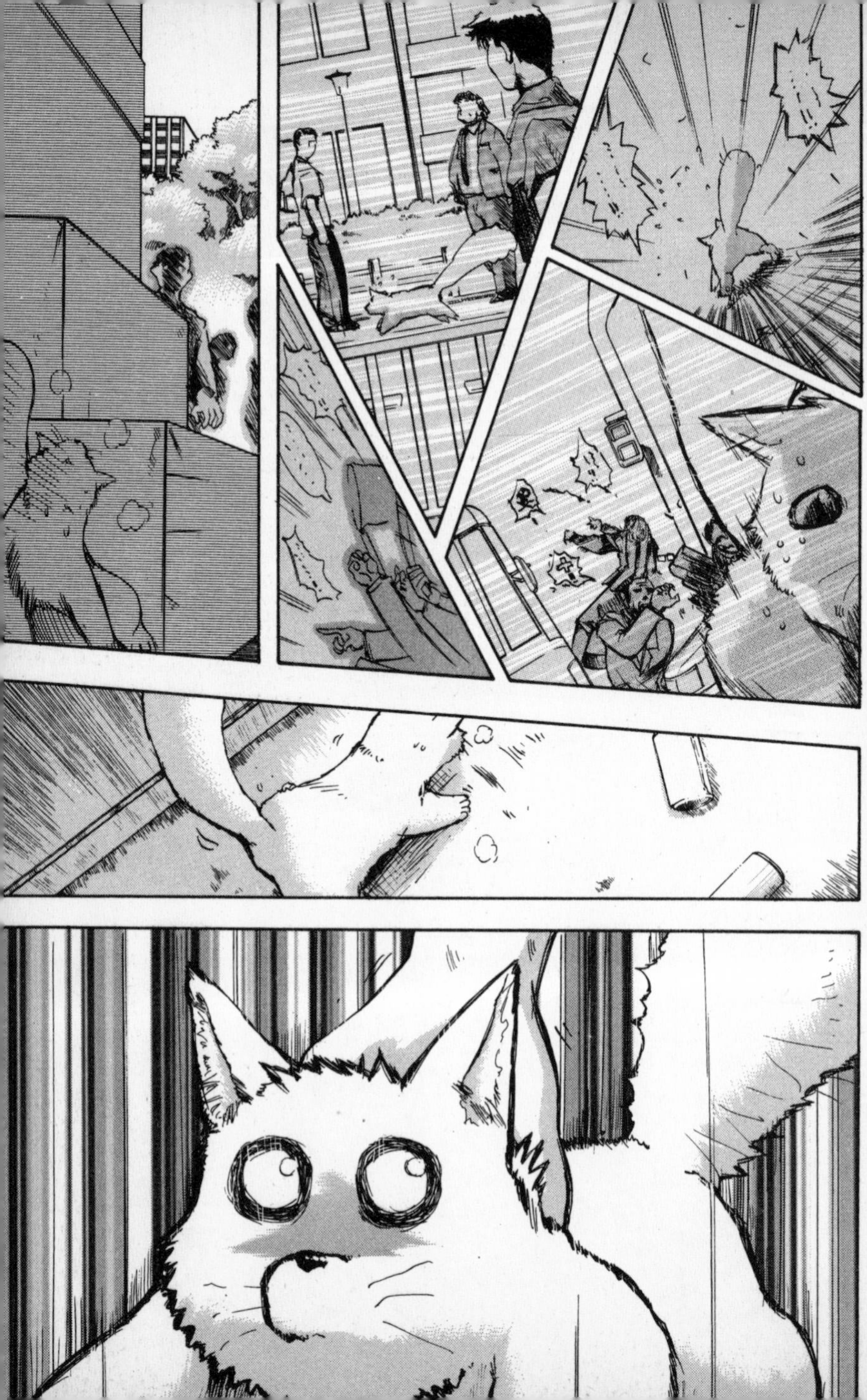

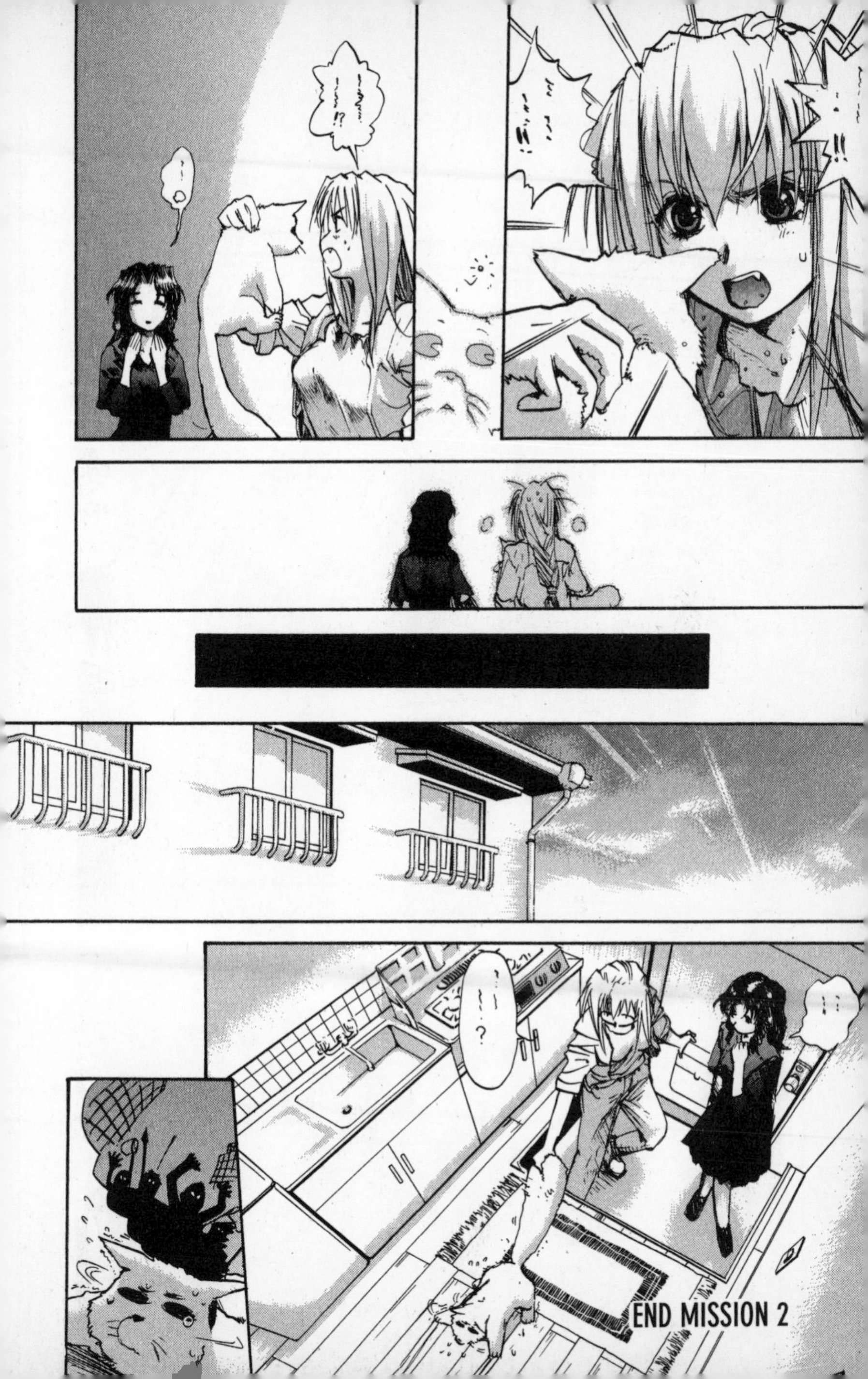
END MISSION 2

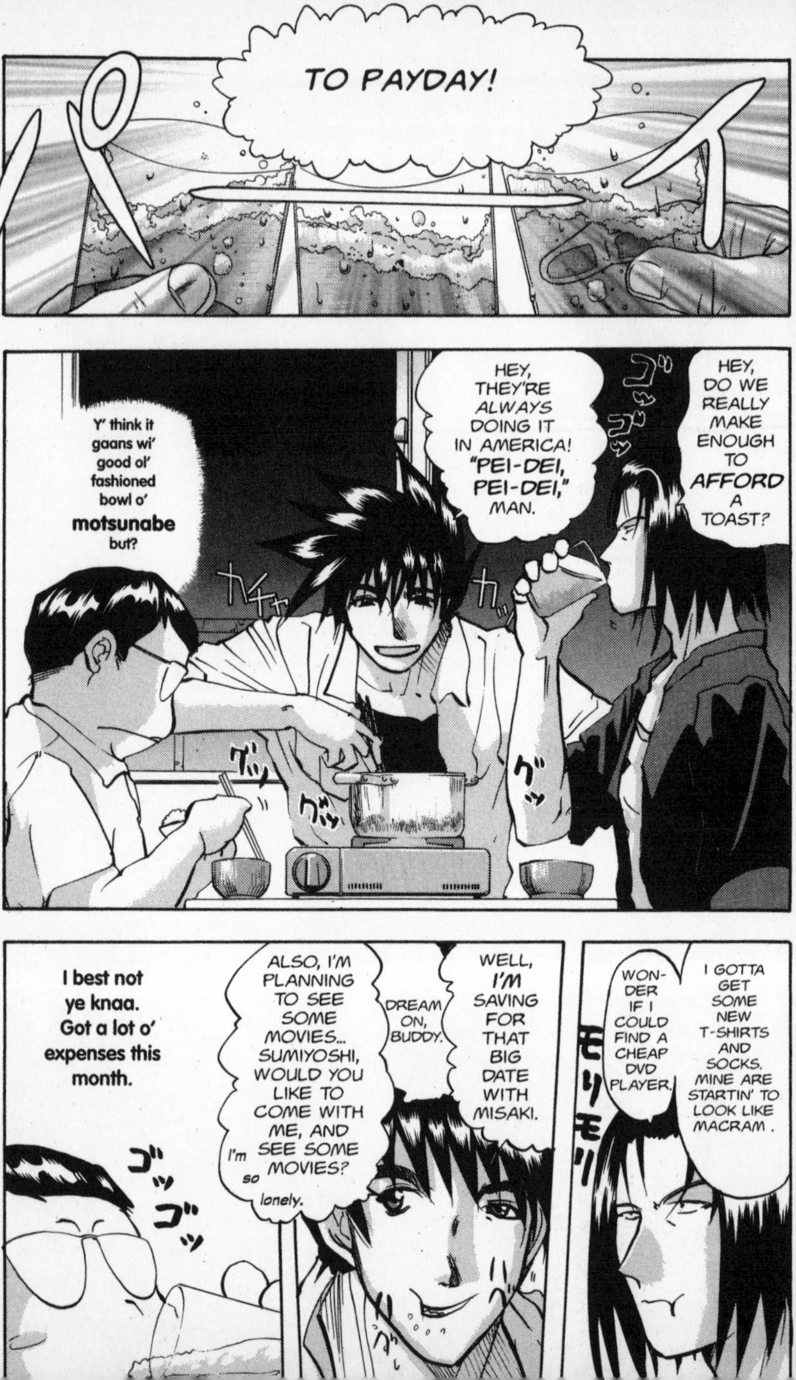
TO PAYDAY!
HEY, DO WE REALLY MAKE ENOUGH TO AFFORD A TOAST?
HEY, THEY'RE ALWAYS DOING IT IN AMERICA! "PEI-DEI, PEI-DEI," MAN.
Y' think it gaans wi' good ol' fashioned bowl o' motsunabe but?
I GOTTA GET SOME NEW T-SHIRTS AND SOCKS. MINE ARE STARTIN' TO LOOK LIKE MACRAM .
WONDER IF I COULD FIND A CHEAP DVD PLAYER.
WELL, I'M SAVING FOR THAT BIG DATE WITH MISAKI.
DREAM ON, BUDDY.
ALSO, I'M PLANNING TO SEE SOME MOVIES... SUMIYOSHI, WOULD YOU LIKE TO COME WITH ME, AND SEE SOME MOVIES?
I'm so lonely.
I best not ye knaa. Got a lot o' expenses this month.

MISSION 3
SCARS UPON A DREAM

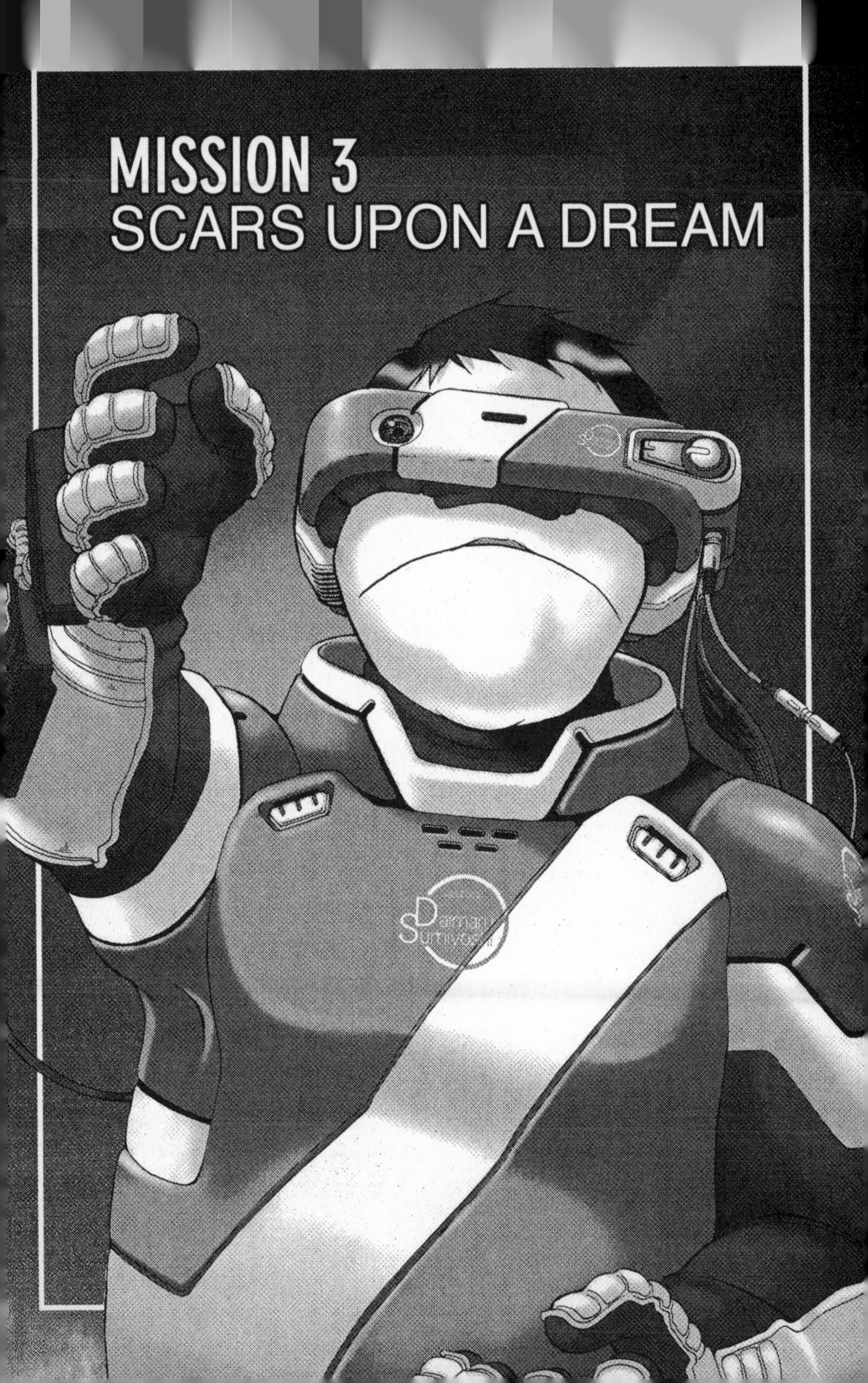

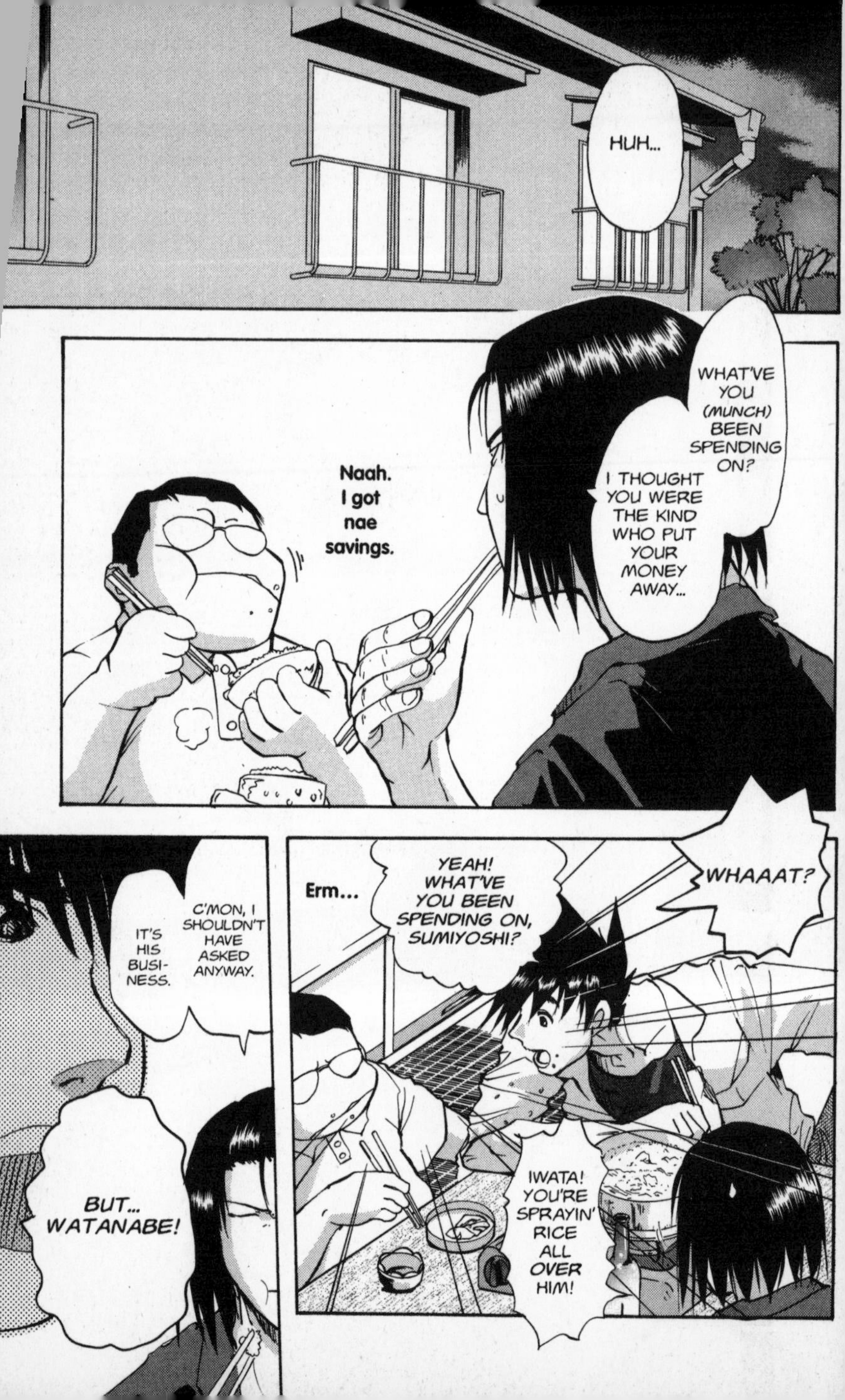
HUH...
WHAT'VE YOU (MUNCH) BEEN SPENDING ON?
I THOUGHT YOU WERE THE KIND WHO PUT YOUR MONEY AWAY...
Naah. I got nae savings.
WHAAAT?
YEAH! WHAT'VE YOU BEEN SPENDING ON, SUMIYOSHI?
Erm...
IWATA! YOU'RE SPRAYIN' RICE ALL OVER HIM!
C'MON, I SHOULDN'T HAVE ASKED ANYWAY.
IT'S HIS BUSINESS.
BUT... WATANABE!

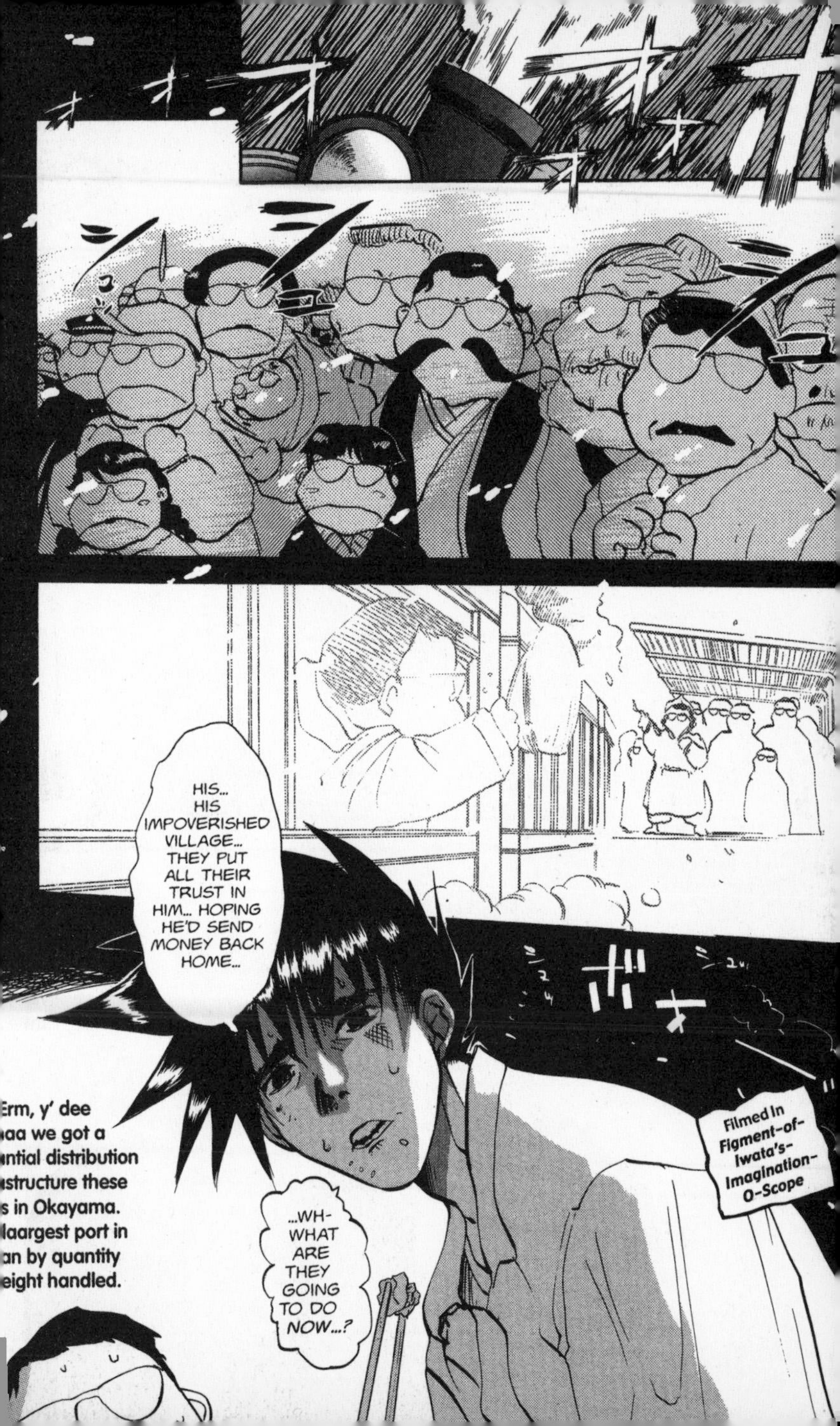
HIS... HIS IMPOVERISHED VILLAGE... THEY PUT ALL THEIR TRUST IN HIM... HOPING HE'D SEND MONEY BACK HOME...
Filmed In Figment-of-Iwata's-Imagination-O-Scope
...WH-WHAT ARE THEY GOING TO DO NOW...?
Erm, y' dee
aa we got a
ntial distribution
structure these
s in Okayama.
largest port in
an by quantity
eight handled.

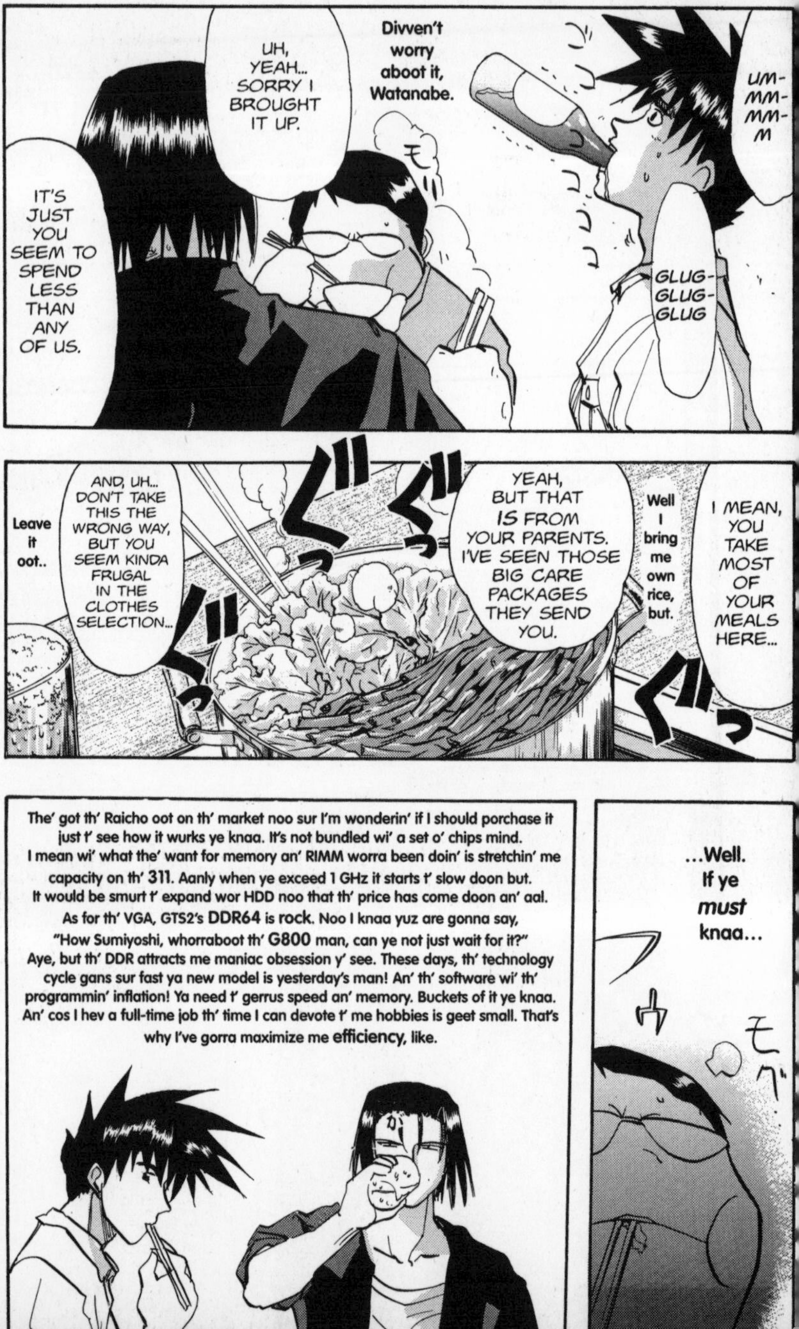
UM-MM-MM-M
Divven't worry aboot it, Watanabe.
UH, YEAH... SORRY I BROUGHT IT UP.
GLUG-GLUG-GLUG
IT'S JUST YOU SEEM TO SPEND LESS THAN ANY OF US.
I MEAN, YOU TAKE MOST OF YOUR MEALS HERE...
Well I bring me own rice, but.
YEAH, BUT THAT IS FROM YOUR PARENTS. I'VE SEEN THOSE BIG CARE PACKAGES THEY SEND YOU.
AND, UH... DON'T TAKE THIS THE WRONG WAY, BUT YOU SEEM KINDA FRUGAL IN THE CLOTHES SELECTION...
Leave it oot..
...Well. If ye must knaa...
The' got th' Raicho oot on th' market noo sur I'm wonderin' if I should porchase it just t' see how it wurks ye knaa. It's not bundled wi' a set o' chips mind. I mean wi' what the' want for memory an' RIMM worra been doin' is stretchin' me capacity on th' 311. Aanly when ye exceed 1 GHz it starts t' slow doon but. It would be smurt t' expand wor HDD noo that th' price has come doon an' aal. As for th' VGA, GTS2's DDR64 is rock. Noo I knaa yuz are gonna say, "How Sumiyoshi, whorraboot th' G800 man, can ye not just wait for it?" Aye, but th' DDR attracts me maniac obsession y' see. These days, th' technology cycle gans sur fast ya new model is yesterday's man! An' th' software wi' th' programmin' inflation! Ya need t' gerrus speed an' memory. Buckets of it ye knaa. An' cos I hev a full-time job th' time I can devote t' me hobbies is geet small. That's why I've gorra maximize me efficiency, like.

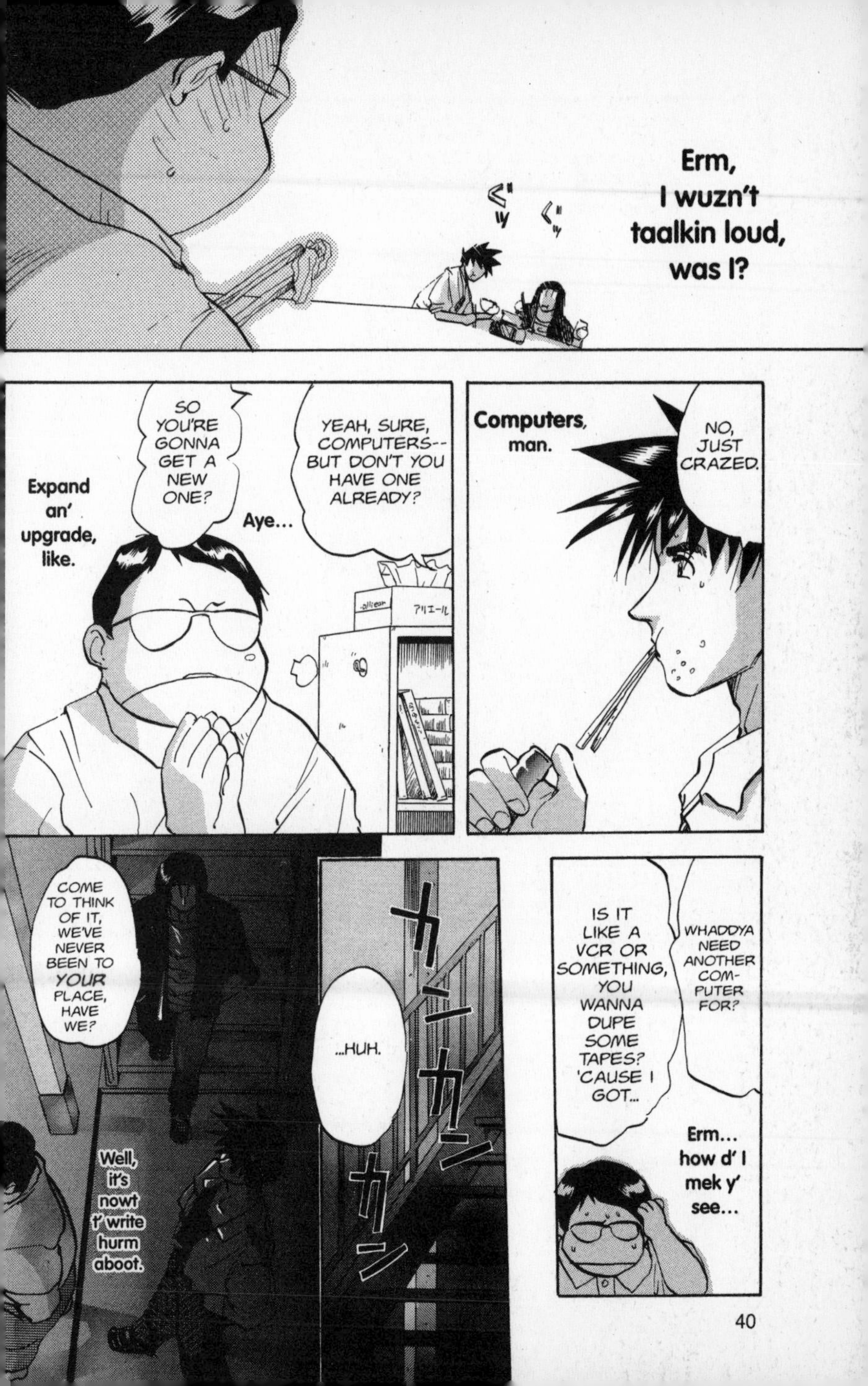
Erm, I wuzn't taalkin loud, was I?
NO, JUST CRAZED.
Computers, man.
YEAH, SURE, COMPUTERS-- BUT DON'T YOU HAVE ONE ALREADY?
Aye...
SO YOU'RE GONNA GET A NEW ONE?
Expand an' upgrade, like.
WHADDYA NEED ANOTHER COM-PUTER FOR?
IS IT LIKE A VCR OR SOMETHING, YOU WANNA DUPE SOME TAPES? 'CAUSE I GOT...
Erm... how d' I mek y' see...
...HUH.
COME TO THINK OF IT, WE'VE NEVER BEEN TO YOUR PLACE, HAVE WE?
Well, it's nowt t' write hurm aboot.

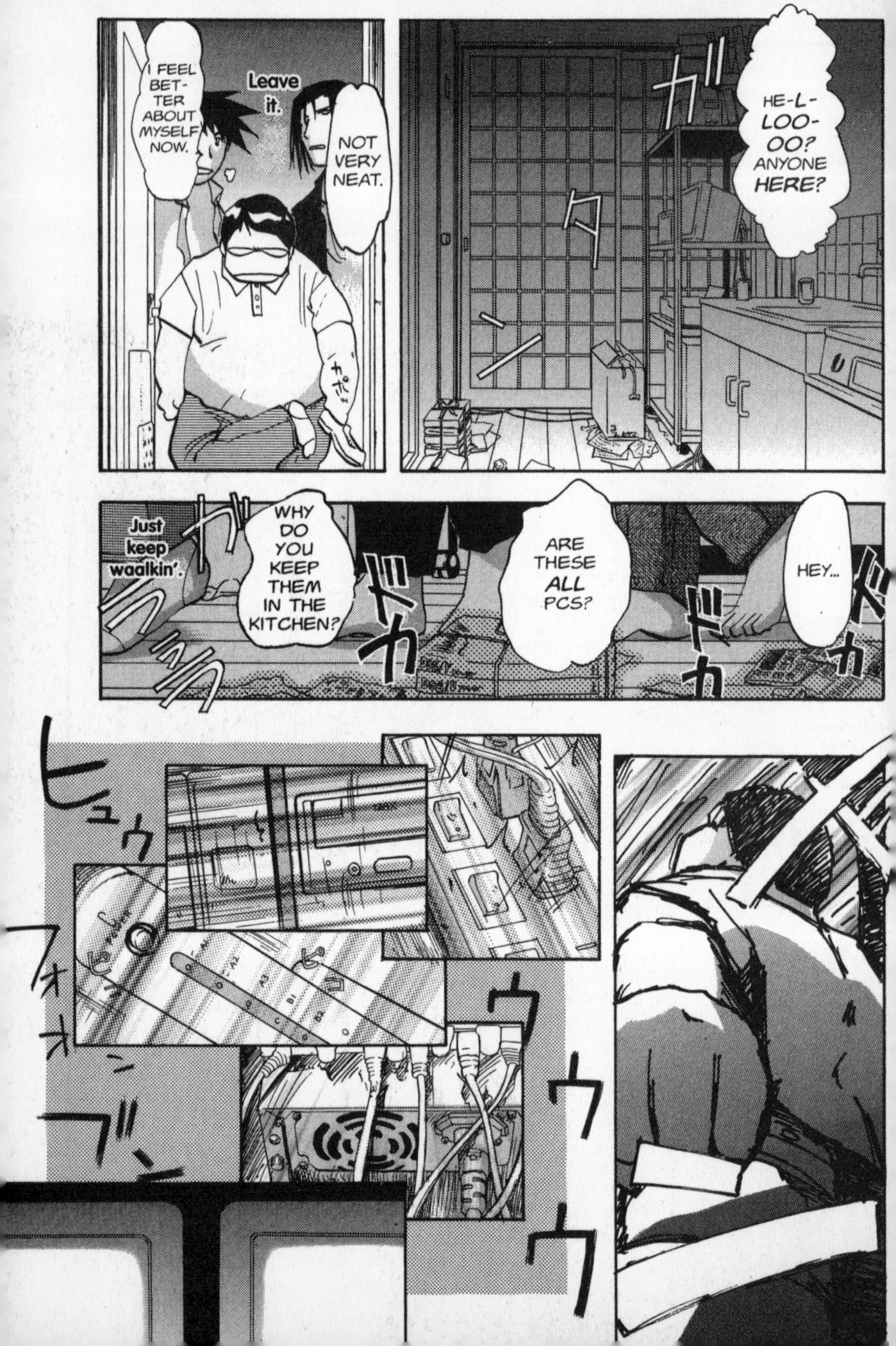
HE-L-LOO-OO? ANYONE HERE?
NOT VERY NEAT.
Leave it.
I FEEL BET-TER ABOUT MYSELF NOW.
HEY...
ARE THESE ALL PCS?
WHY DO YOU KEEP THEM IN THE KITCHEN?
Just keep waalkin'.

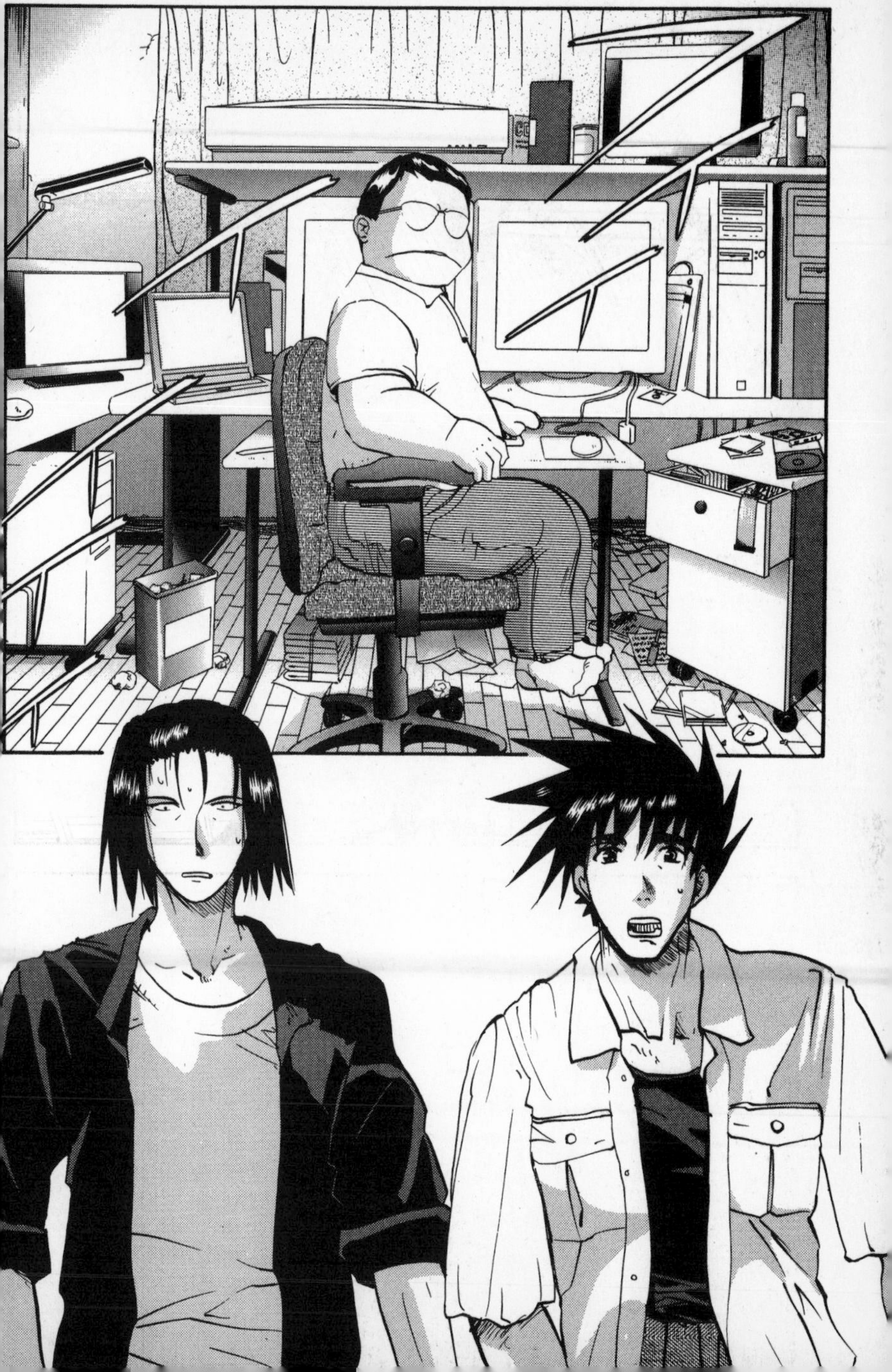

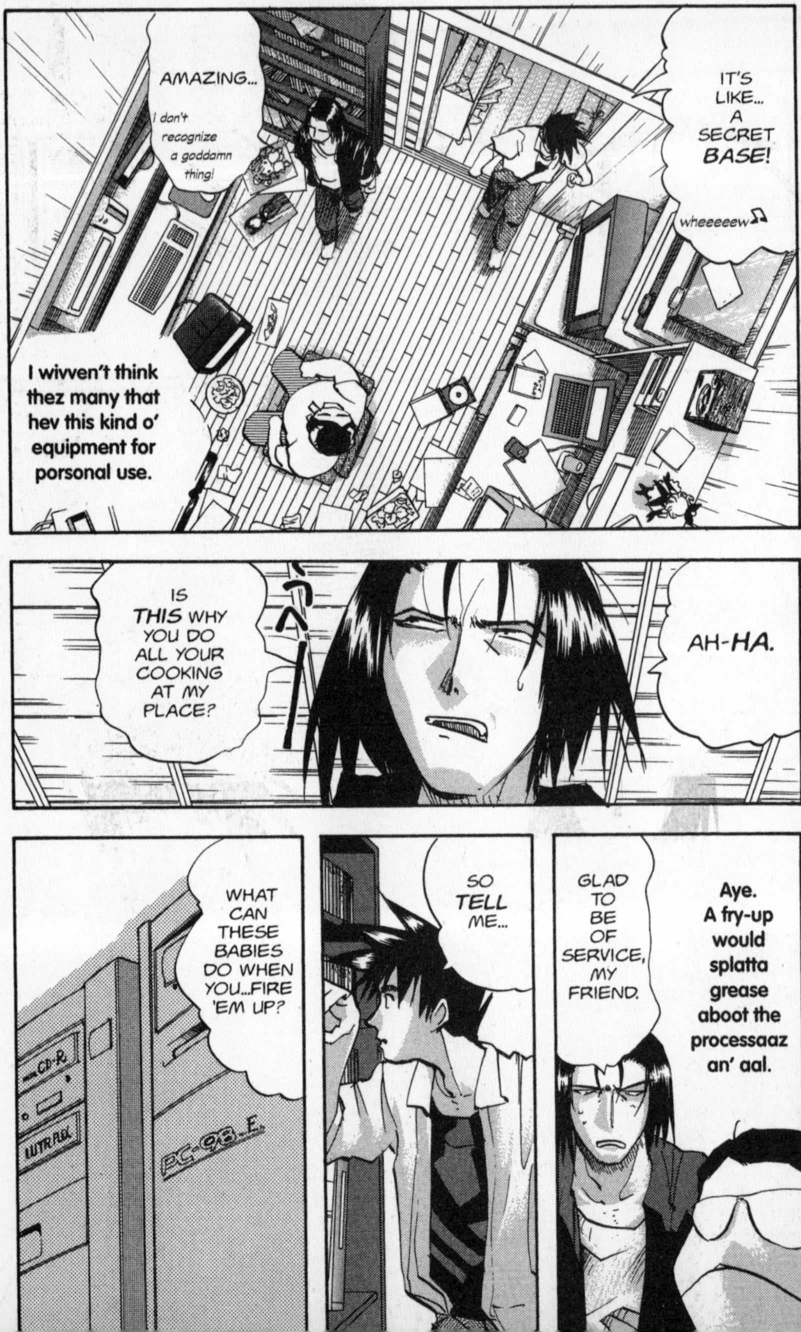
IT'S LIKE... A SECRET BASE!
wheeeeew♫
AMAZING...
I don't recognize a goddamn thing!
I wivven't think thez many that hev this kind o' equipment for porsonal use.
AH-HA.
IS THIS WHY YOU DO ALL YOUR COOKING AT MY PLACE?
Aye. A fry-up would splatta grease aboot the processaaz an' aal.
GLAD TO BE OF SERVICE, MY FRIEND.
SO TELL ME...
WHAT CAN THESE BABIES DO WHEN YOU...FIRE 'EM UP?

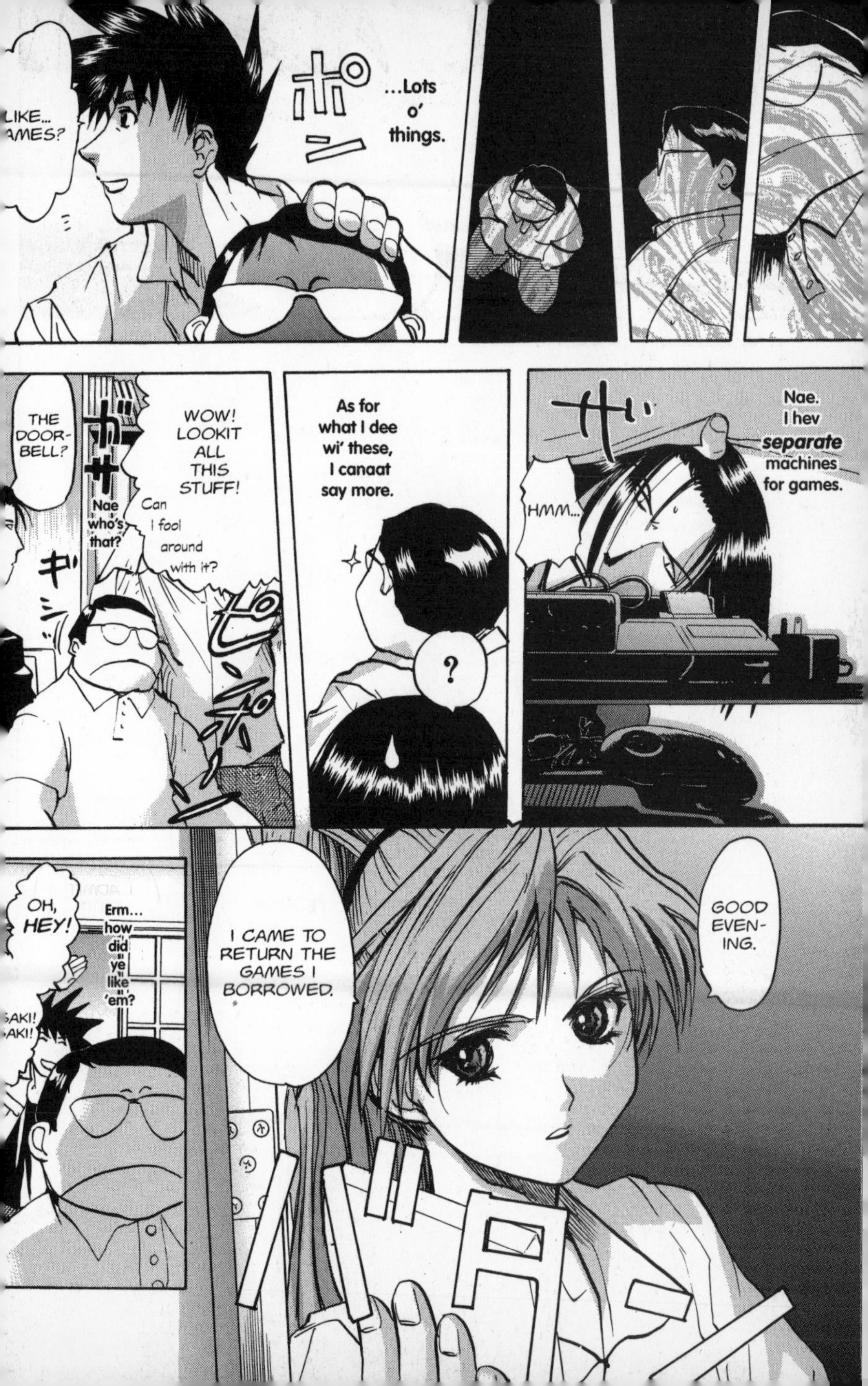
...Lots o' things.
LIKE... AMES?
Nae. I hev *separate* machines for games.
HMM...
As for what I dee wi' these, I canaat say more.
?
WOW! LOOKIT ALL THIS STUFF!
Can I fool around with it?
Nae who's that?
THE DOORBELL?
GOOD EVENING.
I CAME TO RETURN THE GAMES I BORROWED.
Erm... how did ye like 'em?
OH, **HEY!**
SAKI! SAKI!

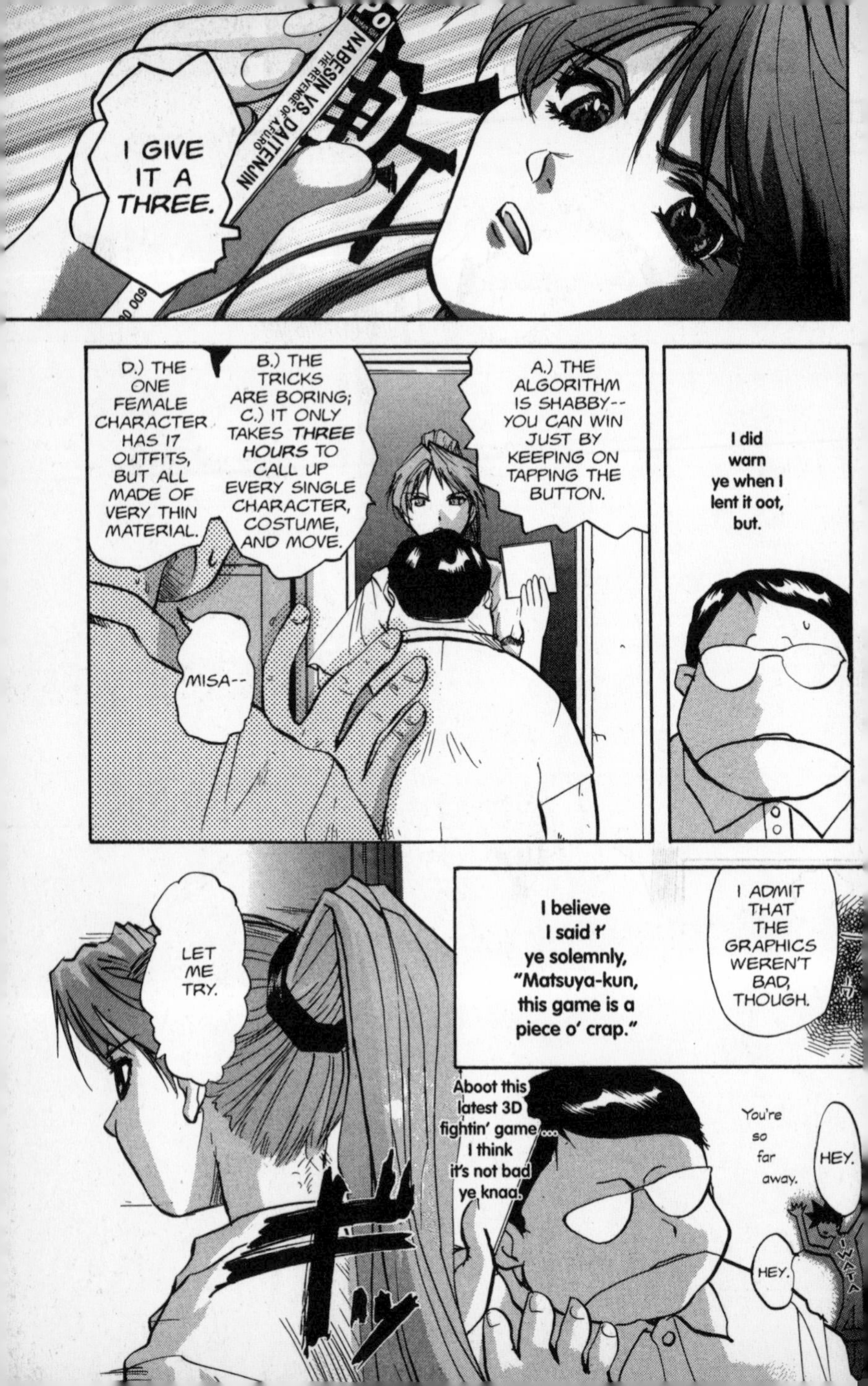
NABESIN VS. DAITENJIN
THE REVENGE OF AJURO
I GIVE IT A THREE.
I did warn ye when I lent it oot, but.
A.) THE ALGORITHM IS SHABBY-- YOU CAN WIN JUST BY KEEPING ON TAPPING THE BUTTON.
B.) THE TRICKS ARE BORING; C.) IT ONLY TAKES **THREE HOURS** TO CALL UP EVERY SINGLE CHARACTER, COSTUME, AND MOVE.
D.) THE ONE FEMALE CHARACTER HAS 17 OUTFITS, BUT ALL MADE OF VERY THIN MATERIAL.
MISA--
I ADMIT THAT THE GRAPHICS WEREN'T BAD, THOUGH.
I believe I said t' ye solemnly, "Matsuya-kun, this game is a piece o' crap."
HEY.
You're so far away.
Aboot this latest 3D fightin' game... I think it's not bad ye knaa.
HEY.
LET ME TRY.

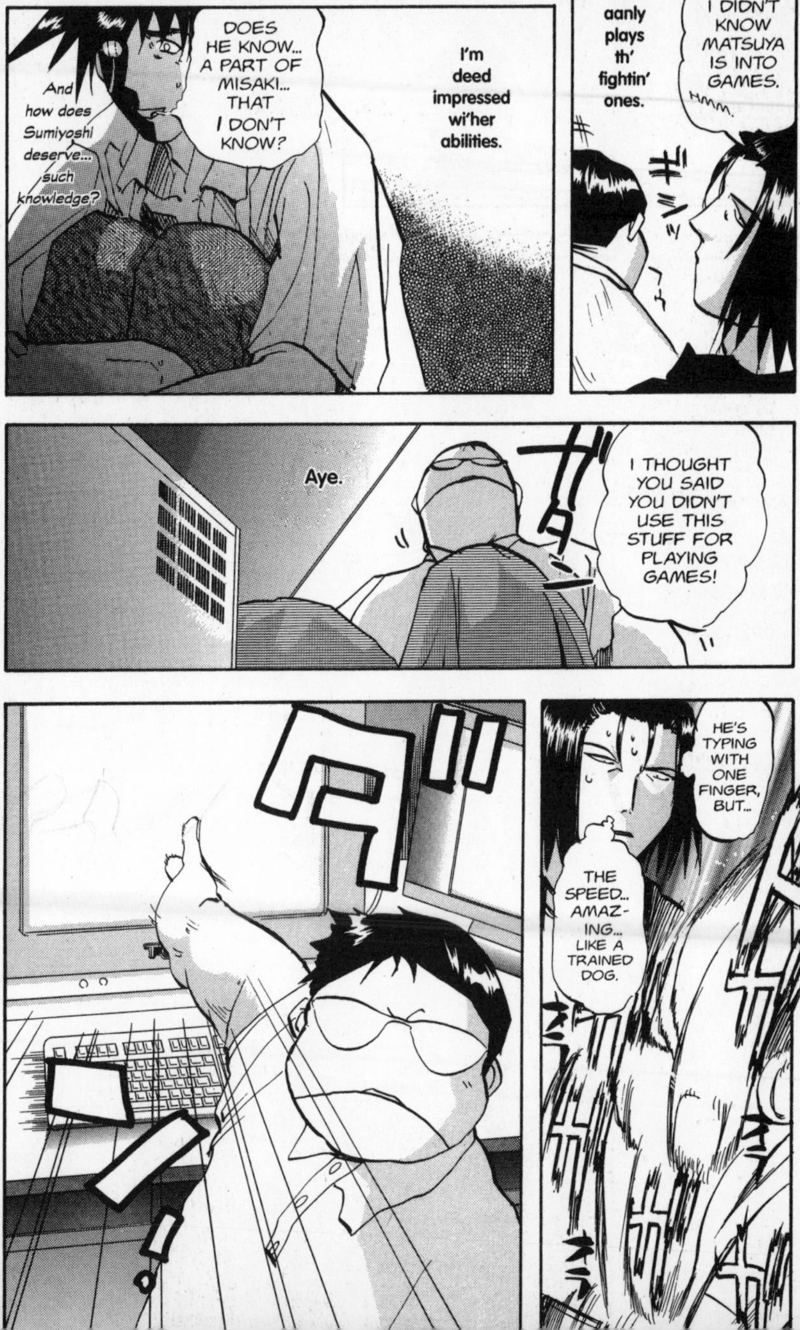
I DIDN'T KNOW MATSUYA IS INTO GAMES.
Hmm.
She aanly plays th' fightin' ones.
I'm deed impressed wi'her abilities.
DOES HE KNOW... A PART OF MISAKI... THAT I DON'T KNOW?
And how does Sumiyoshi deserve... such knowledge?
I THOUGHT YOU SAID YOU DIDN'T USE THIS STUFF FOR PLAYING GAMES!
Aye.
HE'S TYPING WITH ONE FINGER, BUT...
THE SPEED... AMAZ-ING... LIKE A TRAINED DOG.

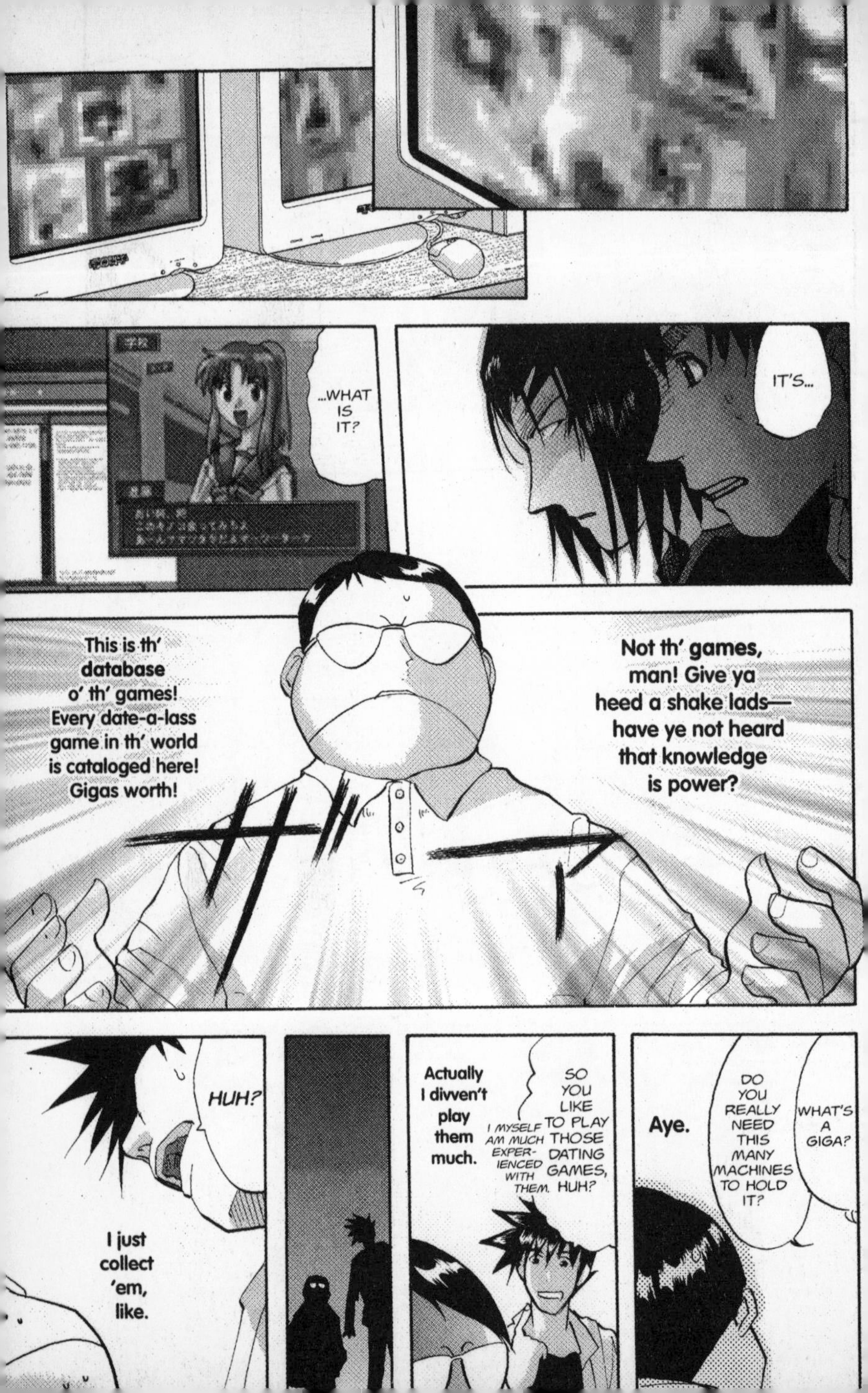
IT'S...
...WHAT IS IT?
Not th' games, man! Give ya heed a shake lads—have ye not heard that knowledge is power?
This is th' database o' th' games! Every date-a-lass game in th' world is cataloged here! Gigas worth!
WHAT'S A GIGA?
DO YOU REALLY NEED THIS MANY MACHINES TO HOLD IT?
Aye.
SO YOU LIKE TO PLAY THOSE DATING GAMES, HUH?
I MYSELF AM MUCH EXPER-IENCED WITH THEM.
Actually I divven't play them much.
HUH?
I just collect 'em, like.

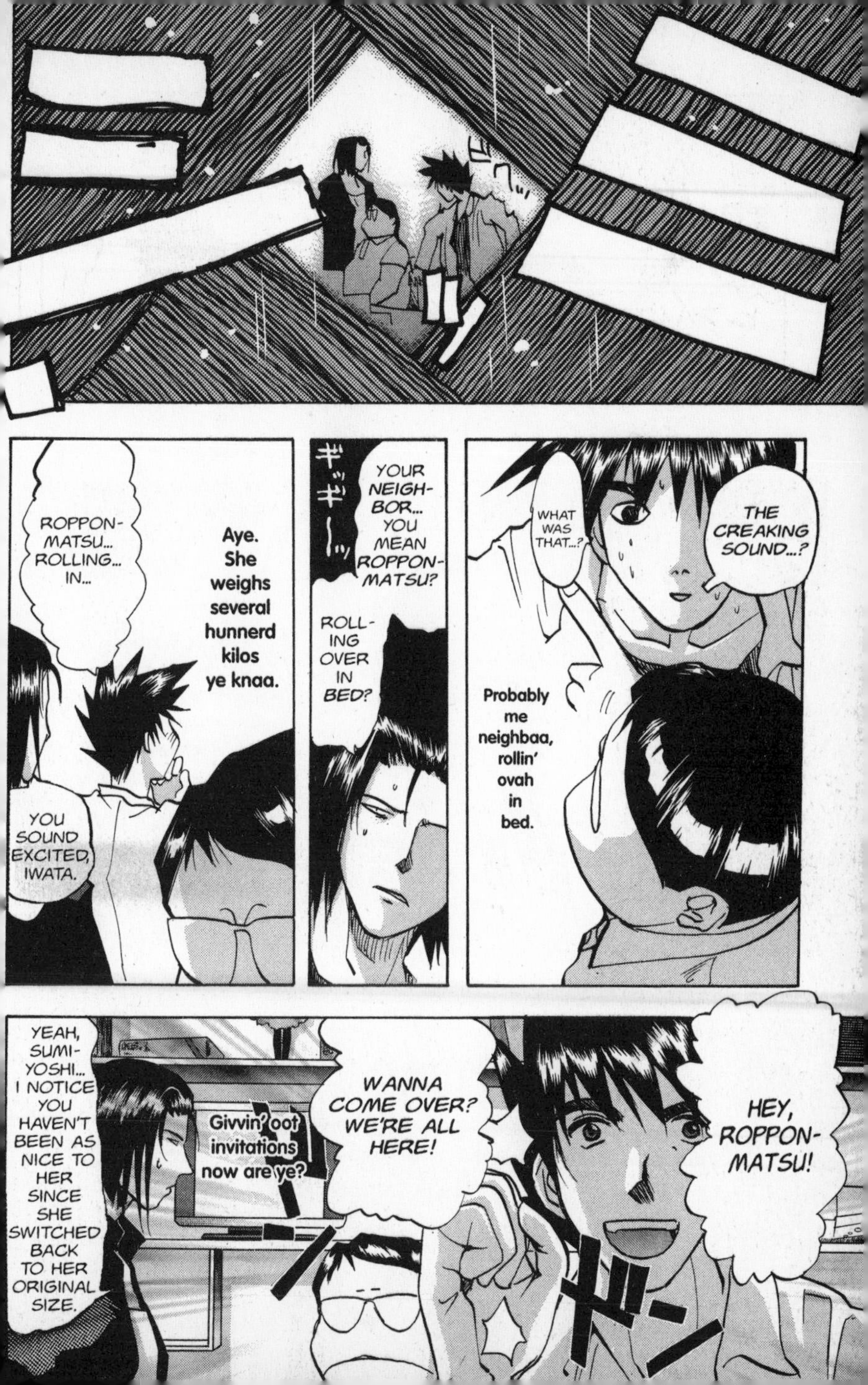
THE CREAKING SOUND...?
WHAT WAS THAT...?
Probably me neighbaa, rollin' ovah in bed.
ギッギーッ
YOUR NEIGHBOR... YOU MEAN ROPPONMATSU?
ROLLING OVER IN BED?
Aye. She weighs several hunnerd kilos ye knaa.
ROPPONMATSU... ROLLING... IN...
YOU SOUND EXCITED, IWATA.
HEY, ROPPONMATSU!
WANNA COME OVER? WE'RE ALL HERE!
Givvin' oot invitations now are ye?
YEAH, SUMIYOSHI... I NOTICE YOU HAVEN'T BEEN AS NICE TO HER SINCE SHE SWITCHED BACK TO HER ORIGINAL SIZE.

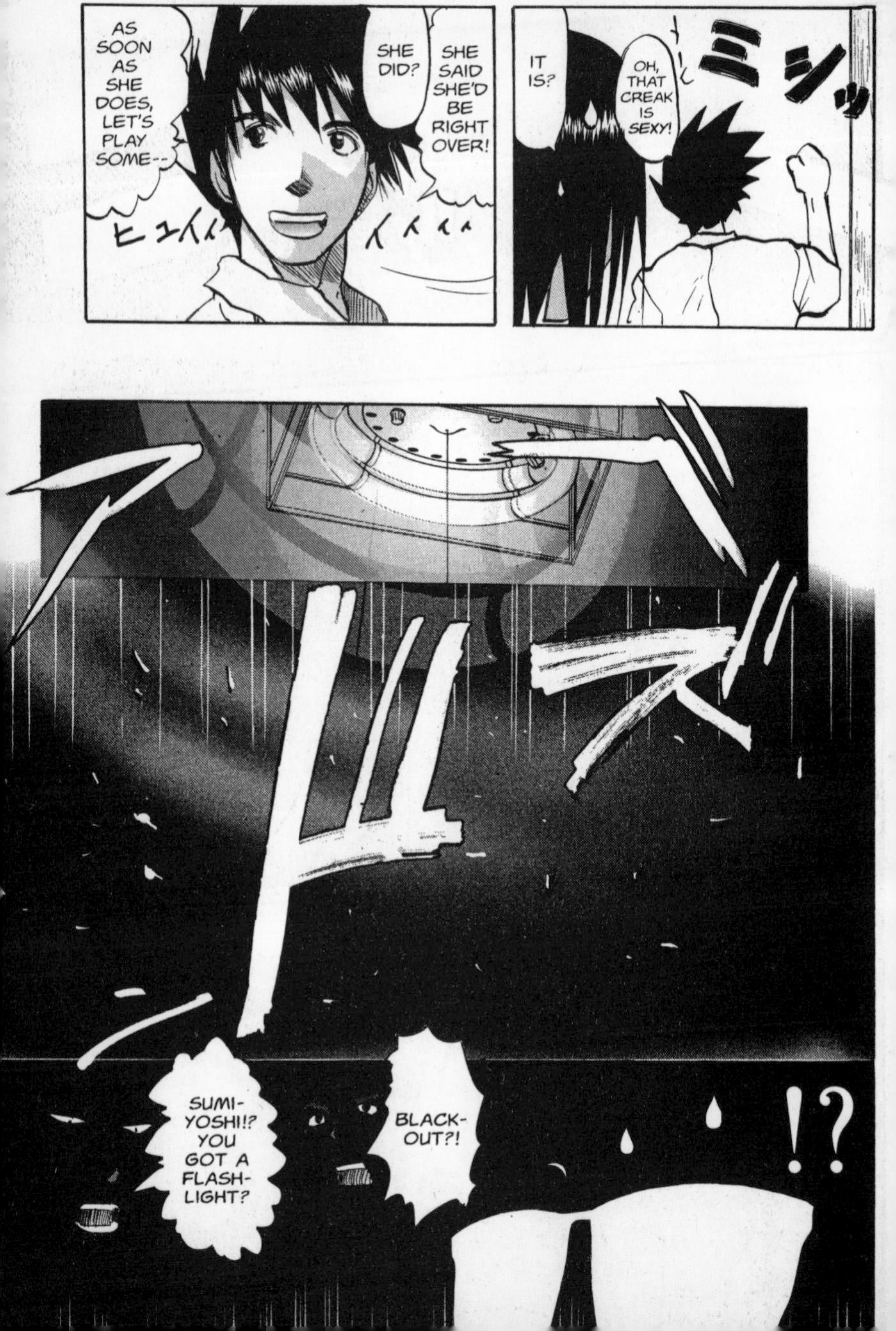
ミシッ
OH, THAT CREAK IS SEXY!
IT IS?
SHE SAID SHE'D BE RIGHT OVER!
SHE DID?
AS SOON AS SHE DOES, LET'S PLAY SOME--
!?
BLACK-OUT?!
SUMI-YOSHI!? YOU GOT A FLASH-LIGHT?

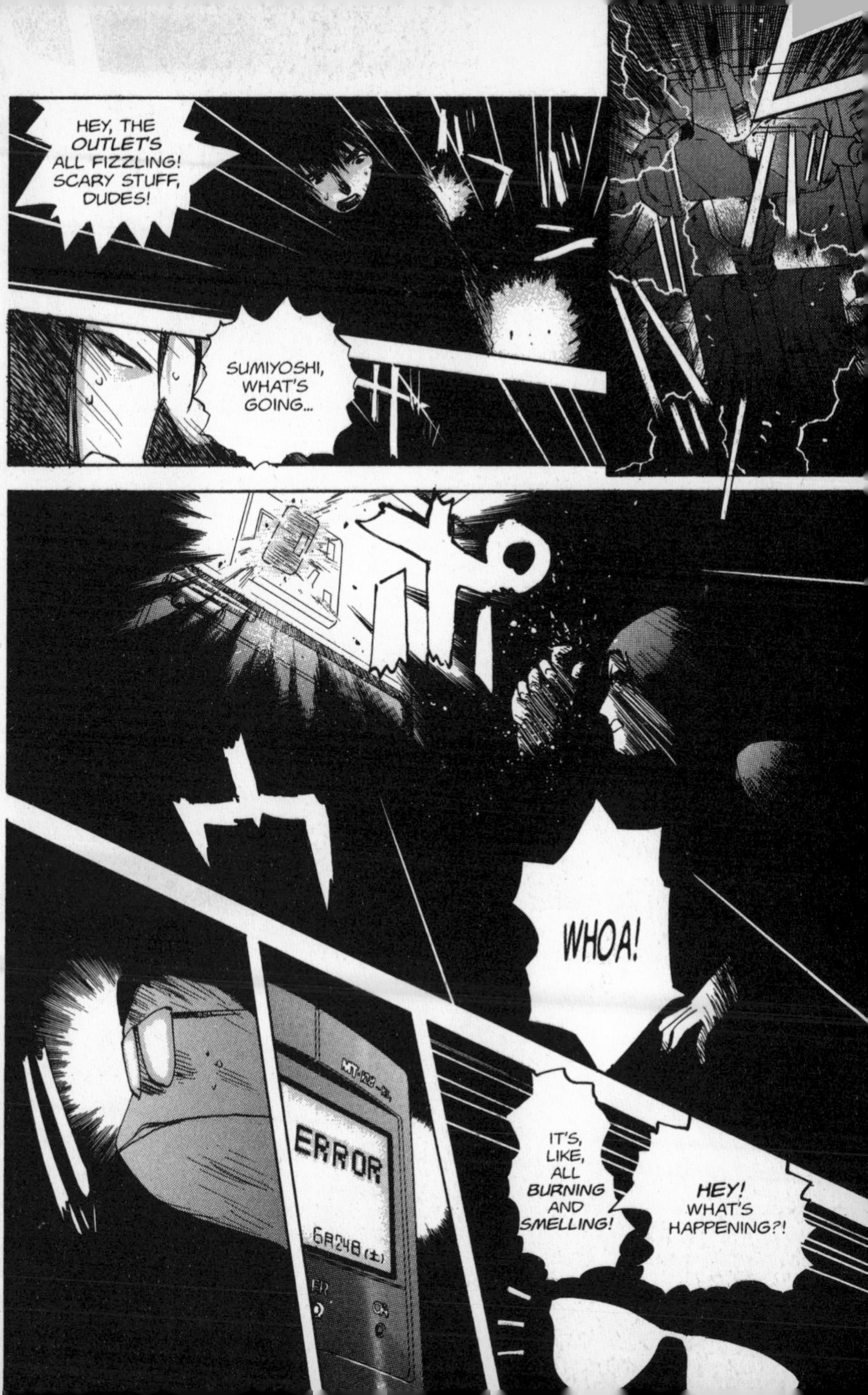
HEY, THE *OUTLET'S* ALL FIZZLING! SCARY STUFF, DUDES!
SUMIYOSHI, WHAT'S GOING...
WHOA!
HEY! WHAT'S HAPPENING?!
IT'S, LIKE, ALL *BURNING* AND *SMELLING!*
ERROR

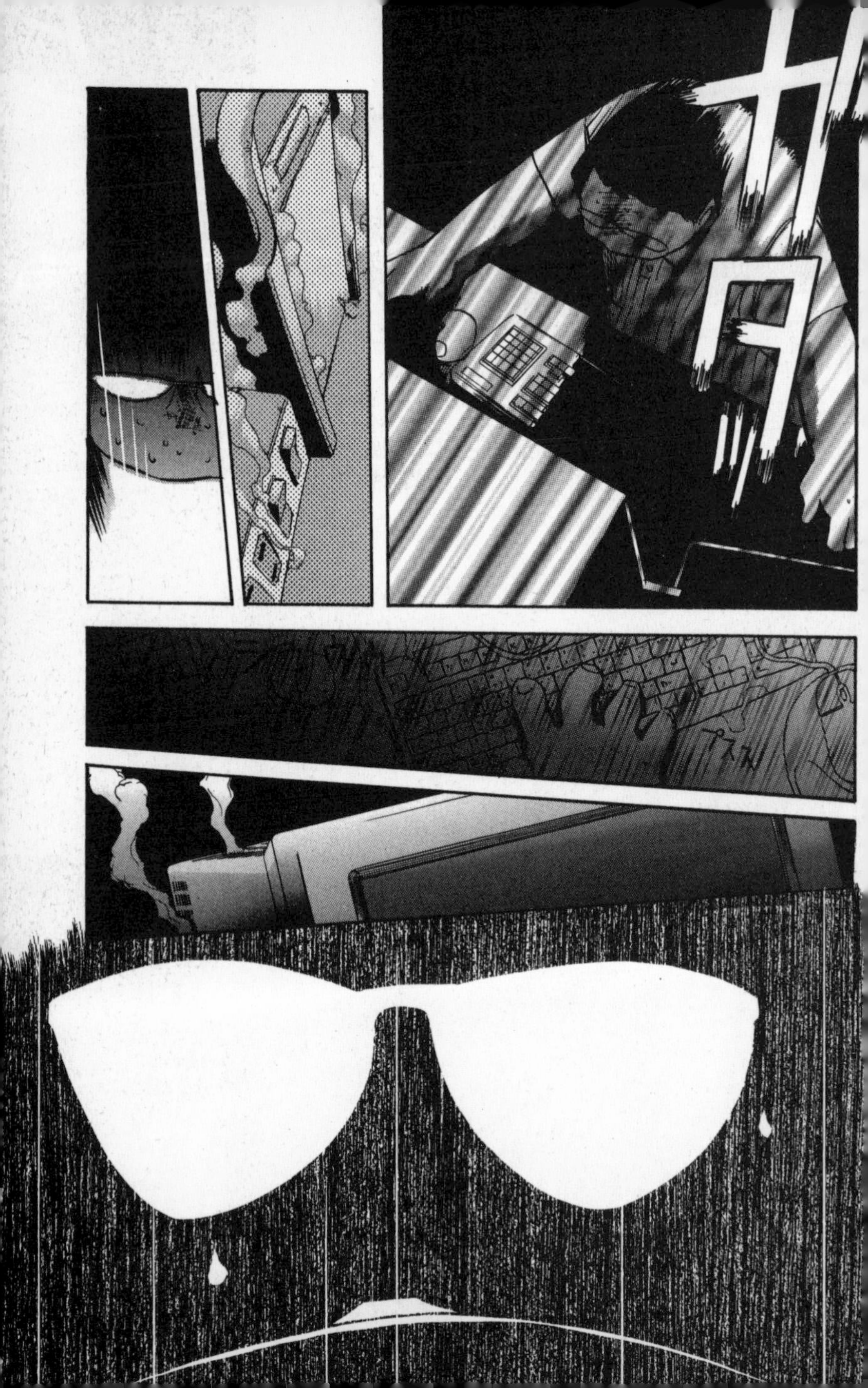
カタ

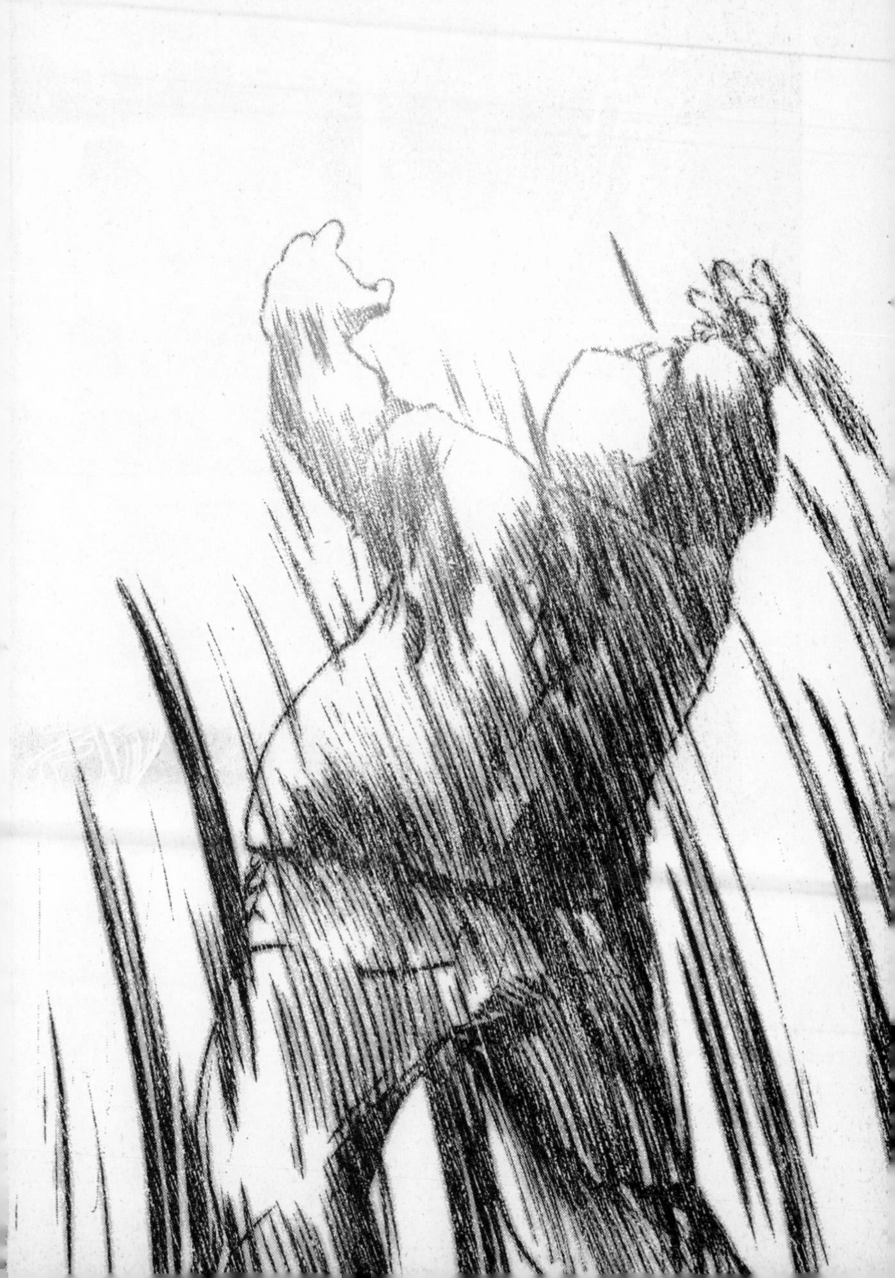

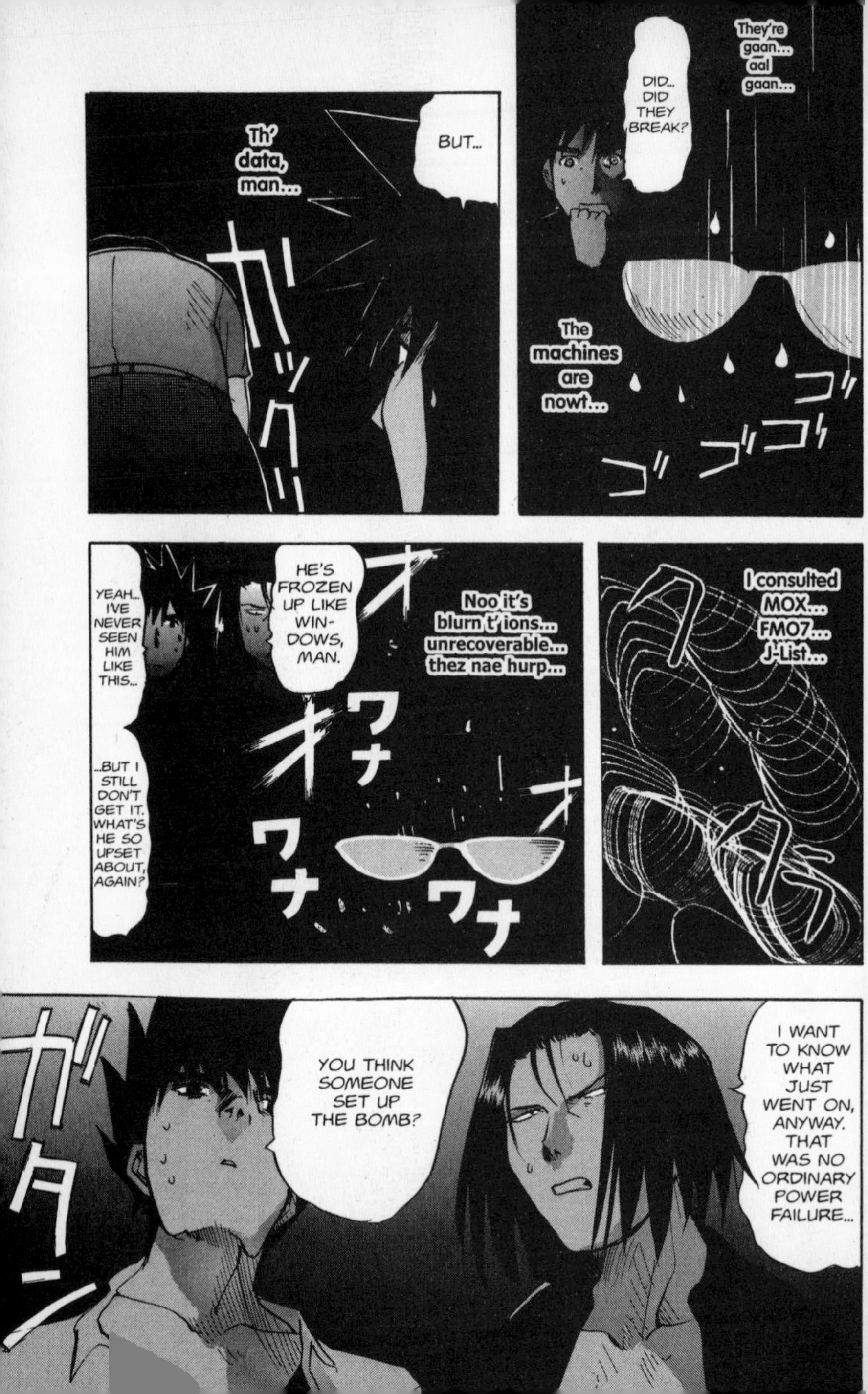
They're gaan... aal gaan...
DID.. DID THEY BREAK?
The machines are nowt...
BUT...
Th' data, man...
I consulted MOX... FM07... J-List...
Noo it's blurn t' ions... unrecoverable... thez nae hurp...
HE'S FROZEN UP LIKE WIN-DOWS, MAN.
YEAH... I'VE NEVER SEEN HIM LIKE THIS...
...BUT I STILL DON'T GET IT. WHAT'S HE SO UPSET ABOUT, AGAIN?
ワナワナ
I WANT TO KNOW WHAT JUST WENT ON, ANYWAY. THAT WAS NO ORDINARY POWER FAILURE...
YOU THINK SOMEONE SET UP THE BOMB?
ガタン

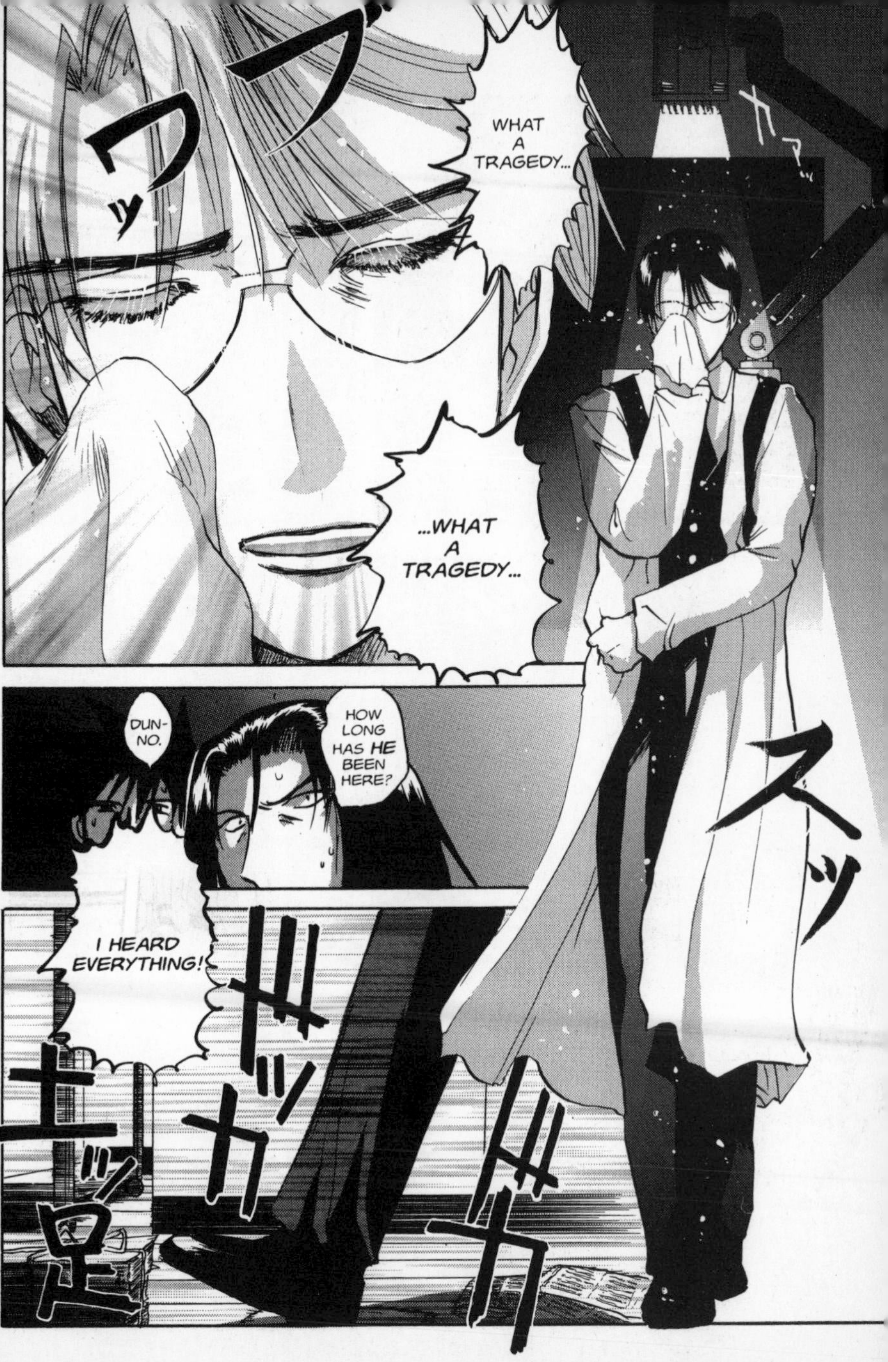
WHAT A TRAGEDY...
...WHAT A TRAGEDY...
HOW LONG HAS HE BEEN HERE?
DUN-NO.
I HEARD EVERYTHING!

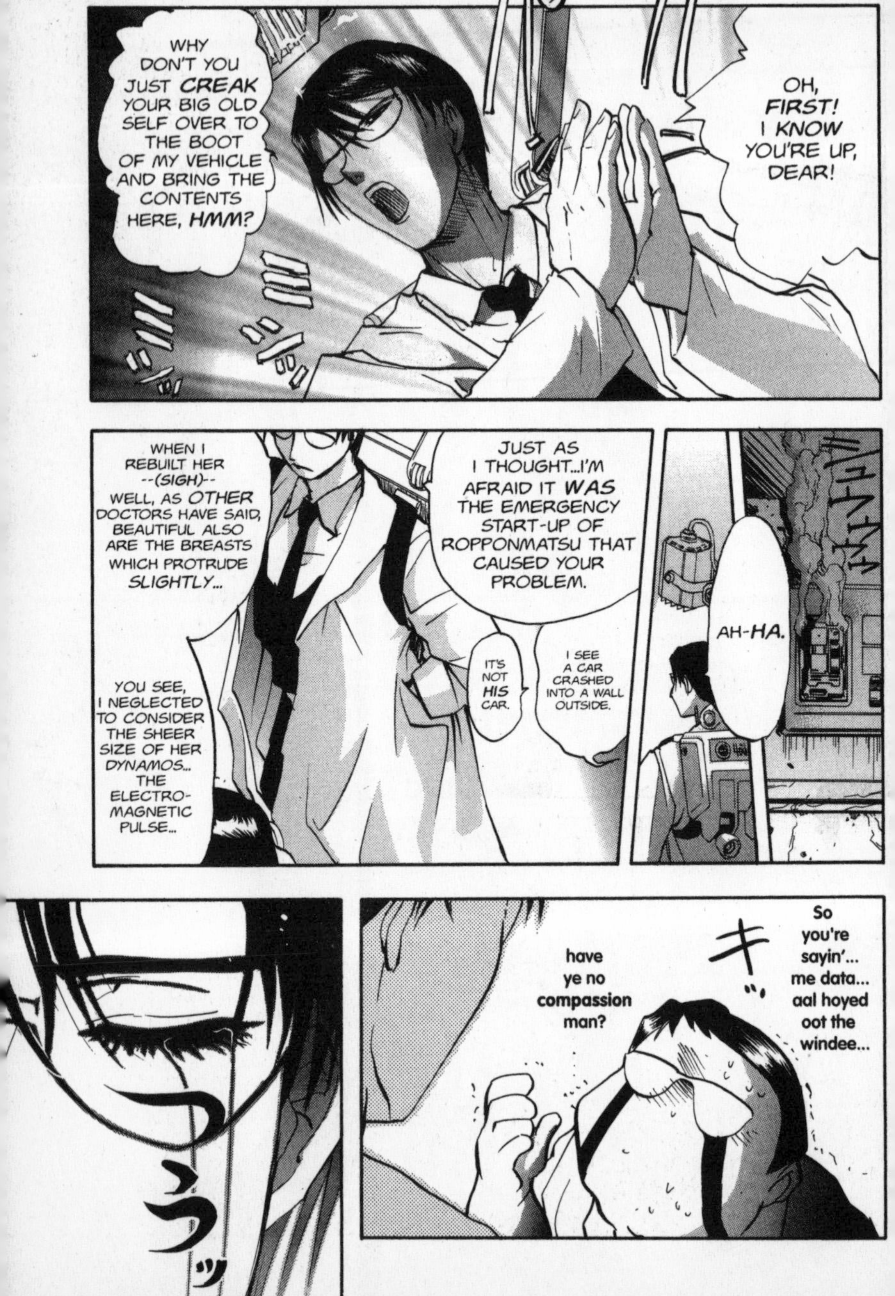
OH, FIRST! I KNOW YOU'RE UP, DEAR!
WHY DON'T YOU JUST CREAK YOUR BIG OLD SELF OVER TO THE BOOT OF MY VEHICLE AND BRING THE CONTENTS HERE, HMM?
AH-HA.
JUST AS I THOUGHT...I'M AFRAID IT WAS THE EMERGENCY START-UP OF ROPPONMATSU THAT CAUSED YOUR PROBLEM.
WHEN I REBUILT HER --(SIGH)-- WELL, AS OTHER DOCTORS HAVE SAID, BEAUTIFUL ALSO ARE THE BREASTS WHICH PROTRUDE SLIGHTLY...
I SEE A CAR CRASHED INTO A WALL OUTSIDE.
IT'S NOT HIS CAR.
YOU SEE, I NEGLECTED TO CONSIDER THE SHEER SIZE OF HER DYNAMOS... THE ELECTRO-MAGNETIC PULSE...
So you're sayin'... me data... aal hoyed oot the windee...
キ
have ye no compassion man?
うッ

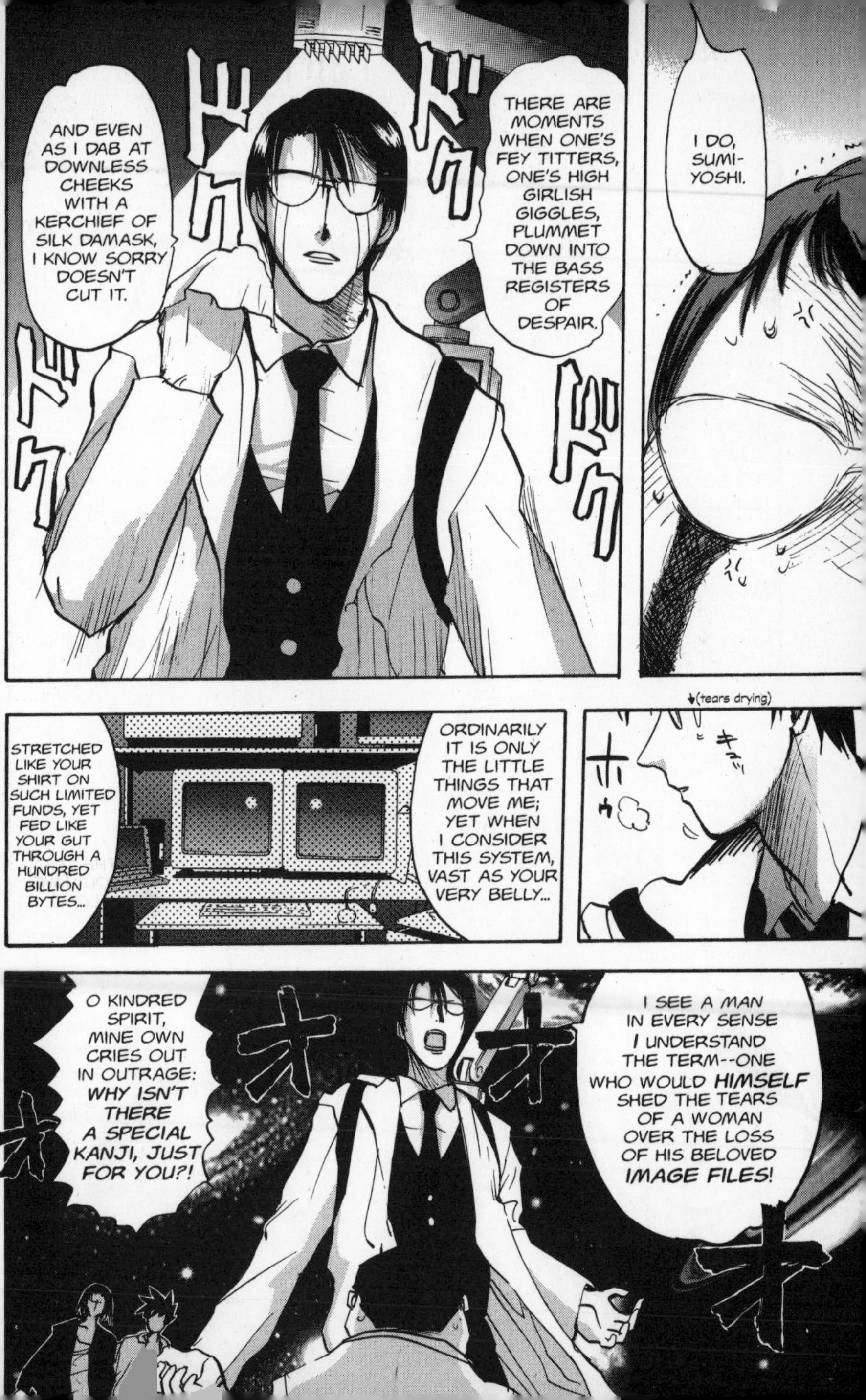
I DO, SUMIYOSHI.
THERE ARE MOMENTS WHEN ONE'S FEY TITTERS, ONE'S HIGH GIRLISH GIGGLES, PLUMMET DOWN INTO THE BASS REGISTERS OF DESPAIR.
AND EVEN AS I DAB AT DOWNLESS CHEEKS WITH A KERCHIEF OF SILK DAMASK, I KNOW SORRY DOESN'T CUT IT.
(tears drying)
ORDINARILY IT IS ONLY THE LITTLE THINGS THAT MOVE ME; YET WHEN I CONSIDER THIS SYSTEM, VAST AS YOUR VERY BELLY...
STRETCHED LIKE YOUR SHIRT ON SUCH LIMITED FUNDS, YET FED LIKE YOUR GUT THROUGH A HUNDRED BILLION BYTES...
I SEE A MAN IN EVERY SENSE I UNDERSTAND THE TERM--ONE WHO WOULD HIMSELF SHED THE TEARS OF A WOMAN OVER THE LOSS OF HIS BELOVED IMAGE FILES!
O KINDRED SPIRIT, MINE OWN CRIES OUT IN OUTRAGE: WHY ISN'T THERE A SPECIAL KANJI, JUST FOR YOU?!

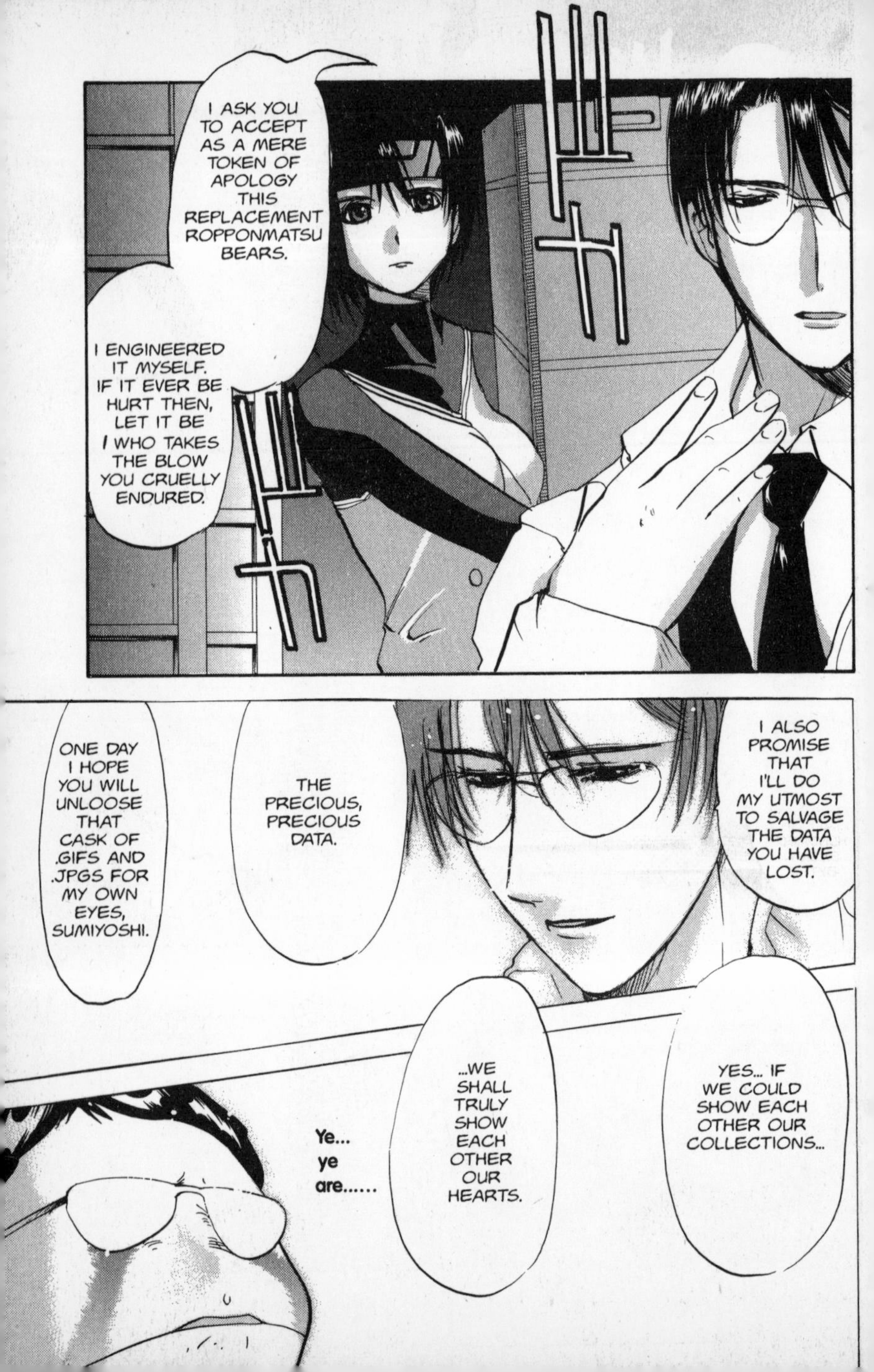
I ASK YOU TO ACCEPT AS A MERE TOKEN OF APOLOGY THIS REPLACEMENT ROPPONMATSU BEARS.
I ENGINEERED IT MYSELF. IF IT EVER BE HURT THEN, LET IT BE I WHO TAKES THE BLOW YOU CRUELLY ENDURED.
I ALSO PROMISE THAT I'LL DO MY UTMOST TO SALVAGE THE DATA YOU HAVE LOST.
THE PRECIOUS, PRECIOUS DATA.
ONE DAY I HOPE YOU WILL UNLOOSE THAT CASK OF .GIFS AND .JPGS FOR MY OWN EYES, SUMIYOSHI.
YES... IF WE COULD SHOW EACH OTHER OUR COLLECTIONS...
...WE SHALL TRULY SHOW EACH OTHER OUR HEARTS.
Ye... ye are......

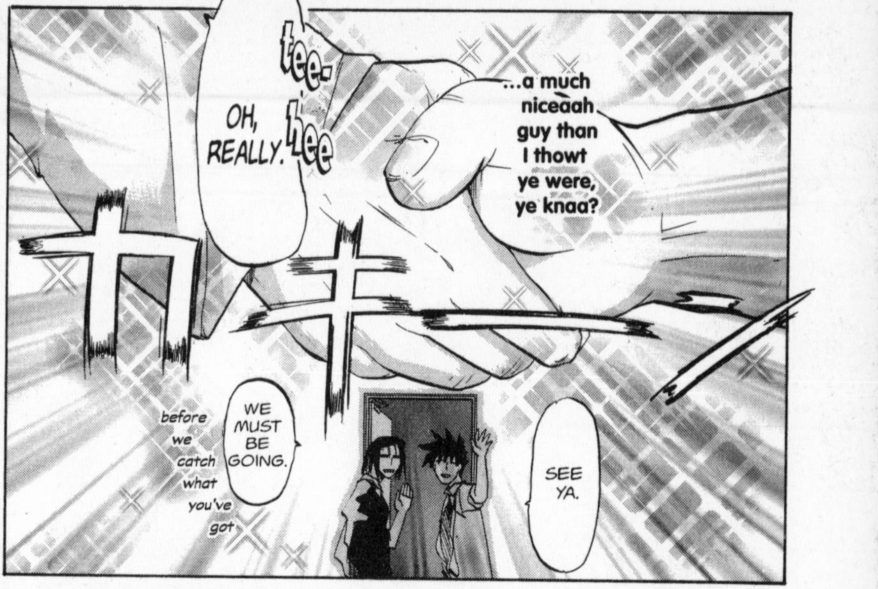
...a much niceaah guy than I thowt ye were, ye knaa?
tee-hee
OH, REALLY.
SEE YA.
WE MUST BE GOING.
before we catch what you've got

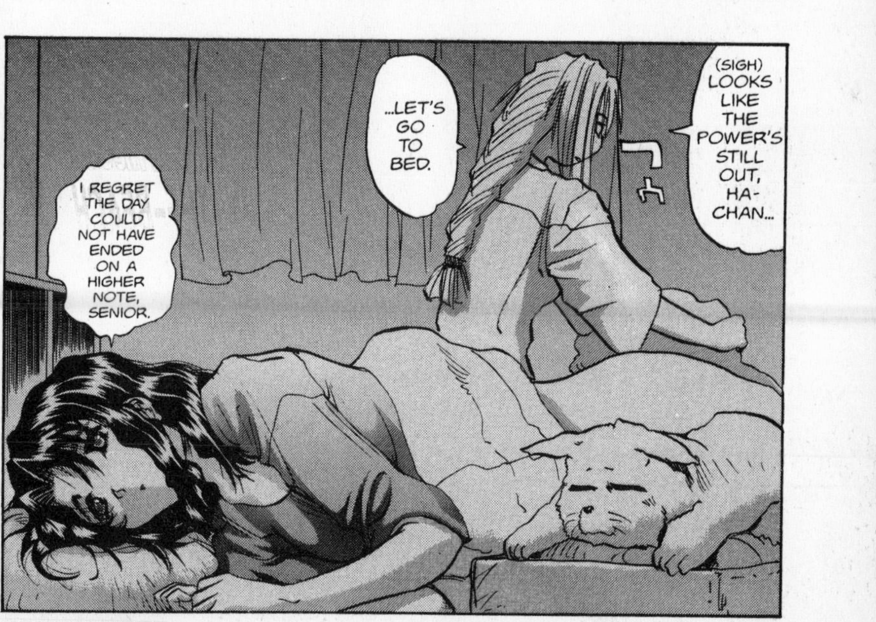
(SIGH) LOOKS LIKE THE POWER'S STILL OUT, HA-CHAN...
...LET'S GO TO BED.
I REGRET THE DAY COULD NOT HAVE ENDED ON A HIGHER NOTE, SENIOR.

END MISSION 3

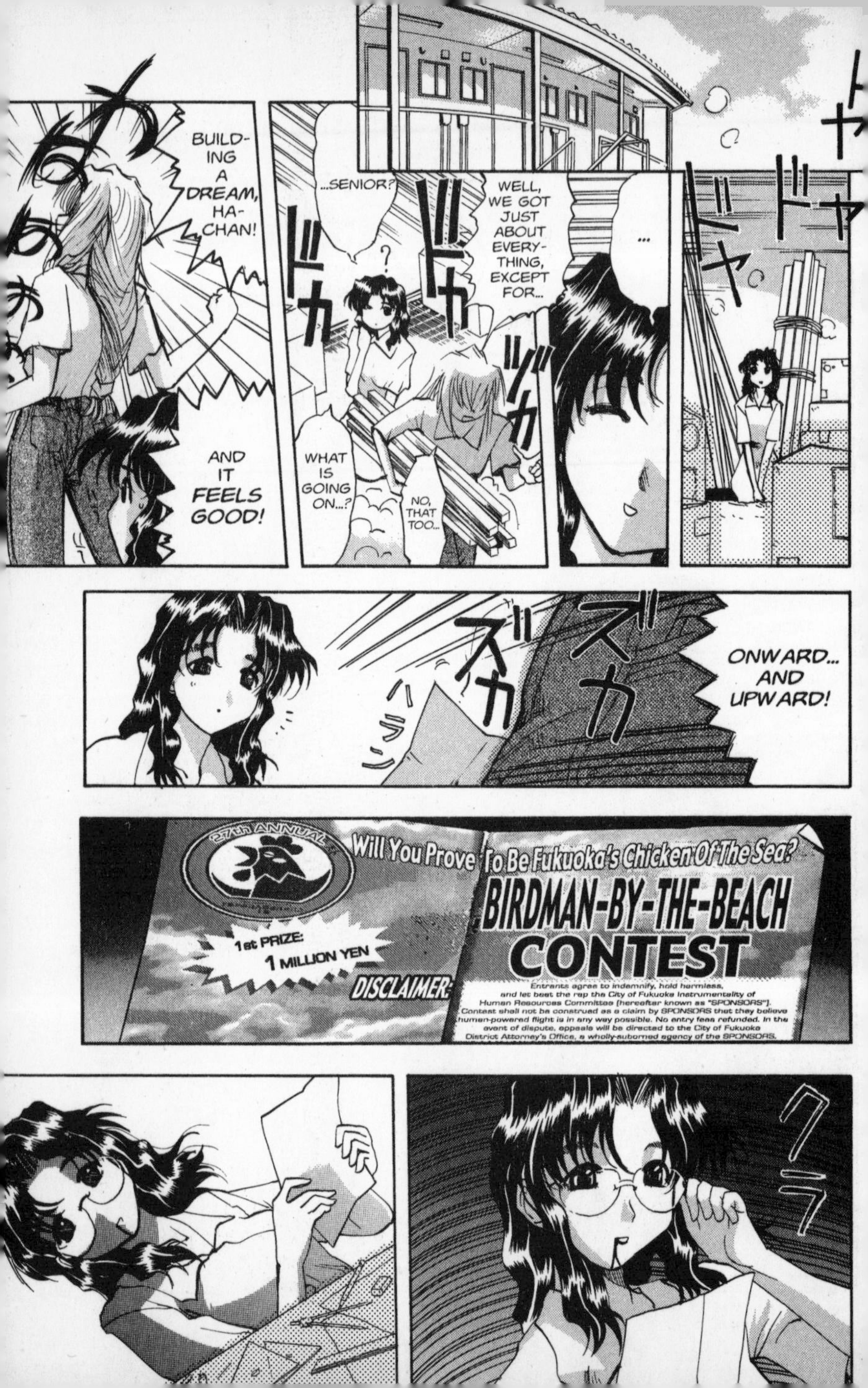
WELL, WE GOT JUST ABOUT EVERYTHING, EXCEPT FOR...
...
...SENIOR?
WHAT IS GOING ON...?
NO, THAT TOO...
BUILDING A DREAM, HA-CHAN!
AND IT FEELS GOOD!
ONWARD... AND UPWARD!
27th ANNUAL
Will You Prove To Be Fukuoka's Chicken Of The Sea?
BIRDMAN-BY-THE-BEACH CONTEST
1st PRIZE: 1 MILLION YEN
DISCLAIMER:
Entrants agree to indemnify, hold harmless, and let beat the rap the City of Fukuoka Instrumentality of Human Resources Committee (hereafter known as "SPONSORS"). Contest shall not be construed as a claim by SPONSORS that they believe human-powered flight is in any way possible. No entry fees refunded. In the event of dispute, appeals will be directed to the City of Fukuoka District Attorney's Office, a wholly-suborned agency of the SPONSORS.

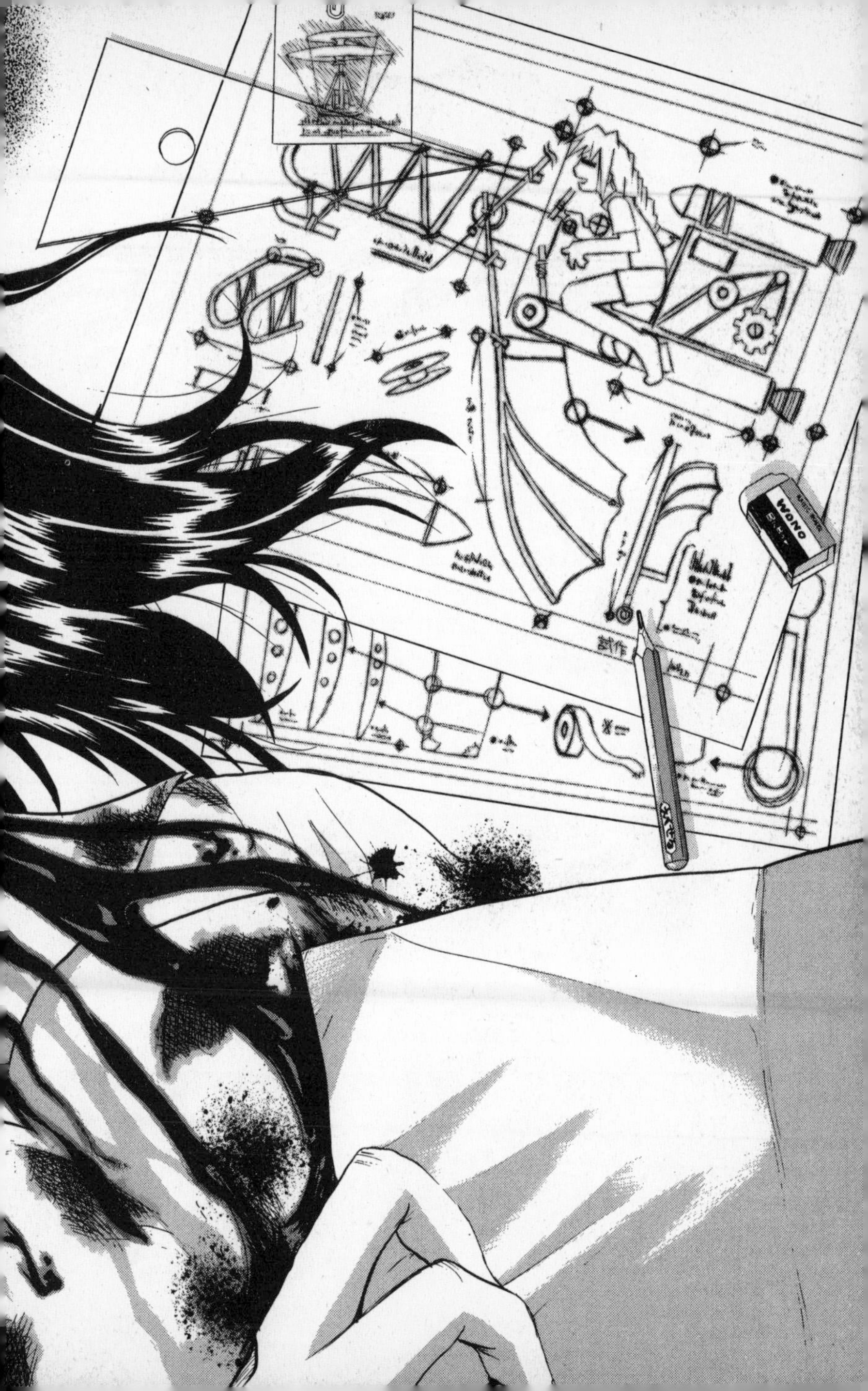
試作
MONO

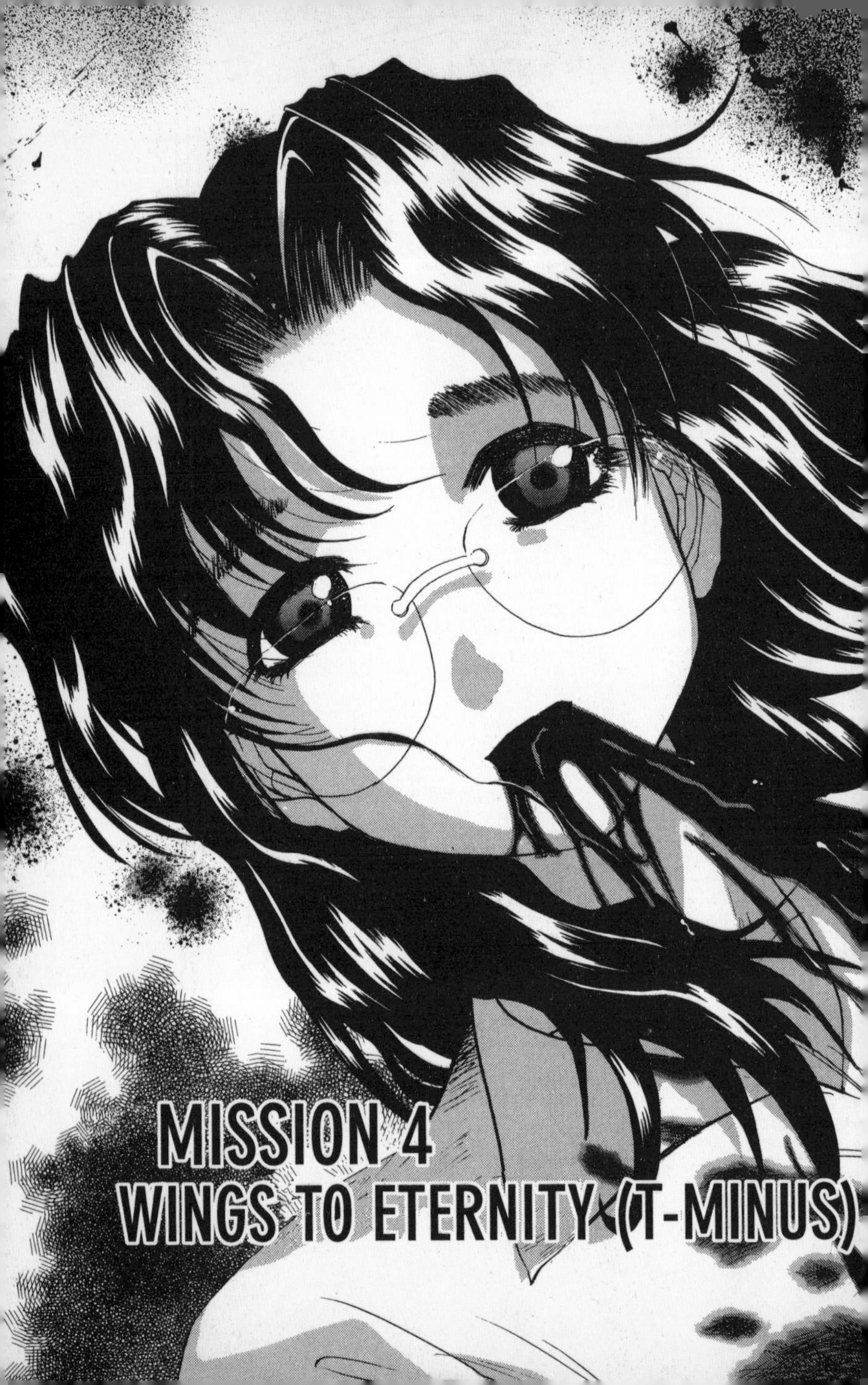

MISSION 4
WINGS TO ETERNITY (T-MINUS)

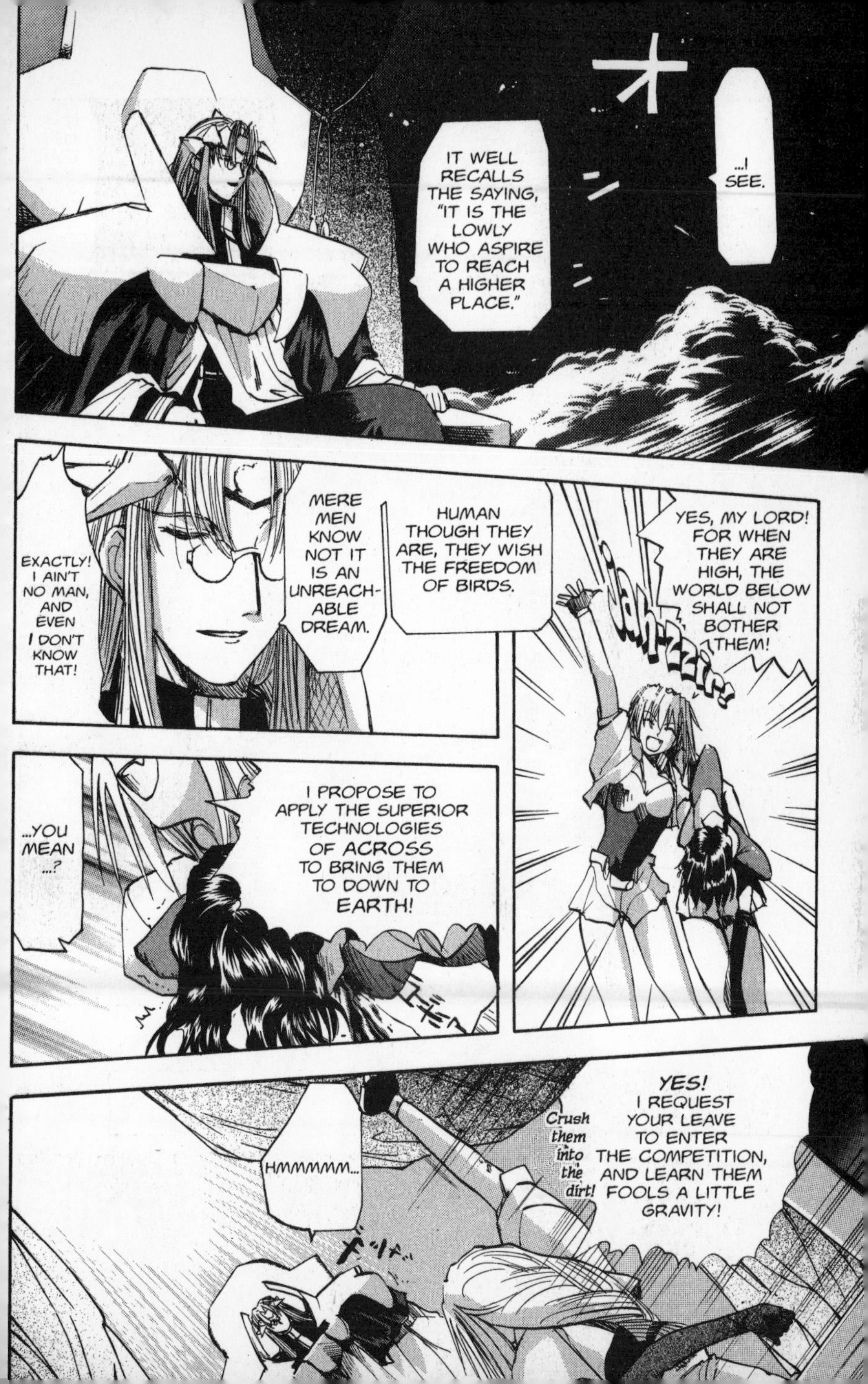
...I SEE.
IT WELL RECALLS THE SAYING, "IT IS THE LOWLY WHO ASPIRE TO REACH A HIGHER PLACE."
YES, MY LORD! FOR WHEN THEY ARE HIGH, THE WORLD BELOW SHALL NOT BOTHER THEM!
HUMAN THOUGH THEY ARE, THEY WISH THE FREEDOM OF BIRDS.
MERE MEN KNOW NOT IT IS AN UNREACH-ABLE DREAM.
EXACTLY! I AIN'T NO MAN, AND EVEN I DON'T KNOW THAT!
I PROPOSE TO APPLY THE SUPERIOR TECHNOLOGIES OF ACROSS TO BRING THEM TO DOWN TO EARTH!
...YOU MEAN ...?
YES! I REQUEST YOUR LEAVE TO ENTER THE COMPETITION, AND LEARN THEM FOOLS A LITTLE GRAVITY!
Crush them into the dirt!
HMMMMM...

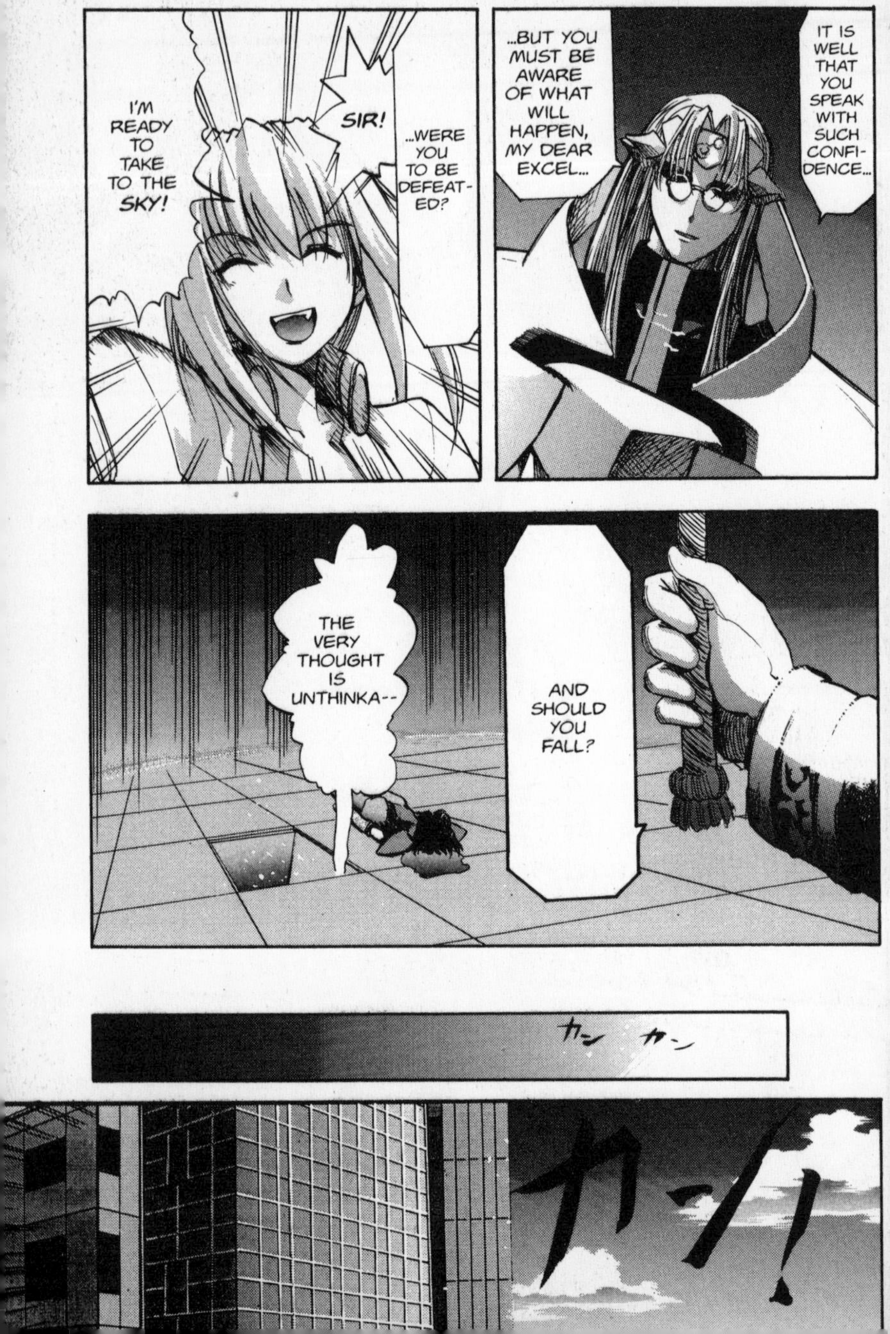
IT IS WELL THAT YOU SPEAK WITH SUCH CONFIDENCE...
...BUT YOU MUST BE AWARE OF WHAT WILL HAPPEN, MY DEAR EXCEL...
...WERE YOU TO BE DEFEATED?
SIR!
I'M READY TO TAKE TO THE SKY!
AND SHOULD YOU FALL?
THE VERY THOUGHT IS UNTHINKA--
カン カン
カーン!

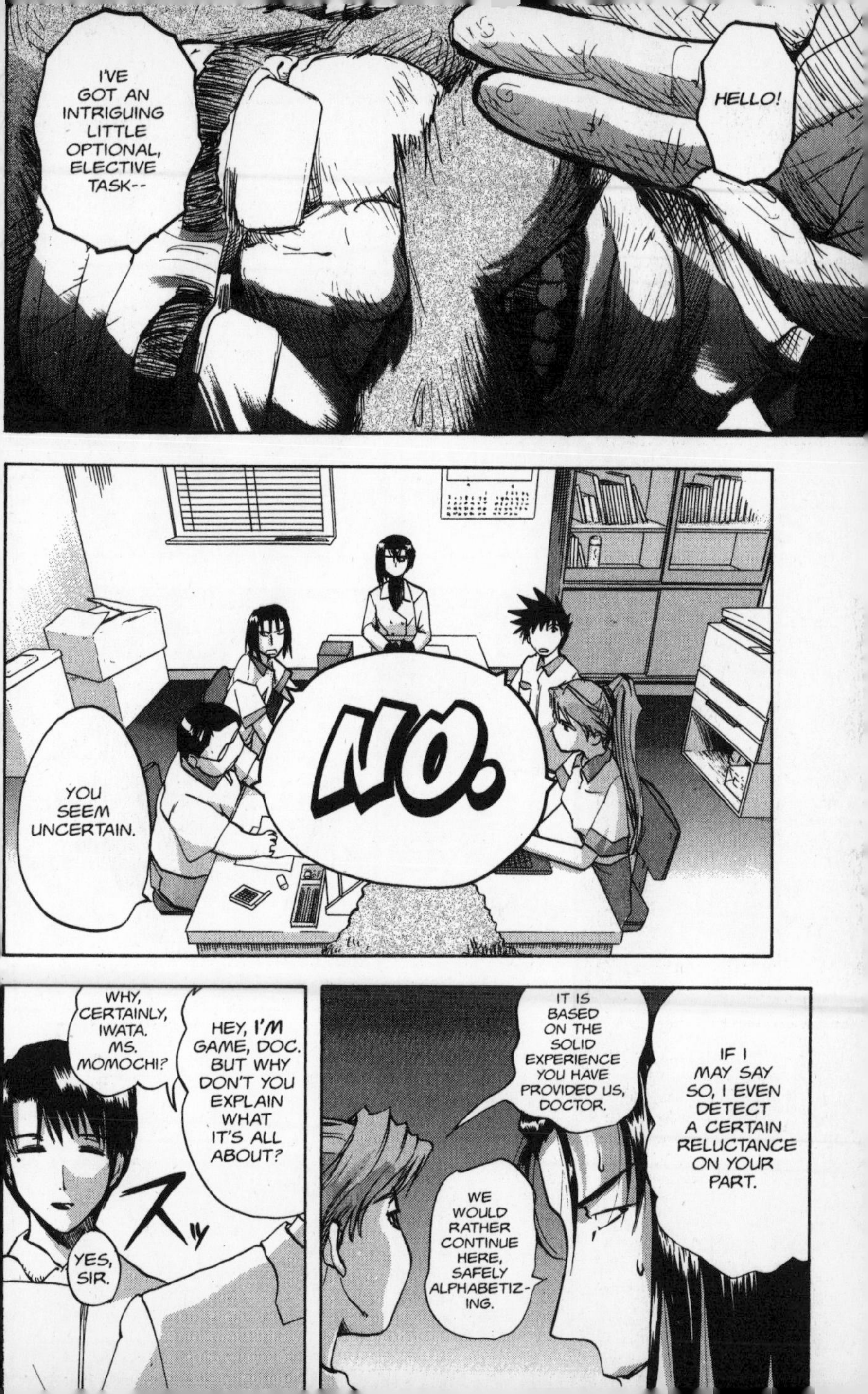
HELLO!
I'VE GOT AN INTRIGUING LITTLE OPTIONAL, ELECTIVE TASK--
NO.
YOU SEEM UNCERTAIN.
IF I MAY SAY SO, I EVEN DETECT A CERTAIN RELUCTANCE ON YOUR PART.
IT IS BASED ON THE SOLID EXPERIENCE YOU HAVE PROVIDED US, DOCTOR.
WE WOULD RATHER CONTINUE HERE, SAFELY ALPHABETIZ-ING.
HEY, I'M GAME, DOC. BUT WHY DON'T YOU EXPLAIN WHAT IT'S ALL ABOUT?
WHY, CERTAINLY, IWATA. MS. MOMOCHI?
YES, SIR.

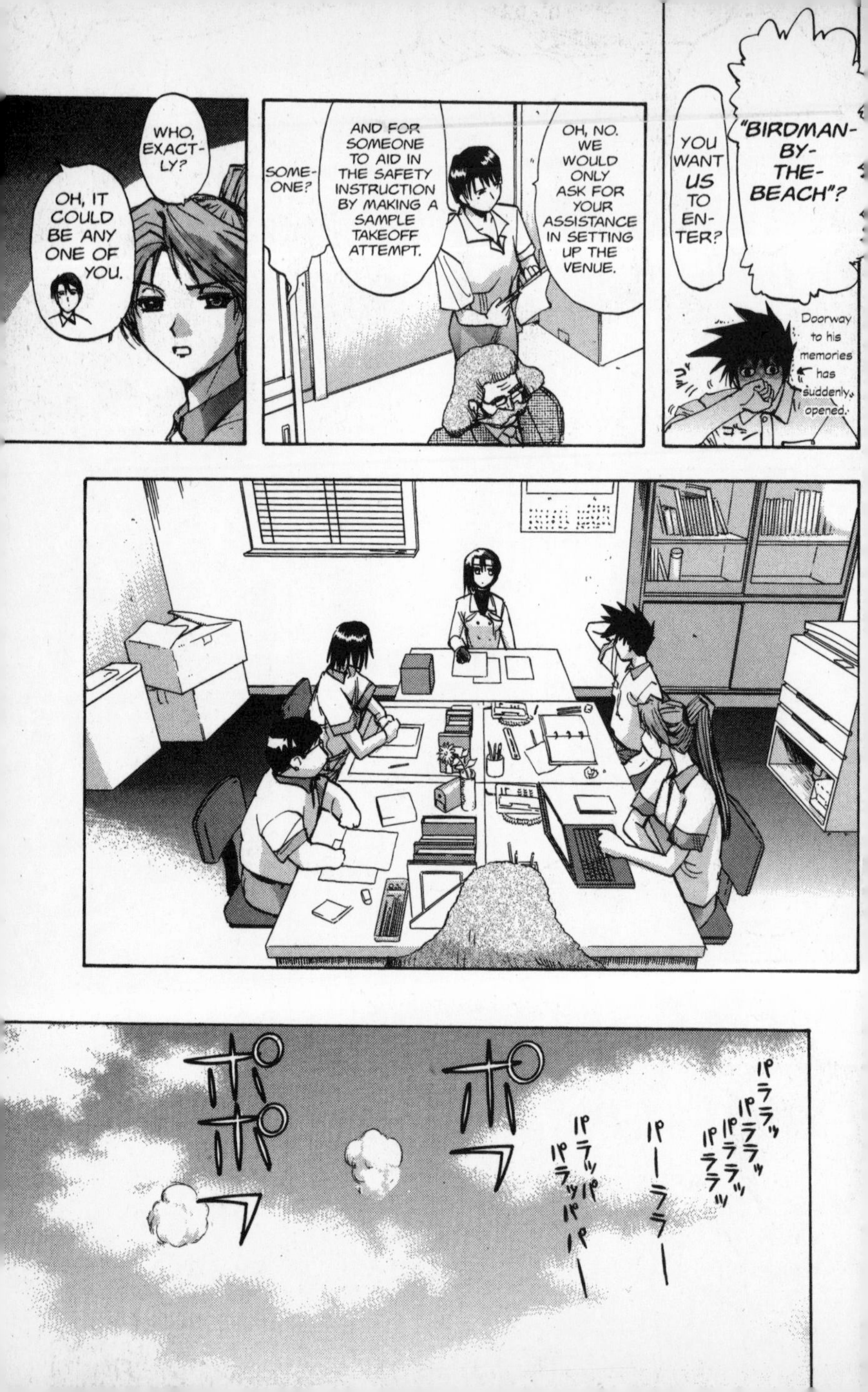
"BIRDMAN-BY-THE-BEACH"?
YOU WANT US TO ENTER?
Doorway to his memories has suddenly opened.
OH, NO. WE WOULD ONLY ASK FOR YOUR ASSISTANCE IN SETTING UP THE VENUE.
AND FOR SOMEONE TO AID IN THE SAFETY INSTRUCTION BY MAKING A SAMPLE TAKEOFF ATTEMPT.
SOME-ONE?
WHO, EXACTLY?
OH, IT COULD BE ANY ONE OF YOU.
パラララッ
パラララッ
パラララッ
パーララー
パラッパ
パラッパパー
ポフ
ポポフ

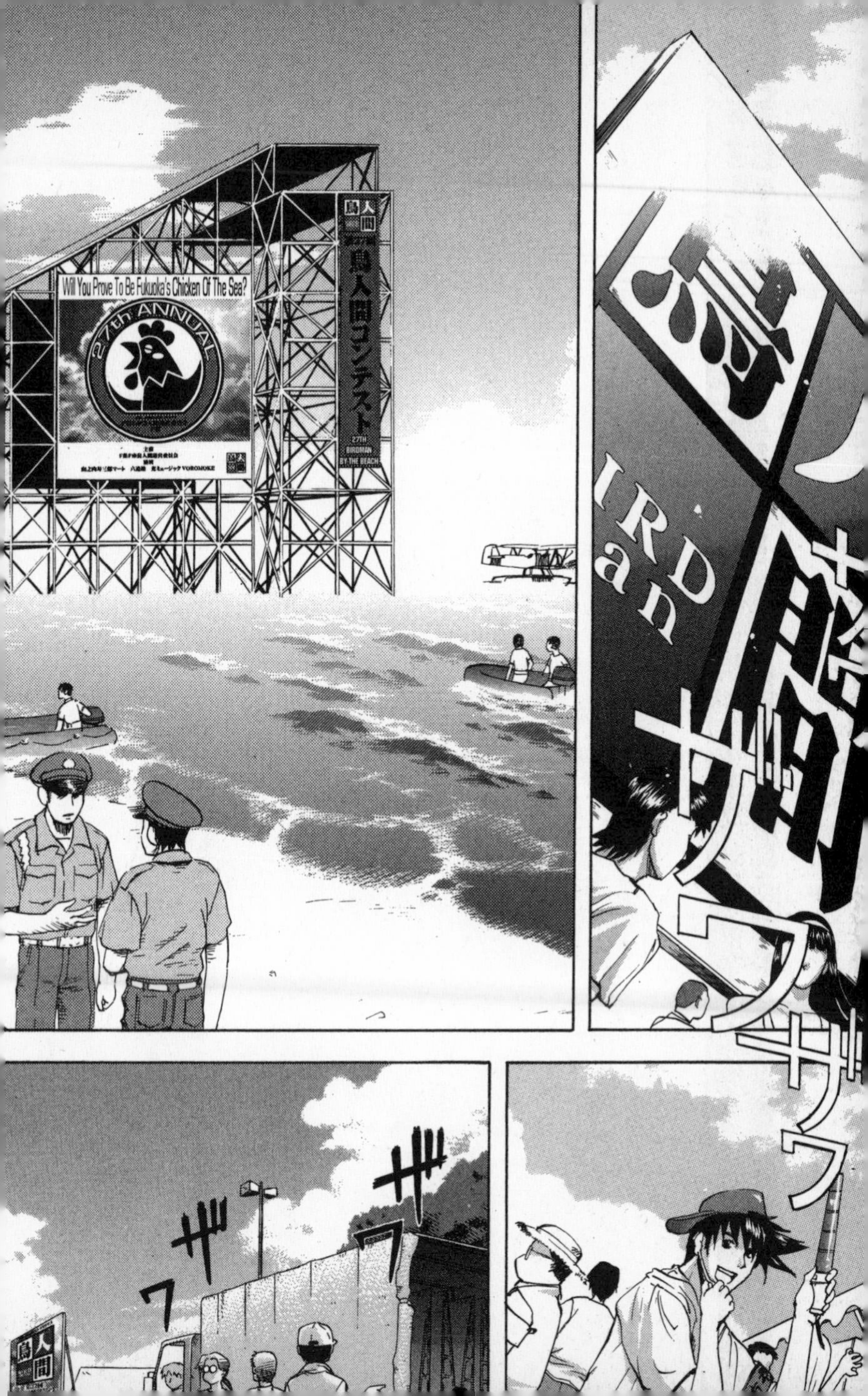
ザワ
ザワ
Will You Prove To Be Fukuoka's Chicken Of The Sea?
27th ANNUAL
鳥人間
第27回
鳥人間コンテスト
27TH
BIRDMAN
BY THE BEACH
ザワ
ザ
ザ
ワ
鳥人間

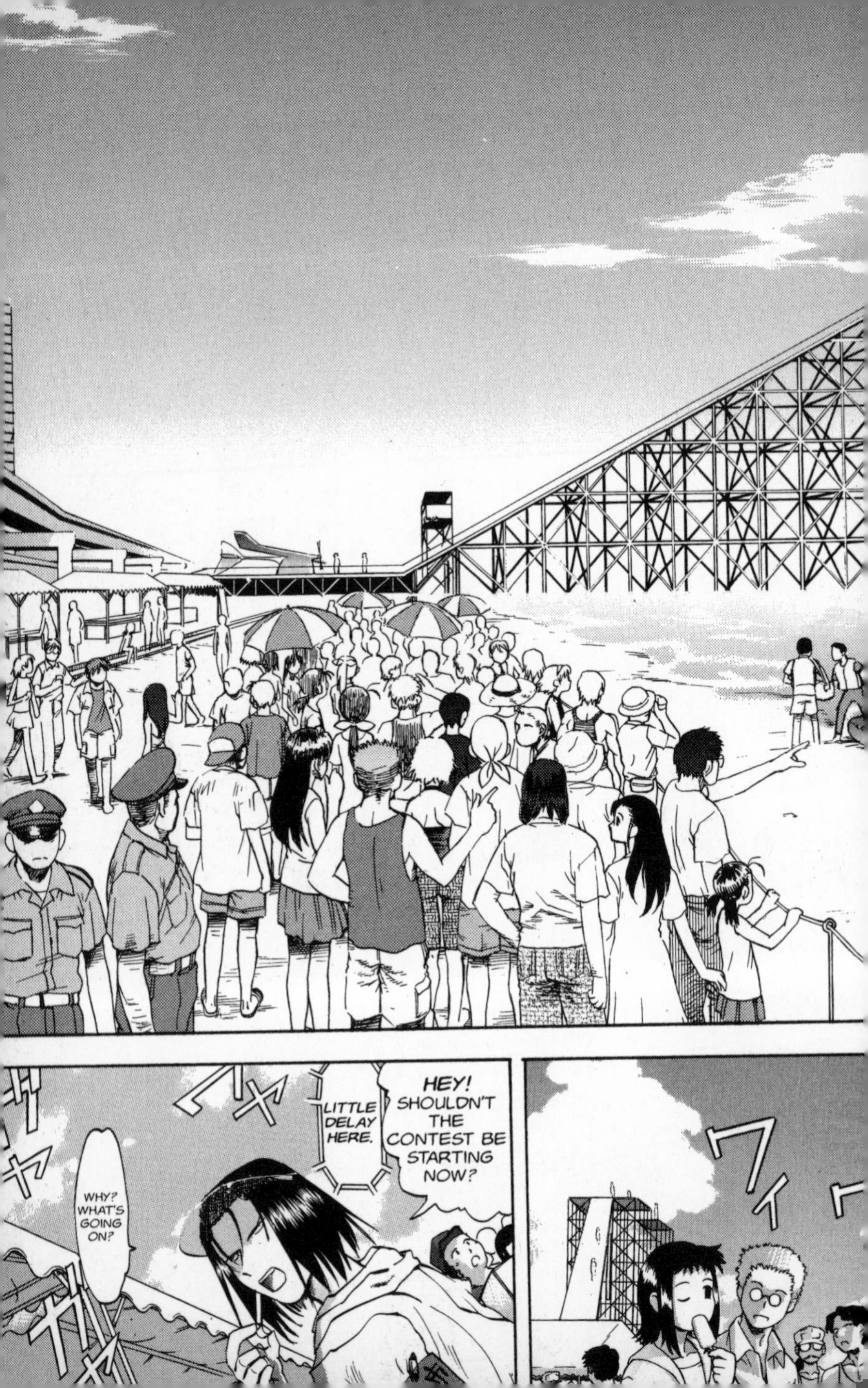
HEY! SHOULDN'T THE CONTEST BE STARTING NOW?
LITTLE DELAY HERE.
WHY? WHAT'S GOING ON?

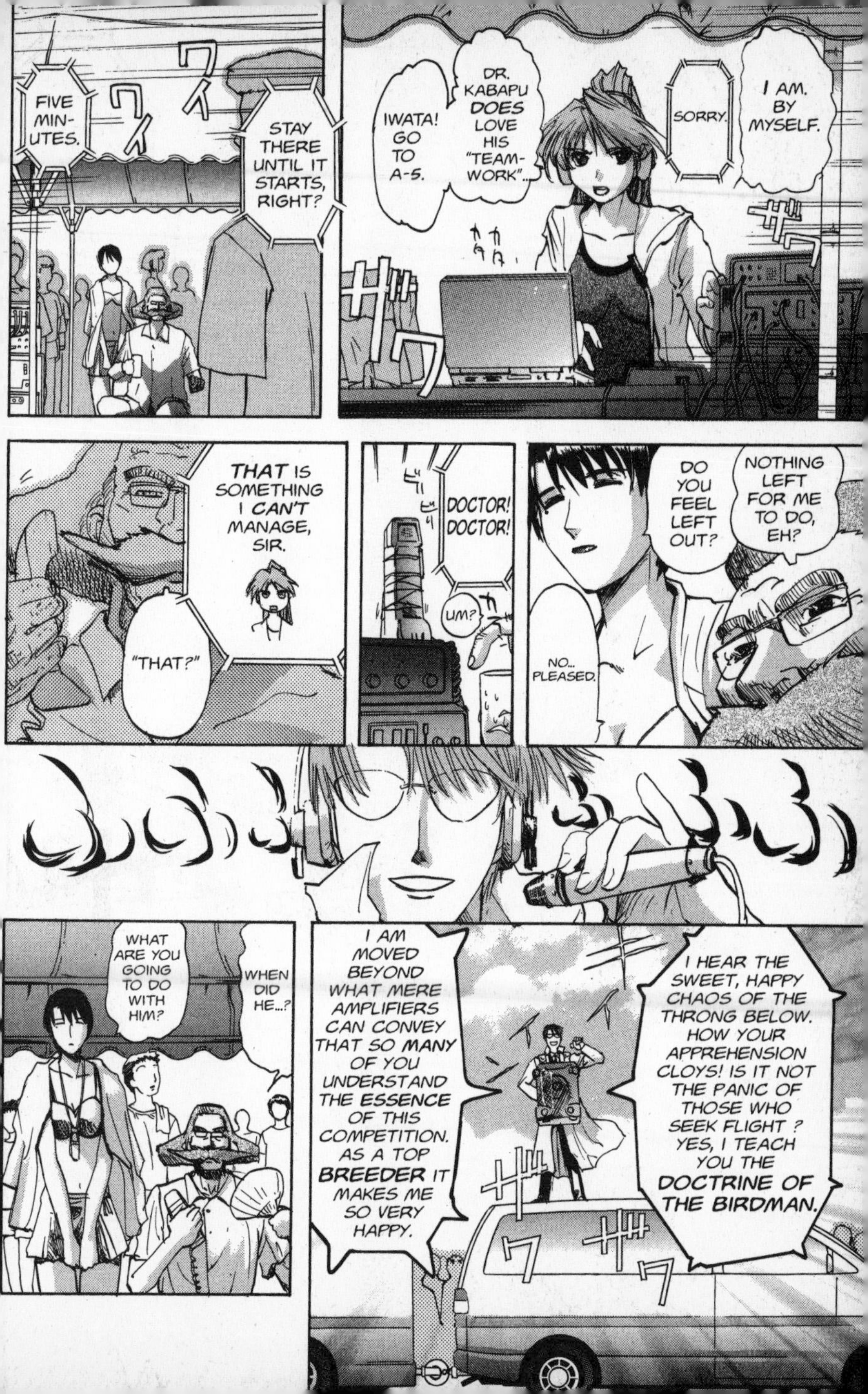
I AM. BY MYSELF.
SORRY.
DR. KABAPU DOES LOVE HIS "TEAM-WORK"...
IWATA! GO TO A-5.
STAY THERE UNTIL IT STARTS, RIGHT?
FIVE MIN-UTES.
NOTHING LEFT FOR ME TO DO, EH?
DO YOU FEEL LEFT OUT?
NO... PLEASED.
DOCTOR! DOCTOR!
UM?
THAT IS SOMETHING I CAN'T MANAGE, SIR.
"THAT?"
I HEAR THE SWEET, HAPPY CHAOS OF THE THRONG BELOW. HOW YOUR APPREHENSION CLOYS! IS IT NOT THE PANIC OF THOSE WHO SEEK FLIGHT ? YES, I TEACH YOU THE DOCTRINE OF THE BIRDMAN.
I AM MOVED BEYOND WHAT MERE AMPLIFIERS CAN CONVEY THAT SO MANY OF YOU UNDERSTAND THE ESSENCE OF THIS COMPETITION. AS A TOP BREEDER IT MAKES ME SO VERY HAPPY.
WHEN DID HE...?
WHAT ARE YOU GOING TO DO WITH HIM?

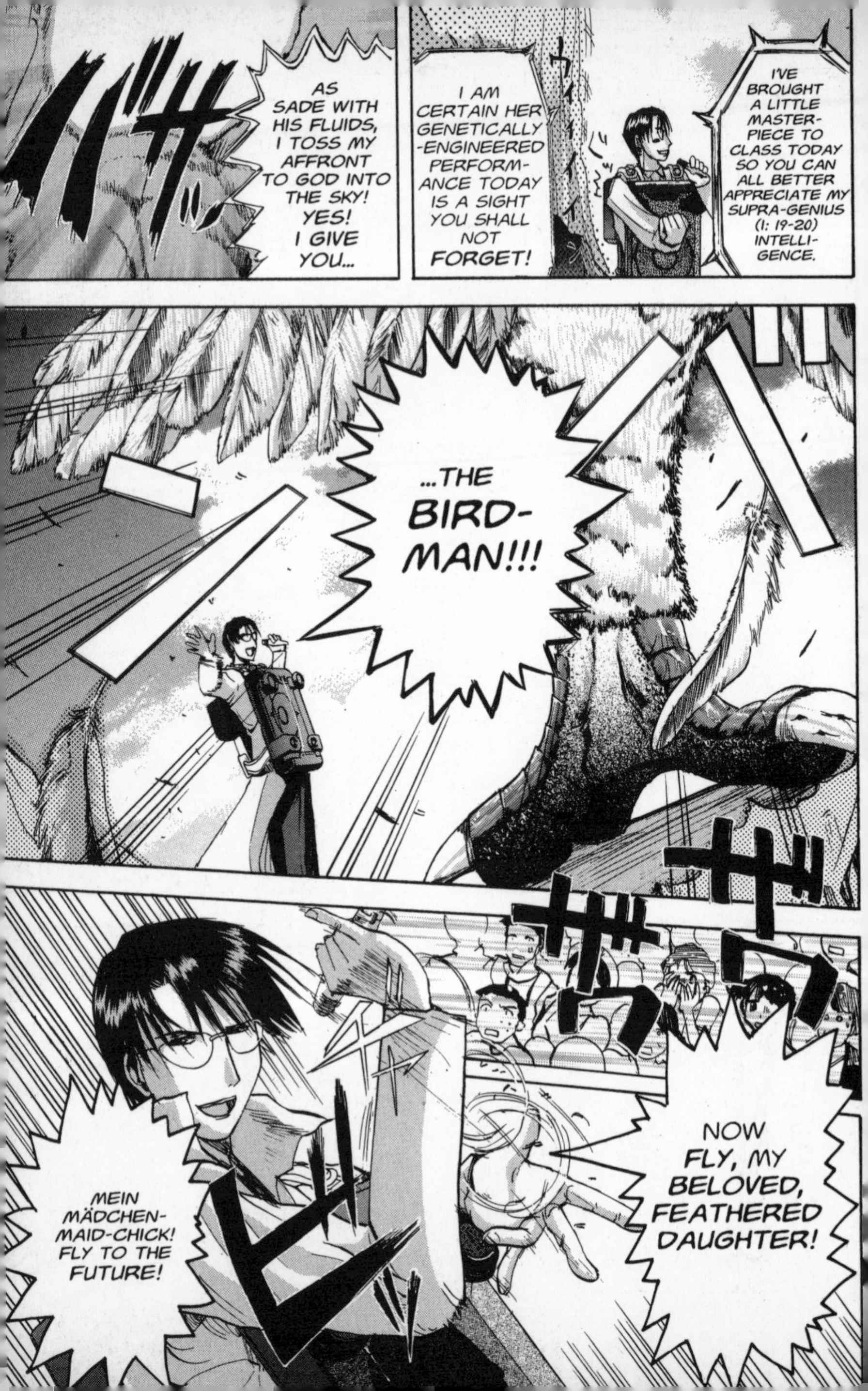
I'VE BROUGHT A LITTLE MASTER-PIECE TO CLASS TODAY SO YOU CAN ALL BETTER APPRECIATE MY SUPRA-GENIUS (I: 19-20) INTELLI-GENCE.
I AM CERTAIN HER GENETICALLY -ENGINEERED PERFORM-ANCE TODAY IS A SIGHT YOU SHALL NOT FORGET!
AS SADE WITH HIS FLUIDS, I TOSS MY AFFRONT TO GOD INTO THE SKY! YES! I GIVE YOU...
...THE BIRD-MAN!!!
NOW FLY, MY BELOVED, FEATHERED DAUGHTER!
MEIN MÄDCHEN-MAID-CHICK! FLY TO THE FUTURE!

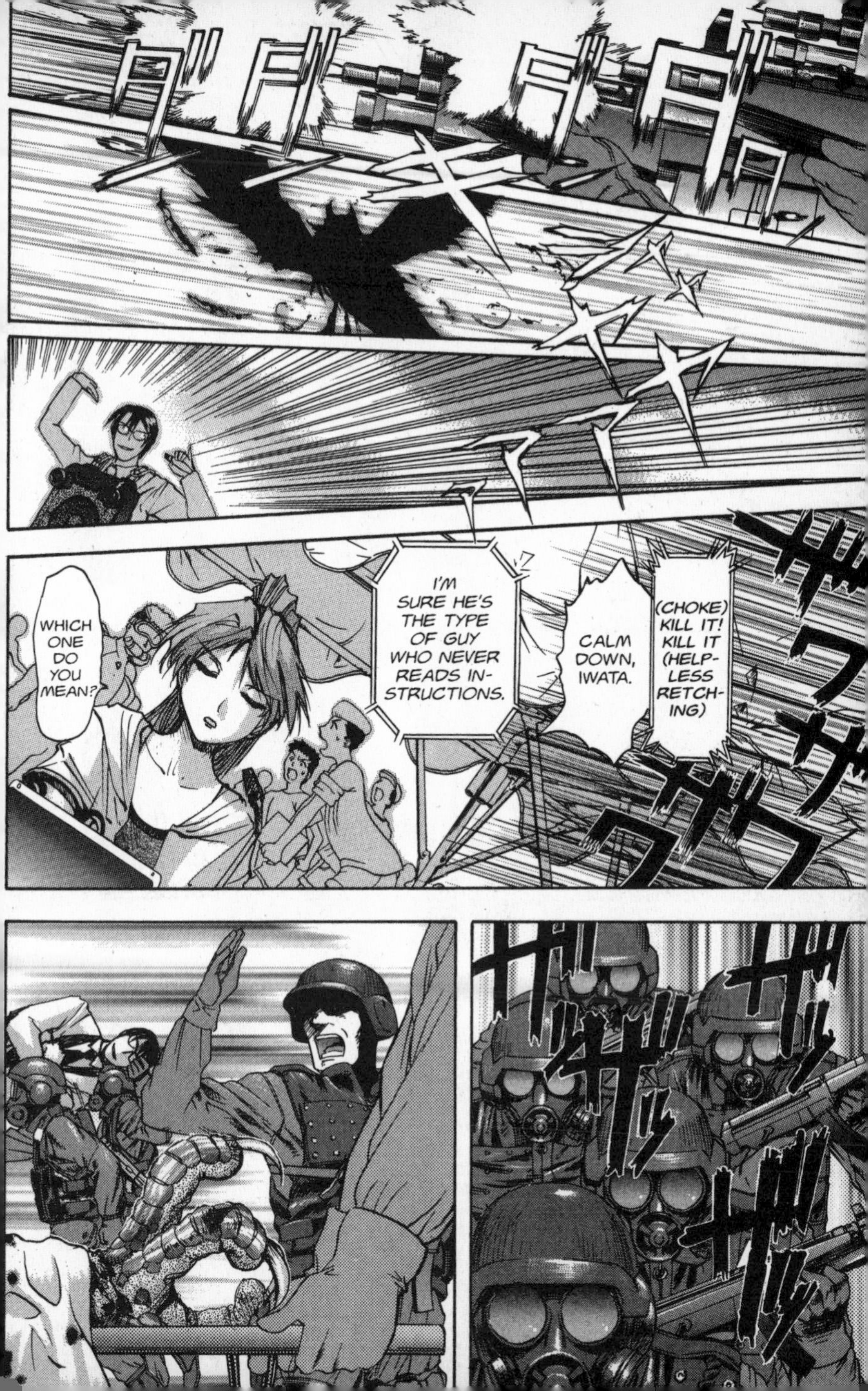
(CHOKE) KILL IT! KILL IT (HELP-LESS RETCHING)
CALM DOWN, IWATA.
I'M SURE HE'S THE TYPE OF GUY WHO NEVER READS IN-STRUCTIONS.
WHICH ONE DO YOU MEAN?

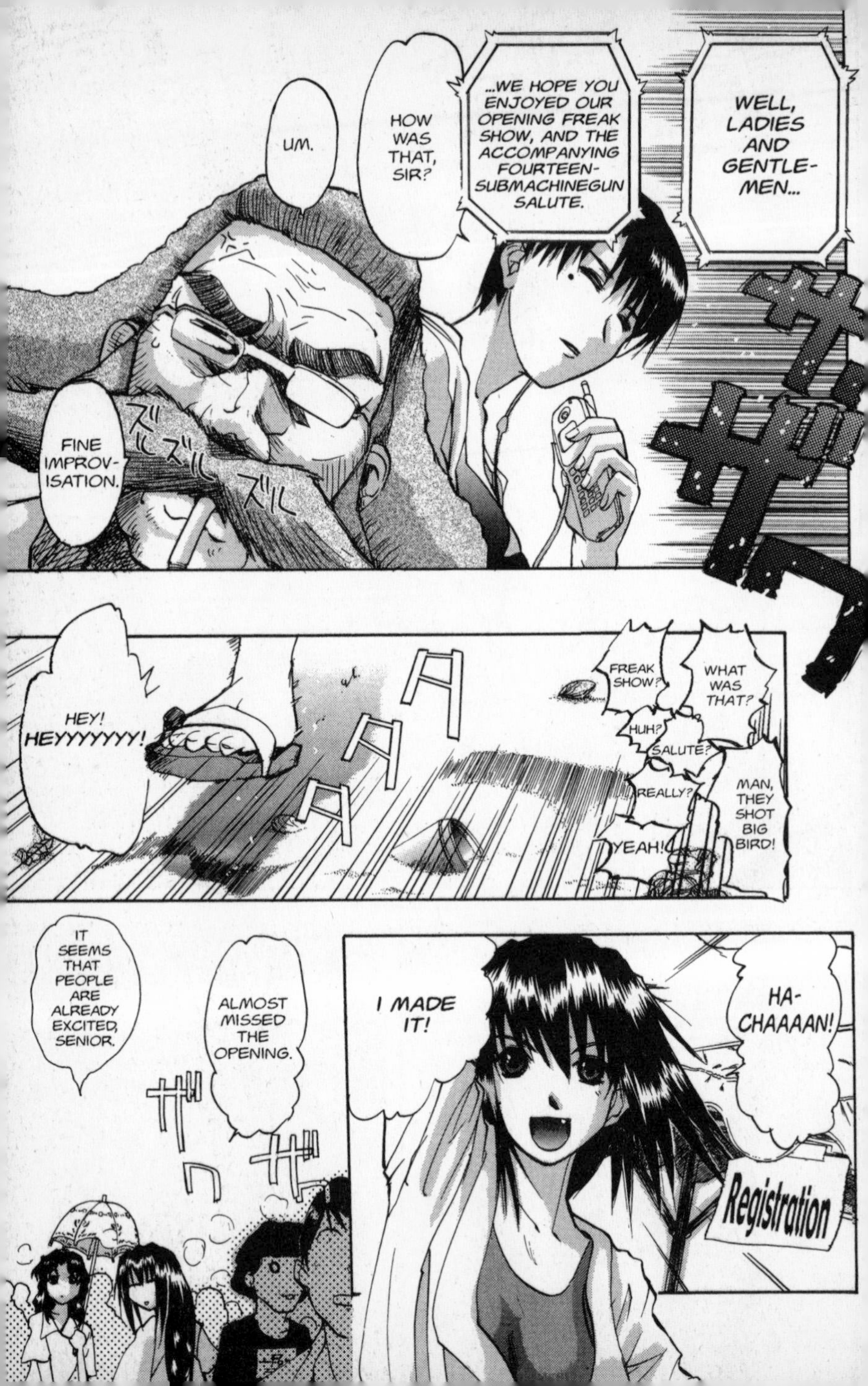
WELL, LADIES AND GENTLE-MEN...
...WE HOPE YOU ENJOYED OUR OPENING FREAK SHOW, AND THE ACCOMPANYING FOURTEEN-SUBMACHINEGUN SALUTE.
HOW WAS THAT, SIR?
UM.
FINE IMPROV-ISATION.
WHAT WAS THAT?
FREAK SHOW?
HUH?
SALUTE?
REALLY?
MAN, THEY SHOT BIG BIRD!
YEAH!
HEY! HEYYYYYYY!
HA-CHAAAAN!
Registration
I MADE IT!
ALMOST MISSED THE OPENING.
IT SEEMS THAT PEOPLE ARE ALREADY EXCITED, SENIOR.

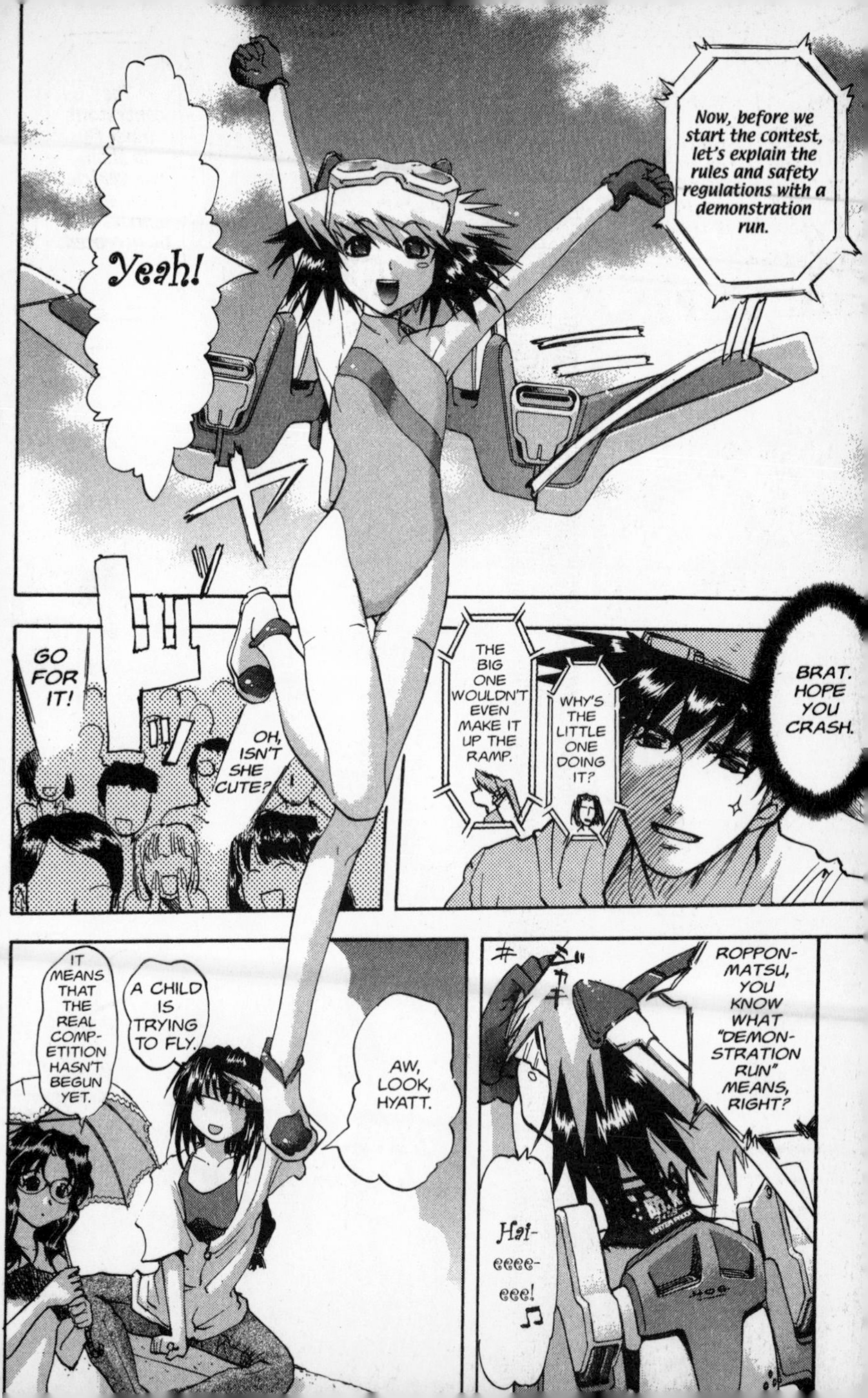

Now, before we start the contest, let's explain the rules and safety regulations with a demonstration run.
Yeah!
BRAT. HOPE YOU CRASH.
WHY'S THE LITTLE ONE DOING IT?
THE BIG ONE WOULDN'T EVEN MAKE IT UP THE RAMP.
OH, ISN'T SHE CUTE?
GO FOR IT!
ROPPON-MATSU, YOU KNOW WHAT "DEMON-STRATION RUN" MEANS, RIGHT?
Hai-eeee-eee! ♪
AW, LOOK, HYATT.
A CHILD IS TRYING TO FLY.
IT MEANS THAT THE REAL COMP-ETITION HASN'T BEGUN YET.

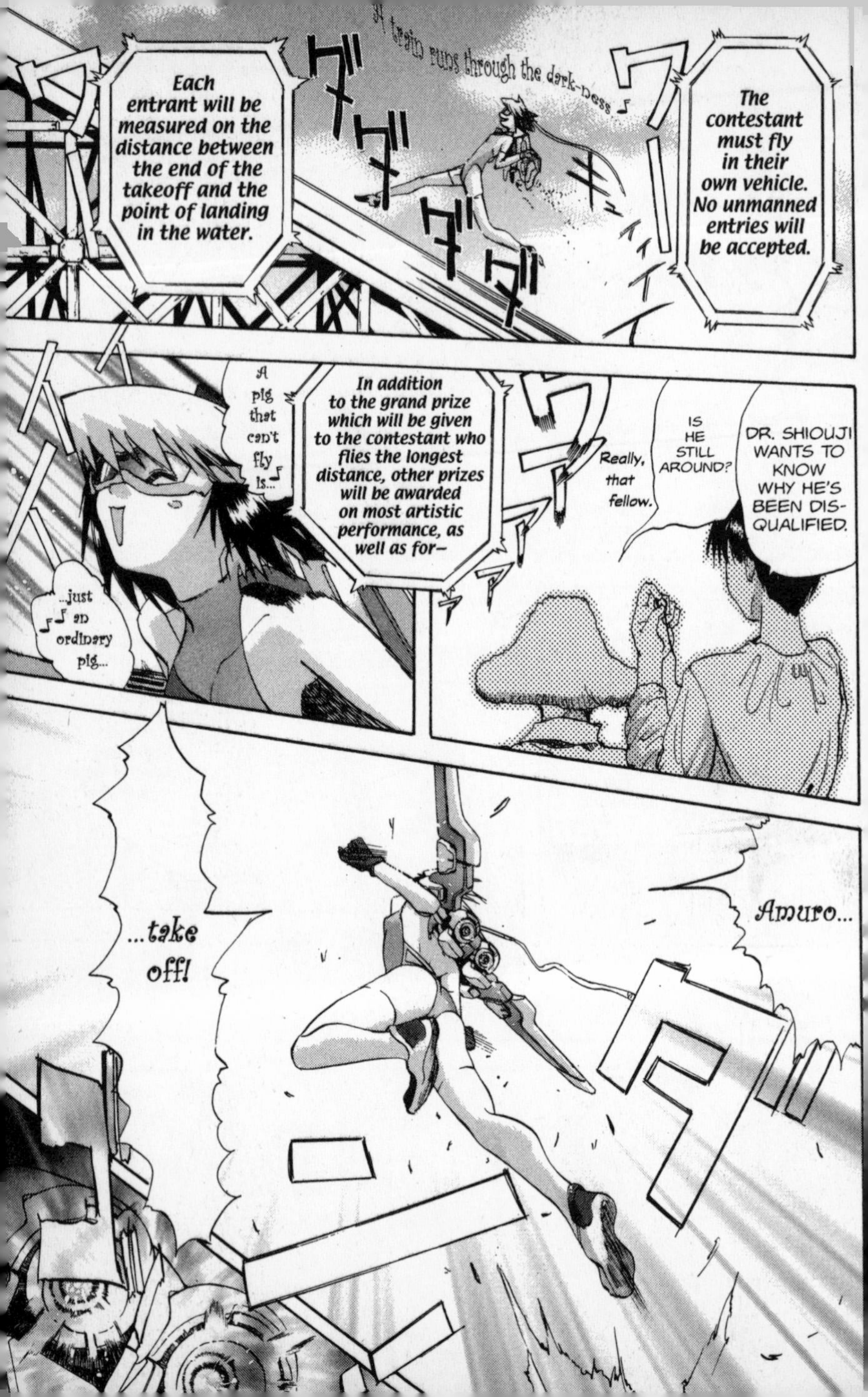
The contestant must fly in their own vehicle. No unmanned entries will be accepted.
A train runs through the dark-ness ♪
Each entrant will be measured on the distance between the end of the takeoff and the point of landing in the water.
DR. SHIOUJI WANTS TO KNOW WHY HE'S BEEN DIS-QUALIFIED.
IS HE STILL AROUND?
Really, that fellow.
In addition to the grand prize which will be given to the contestant who flies the longest distance, other prizes will be awarded on most artistic performance, as well as for–
A pig that can't fly is...♪
...just ♪♪ an ordinary pig...
Amuro...
...take off!

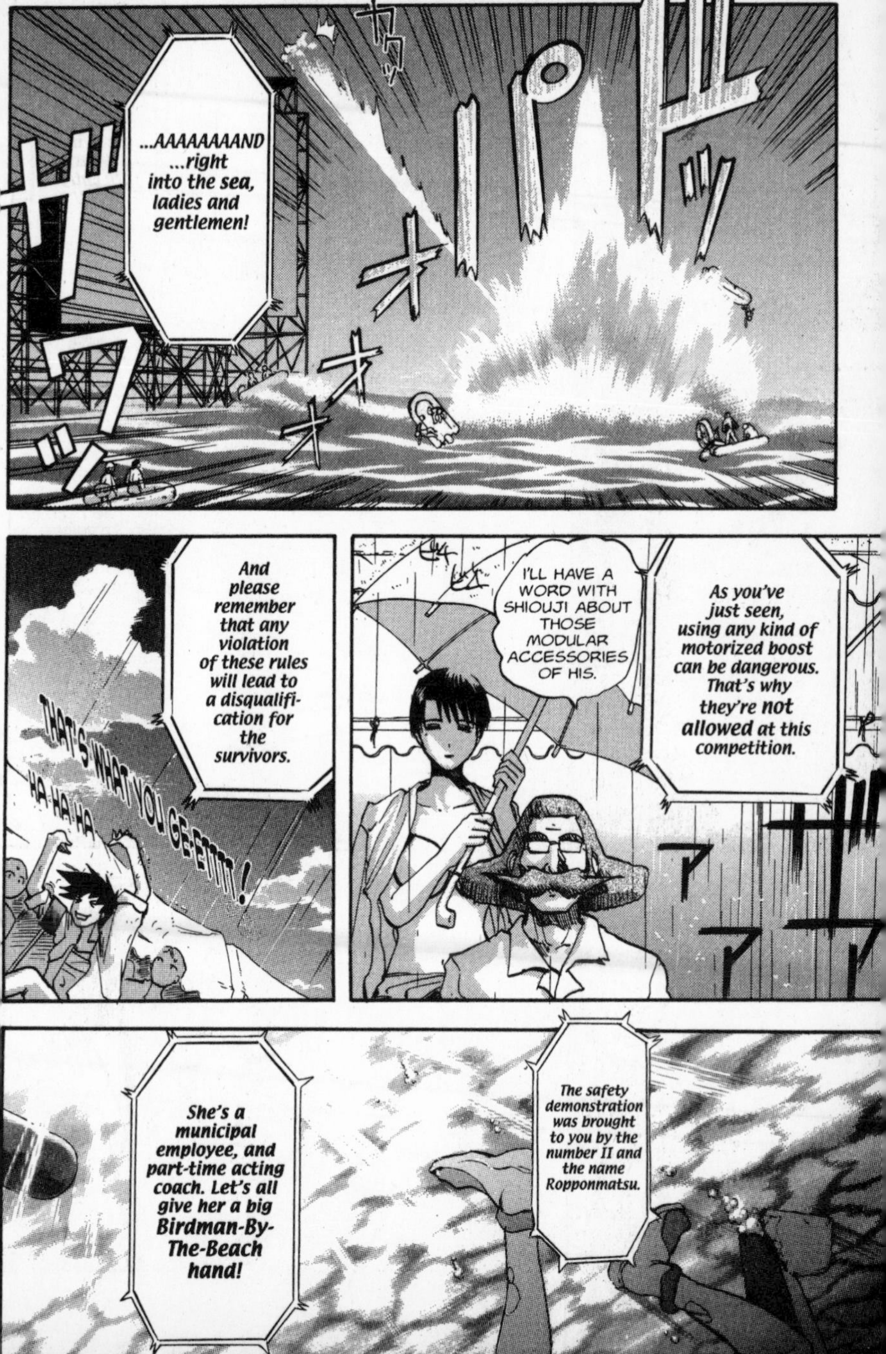

...AAAAAAAAND ...right into the sea, ladies and gentlemen!
As you've just seen, using any kind of motorized boost can be dangerous. That's why they're not allowed at this competition.
I'LL HAVE A WORD WITH SHIOUJI ABOUT THOSE MODULAR ACCESSORIES OF HIS.
And please remember that any violation of these rules will lead to a disqualification for the survivors.
THAT'S WHAT YOU GE-ETTTT!
HA HA HA
The safety demonstration was brought to you by the number II and the name Ropponmatsu.
She's a municipal employee, and part-time acting coach. Let's all give her a big Birdman-By-The-Beach hand!

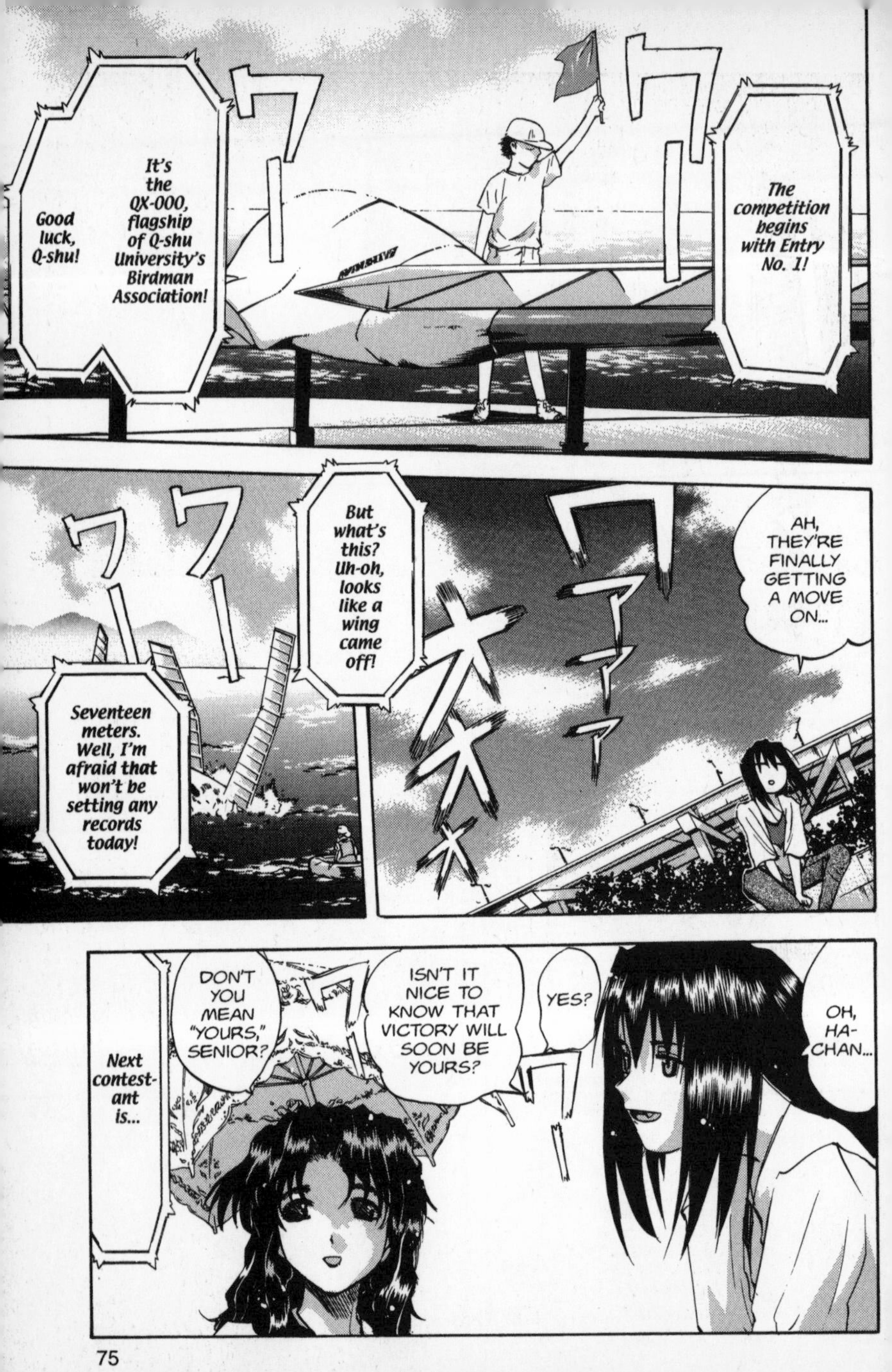
The competition begins with Entry No. 1!
It's the QX-000, flagship of Q-shu University's Birdman Association!
Good luck, Q-shu!
AH, THEY'RE FINALLY GETTING A MOVE ON...
But what's this? Uh-oh, looks like a wing came off!
Seventeen meters. Well, I'm afraid that won't be setting any records today!
OH, HA-CHAN...
YES?
ISN'T IT NICE TO KNOW THAT VICTORY WILL SOON BE YOURS?
DON'T YOU MEAN "YOURS," SENIOR?
Next contest-ant is...

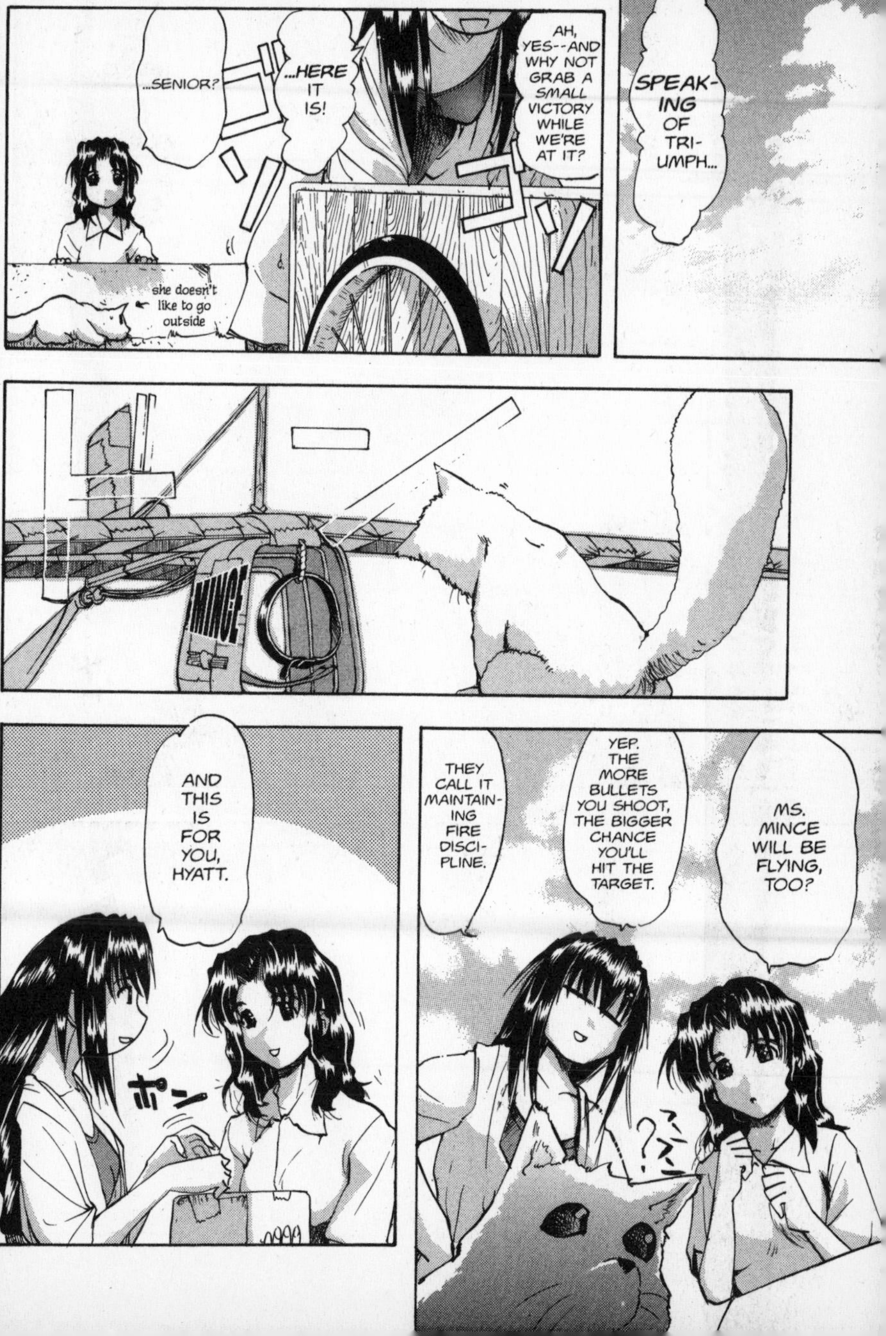
SPEAK-ING OF TRI-UMPH...
AH, YES--AND WHY NOT GRAB A SMALL VICTORY WHILE WE'RE AT IT?
...HERE IT IS!
...SENIOR?
she doesn't like to go outside
MINCE
MS. MINCE WILL BE FLYING, TOO?
YEP. THE MORE BULLETS YOU SHOOT, THE BIGGER CHANCE YOU'LL HIT THE TARGET.
THEY CALL IT MAINTAIN-ING FIRE DISCI-PLINE.
AND THIS IS FOR YOU, HYATT.
ポン

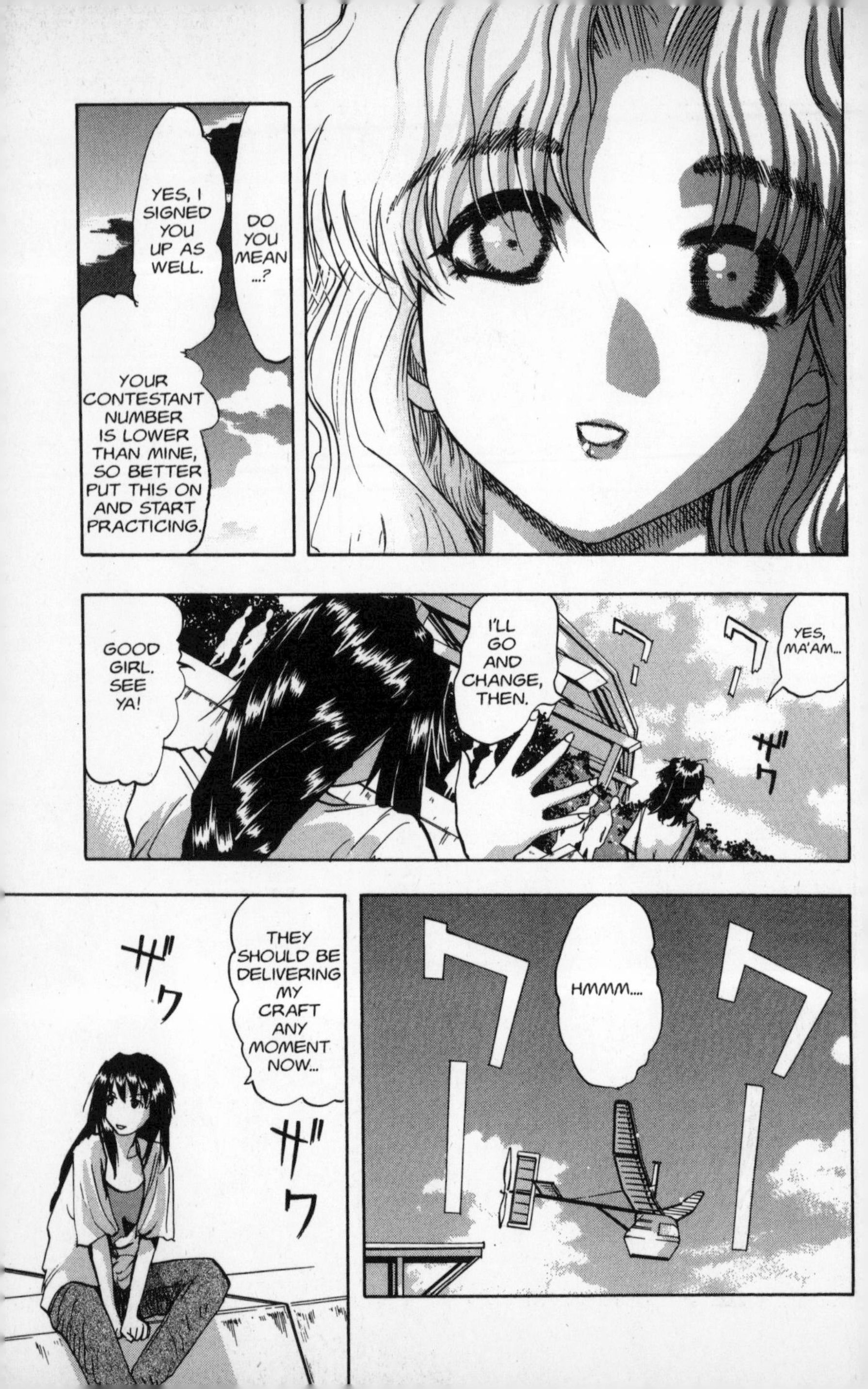
DO YOU MEAN ...?
YES, I SIGNED YOU UP AS WELL.
YOUR CONTESTANT NUMBER IS LOWER THAN MINE, SO BETTER PUT THIS ON AND START PRACTICING.
YES, MA'AM...
クー
クー
ザワ
I'LL GO AND CHANGE, THEN.
GOOD GIRL. SEE YA!
クー
HMMM....
クー
THEY SHOULD BE DELIVERING MY CRAFT ANY MOMENT NOW...
ザワ
ザワ

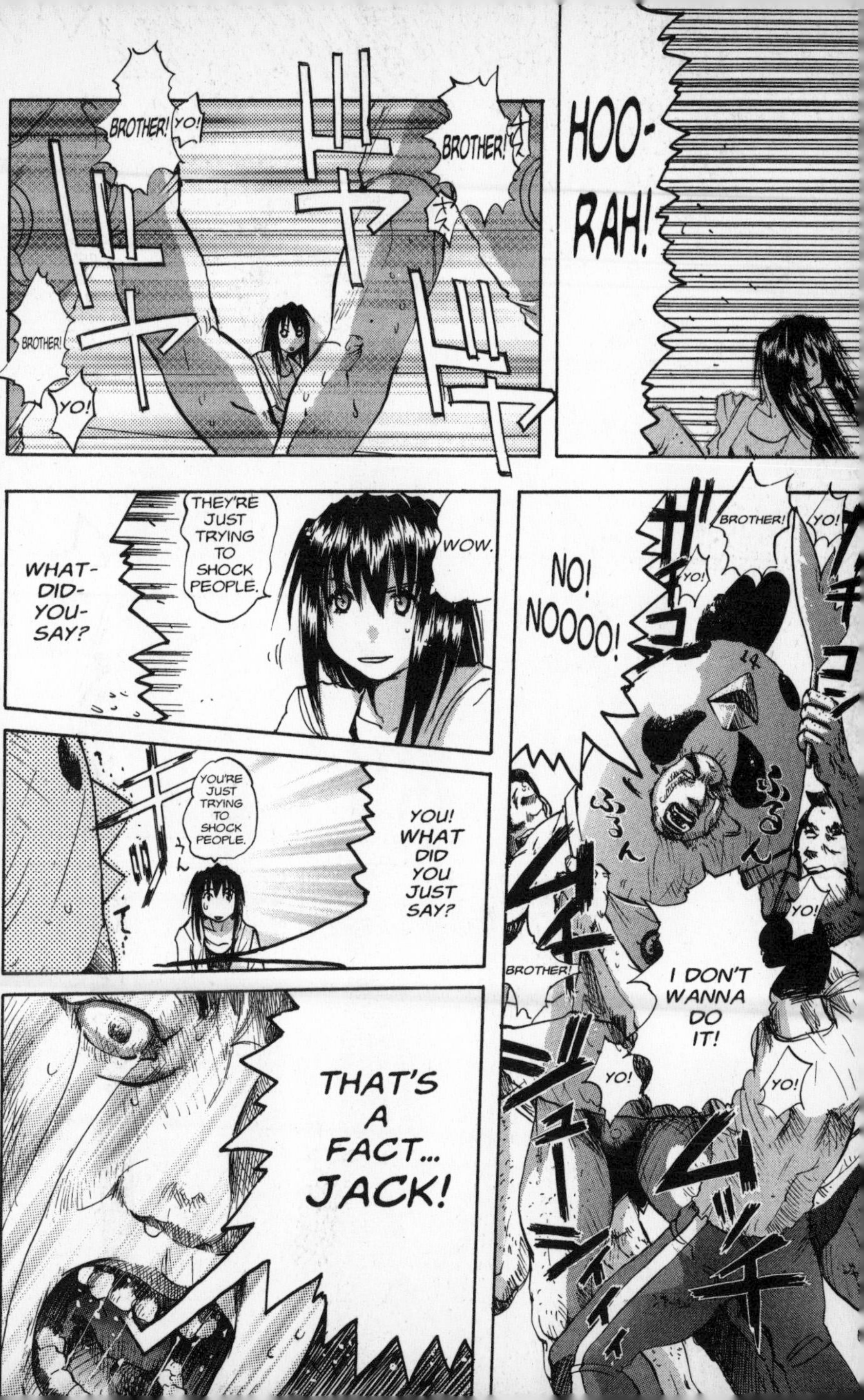

HOO-RAH!
BROTHER!
YO!
BROTHER!
YO!
BROTHER!
YO!
YO!
BROTHER!
YO!
NO! NOOOO!
YO!
I DON'T WANNA DO IT!
BROTHER!
YO!
YO!
WOW.
THEY'RE JUST TRYING TO SHOCK PEOPLE.
WHAT-DID-YOU-SAY?
YOU! WHAT DID YOU JUST SAY?
YOU'RE JUST TRYING TO SHOCK PEOPLE.
THAT'S A FACT... JACK!

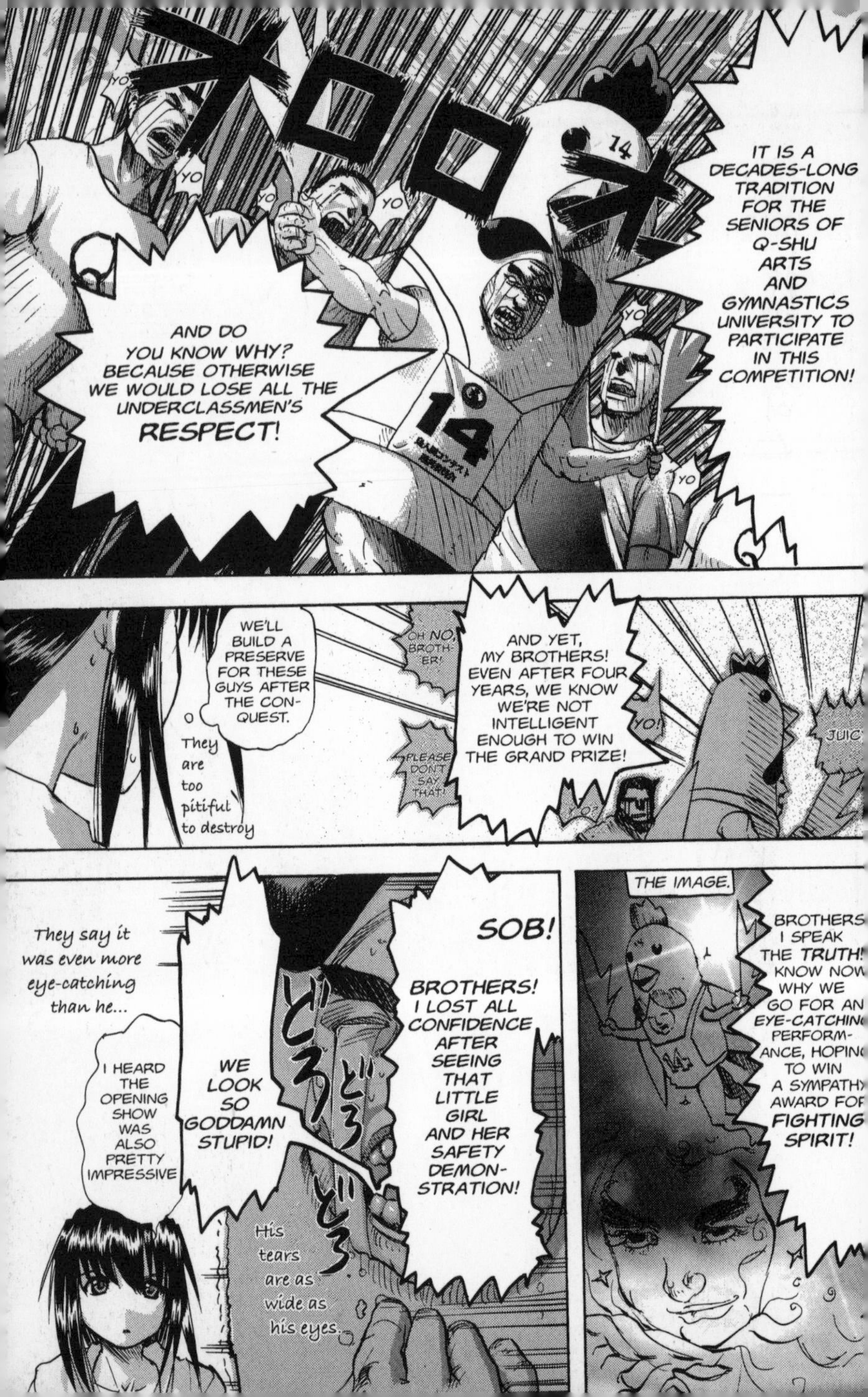
IT IS A DECADES-LONG TRADITION FOR THE SENIORS OF Q-SHU ARTS AND GYMNASTICS UNIVERSITY TO PARTICIPATE IN THIS COMPETITION!
YO
YO
YO
YO
YO
YO
14
AND DO YOU KNOW WHY? BECAUSE OTHERWISE WE WOULD LOSE ALL THE UNDERCLASSMEN'S **RESPECT**!
14
JUIC
YO!
AND YET, MY BROTHERS! EVEN AFTER FOUR YEARS, WE KNOW WE'RE NOT INTELLIGENT ENOUGH TO WIN THE GRAND PRIZE!
OH NO, BROTHER!
PLEASE DON'T SAY THAT!
YO?
WE'LL BUILD A PRESERVE FOR THESE GUYS AFTER THE CON-QUEST.
They are too pitiful to destroy
THE IMAGE.
BROTHERS I SPEAK THE **TRUTH**! KNOW NOW WHY WE GO FOR AN EYE-CATCHIN PERFORM-ANCE, HOPIN TO WIN A SYMPATH AWARD FOF **FIGHTING SPIRIT**!
SOB!
BROTHERS! I LOST ALL CONFIDENCE AFTER SEEING THAT LITTLE GIRL AND HER SAFETY DEMON-STRATION!
WE LOOK SO GODDAMN STUPID!
His tears are as wide as his eyes.
They say it was even more eye-catching than he...
I HEARD THE OPENING SHOW WAS ALSO PRETTY IMPRESSIVE

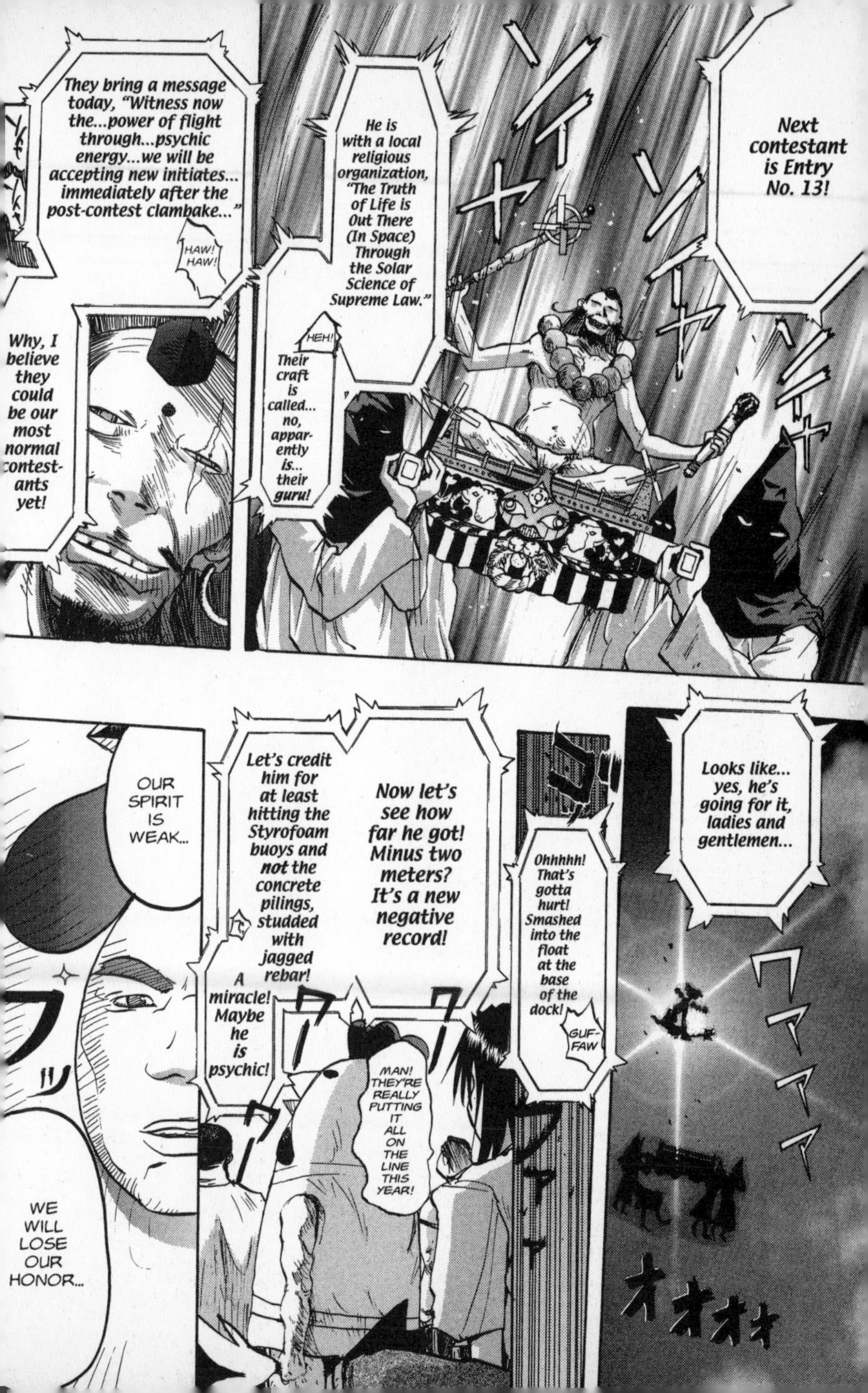
Next contestant is Entry No. 13!
He is with a local religious organization, "The Truth of Life is Out There (In Space) Through the Solar Science of Supreme Law."
HEH!
Their craft is called... no, apparently is... their guru!
They bring a message today, "Witness now the...power of flight through...psychic energy...we will be accepting new initiates... immediately after the post-contest clambake..."
HAW! HAW!
Why, I believe they could be our most normal contest-ants yet!
Looks like... yes, he's going for it, ladies and gentlemen...
Ohhhhh! That's gotta hurt! Smashed into the float at the base of the dock!
Now let's see how far he got! Minus two meters? It's a new negative record!
Let's credit him for at least hitting the Styrofoam buoys and *not* the concrete pilings, studded with jagged rebar!
GUF-FAW
A miracle! Maybe he *is* psychic!
MAN! THEY'RE REALLY PUTTING IT ALL ON THE LINE THIS YEAR!
OUR SPIRIT IS WEAK...
WE WILL LOSE OUR HONOR...

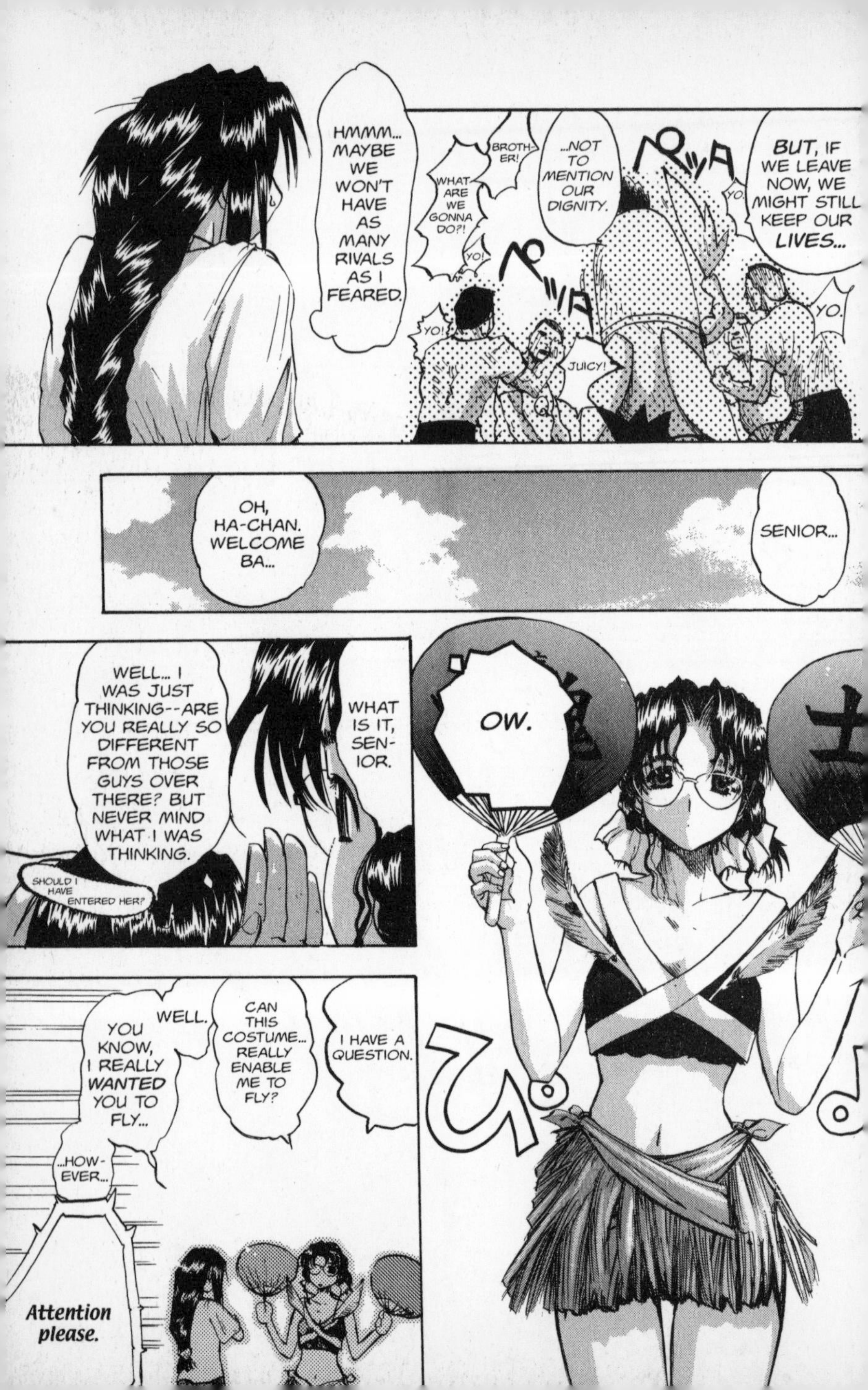
BUT, IF WE LEAVE NOW, WE MIGHT STILL KEEP OUR LIVES...
YO.
...NOT TO MENTION OUR DIGNITY.
BROTH-ER!
WHAT ARE WE GONNA DO?!
YO!
YO!
JUICY!
YO.
HMMM... MAYBE WE WON'T HAVE AS MANY RIVALS AS I FEARED.
SENIOR...
OH, HA-CHAN. WELCOME BA...
OW.
WHAT IS IT, SEN-IOR.
WELL... I WAS JUST THINKING--ARE YOU REALLY SO DIFFERENT FROM THOSE GUYS OVER THERE? BUT NEVER MIND WHAT I WAS THINKING.
SHOULD I HAVE ENTERED HER?
I HAVE A QUESTION.
CAN THIS COSTUME... REALLY ENABLE ME TO FLY?
WELL.
YOU KNOW, I REALLY WANTED YOU TO FLY...
...HOW-EVER...
Attention please.

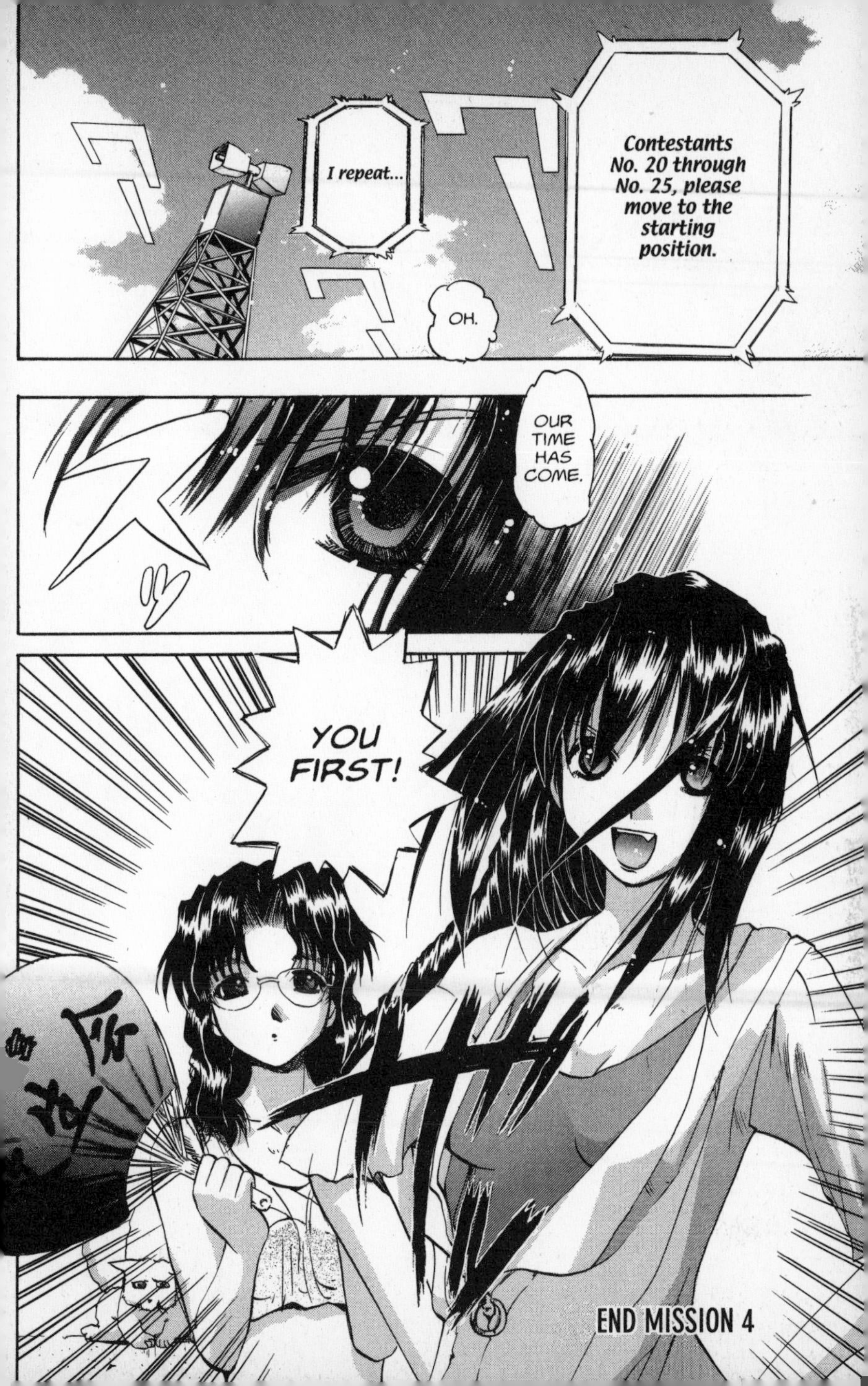
Contestants No. 20 through No. 25, please move to the starting position.
I repeat...
OH.
OUR TIME HAS COME.
YOU FIRST!
END MISSION 4

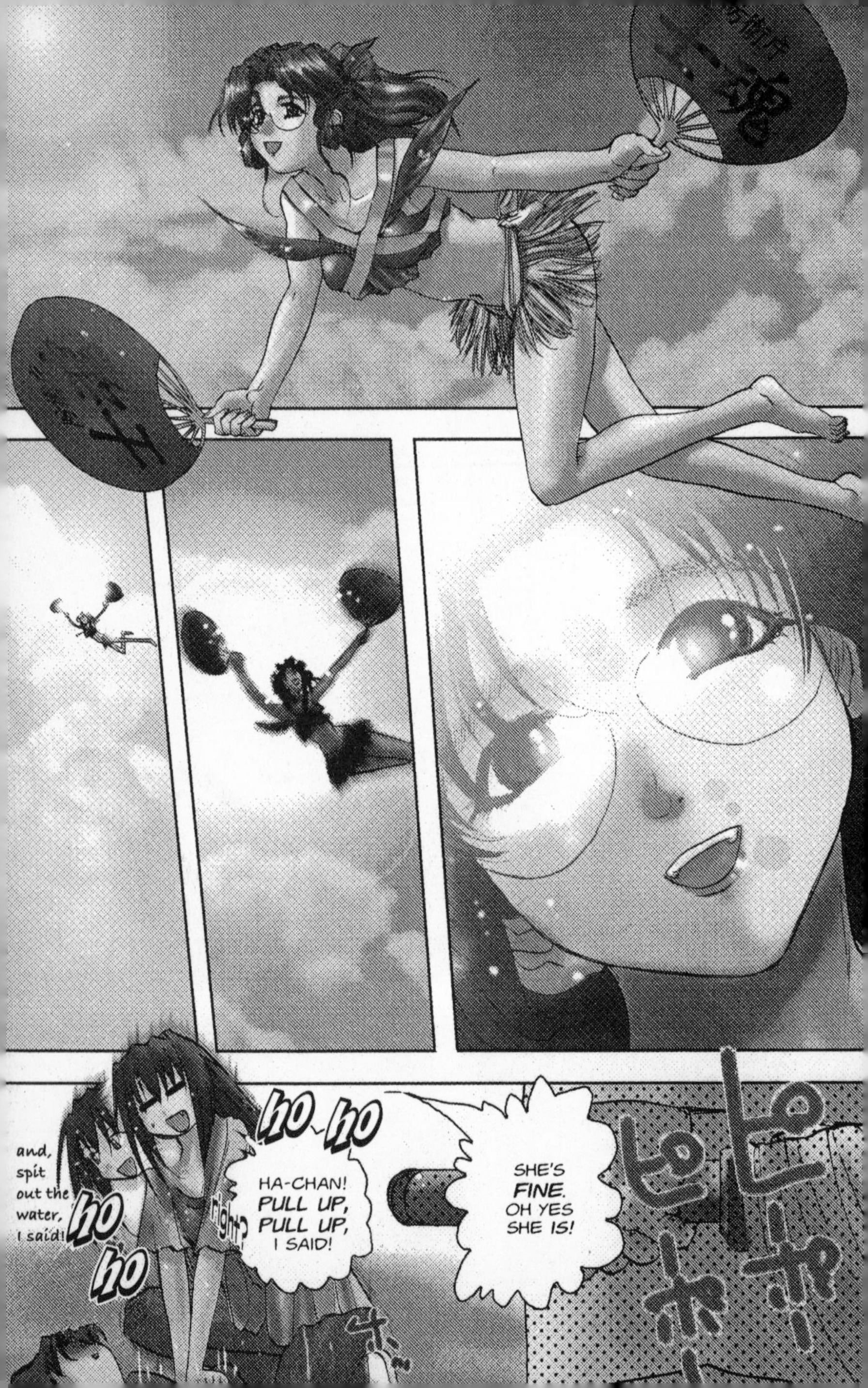
SHE'S FINE. OH YES SHE IS!
HA-CHAN! PULL UP, PULL UP, I SAID!
ho ho
right?
ho ho
and, spit out the water, I said!

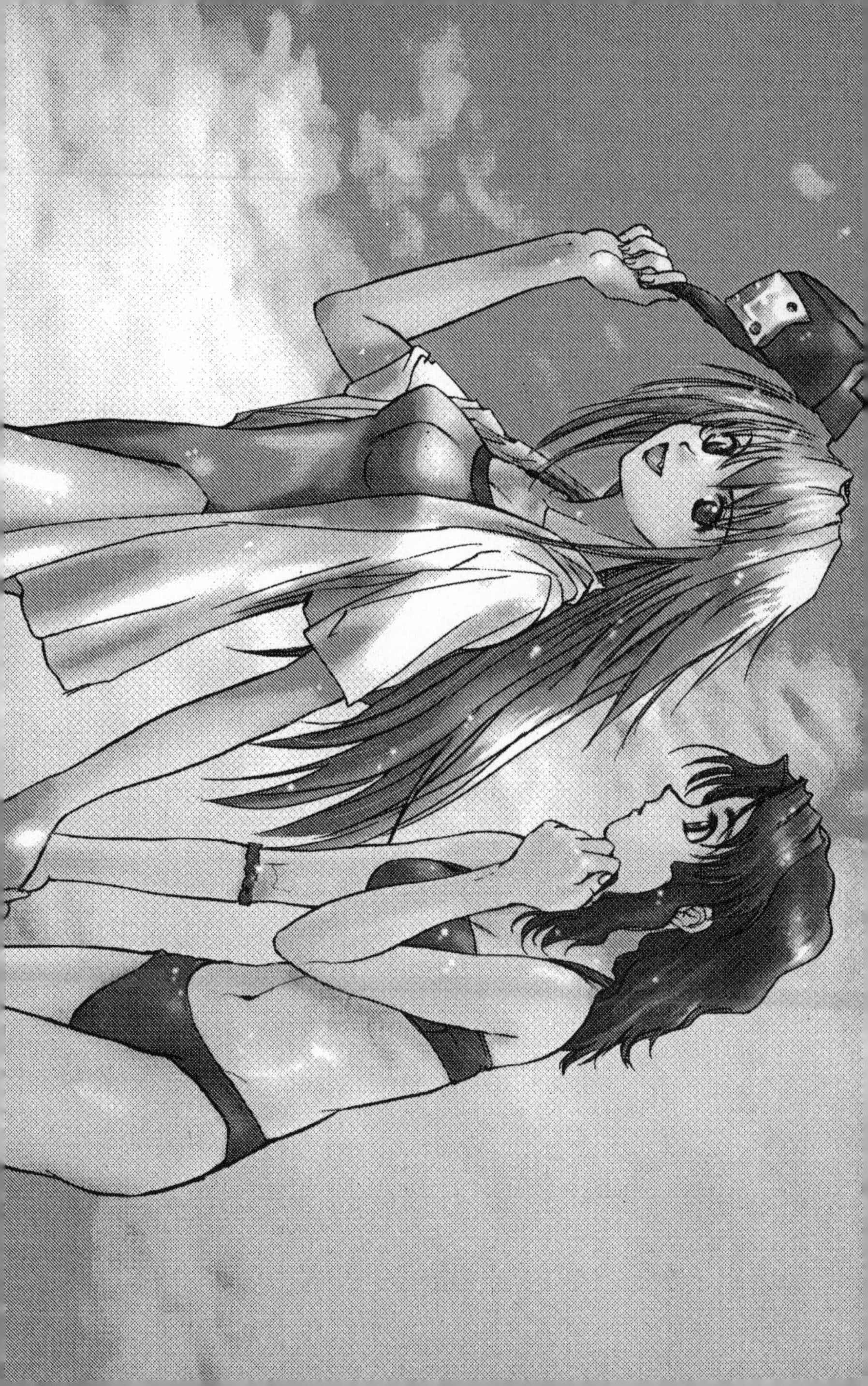

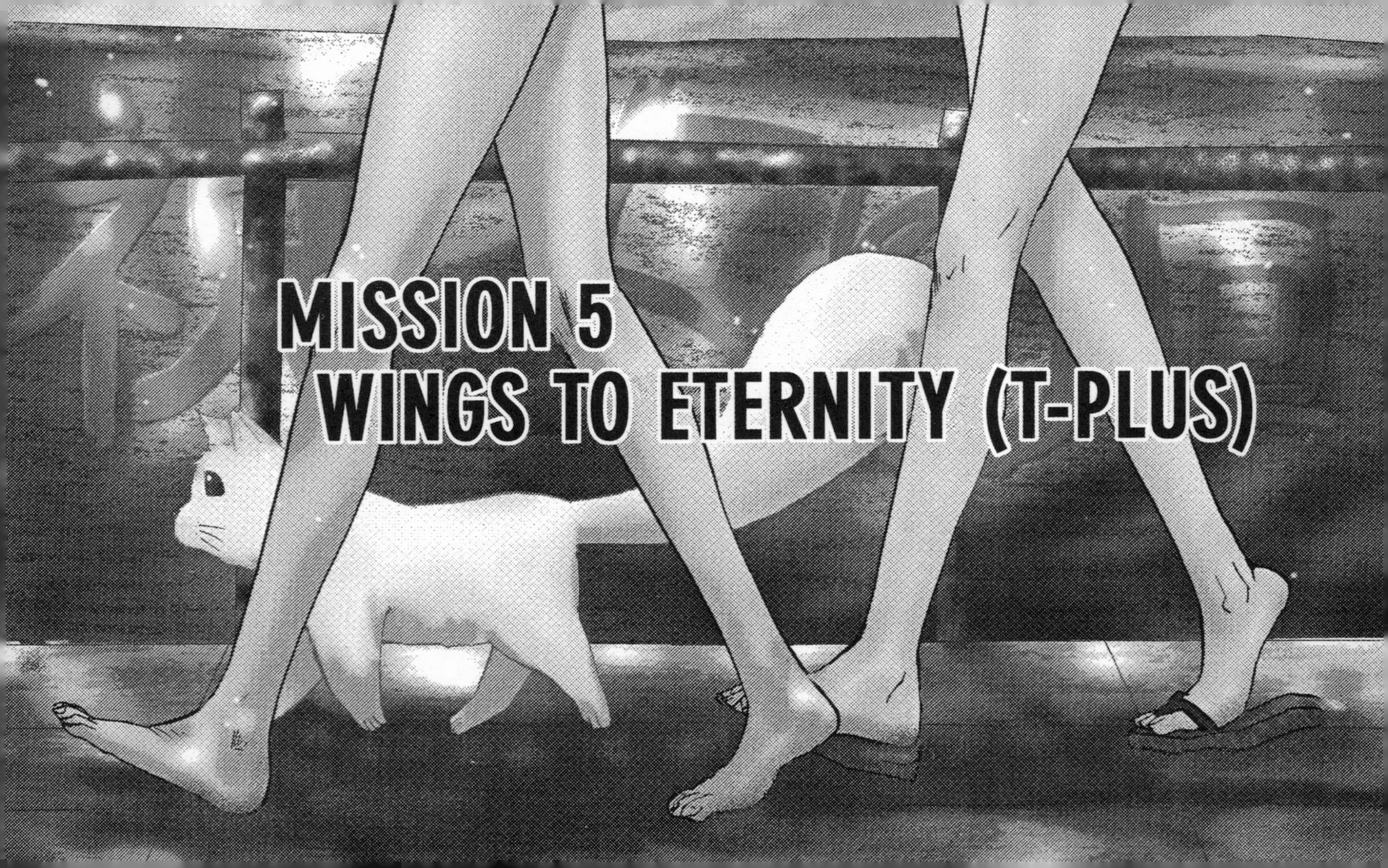
MISSION 5
WINGS TO ETERNITY (T-PLUS)

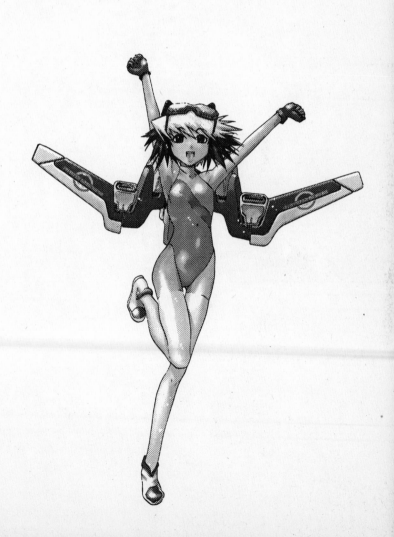

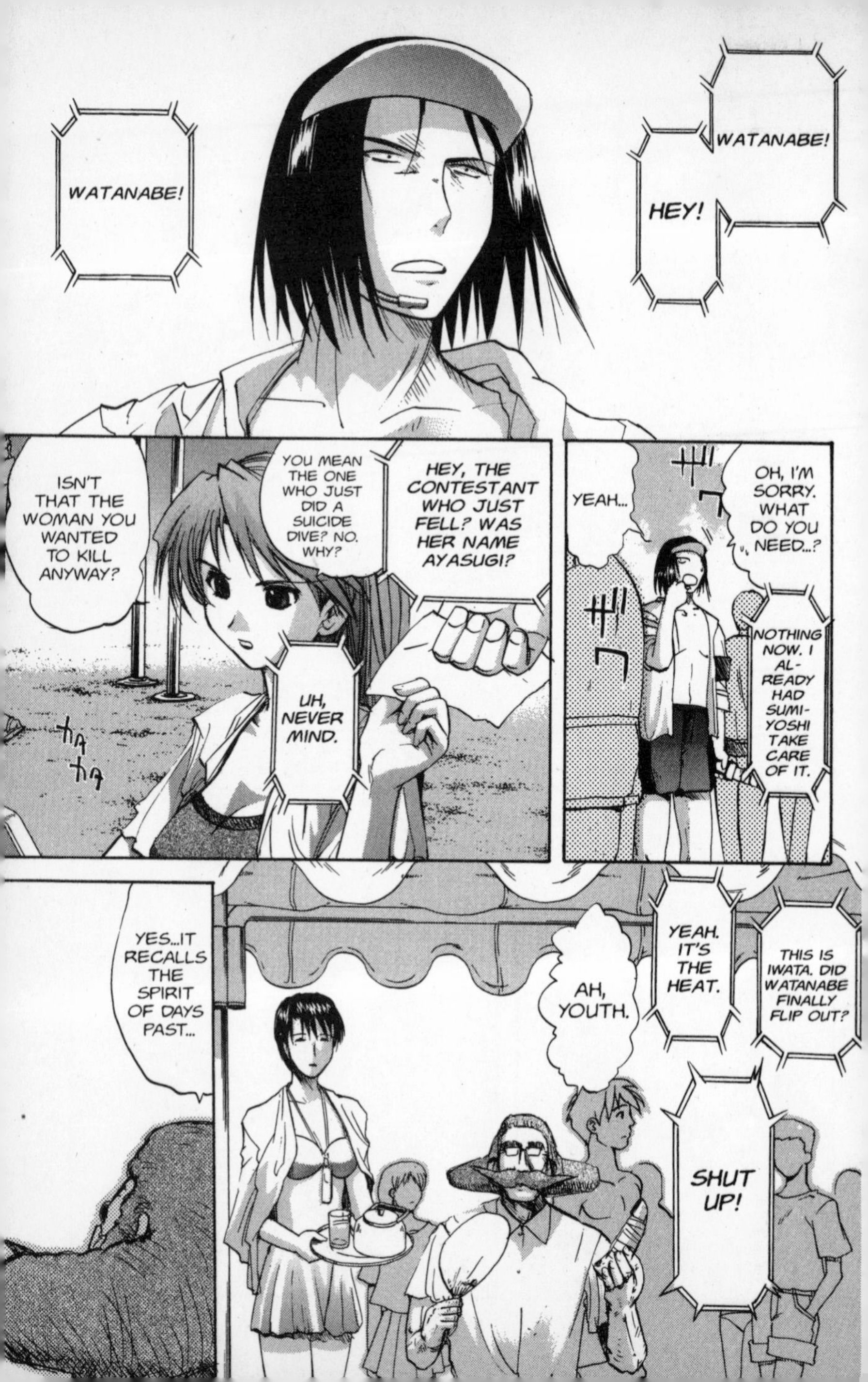
WATANABE!
HEY!
WATANABE!
OH, I'M SORRY. WHAT DO YOU NEED...?
YEAH...
NOTHING NOW. I AL-READY HAD SUMI-YOSHI TAKE CARE OF IT.
HEY, THE CONTESTANT WHO JUST FELL? WAS HER NAME AYASUGI?
YOU MEAN THE ONE WHO JUST DID A SUICIDE DIVE? NO. WHY?
ISN'T THAT THE WOMAN YOU WANTED TO KILL ANYWAY?
UH, NEVER MIND.
THIS IS IWATA. DID WATANABE FINALLY FLIP OUT?
YEAH. IT'S THE HEAT.
AH, YOUTH.
YES...IT RECALLS THE SPIRIT OF DAYS PAST...
SHUT UP!

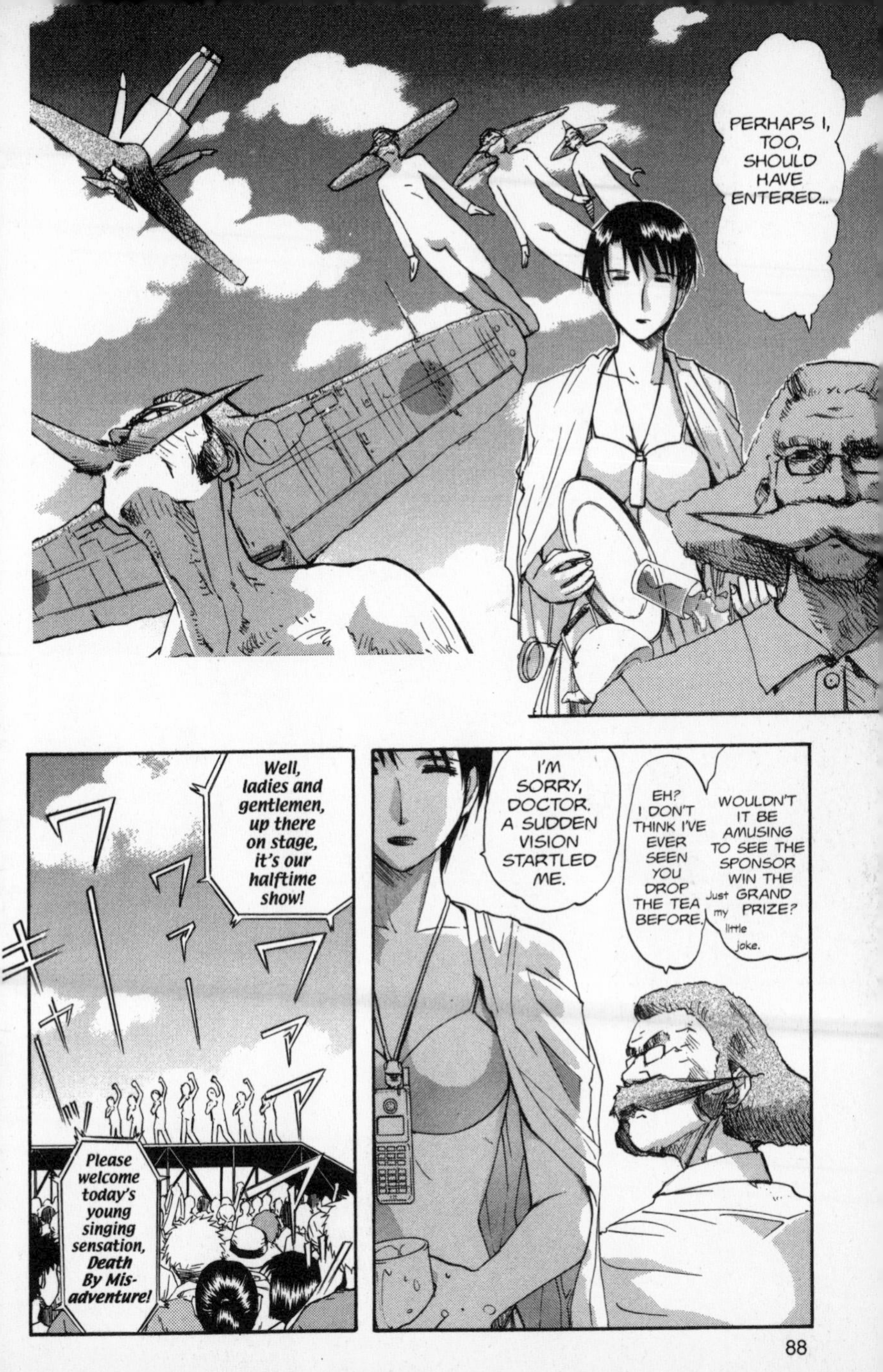
PERHAPS I, TOO, SHOULD HAVE ENTERED...
WOULDN'T IT BE AMUSING TO SEE THE SPONSOR WIN THE GRAND PRIZE?
Just my little joke.
EH? I DON'T THINK I'VE EVER SEEN YOU DROP THE TEA BEFORE.
I'M SORRY, DOCTOR. A SUDDEN VISION STARTLED ME.
Well, ladies and gentlemen, up there on stage, it's our halftime show!
Please welcome today's young singing sensation, Death By Mis-adventure!

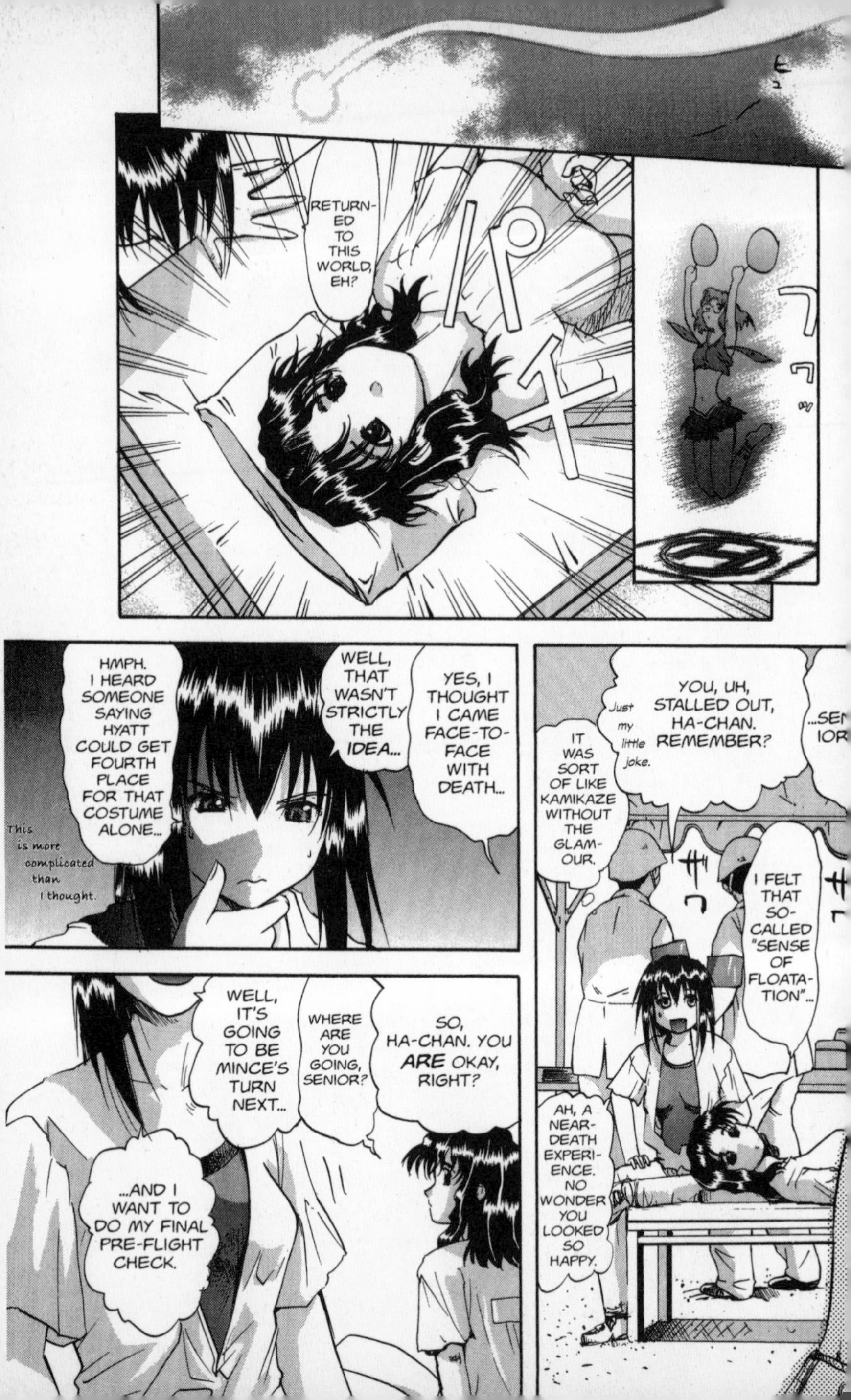
RETURNED TO THIS WORLD, EH?
...SENIOR
YOU, UH, STALLED OUT, HA-CHAN. REMEMBER?
Just my little joke.
IT WAS SORT OF LIKE KAMIKAZE WITHOUT THE GLAMOUR.
I FELT THAT SO-CALLED "SENSE OF FLOATATION"...
AH, A NEAR-DEATH EXPERIENCE. NO WONDER YOU LOOKED SO HAPPY.
YES, I THOUGHT I CAME FACE-TO-FACE WITH DEATH...
WELL, THAT WASN'T STRICTLY THE IDEA...
HMPH. I HEARD SOMEONE SAYING HYATT COULD GET FOURTH PLACE FOR THAT COSTUME ALONE...
This is more complicated than I thought.
SO, HA-CHAN. YOU ARE OKAY, RIGHT?
WHERE ARE YOU GOING, SENIOR?
WELL, IT'S GOING TO BE MINCE'S TURN NEXT...
...AND I WANT TO DO MY FINAL PRE-FLIGHT CHECK.

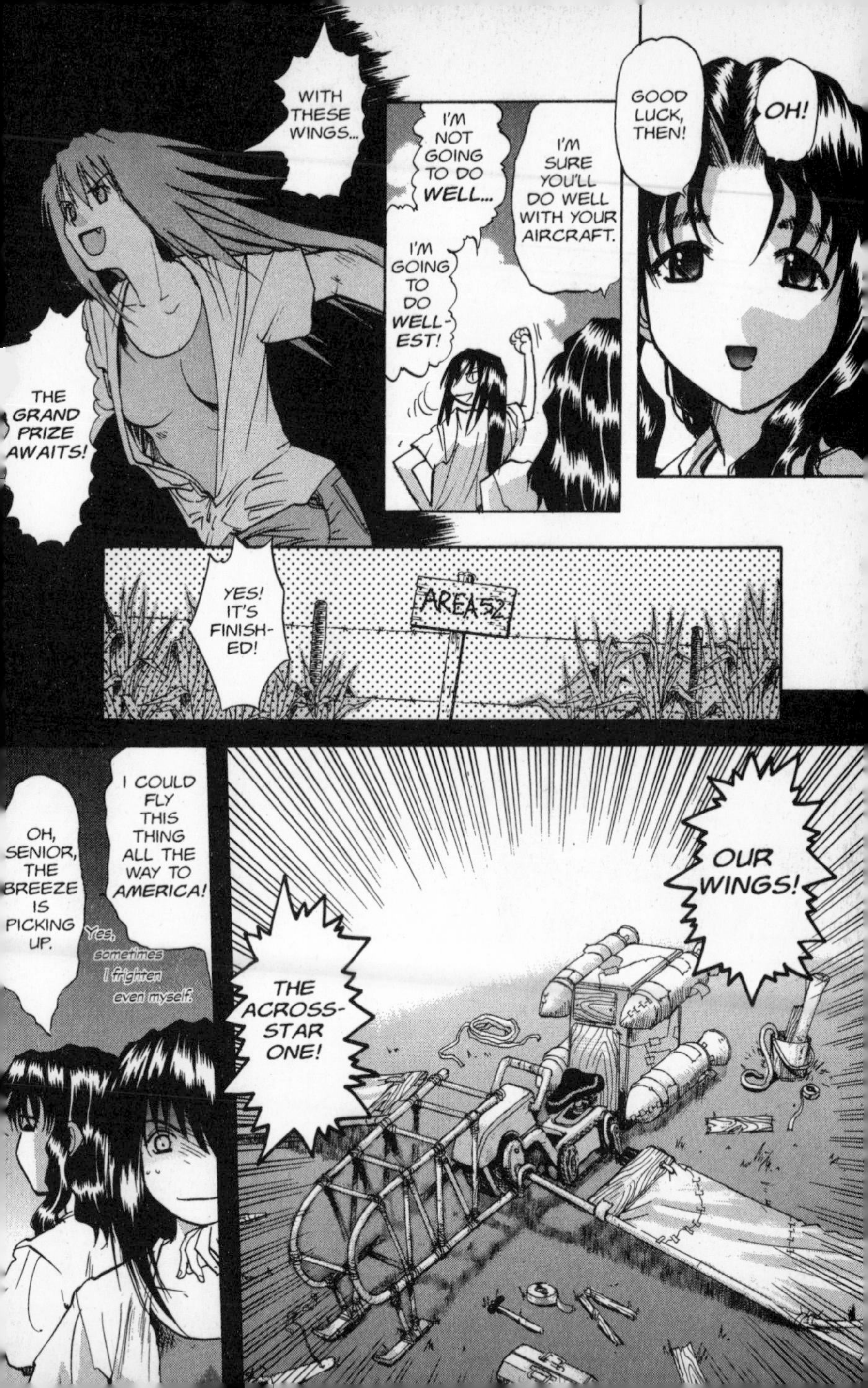
GOOD LUCK, THEN!
OH!
I'M SURE YOU'LL DO WELL WITH YOUR AIRCRAFT.
I'M NOT GOING TO DO WELL...
I'M GOING TO DO WELL-EST!
WITH THESE WINGS...
THE GRAND PRIZE AWAITS!
AREA 52
YES! IT'S FINISHED!
OUR WINGS!
THE ACROSS-STAR ONE!
I COULD FLY THIS THING ALL THE WAY TO AMERICA!
OH, SENIOR, THE BREEZE IS PICKING UP.
Yes, sometimes I frighten even myself.

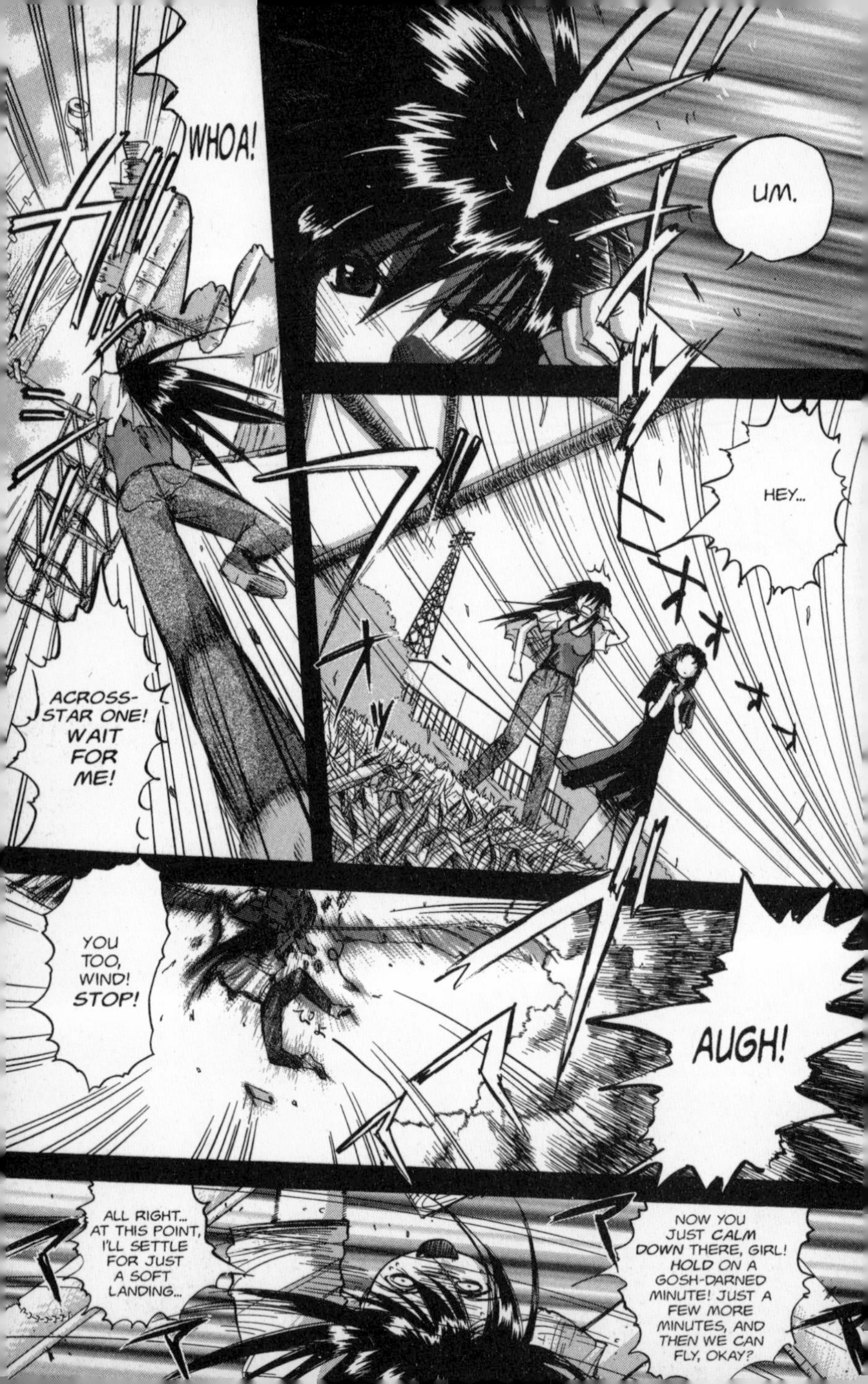
UM.
HEY...
WHOA!
ACROSS-STAR ONE! WAIT FOR ME!
AUGH!
YOU TOO, WIND! STOP!
NOW YOU JUST CALM DOWN THERE, GIRL! HOLD ON A GOSH-DARNED MINUTE! JUST A FEW MORE MINUTES, AND THEN WE CAN FLY, OKAY?
ALL RIGHT... AT THIS POINT, I'LL SETTLE FOR JUST A SOFT LANDING...

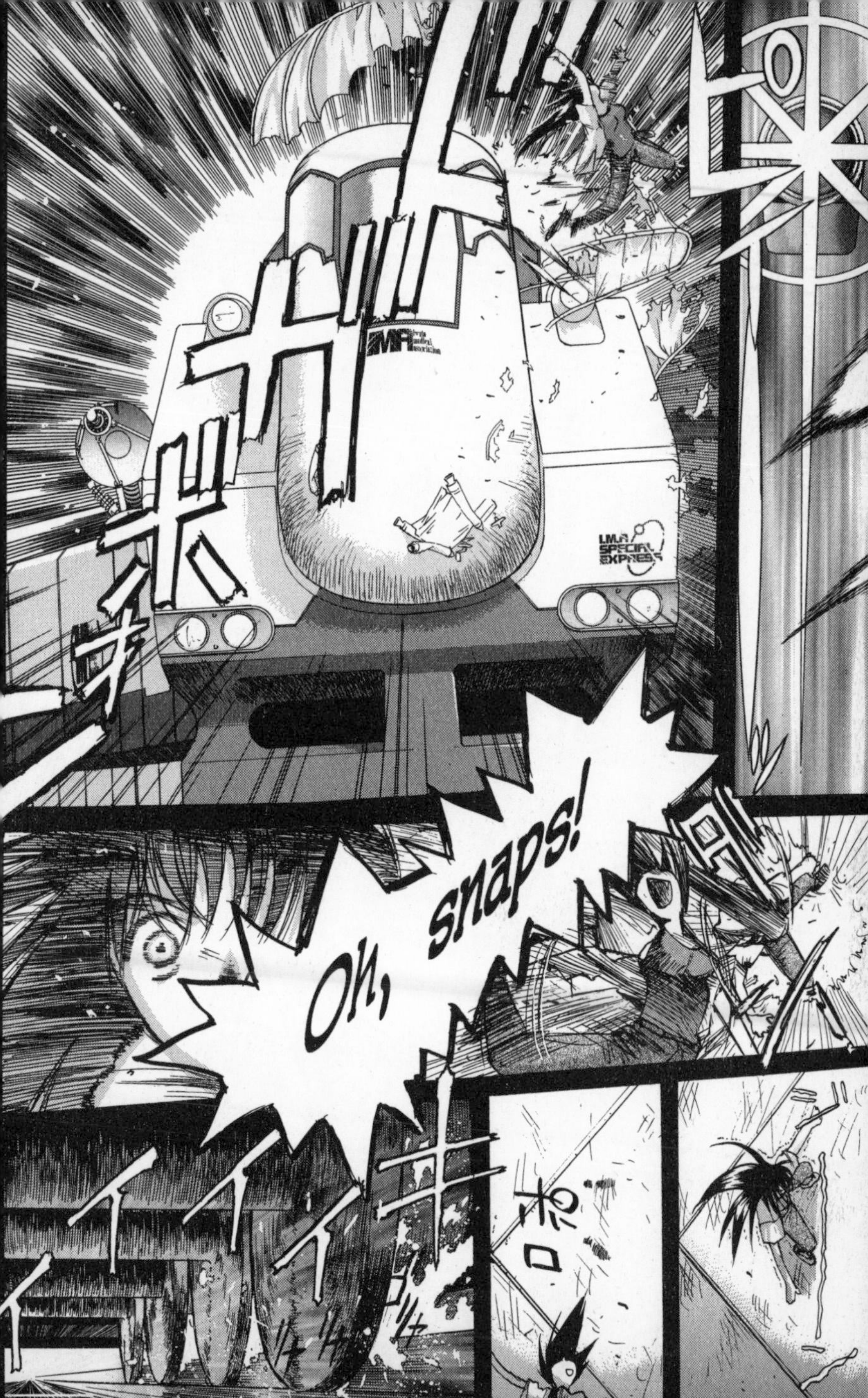
IMA SPECIAL EXPRESS
Oh, snaps!

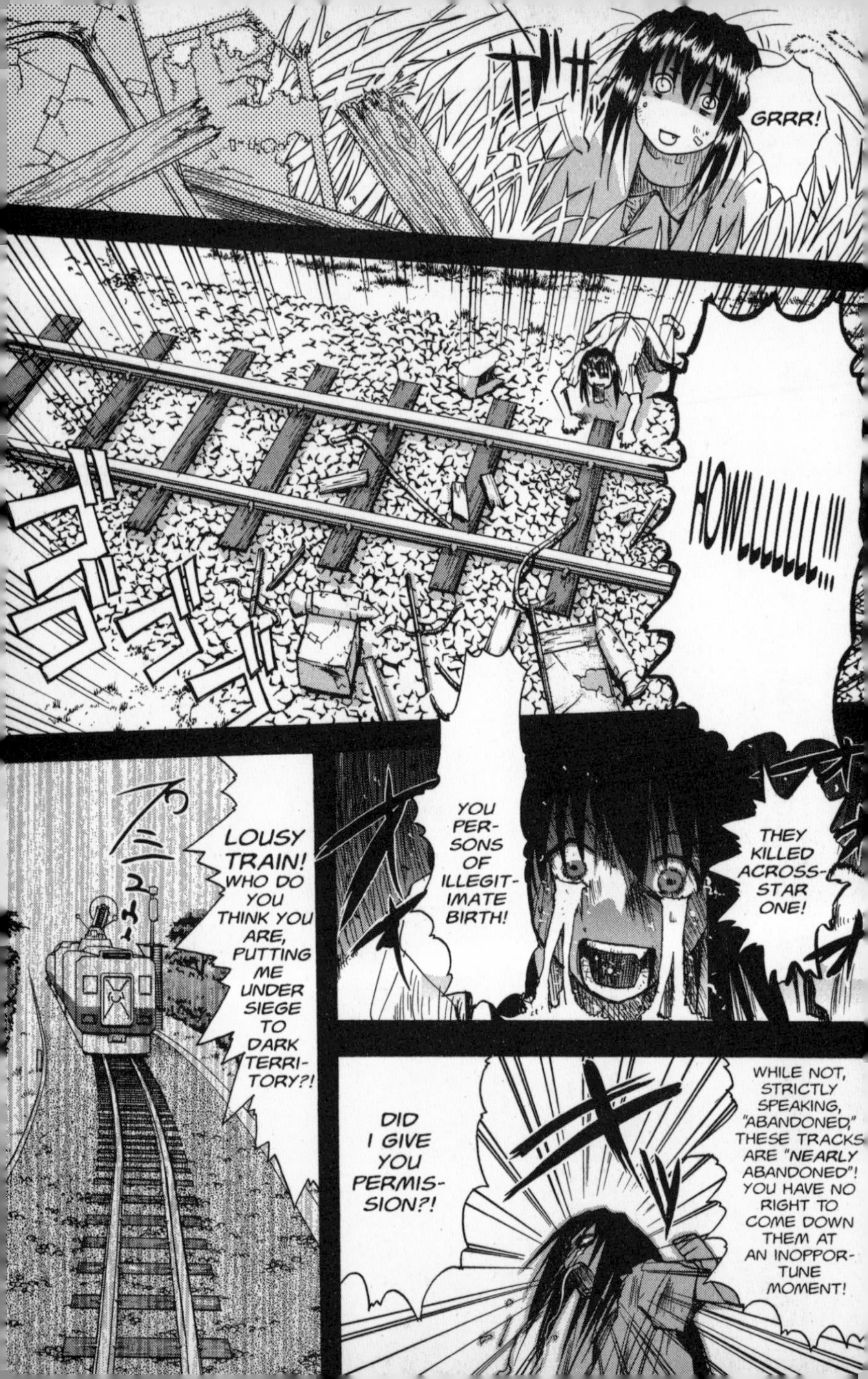
GRRR!
HOWLLLLLLLL!!!
THEY KILLED ACROSS-STAR ONE!
YOU PERSONS OF ILLEGITIMATE BIRTH!
LOUSY TRAIN! WHO DO YOU THINK YOU ARE, PUTTING ME UNDER SIEGE TO DARK TERRITORY?!
WHILE NOT, STRICTLY SPEAKING, "ABANDONED," THESE TRACKS ARE "NEARLY ABANDONED"! YOU HAVE NO RIGHT TO COME DOWN THEM AT AN INOPPORTUNE MOMENT!
DID I GIVE YOU PERMISSION?!

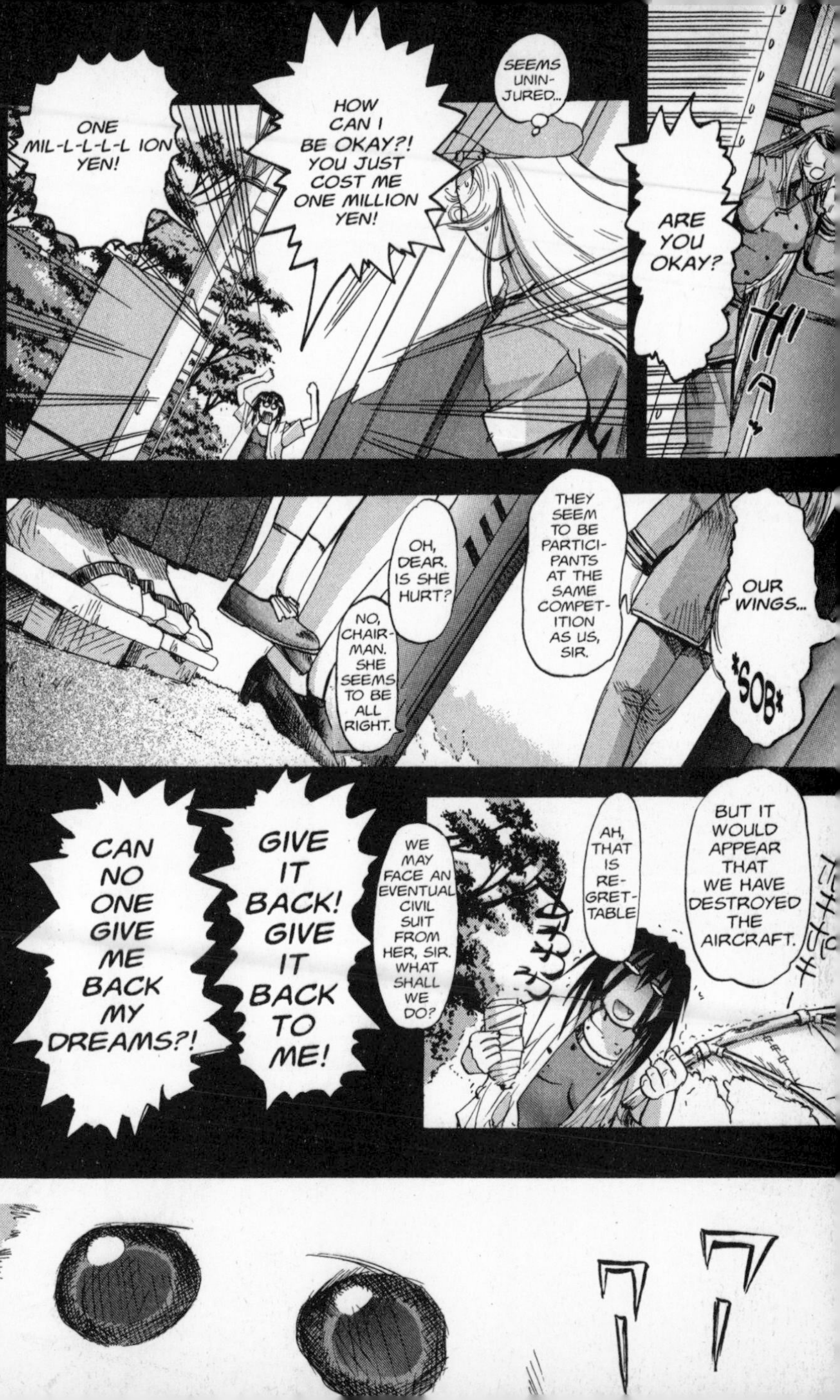
ARE YOU OKAY?
SEEMS UNINJURED...
HOW CAN I BE OKAY?! YOU JUST COST ME ONE MILLION YEN!
ONE MIL-L-L-L-L ION YEN!
OUR WINGS...
SOB
THEY SEEM TO BE PARTICIPANTS AT THE SAME COMPETITION AS US, SIR.
OH, DEAR. IS SHE HURT?
NO, CHAIRMAN. SHE SEEMS TO BE ALL RIGHT.
BUT IT WOULD APPEAR THAT WE HAVE DESTROYED THE AIRCRAFT.
AH, THAT IS REGRETTABLE
WE MAY FACE AN EVENTUAL CIVIL SUIT FROM HER, SIR. WHAT SHALL WE DO?
GIVE IT BACK! GIVE IT BACK TO ME!
CAN NO ONE GIVE ME BACK MY DREAMS?!

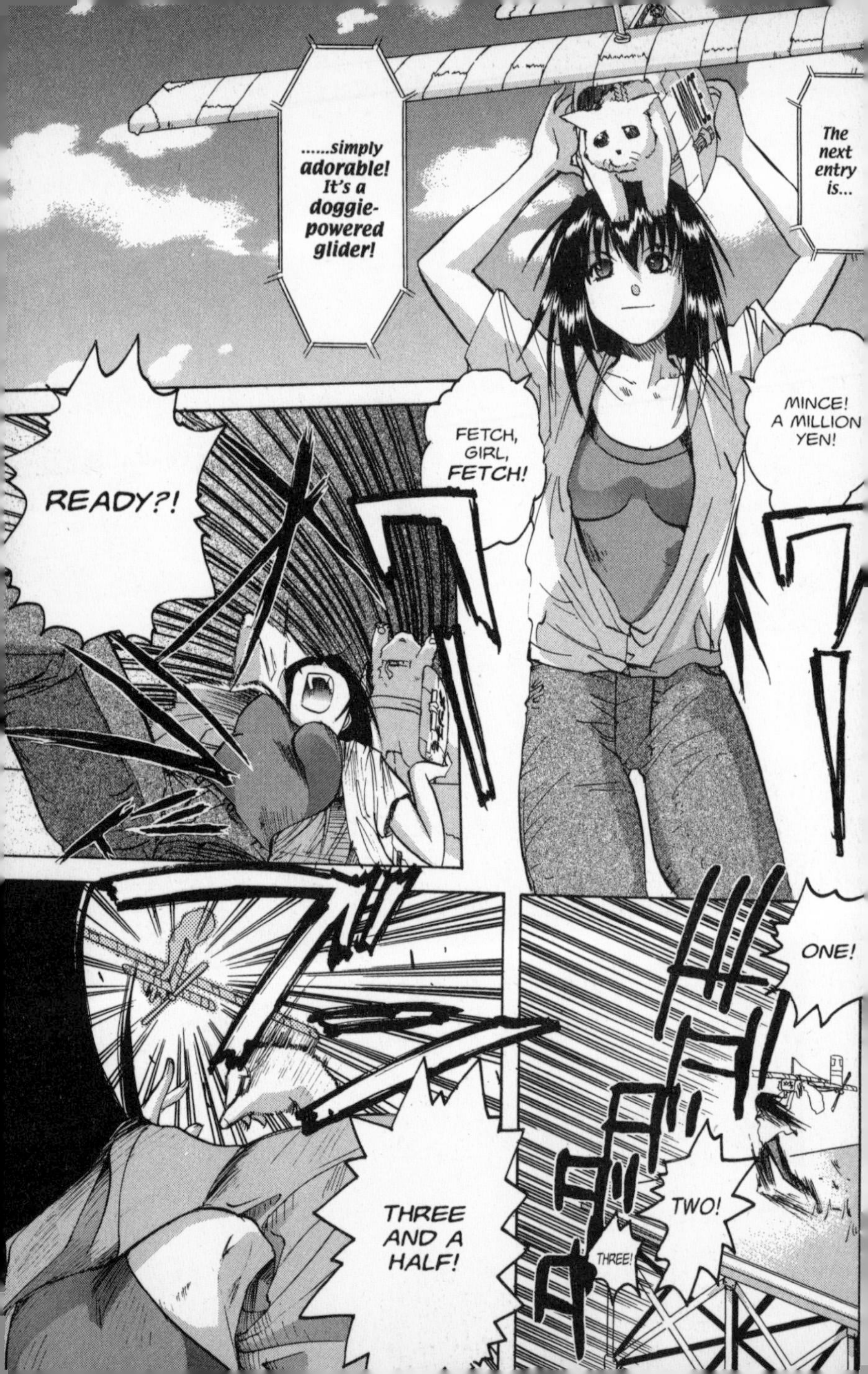
The next entry is...
......simply adorable! It's a doggie-powered glider!
MINCE! A MILLION YEN!
FETCH, GIRL, FETCH!
READY?!
ONE!
TWO!
THREE!
THREE AND A HALF!

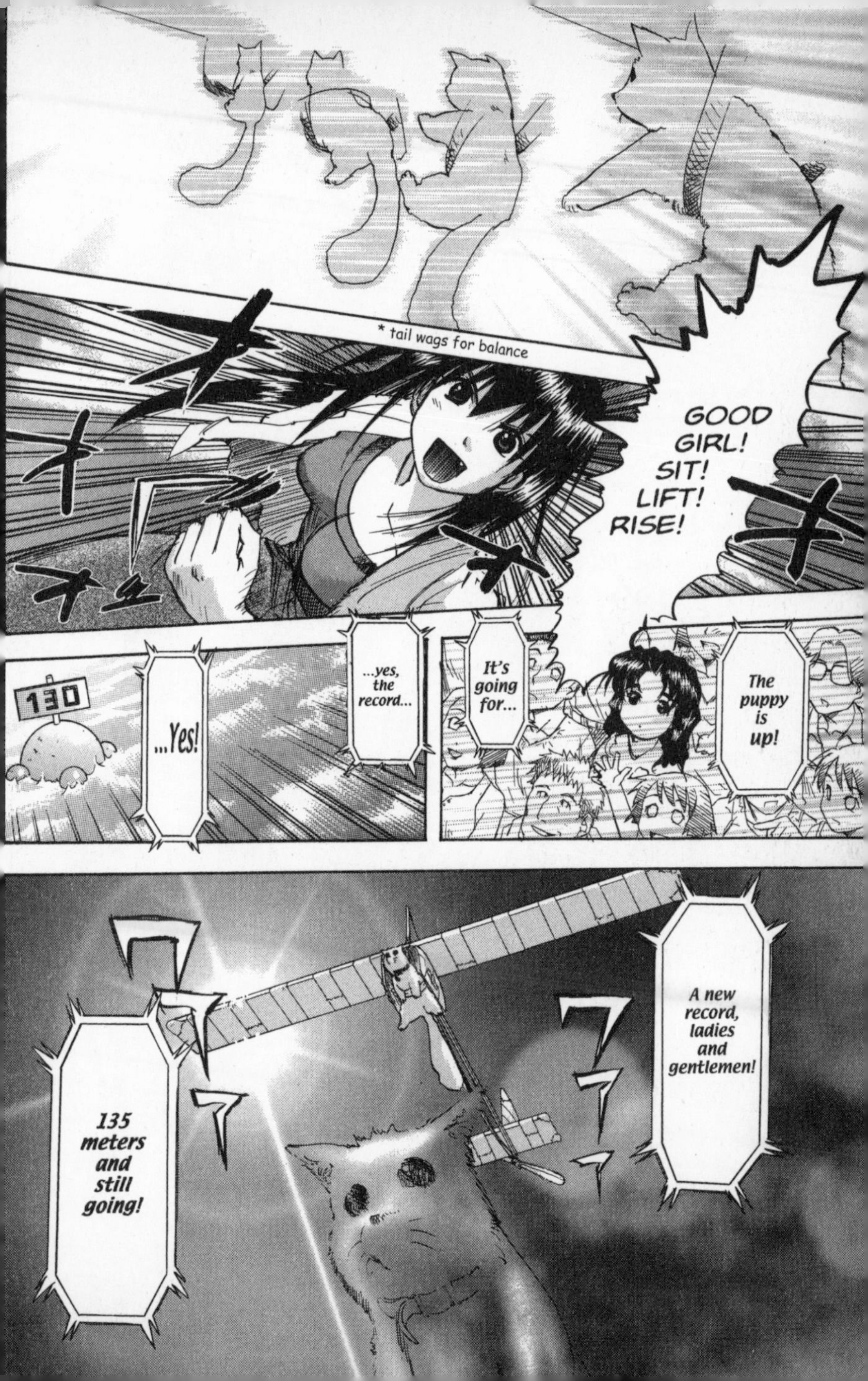
GOOD GIRL! SIT! LIFT! RISE!
* tail wags for balance
The puppy is up!
It's going for...
...yes, the record...
...Yes!
130
A new record, ladies and gentlemen!
135 meters and still going!

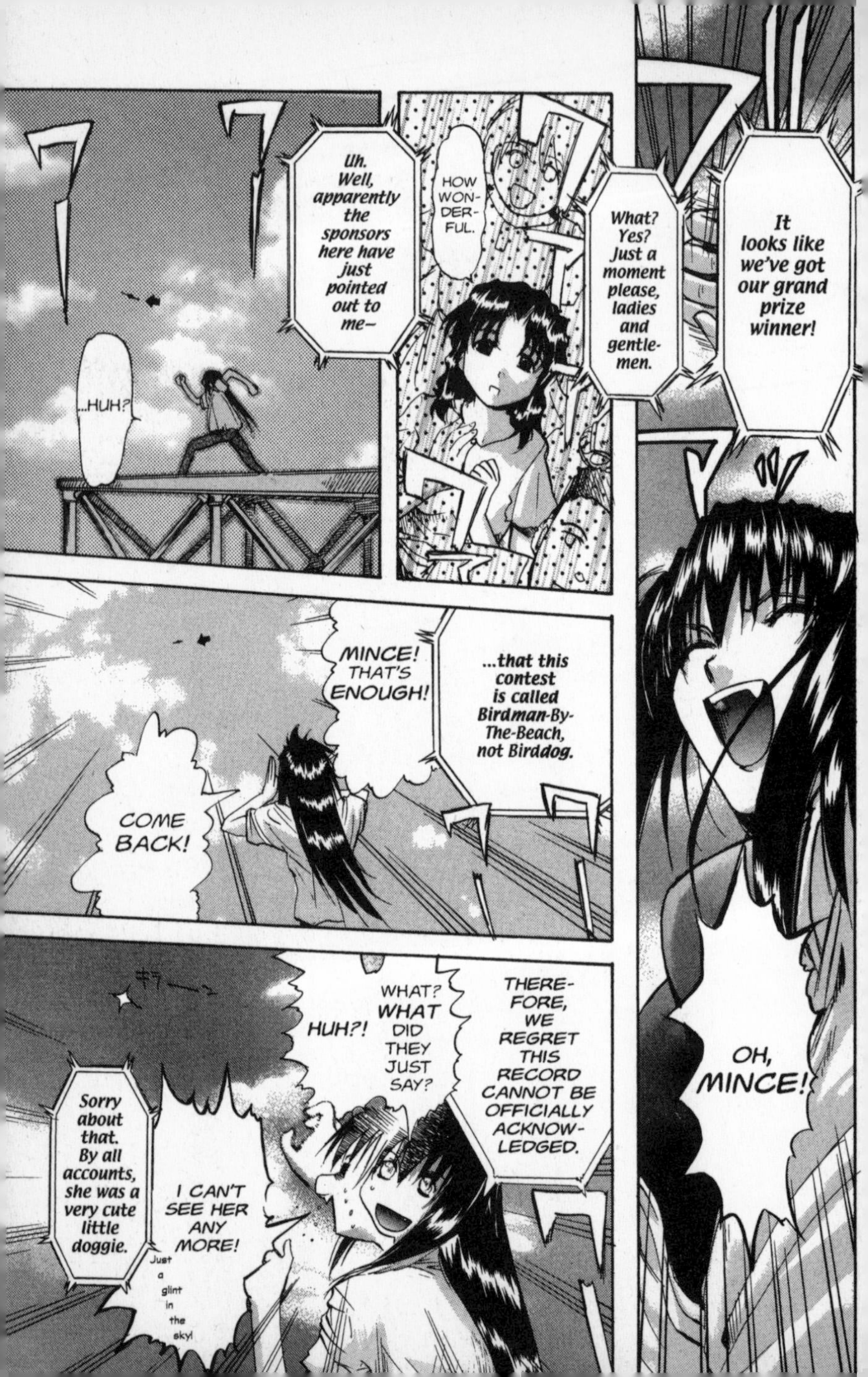
It looks like we've got our grand prize winner!
OH, MINCE!
What? Yes? Just a moment please, ladies and gentlemen.
HOW WONDERFUL.
Uh. Well, apparently the sponsors here have just pointed out to me—
...HUH?
...that this contest is called Birdman-By-The-Beach, not Birddog.
MINCE! THAT'S ENOUGH!
COME BACK!
THEREFORE, WE REGRET THIS RECORD CANNOT BE OFFICIALLY ACKNOWLEDGED.
WHAT? WHAT DID THEY JUST SAY?
HUH?!
I CAN'T SEE HER ANY MORE!
Sorry about that. By all accounts, she was a very cute little doggie.
Just a glint in the sky!

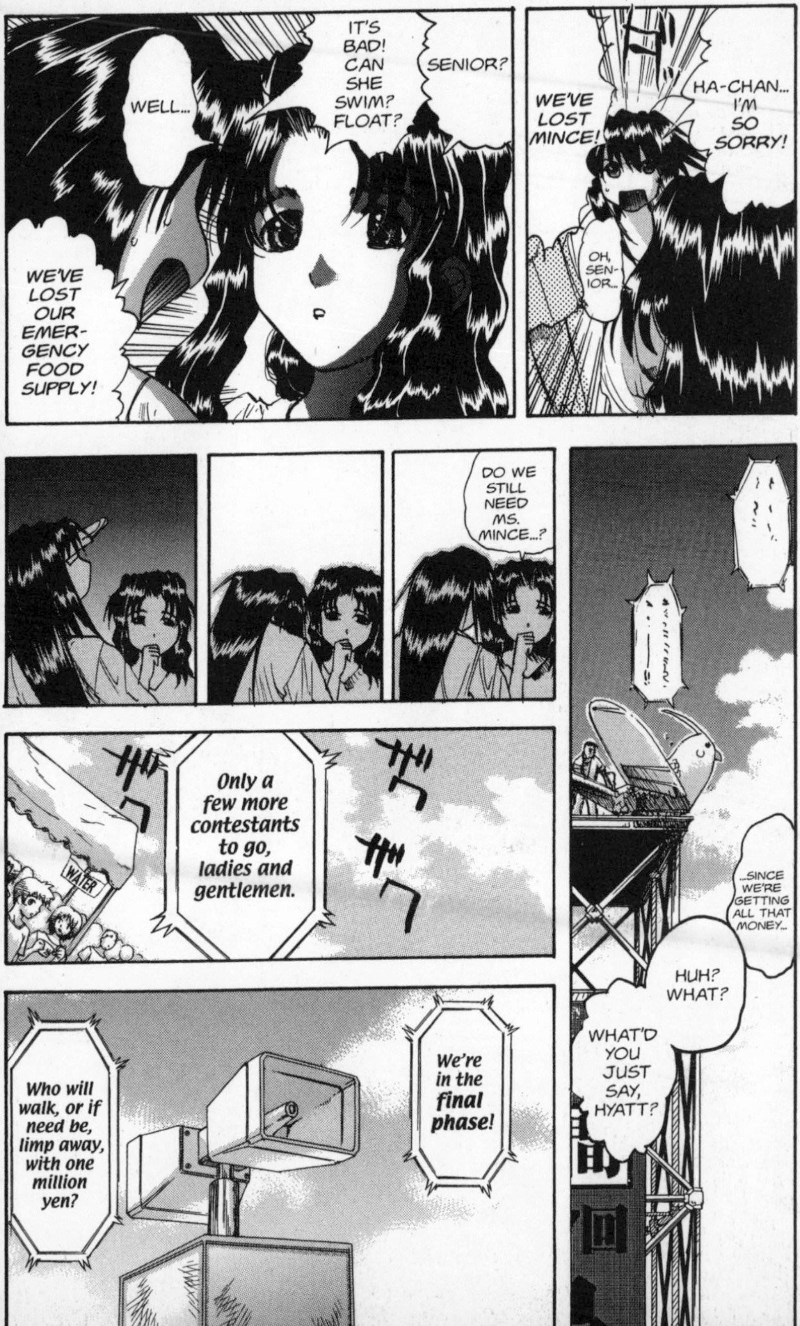
HA-CHAN... I'M SO SORRY!
WE'VE LOST MINCE!
OH, SENIOR...
SENIOR?
IT'S BAD! CAN SHE SWIM? FLOAT?
WELL...
WE'VE LOST OUR EMERGENCY FOOD SUPPLY!
...SINCE WE'RE GETTING ALL THAT MONEY...
HUH? WHAT?
WHAT'D YOU JUST SAY, HYATT?
DO WE STILL NEED MS. MINCE...?
Only a few more contestants to go, ladies and gentlemen.
WATER
We're in the final phase!
Who will walk, or if need be, limp away, with one million yen?

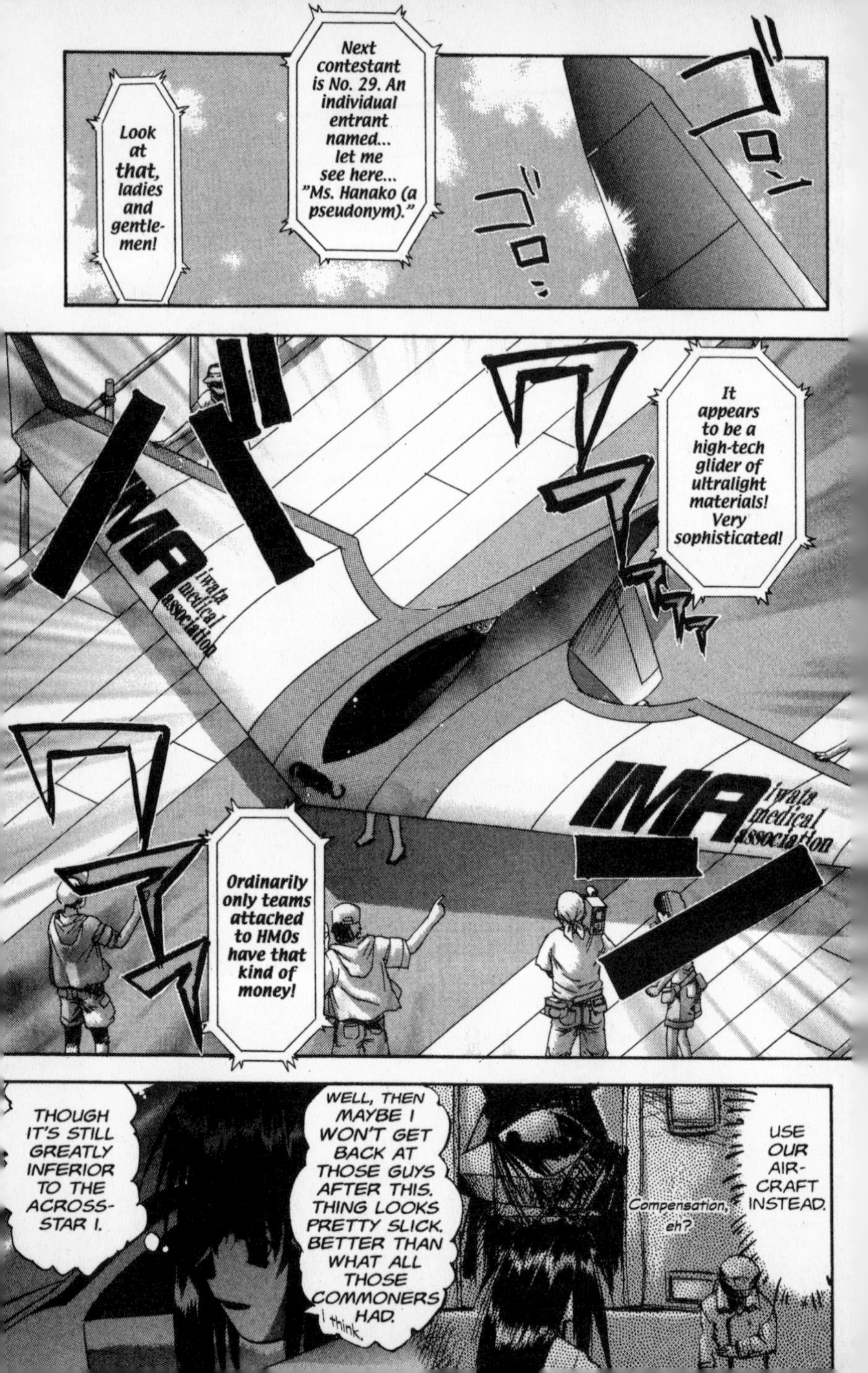
Next contestant is No. 29. An individual entrant named... let me see here... "Ms. Hanako (a pseudonym)."
Look at that, ladies and gentle-men!
It appears to be a high-tech glider of ultralight materials! Very sophisticated!
IMA iwata medical association
Ordinarily only teams attached to HMOs have that kind of money!
USE OUR AIR-CRAFT INSTEAD.
Compensation, eh?
WELL, THEN MAYBE I WON'T GET BACK AT THOSE GUYS AFTER THIS. THING LOOKS PRETTY SLICK. BETTER THAN WHAT ALL THOSE COMMONERS HAD.
I think.
THOUGH IT'S STILL GREATLY INFERIOR TO THE ACROSS-STAR I.

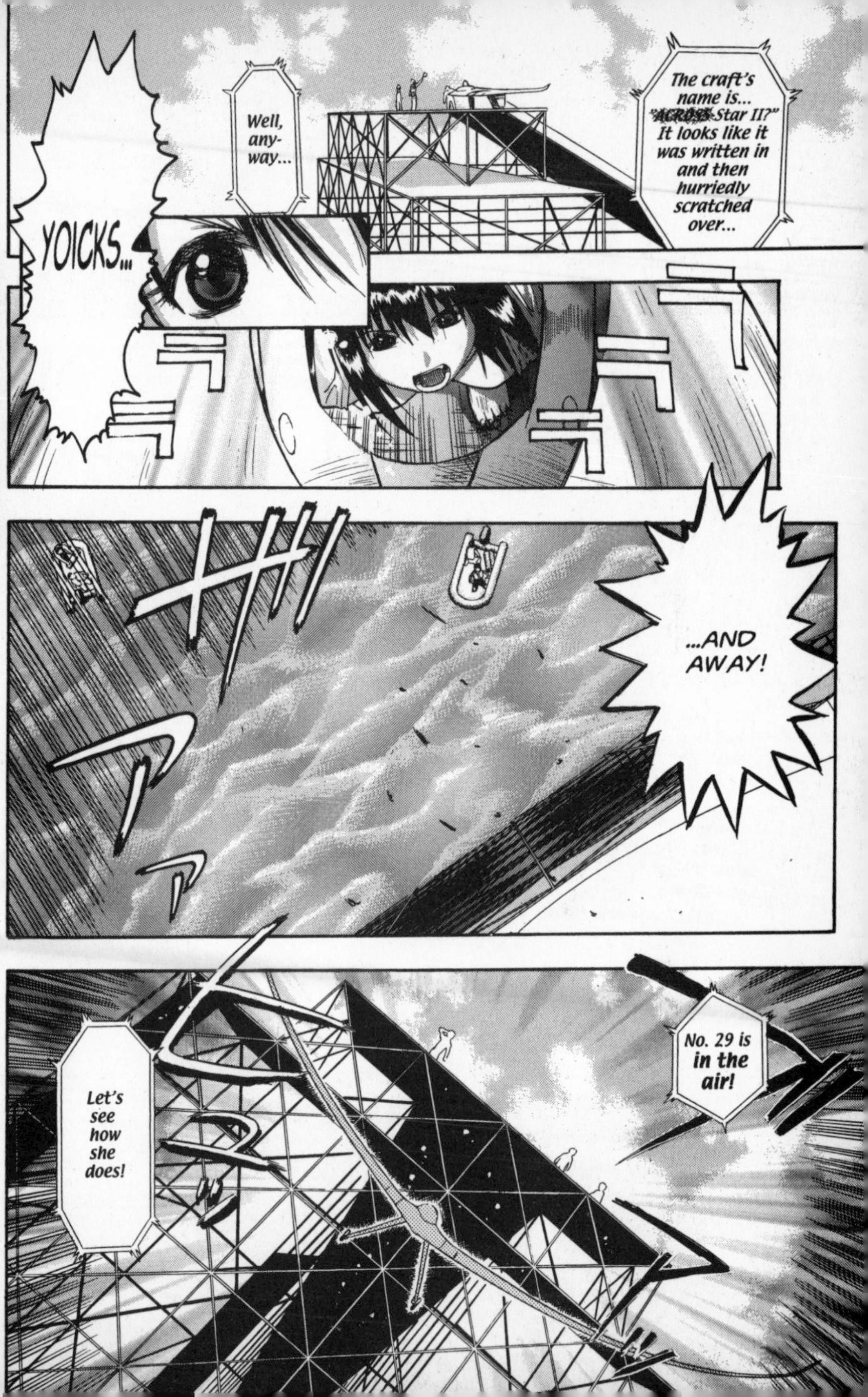
The craft's name is... "~~ACROSS~~ Star II?" It looks like it was written in and then hurriedly scratched over...
Well, anyway...
YOICKS...
...AND AWAY!
No. 29 is **in the air!**
Let's see how she does!

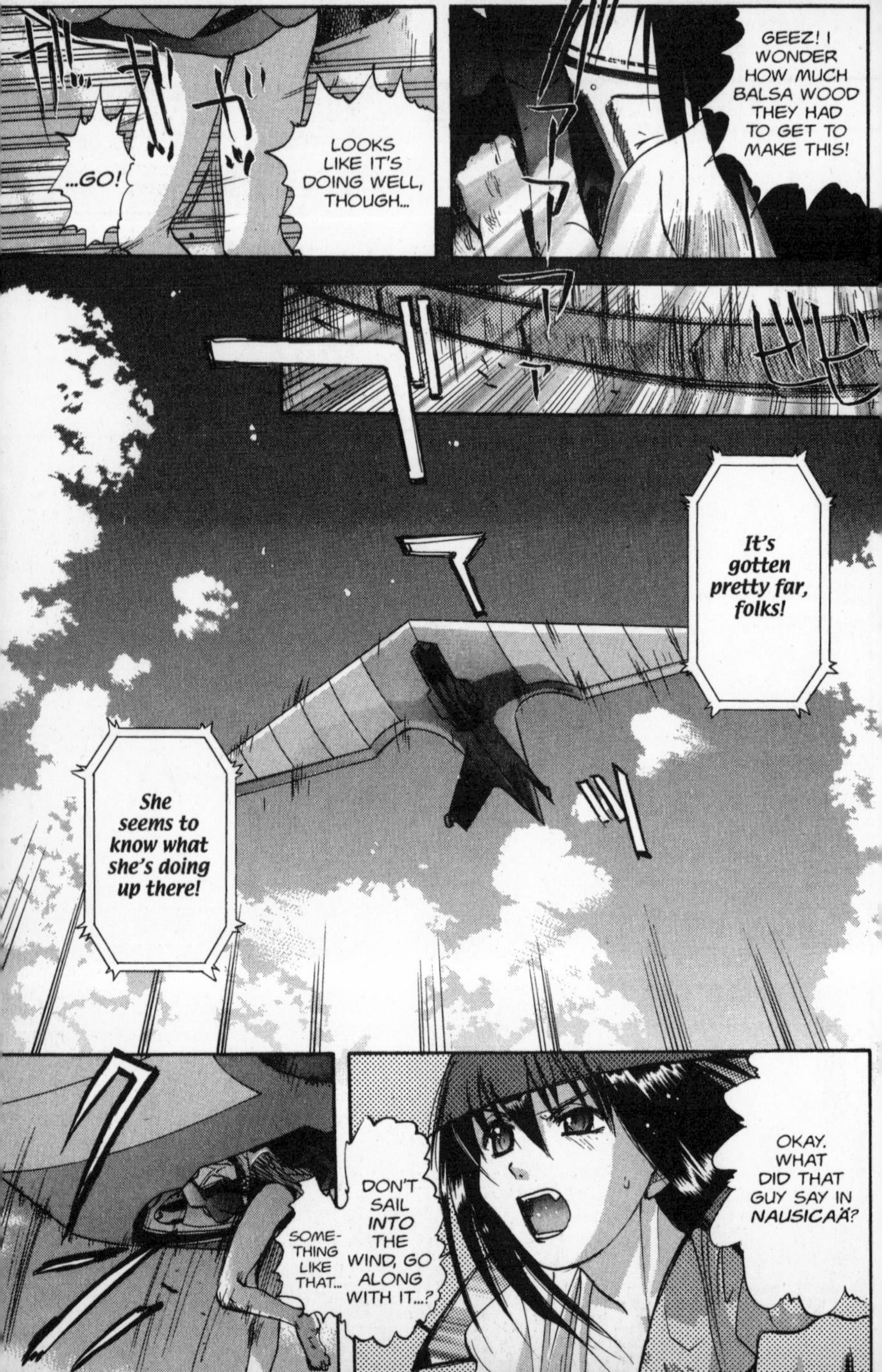
GEEZ! I WONDER HOW MUCH BALSA WOOD THEY HAD TO GET TO MAKE THIS!
LOOKS LIKE IT'S DOING WELL, THOUGH...
...GO!
It's gotten pretty far, folks!
She seems to know what she's doing up there!
OKAY. WHAT DID THAT GUY SAY IN NAUSICAÄ?
DON'T SAIL INTO THE WIND, GO ALONG WITH IT...?
SOMETHING LIKE THAT...

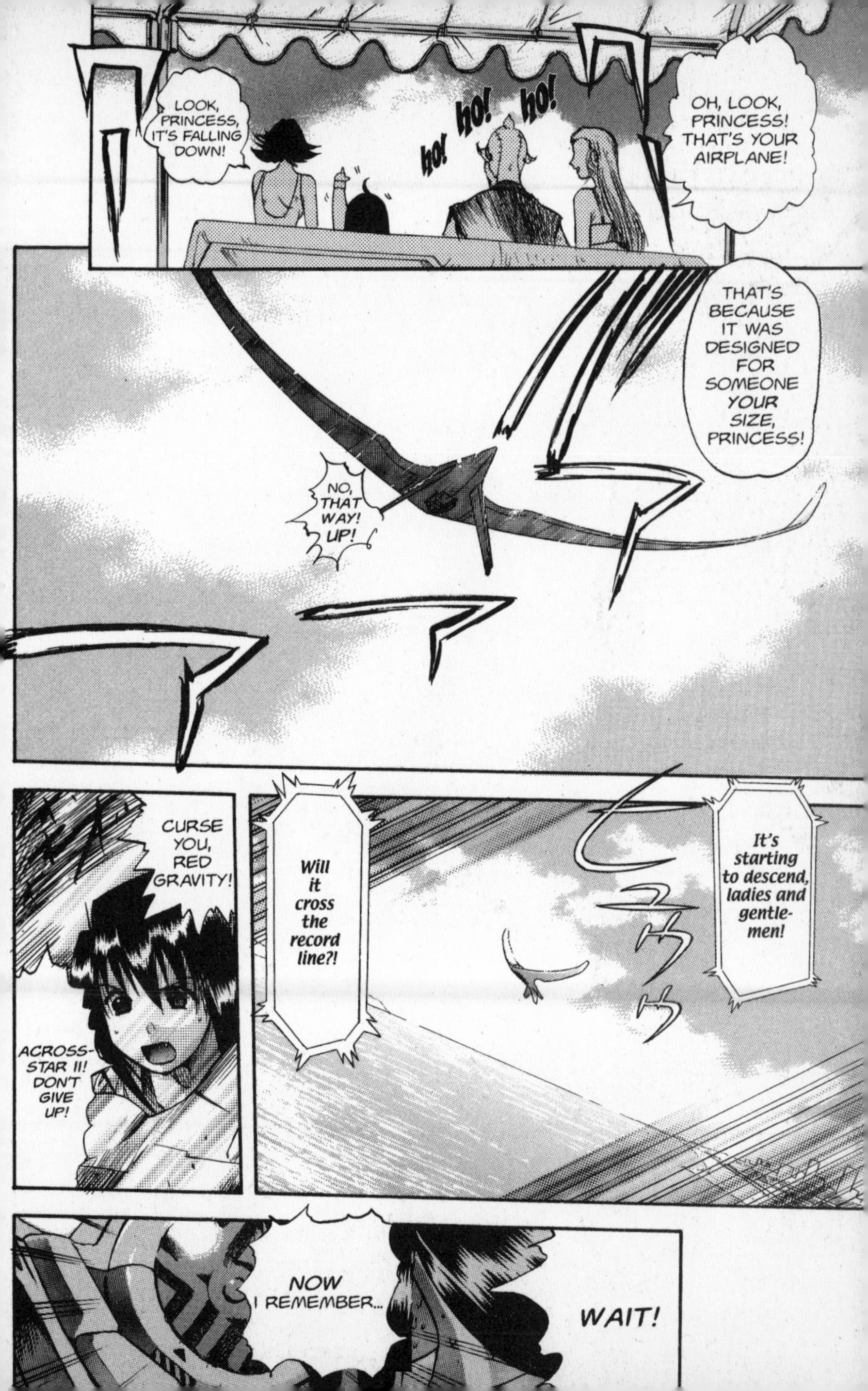
OH, LOOK, PRINCESS! THAT'S YOUR AIRPLANE!
ho! ho! ho!
LOOK, PRINCESS, IT'S FALLING DOWN!
THAT'S BECAUSE IT WAS DESIGNED FOR SOMEONE YOUR SIZE, PRINCESS!
NO, THAT WAY! UP!
It's starting to descend, ladies and gentle-men!
Will it cross the record line?!
CURSE YOU, RED GRAVITY!
ACROSS-STAR II! DON'T GIVE UP!
WAIT!
NOW I REMEMBER...

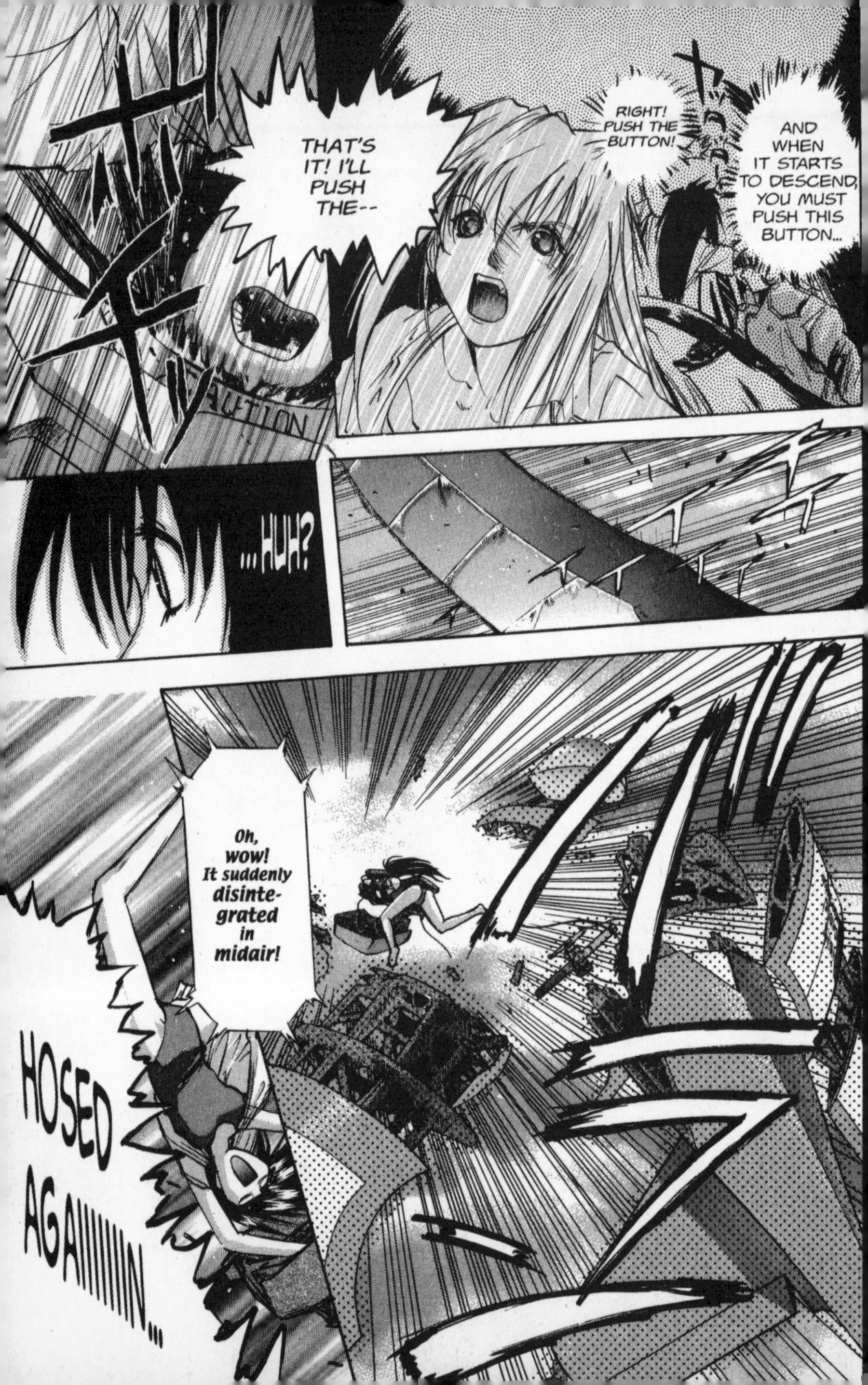

AND WHEN IT STARTS TO DESCEND, YOU MUST PUSH THIS BUTTON...
RIGHT! PUSH THE BUTTON!
THAT'S IT! I'LL PUSH THE--
CAUTION
...HUH?
Oh, wow! It suddenly disinte-grated in midair!
HOSED AGAIIIIIIN...

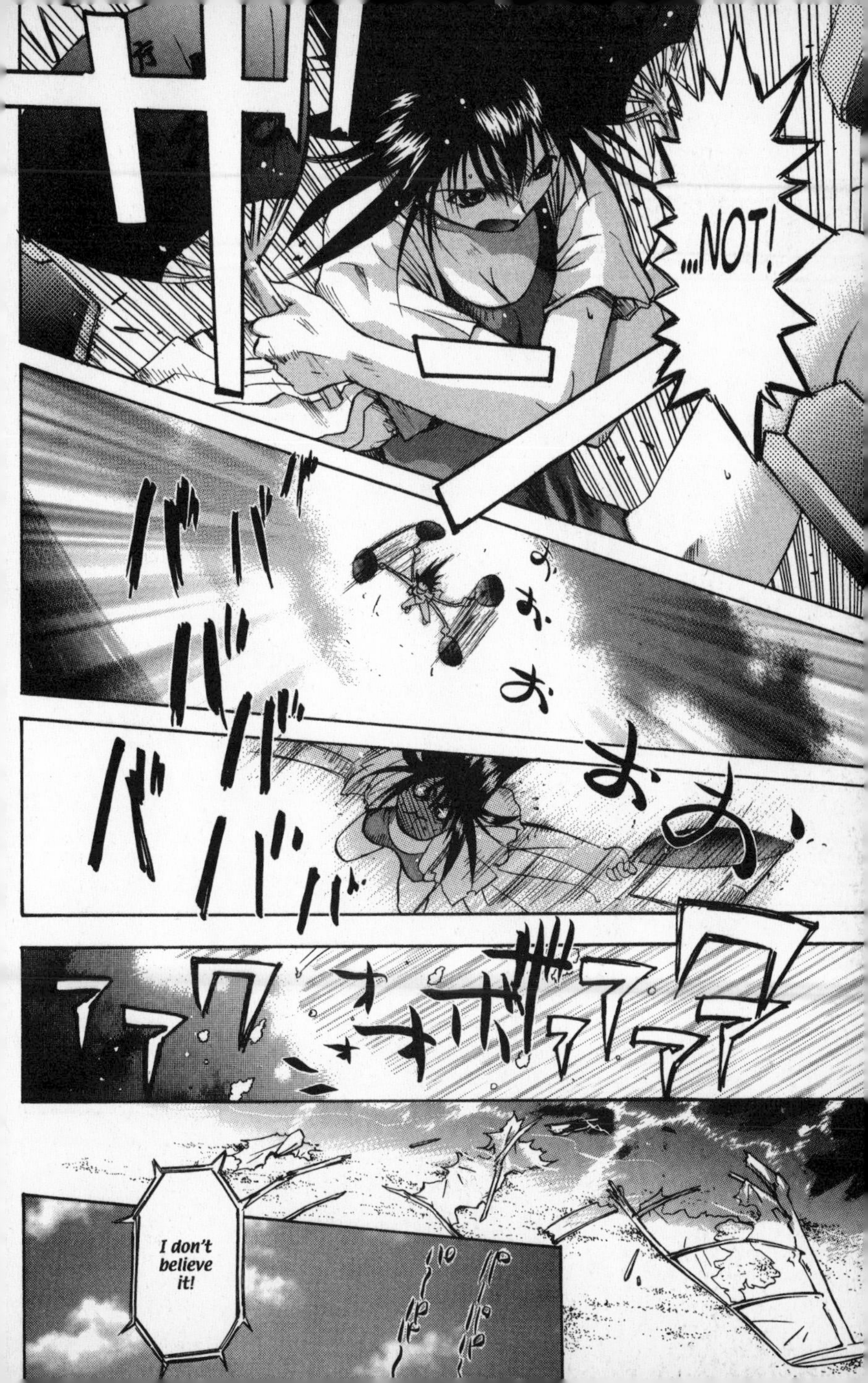
...NOT!
I don't believe it!

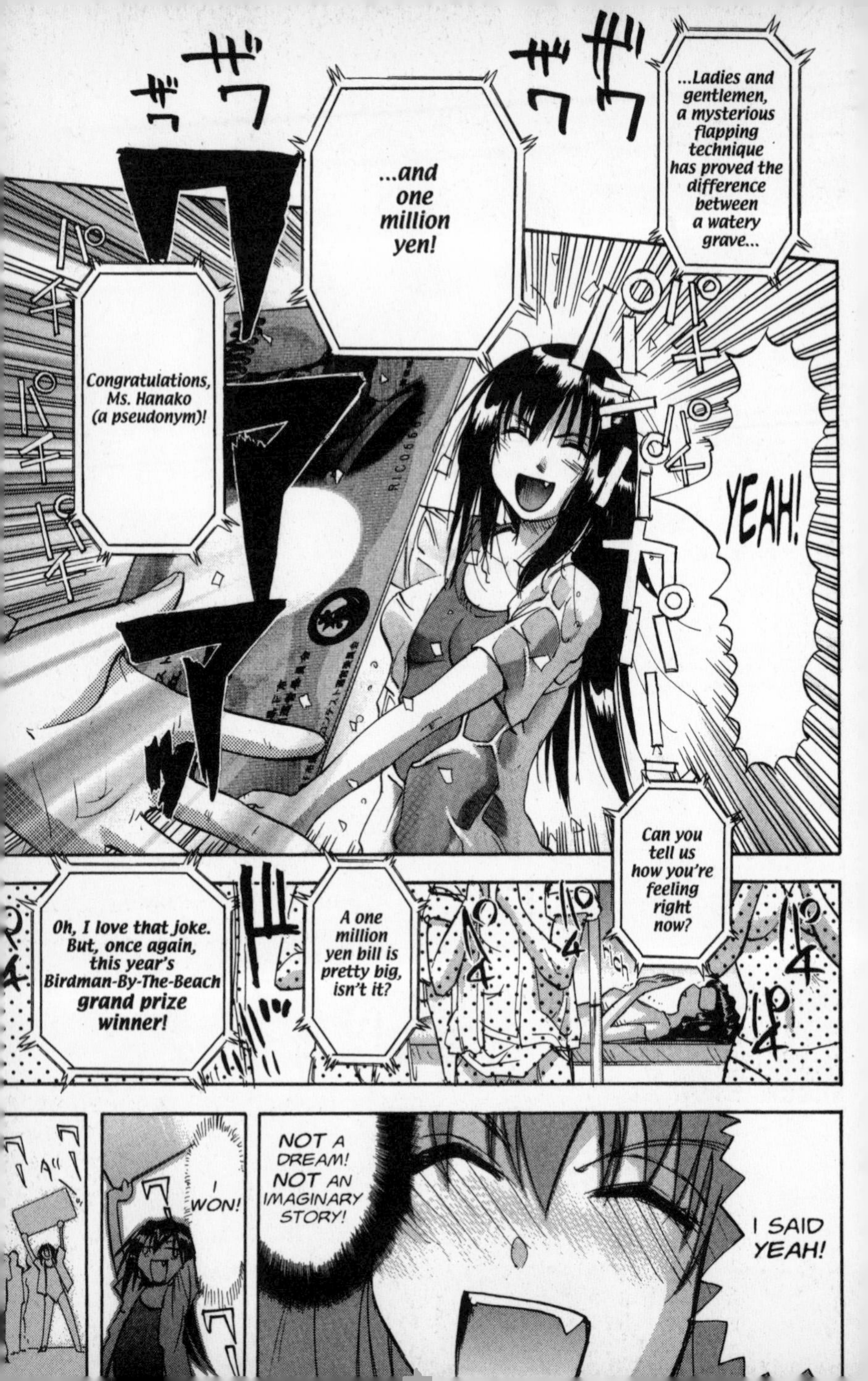
...Ladies and gentlemen, a mysterious flapping technique has proved the difference between a watery grave...
...and one million yen!
Congratulations, Ms. Hanako (a pseudonym)!
YEAH!
Can you tell us how you're feeling right now?
A one million yen bill is pretty big, isn't it?
Oh, I love that joke. But, once again, this year's Birdman-By-The-Beach grand prize winner!
I SAID YEAH!
NOT A DREAM! NOT AN IMAGINARY STORY!
I WON!

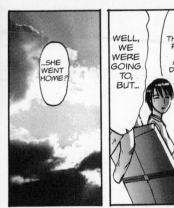

AH, THE SUN SETS UPON ANOTHER THRILLING CONTEST...
オーライ
UM, DOCTOR?
HMM?
ISN'T THAT THE CHECK FOR THE PRIZE MONEY? DIDN'T WE GIVE IT TO HER?
WELL, WE WERE GOING TO, BUT...
...SHE WENT HOME?
ハッ ハッ ハッ
EAT AS MUCH AS YOU WANT, HA-CHAN! NO NEED TO ECONOMIZE!
1000000
金百萬円
A ONE MILLION YEN BILL IS PRETTY BIG, ISN'T IT?
TO-MORROW WE'RE TAKING THAT THING TO THE SUPER-MARKET, AND I HOPE THEY GOT CHANGE!

...Hey...what did happen to Mince?

END MISSION 5

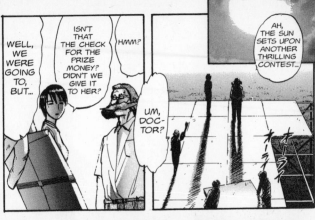

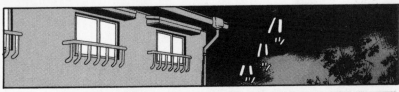

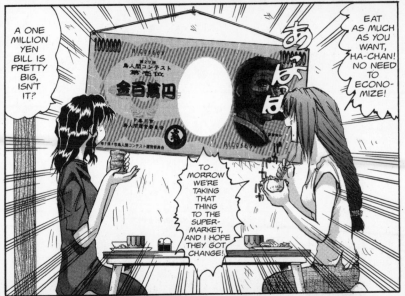

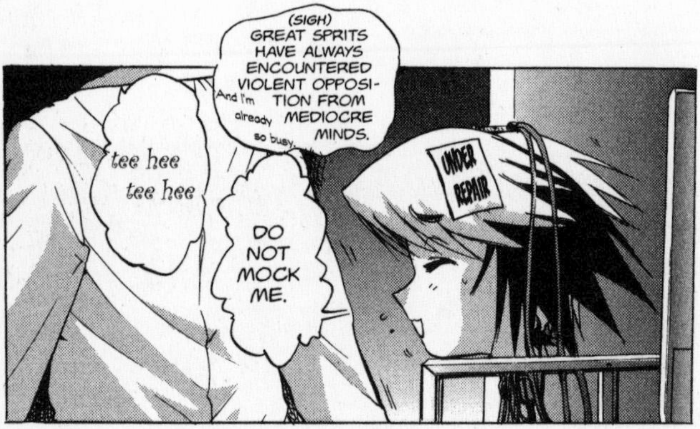
(SIGH) GREAT SPRITS HAVE ALWAYS ENCOUNTERED VIOLENT OPPOSITION FROM MEDIOCRE MINDS.
UNDER REPAIR
And I'm already so busy.
DO NOT MOCK ME.
tee hee tee hee

EXCEL SAGA

EXCEL SAGA

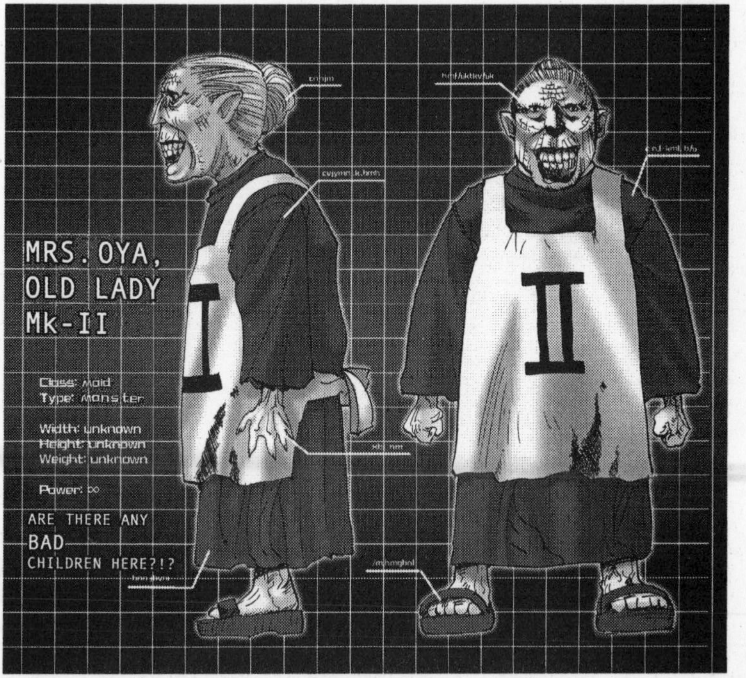
MRS. OYA,
OLD LADY
Mk-II
Class: maid
Type: monster
Width: unknown
Height: unknown
Weight: unknown
Power: ∞
ARE THERE ANY
BAD
CHILDREN HERE?!?

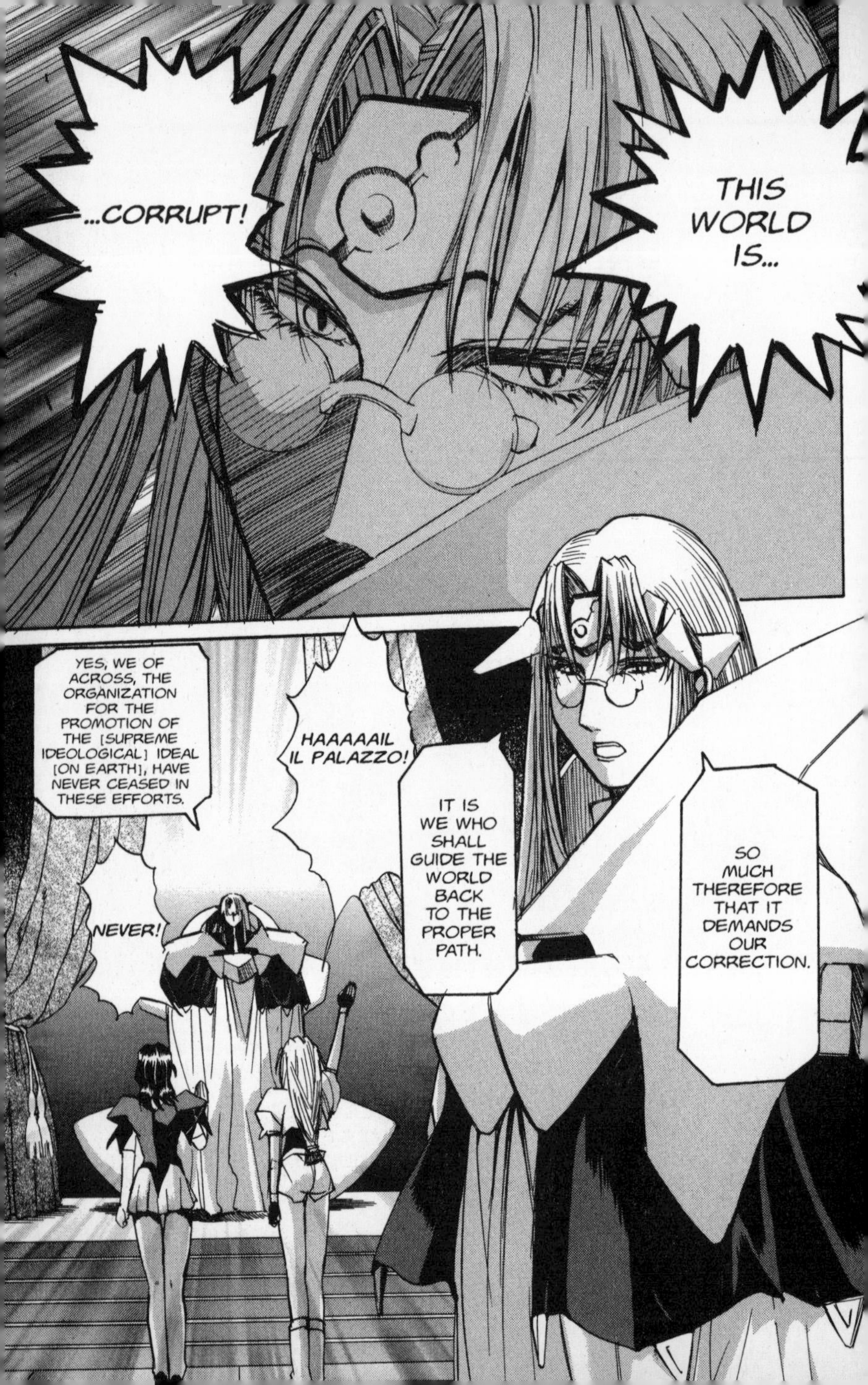
THIS WORLD IS...
...CORRUPT!
SO MUCH THEREFORE THAT IT DEMANDS OUR CORRECTION.
IT IS WE WHO SHALL GUIDE THE WORLD BACK TO THE PROPER PATH.
YES, WE OF ACROSS, THE ORGANIZATION FOR THE PROMOTION OF THE [SUPREME IDEOLOGICAL] IDEAL [ON EARTH], HAVE NEVER CEASED IN THESE EFFORTS.
NEVER!
HAAAAAIL IL PALAZZO!

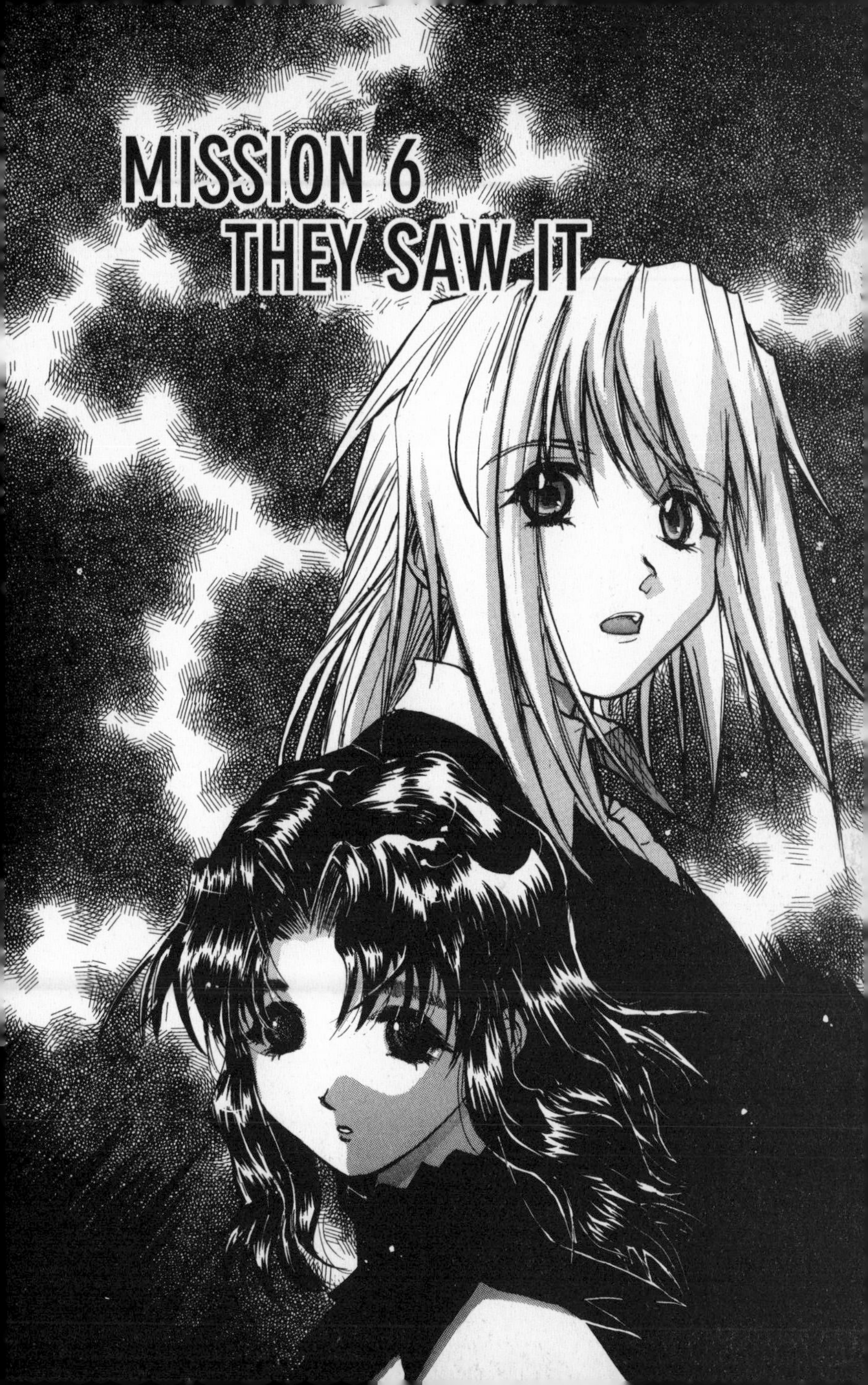
MISSION 6
THEY SAW IT

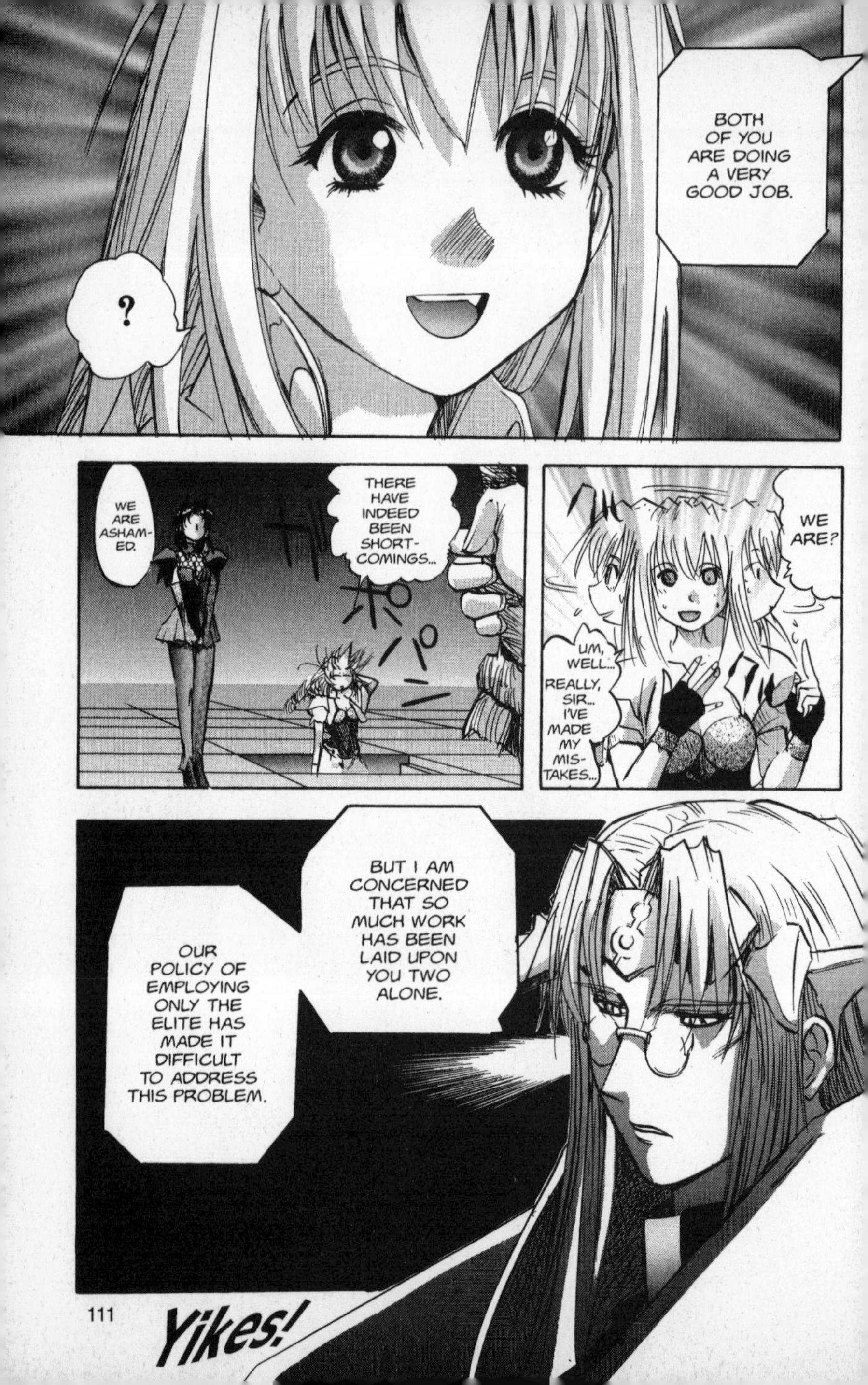
BOTH OF YOU ARE DOING A VERY GOOD JOB.
?
WE ARE?
UM, WELL... REALLY, SIR... I'VE MADE MY MIS-TAKES...
THERE HAVE INDEED BEEN SHORT-COMINGS...
WE ARE ASHAM-ED.
BUT I AM CONCERNED THAT SO MUCH WORK HAS BEEN LAID UPON YOU TWO ALONE.
OUR POLICY OF EMPLOYING ONLY THE ELITE HAS MADE IT DIFFICULT TO ADDRESS THIS PROBLEM.
Yikes!

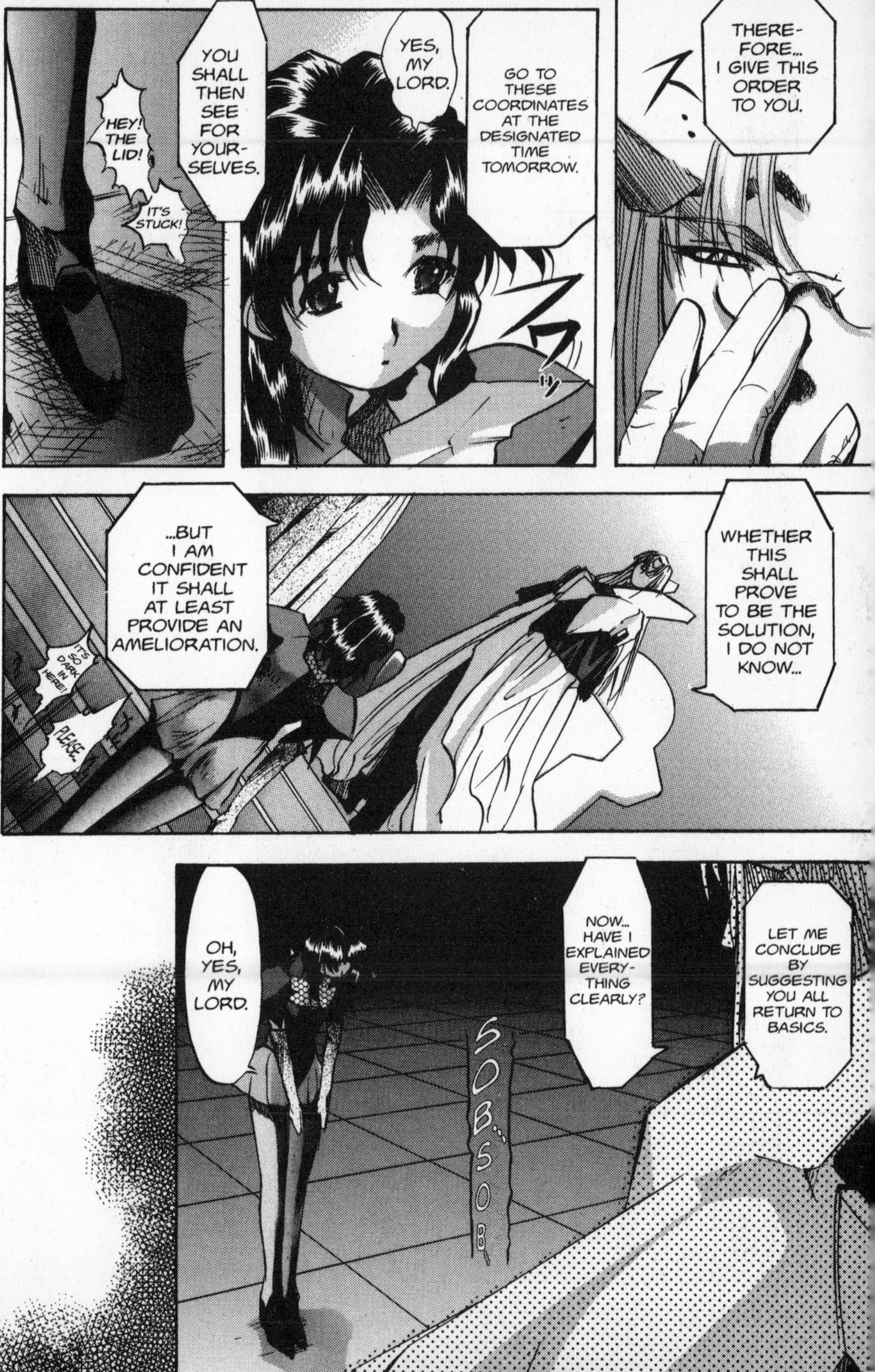
THEREFORE... I GIVE THIS ORDER TO YOU.
GO TO THESE COORDINATES AT THE DESIGNATED TIME TOMORROW.
YES, MY LORD.
YOU SHALL THEN SEE FOR YOURSELVES.
HEY! THE LID!
IT'S STUCK!
WHETHER THIS SHALL PROVE TO BE THE SOLUTION, I DO NOT KNOW...
...BUT I AM CONFIDENT IT SHALL AT LEAST PROVIDE AN AMELIORATION.
IT'S SO DARK IN HERE!
PLEASE, PLEASE.
LET ME CONCLUDE BY SUGGESTING YOU ALL RETURN TO BASICS.
NOW... HAVE I EXPLAINED EVERYTHING CLEARLY?
SOB... SOB
OH, YES, MY LORD.

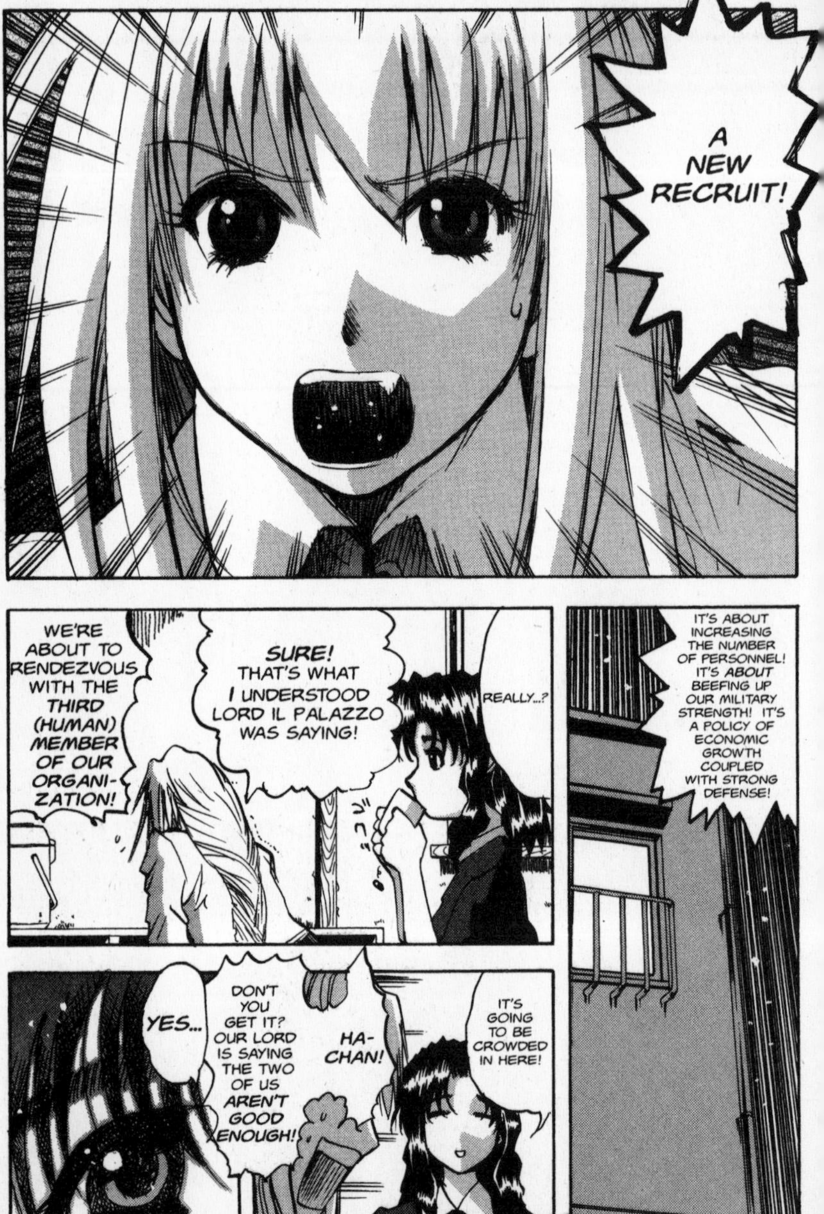
A NEW RECRUIT!
IT'S ABOUT INCREASING THE NUMBER OF PERSONNEL! IT'S ABOUT BEEFING UP OUR MILITARY STRENGTH! IT'S A POLICY OF ECONOMIC GROWTH COUPLED WITH STRONG DEFENSE!
REALLY...?
SURE! THAT'S WHAT I UNDERSTOOD LORD IL PALAZZO WAS SAYING!
WE'RE ABOUT TO RENDEZVOUS WITH THE THIRD (HUMAN) MEMBER OF OUR ORGANI-ZATION!
IT'S GOING TO BE CROWDED IN HERE!
HA-CHAN!
DON'T YOU GET IT? OUR LORD IS SAYING THE TWO OF US AREN'T GOOD ENOUGH!
YES...

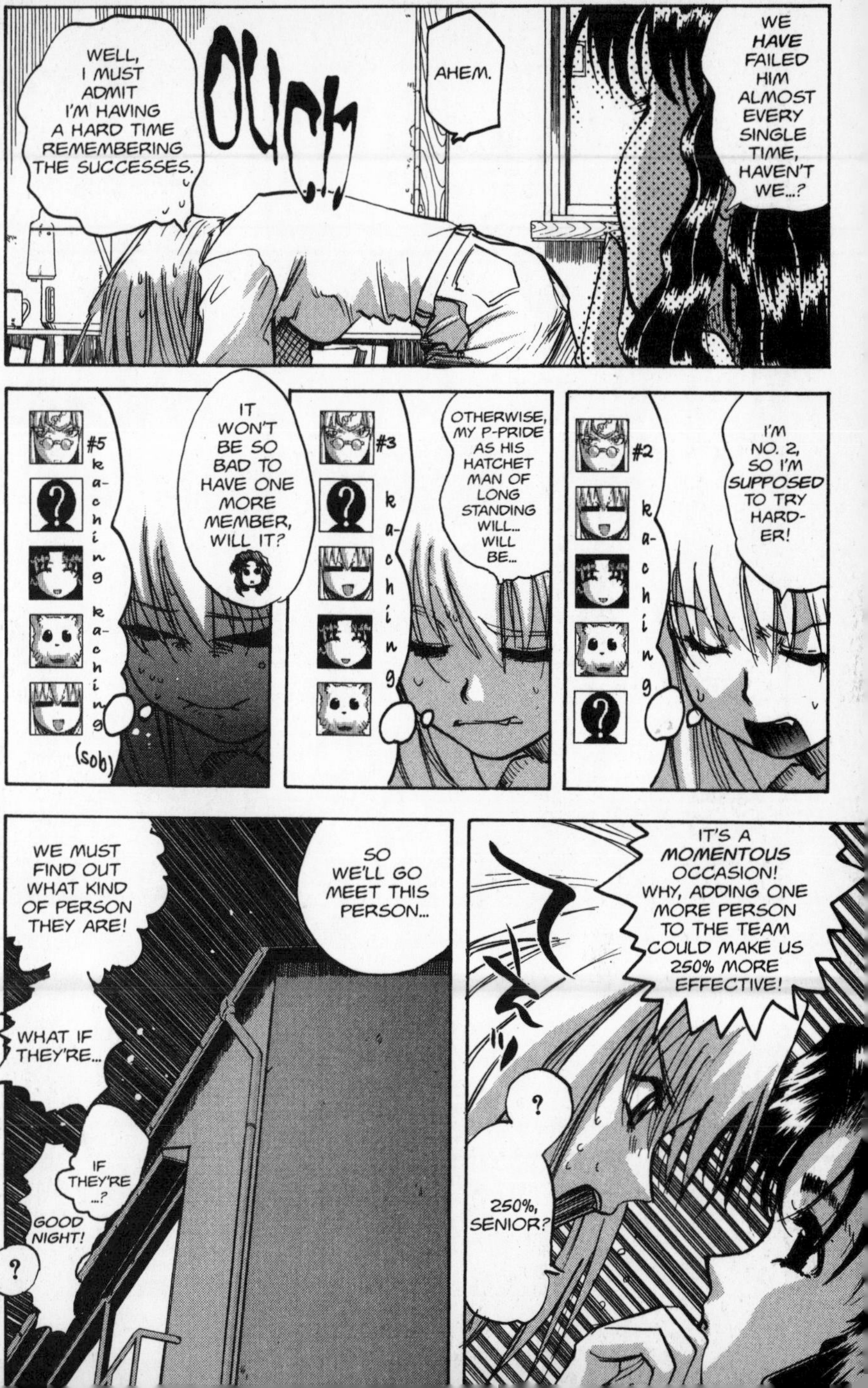
WE HAVE FAILED HIM ALMOST EVERY SINGLE TIME, HAVEN'T WE...?
AHEM.
OUCH
WELL, I MUST ADMIT I'M HAVING A HARD TIME REMEMBERING THE SUCCESSES.
I'M NO. 2, SO I'M SUPPOSED TO TRY HARDER!
#2
ka-ching
OTHERWISE, MY P-PRIDE AS HIS HATCHET MAN OF LONG STANDING WILL... WILL BE...
#3
ka-ching
IT WON'T BE SO BAD TO HAVE ONE MORE MEMBER, WILL IT?
#5
ka-ching ka-ching
(sob)
IT'S A MOMENTOUS OCCASION! WHY, ADDING ONE MORE PERSON TO THE TEAM COULD MAKE US 250% MORE EFFECTIVE!
?
250%, SENIOR?
SO WE'LL GO MEET THIS PERSON...
WE MUST FIND OUT WHAT KIND OF PERSON THEY ARE!
WHAT IF THEY'RE...
IF THEY'RE ...?
GOOD NIGHT!
?

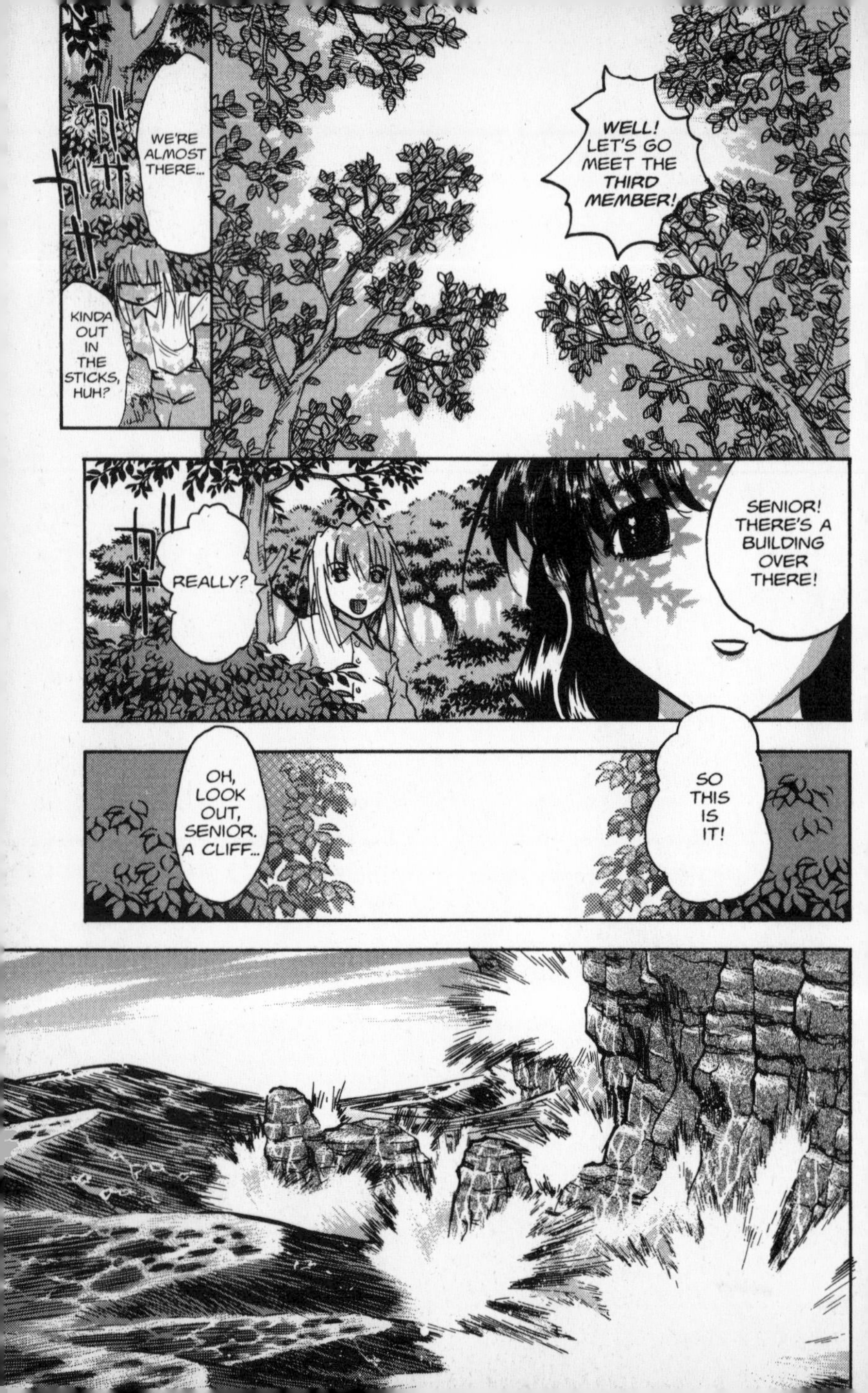
WELL! LET'S GO MEET THE THIRD MEMBER!
WE'RE ALMOST THERE...
KINDA OUT IN THE STICKS, HUH?
SENIOR! THERE'S A BUILDING OVER THERE!
REALLY?
SO THIS IS IT!
OH, LOOK OUT, SENIOR. A CLIFF...

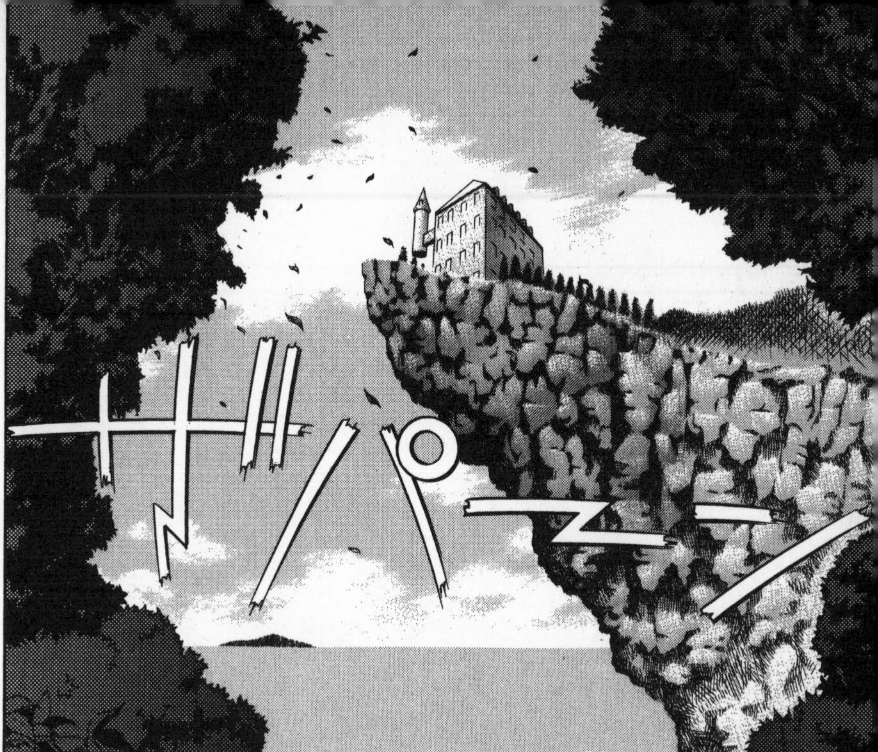

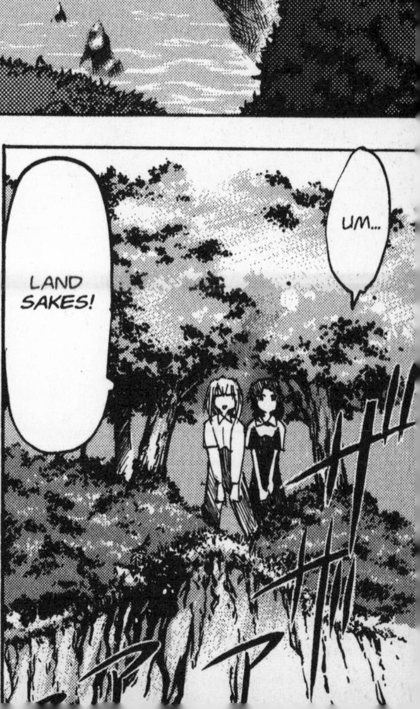
UM...
LAND SAKES!

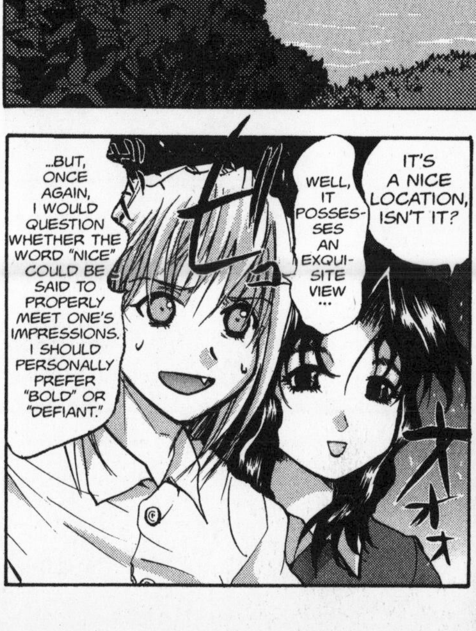
IT'S A NICE LOCATION, ISN'T IT?
WELL, IT POSSESSES AN EXQUISITE VIEW...
...BUT, ONCE AGAIN, I WOULD QUESTION WHETHER THE WORD "NICE" COULD BE SAID TO PROPERLY MEET ONE'S IMPRESSIONS. I SHOULD PERSONALLY PREFER "BOLD" OR "DEFIANT."

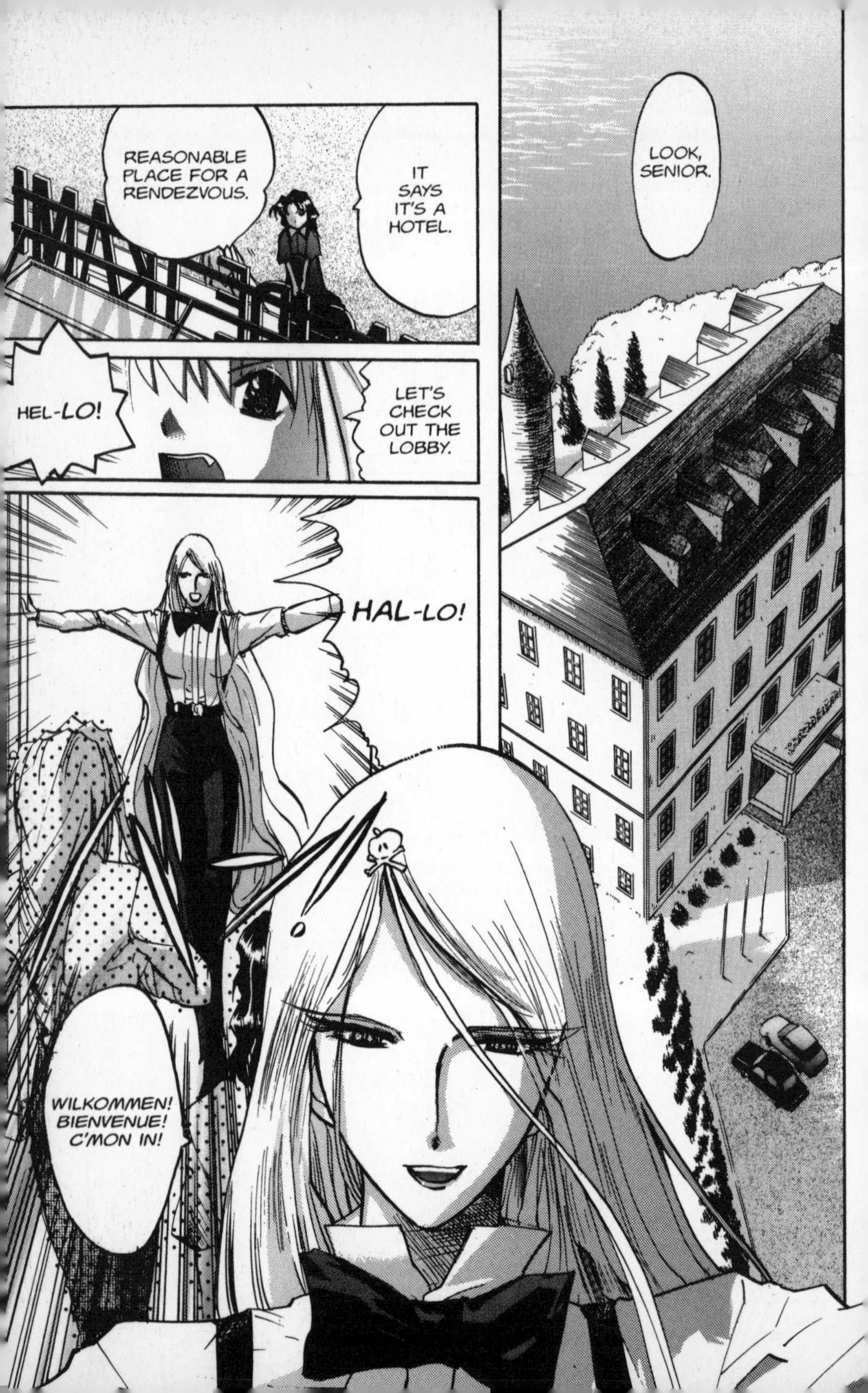
LOOK, SENIOR.
IT SAYS IT'S A HOTEL.
REASONABLE PLACE FOR A RENDEZVOUS.
LET'S CHECK OUT THE LOBBY.
HEL-LO!
HAL-LO!
WILKOMMEN! BIENVENUE! C'MON IN!

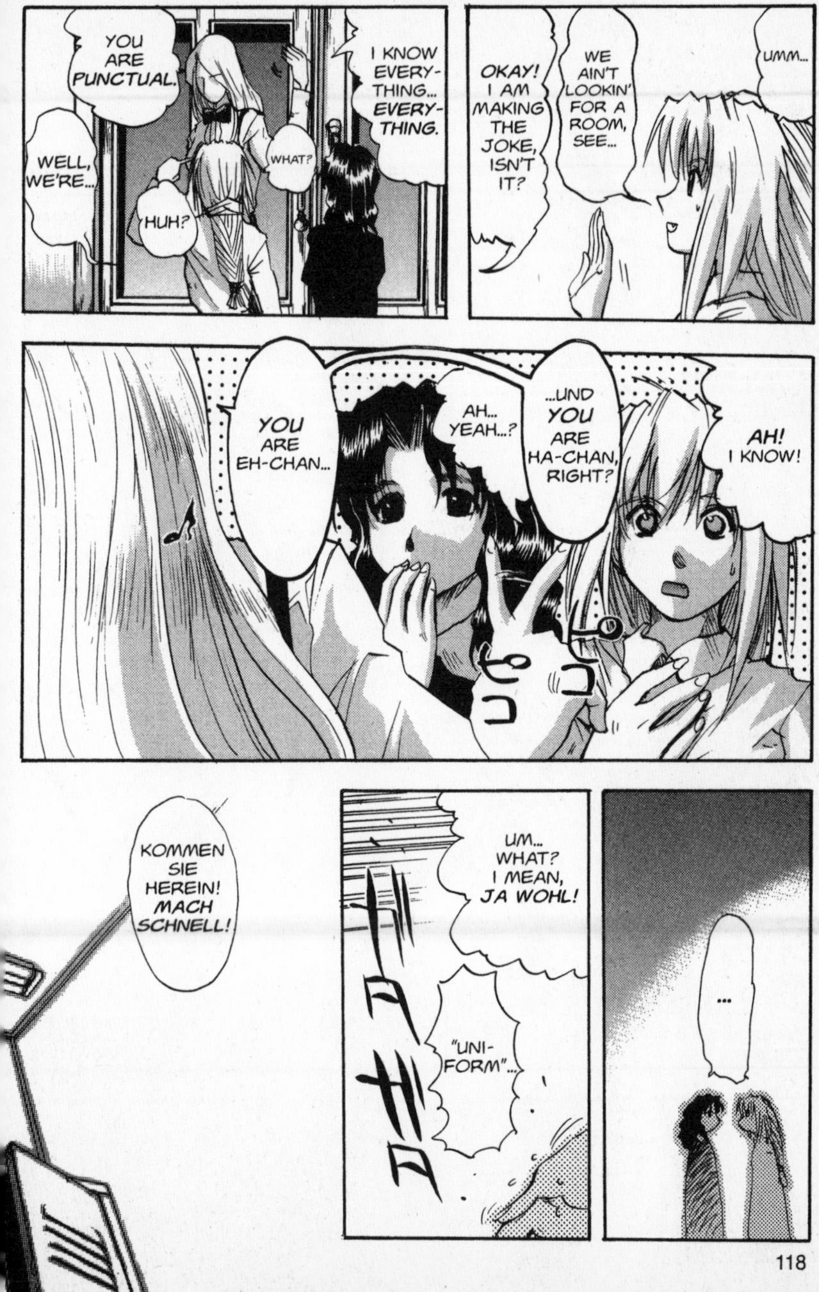
UMM...
WE AIN'T LOOKIN' FOR A ROOM, SEE...
OKAY! I AM MAKING THE JOKE, ISN'T IT?
I KNOW EVERY-THING... EVERY-THING.
YOU ARE PUNCTUAL.
WHAT?
WELL, WE'RE...
HUH?
AH! I KNOW!
...UND YOU ARE HA-CHAN, RIGHT?
AH... YEAH...?
YOU ARE EH-CHAN...
...
UM... WHAT? I MEAN, JA WOHL!
"UNI-FORM"...
KOMMEN SIE HEREIN! MACH SCHNELL!

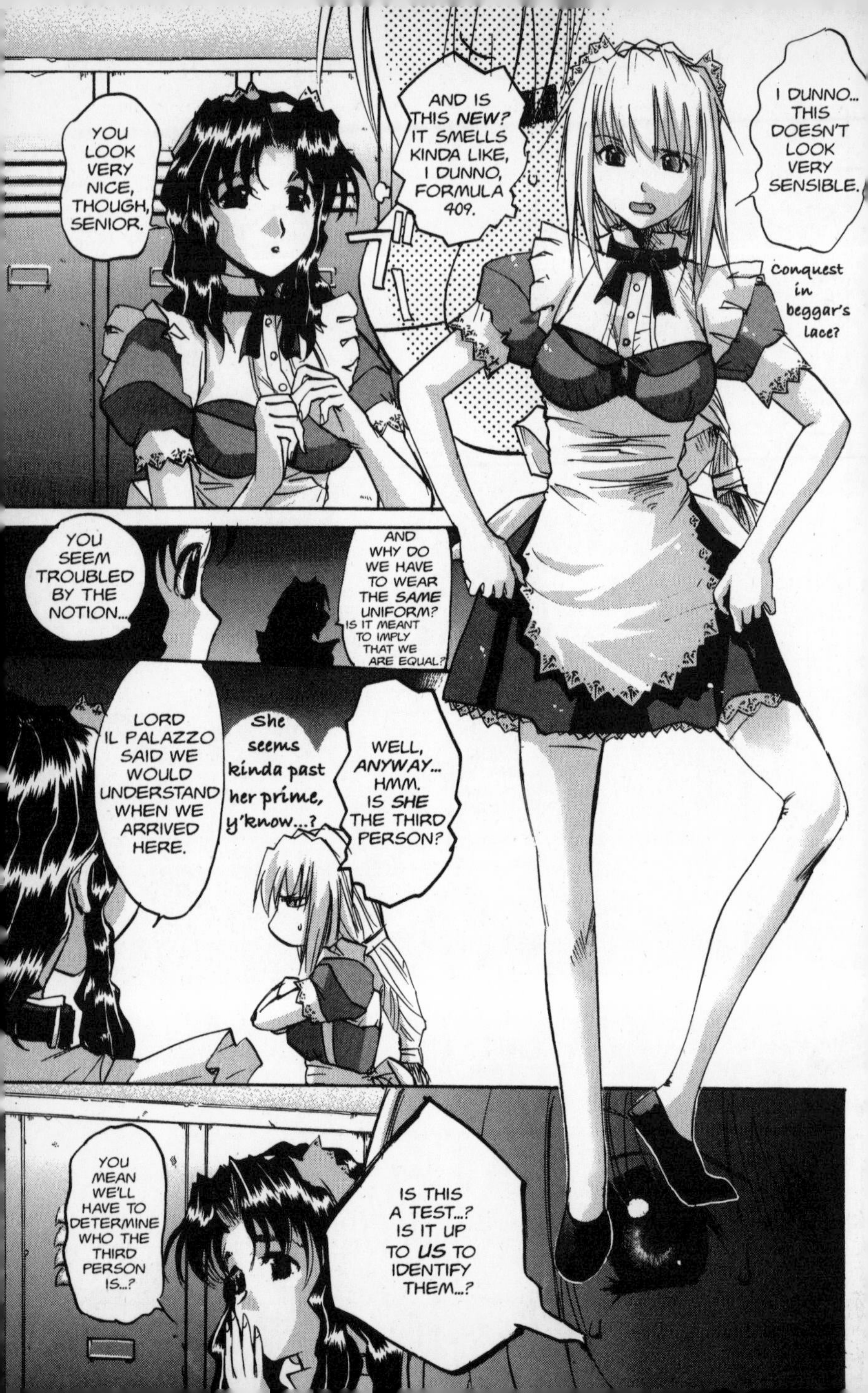
I DUNNO... THIS DOESN'T LOOK VERY SENSIBLE.
Conquest in beggar's lace?
AND IS THIS NEW? IT SMELLS KINDA LIKE, I DUNNO, FORMULA 409.
YOU LOOK VERY NICE, THOUGH, SENIOR.
AND WHY DO WE HAVE TO WEAR THE SAME UNIFORM? IS IT MEANT TO IMPLY THAT WE ARE EQUAL?
YOU SEEM TROUBLED BY THE NOTION...
WELL, ANYWAY... HMM. IS SHE THE THIRD PERSON?
She seems kinda past her prime, y'know...?
LORD IL PALAZZO SAID WE WOULD UNDERSTAND WHEN WE ARRIVED HERE.
IS THIS A TEST...? IS IT UP TO US TO IDENTIFY THEM...?
YOU MEAN WE'LL HAVE TO DETERMINE WHO THE THIRD PERSON IS...?

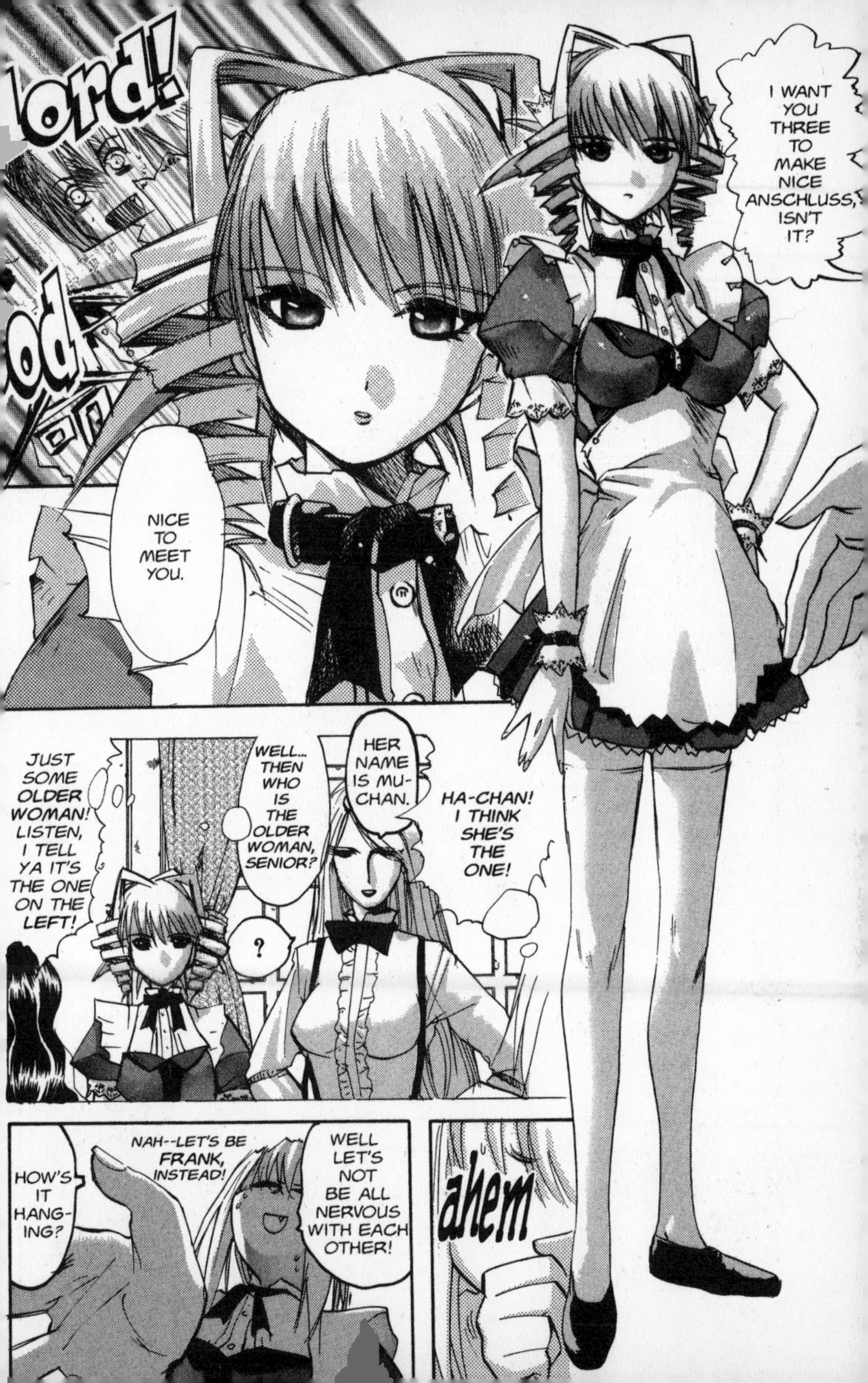
I WANT YOU THREE TO MAKE NICE ANSCHLUSS, ISN'T IT?
ord!
od
NICE TO MEET YOU.
HA-CHAN! I THINK SHE'S THE ONE!
HER NAME IS MU-CHAN.
WELL... THEN WHO IS THE OLDER WOMAN, SENIOR?
JUST SOME OLDER WOMAN! LISTEN, I TELL YA IT'S THE ONE ON THE LEFT!
?
ahem
WELL LET'S NOT BE ALL NERVOUS WITH EACH OTHER!
NAH--LET'S BE FRANK, INSTEAD!
HOW'S IT HANGING?

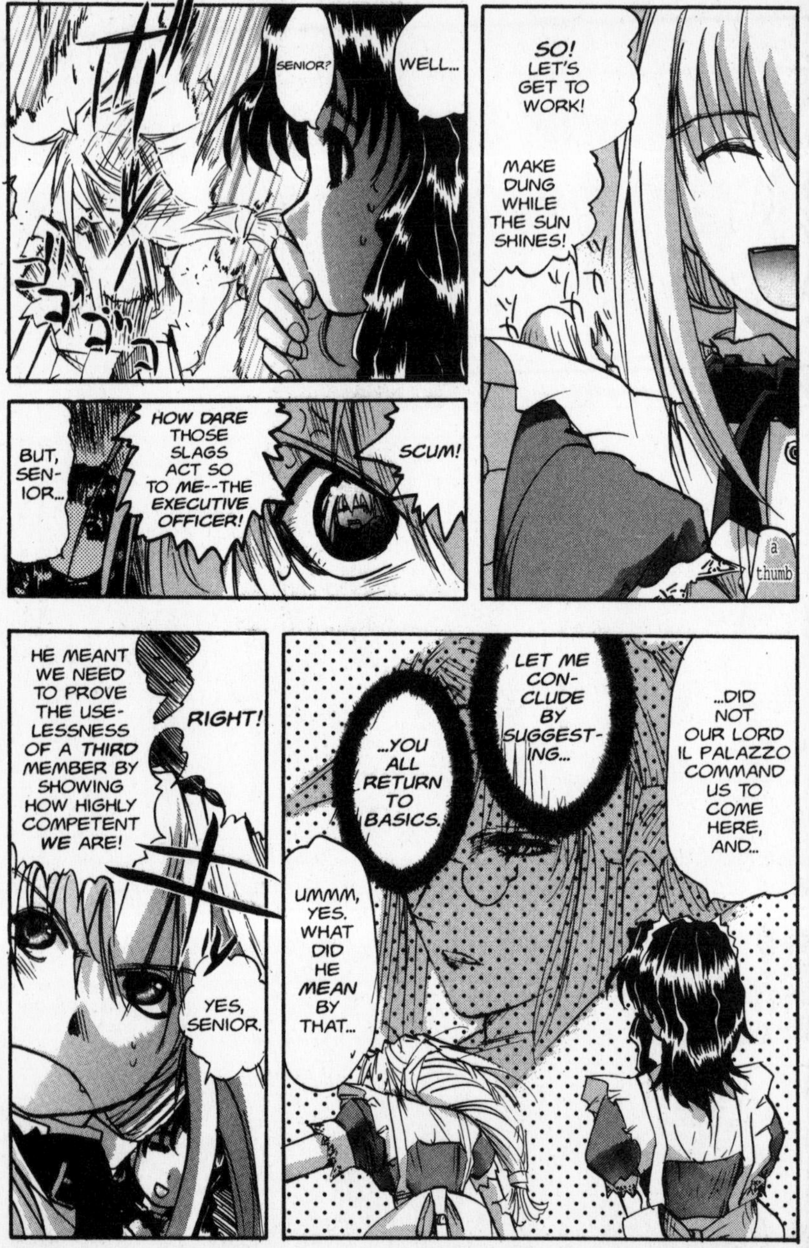
SO! LET'S GET TO WORK!
MAKE DUNG WHILE THE SUN SHINES!
a thumb
WELL...
SENIOR?
SCUM!
HOW DARE THOSE SLAGS ACT SO TO ME--THE EXECUTIVE OFFICER!
BUT, SENIOR...
...DID NOT OUR LORD IL PALAZZO COMMAND US TO COME HERE, AND...
LET ME CONCLUDE BY SUGGESTING...
...YOU ALL RETURN TO BASICS.
UMMM, YES. WHAT DID HE MEAN BY THAT...
RIGHT!
HE MEANT WE NEED TO PROVE THE USELESSNESS OF A THIRD MEMBER BY SHOWING HOW HIGHLY COMPETENT WE ARE!
YES, SENIOR.

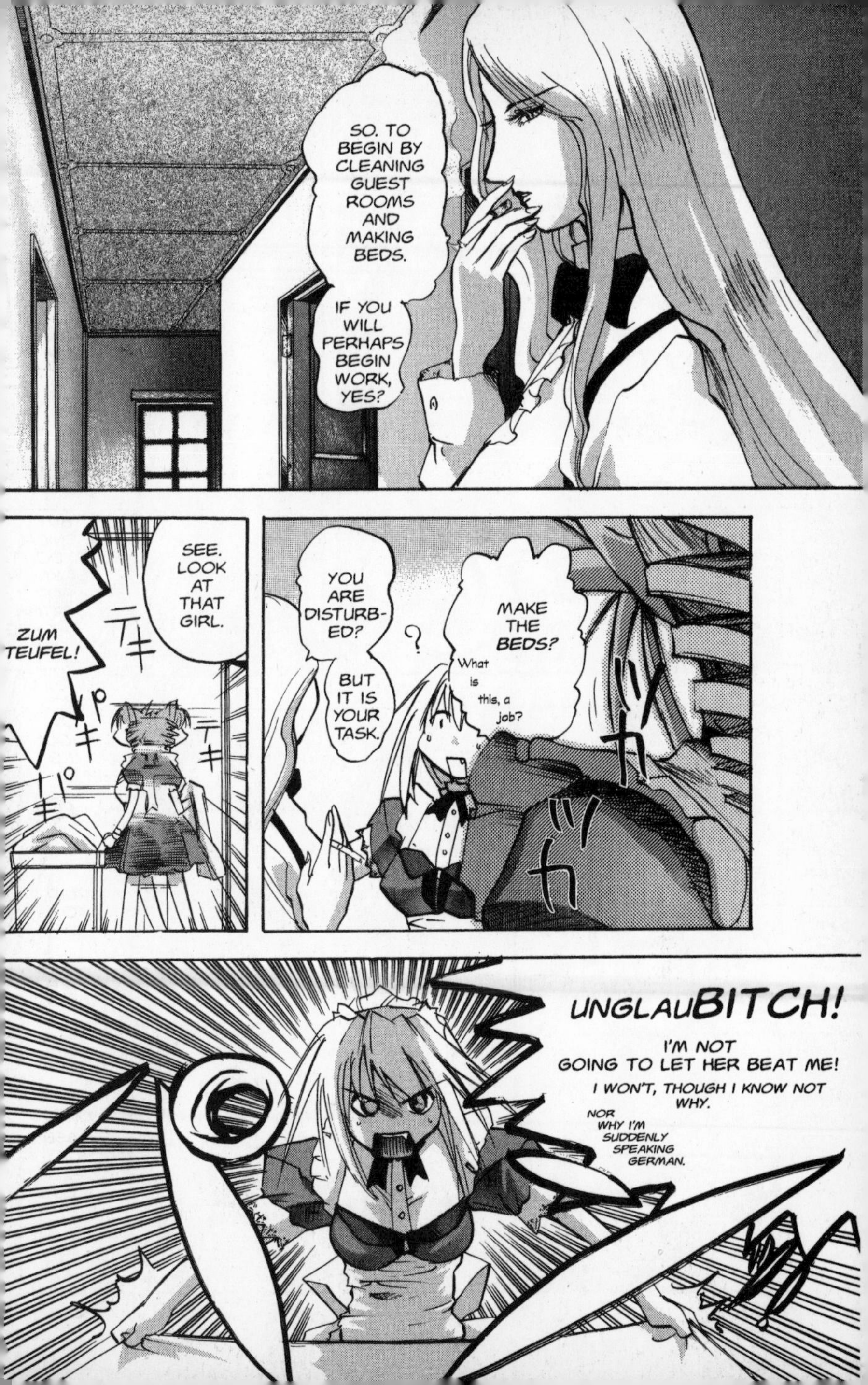
SO. TO BEGIN BY CLEANING GUEST ROOMS AND MAKING BEDS.
IF YOU WILL PERHAPS BEGIN WORK, YES?
MAKE THE *BEDS?*
What is this, a job?
YOU ARE DISTURB-ED?
BUT IT IS YOUR TASK.
SEE. LOOK AT THAT GIRL.
ZUM TEUFEL!
UNGLAUBITCH!
I'M NOT GOING TO LET HER BEAT ME!
I WON'T, THOUGH I KNOW NOT WHY.
NOR WHY I'M SUDDENLY SPEAKING GERMAN.

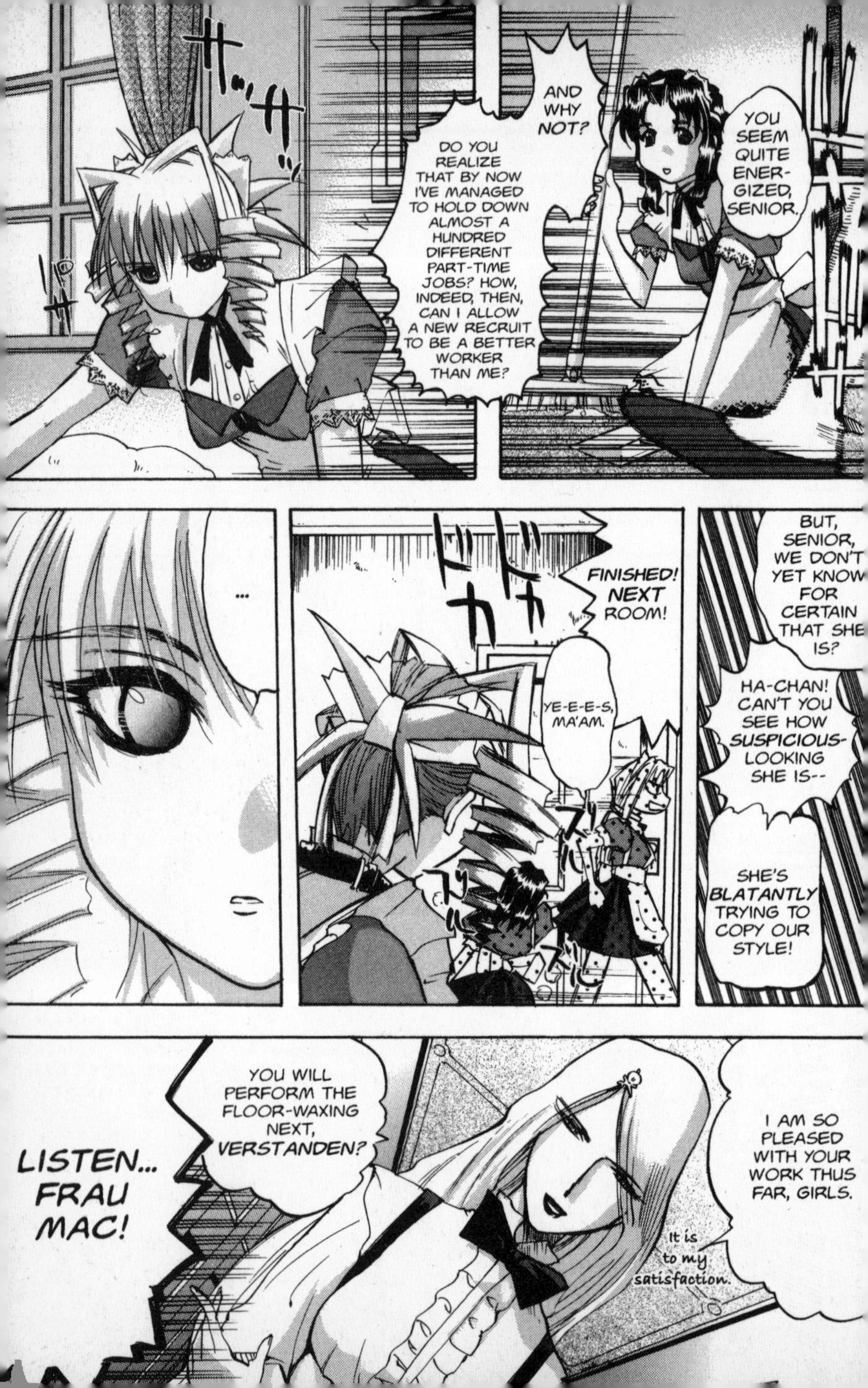
YOU SEEM QUITE ENERGIZED, SENIOR.
AND WHY NOT?
DO YOU REALIZE THAT BY NOW I'VE MANAGED TO HOLD DOWN ALMOST A HUNDRED DIFFERENT PART-TIME JOBS? HOW, INDEED, THEN, CAN I ALLOW A NEW RECRUIT TO BE A BETTER WORKER THAN ME?
BUT, SENIOR, WE DON'T YET KNOW FOR CERTAIN THAT SHE IS?
HA-CHAN! CAN'T YOU SEE HOW SUSPICIOUS-LOOKING SHE IS--
SHE'S BLATANTLY TRYING TO COPY OUR STYLE!
FINISHED! NEXT ROOM!
YE-E-E-S, MA'AM.
...
I AM SO PLEASED WITH YOUR WORK THUS FAR, GIRLS.
It is to my satisfaction.
YOU WILL PERFORM THE FLOOR-WAXING NEXT, VERSTANDEN?
LISTEN... FRAU MAC!

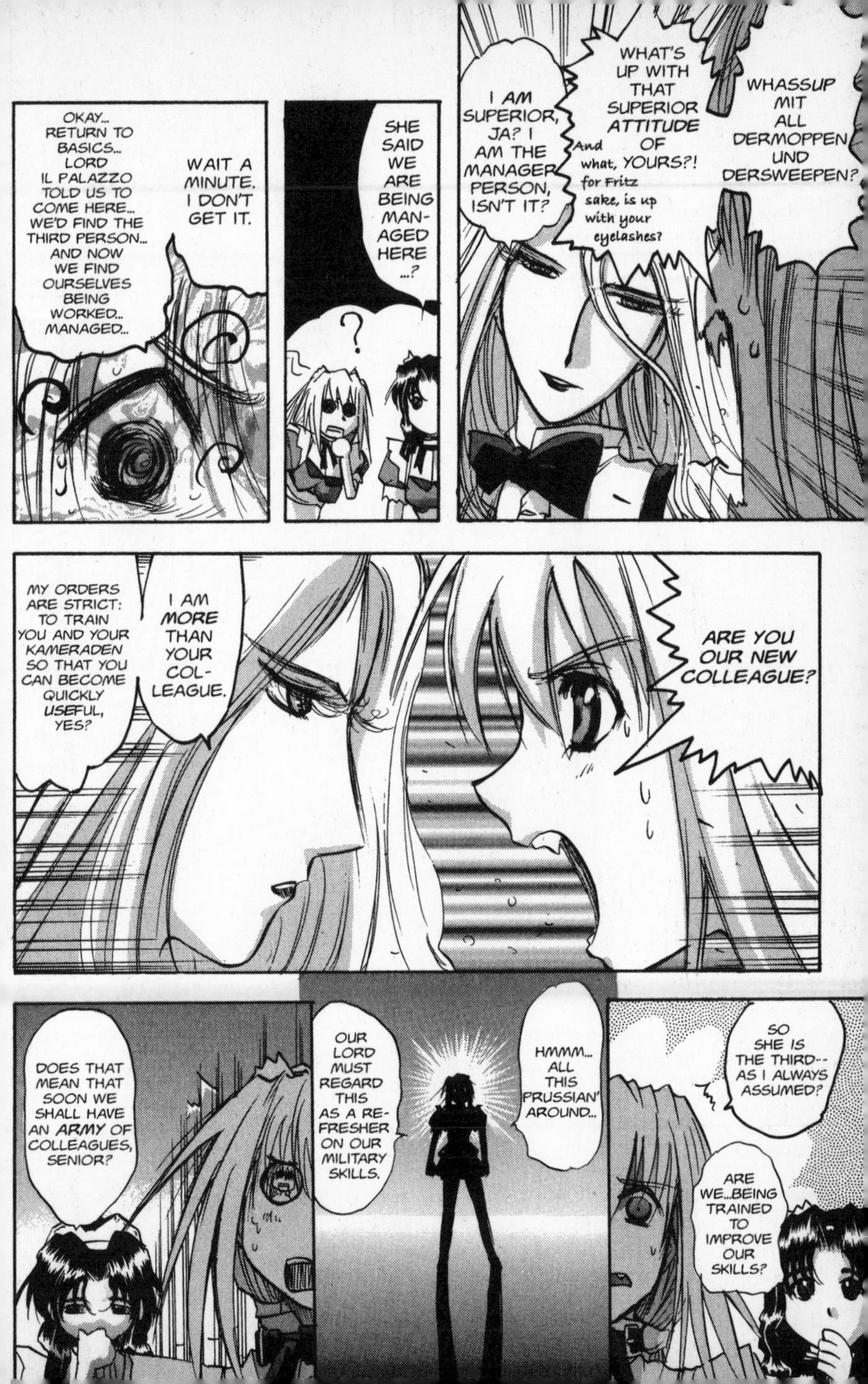
WHASSUP MIT ALL DERMOPPEN UND DERSWEEPEN?
WHAT'S UP WITH THAT SUPERIOR ATTITUDE OF YOURS?!
And what, for Fritz sake, is up with your eyelashes?
I AM SUPERIOR, JA? I AM THE MANAGER PERSON, ISN'T IT?
SHE SAID WE ARE BEING MANAGED HERE ...?
?
WAIT A MINUTE. I DON'T GET IT.
OKAY... RETURN TO BASICS... LORD IL PALAZZO TOLD US TO COME HERE... WE'D FIND THE THIRD PERSON... AND NOW WE FIND OURSELVES BEING WORKED.. MANAGED...
ARE YOU OUR NEW COLLEAGUE?
I AM MORE THAN YOUR COLLEAGUE.
MY ORDERS ARE STRICT: TO TRAIN YOU AND YOUR KAMERADEN SO THAT YOU CAN BECOME QUICKLY USEFUL, YES?
SO SHE IS THE THIRD-- AS I ALWAYS ASSUMED?
ARE WE...BEING TRAINED TO IMPROVE OUR SKILLS?
HMMM... ALL THIS PRUSSIAN' AROUND..
OUR LORD MUST REGARD THIS AS A REFRESHER ON OUR MILITARY SKILLS.
DOES THAT MEAN THAT SOON WE SHALL HAVE AN ARMY OF COLLEAGUES, SENIOR?

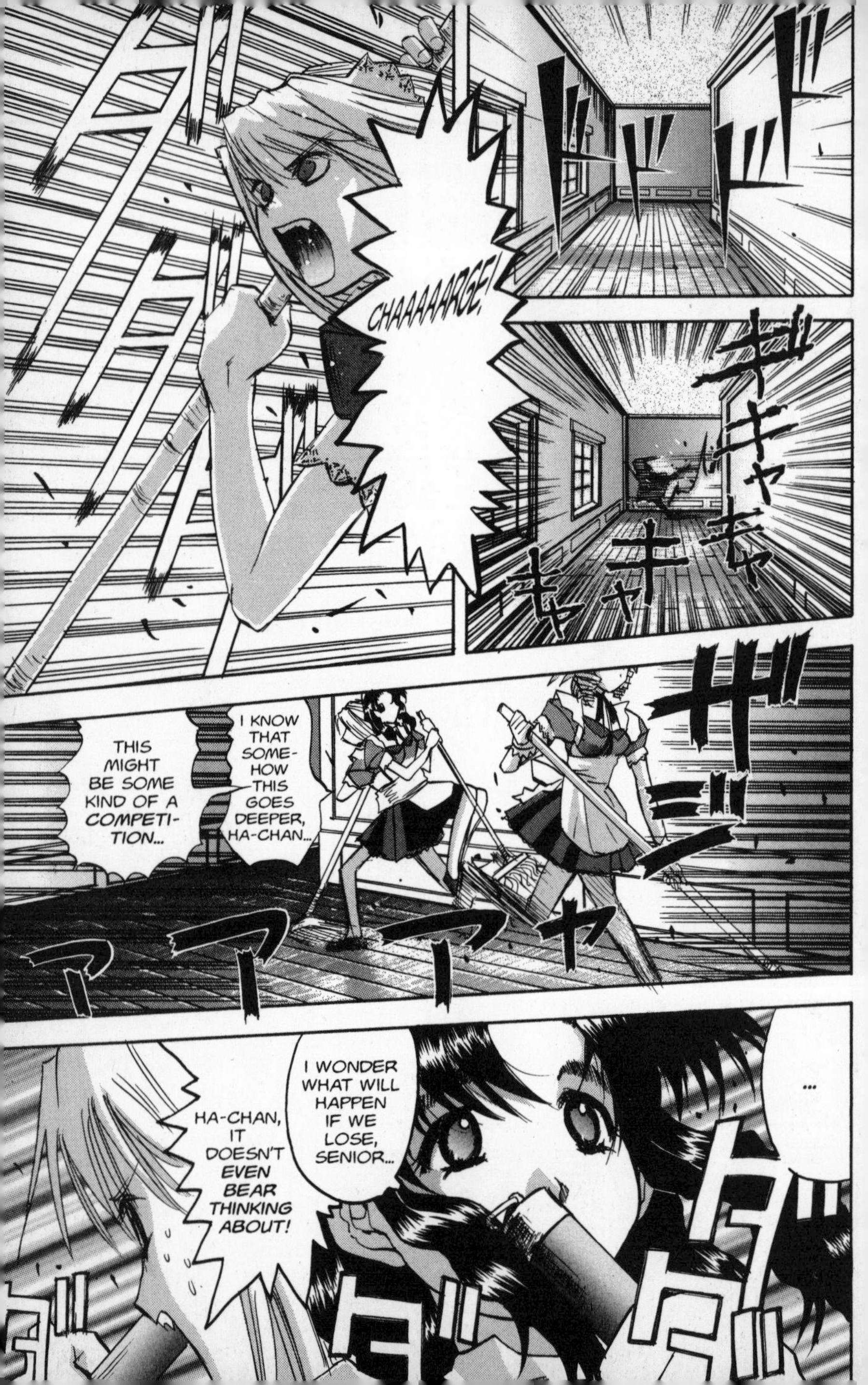

CHAAAAARGE!
I KNOW THAT SOMEHOW THIS GOES DEEPER, HA-CHAN...
THIS MIGHT BE SOME KIND OF A COMPETITION...
...
I WONDER WHAT WILL HAPPEN IF WE LOSE, SENIOR...
HA-CHAN, IT DOESN'T EVEN BEAR THINKING ABOUT!

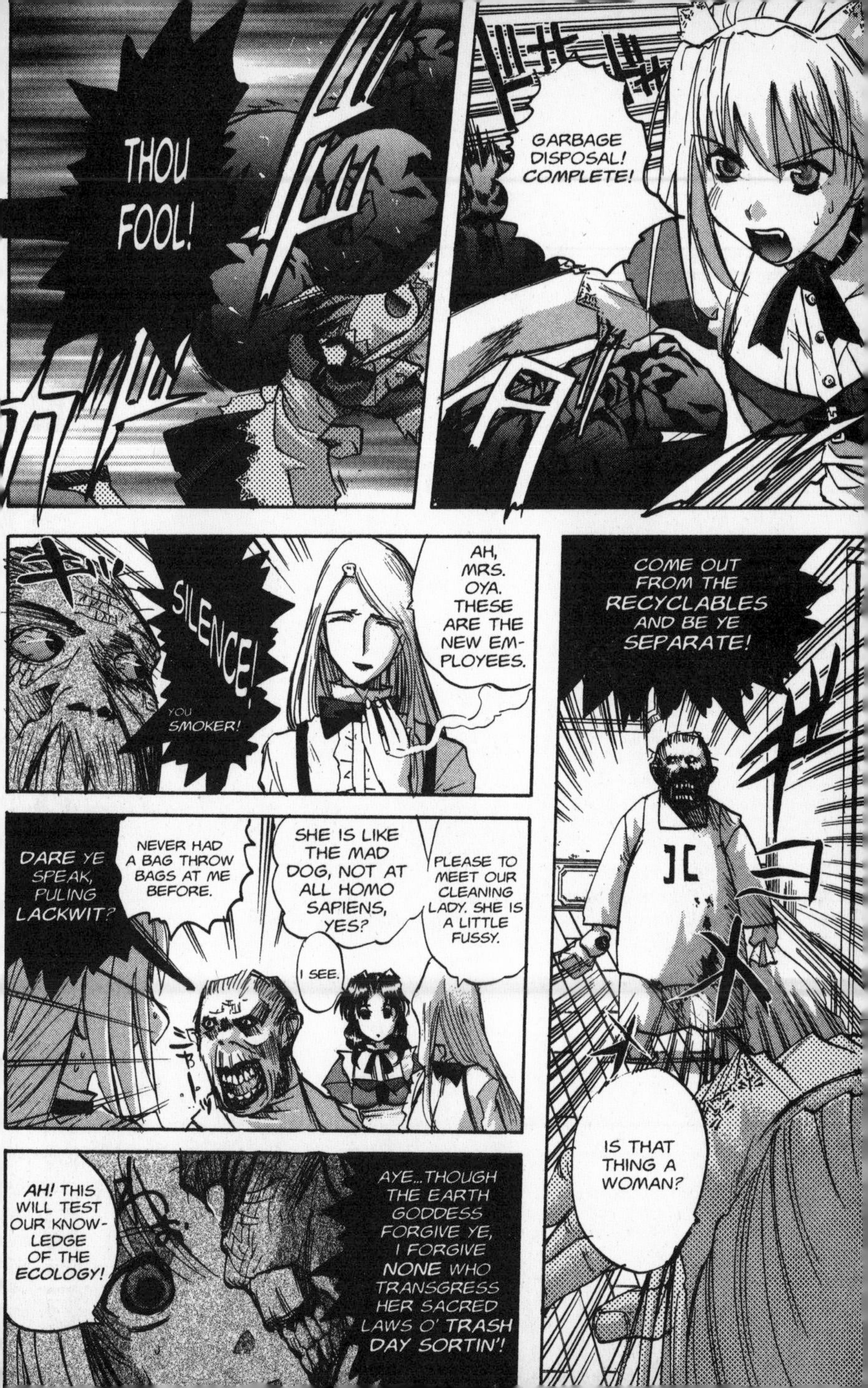
GARBAGE DISPOSAL! COMPLETE!
THOU FOOL!
COME OUT FROM THE RECYCLABLES AND BE YE SEPARATE!
IS THAT THING A WOMAN?
AH, MRS. OYA. THESE ARE THE NEW EM-PLOYEES.
SILENCE! YOU SMOKER!
PLEASE TO MEET OUR CLEANING LADY. SHE IS A LITTLE FUSSY.
SHE IS LIKE THE MAD DOG, NOT AT ALL HOMO SAPIENS, YES?
I SEE.
NEVER HAD A BAG THROW BAGS AT ME BEFORE.
DARE YE SPEAK, PULING LACKWIT?
AYE...THOUGH THE EARTH GODDESS FORGIVE YE, I FORGIVE NONE WHO TRANSGRESS HER SACRED LAWS O' TRASH DAY SORTIN'!
AH! THIS WILL TEST OUR KNOW-LEDGE OF THE ECOLOGY!

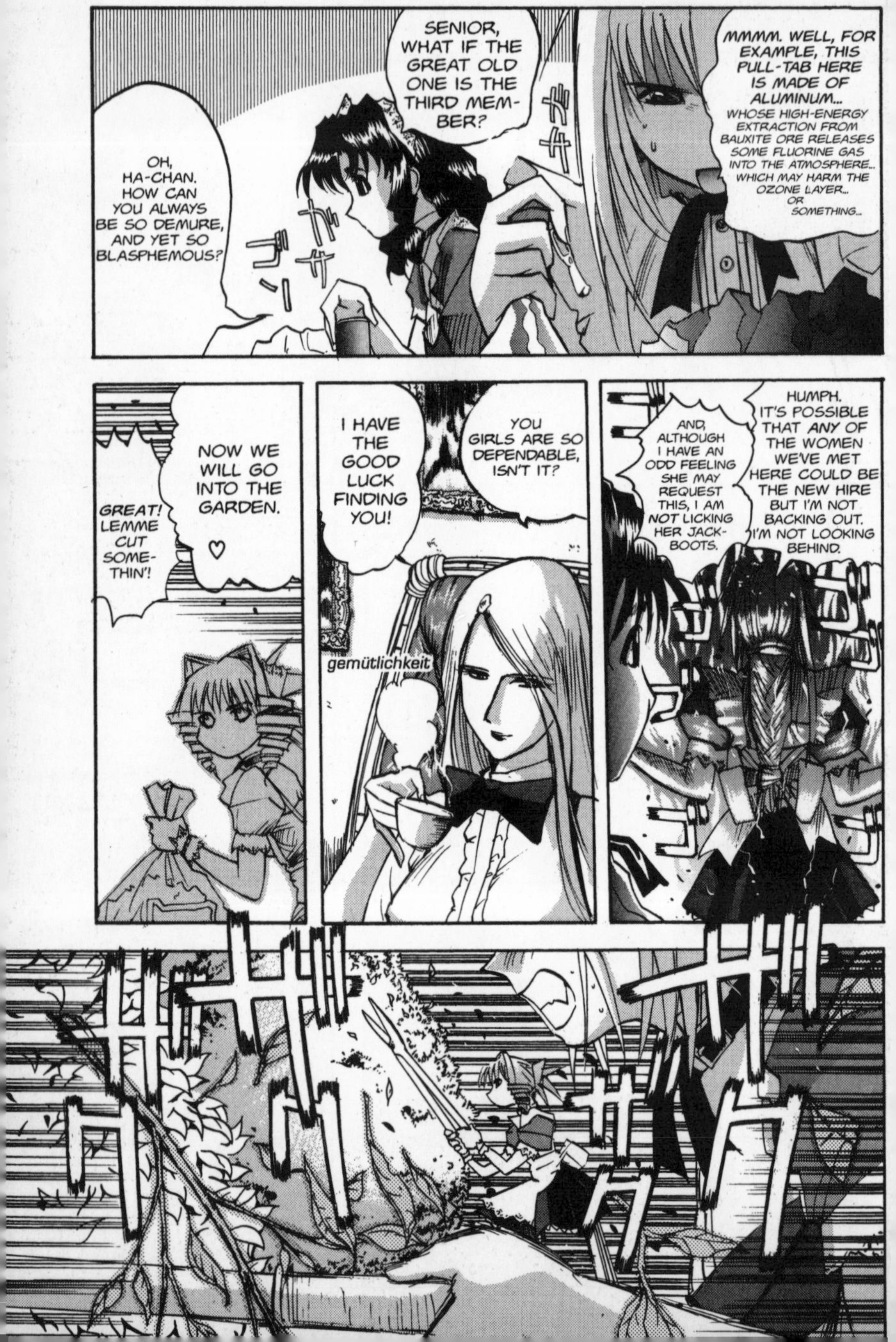
MMMM. WELL, FOR EXAMPLE, THIS PULL-TAB HERE IS MADE OF ALUMINUM... WHOSE HIGH-ENERGY EXTRACTION FROM BAUXITE ORE RELEASES SOME FLUORINE GAS INTO THE ATMOSPHERE... WHICH MAY HARM THE OZONE LAYER... OR SOMETHING...
SENIOR, WHAT IF THE GREAT OLD ONE IS THE THIRD MEM-BER?
OH, HA-CHAN. HOW CAN YOU ALWAYS BE SO DEMURE, AND YET SO BLASPHEMOUS?
HUMPH. IT'S POSSIBLE THAT ANY OF THE WOMEN WE'VE MET HERE COULD BE THE NEW HIRE BUT I'M NOT BACKING OUT. I'M NOT LOOKING BEHIND.
AND, ALTHOUGH I HAVE AN ODD FEELING SHE MAY REQUEST THIS, I AM NOT LICKING HER JACK-BOOTS.
YOU GIRLS ARE SO DEPENDABLE, ISN'T IT?
I HAVE THE GOOD LUCK FINDING YOU!
gemütlichkeit
NOW WE WILL GO INTO THE GARDEN. ♡
GREAT! LEMME CUT SOME-THIN'!

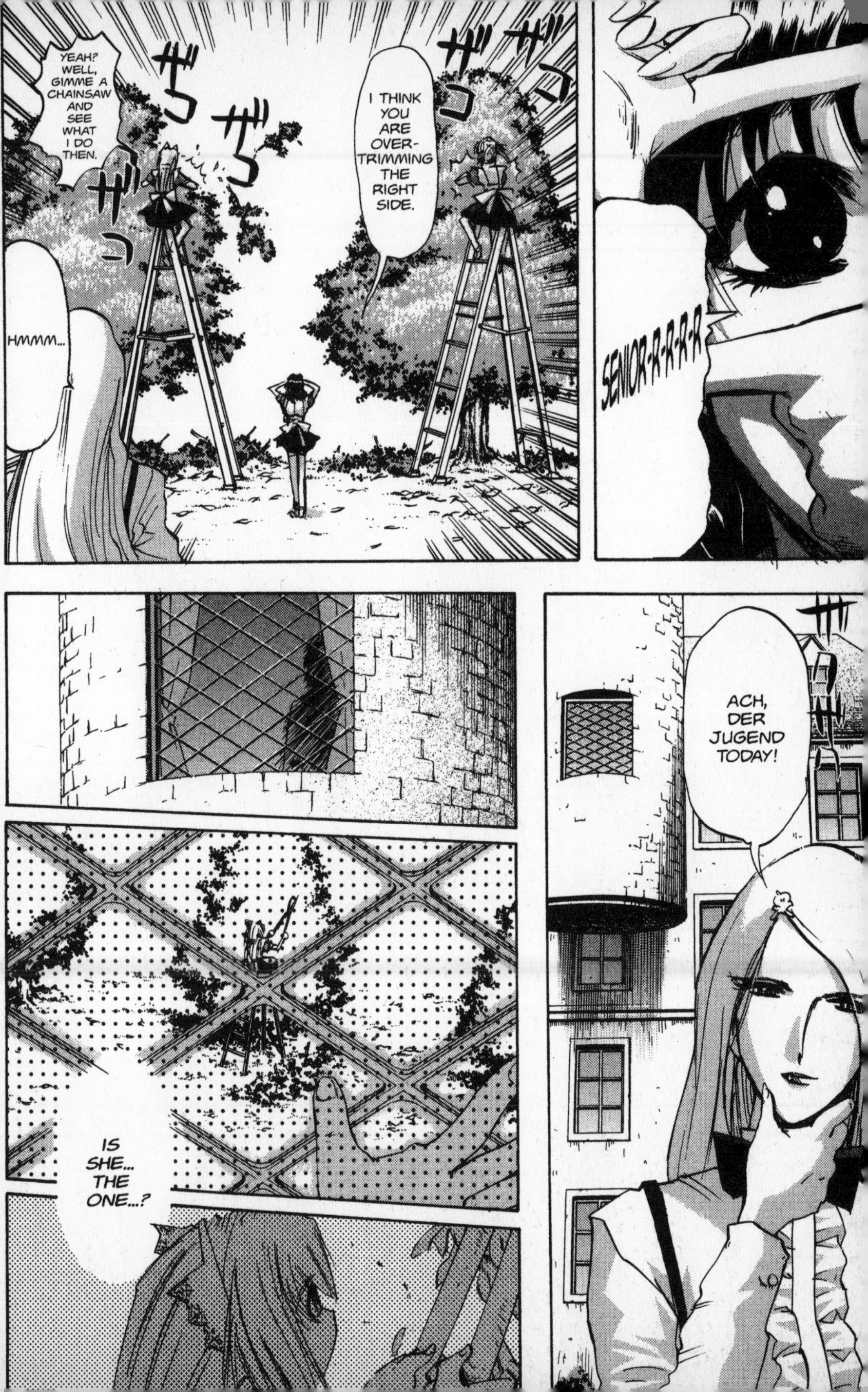
SENIOR-R-R-R
I THINK YOU ARE OVER-TRIMMING THE RIGHT SIDE.
YEAH? WELL, GIMME A CHAINSAW AND SEE WHAT I DO THEN.
HMMM...
ACH, DER JUGEND TODAY!
IS SHE... THE ONE...?

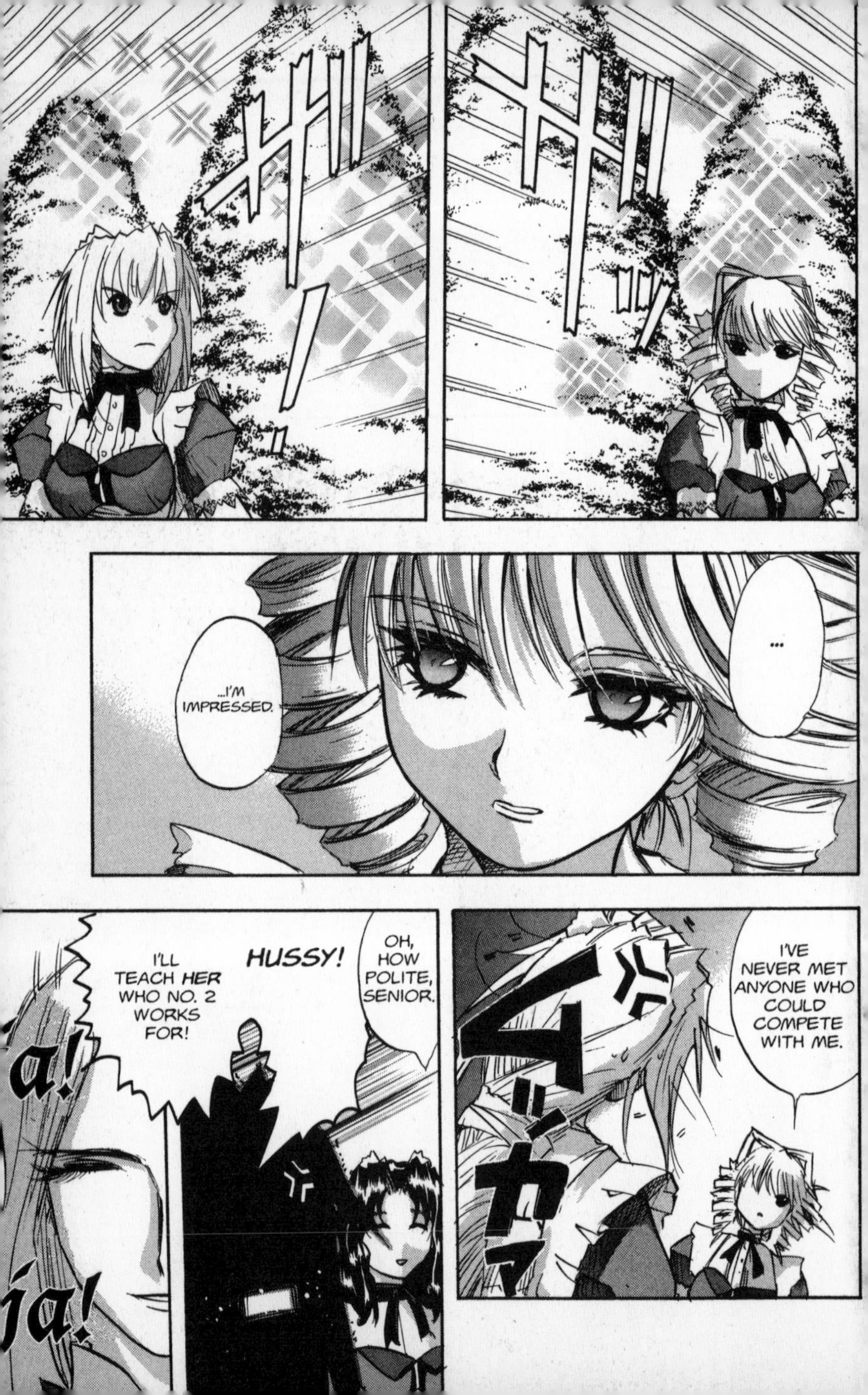
...
...I'M IMPRESSED.
I'VE NEVER MET ANYONE WHO COULD COMPETE WITH ME.
OH, HOW POLITE, SENIOR.
HUSSY!
I'LL TEACH HER WHO NO. 2 WORKS FOR!

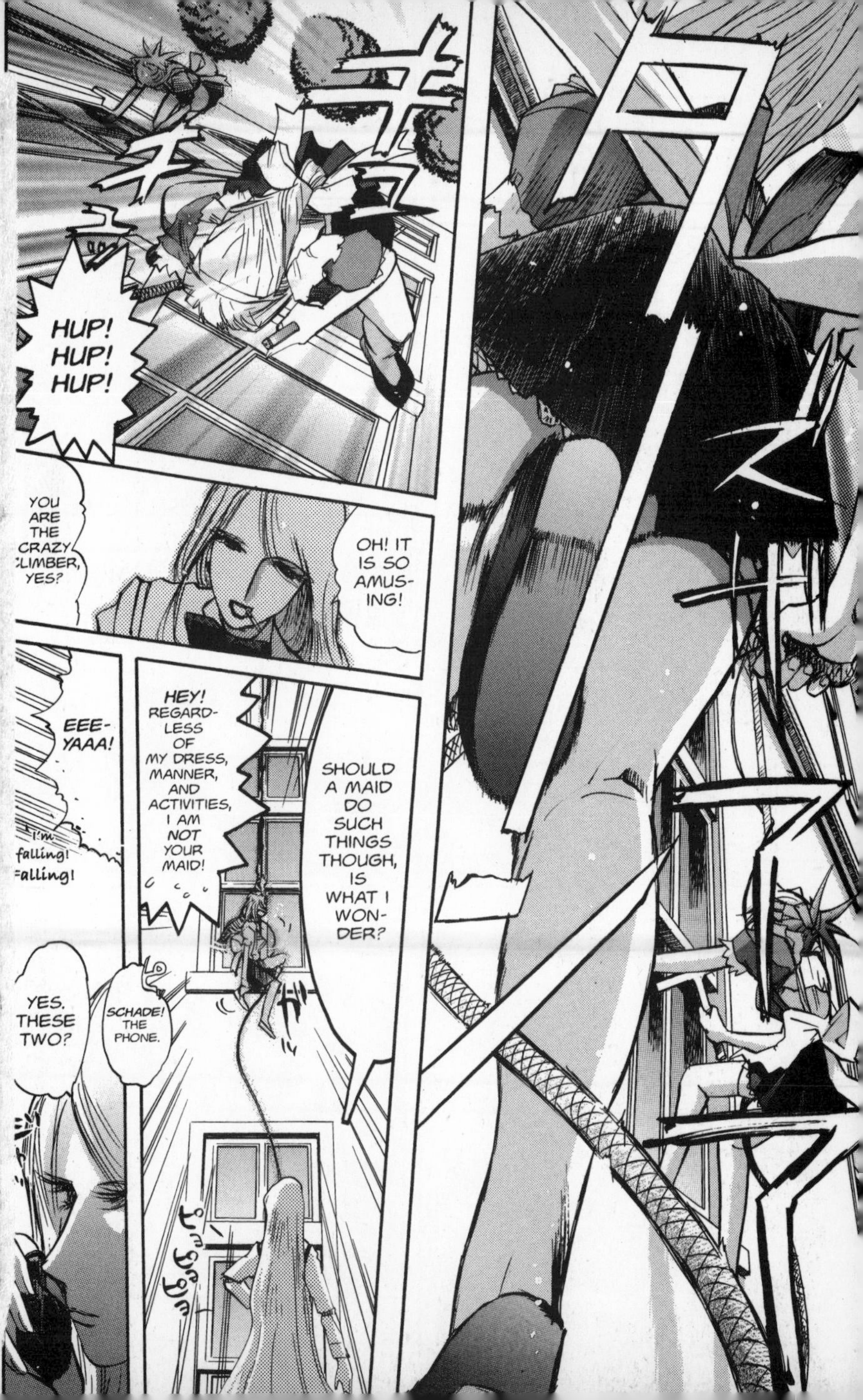
HUP! HUP! HUP!
OH! IT IS SO AMUSING!
YOU ARE THE CRAZY CLIMBER, YES?
SHOULD A MAID DO SUCH THINGS THOUGH, IS WHAT I WONDER?
HEY! REGARDLESS OF MY DRESS, MANNER, AND ACTIVITIES, I AM NOT YOUR MAID!
EEE-YAAA!
I'm falling! Falling!
SCHADE! THE PHONE.
YES. THESE TWO?

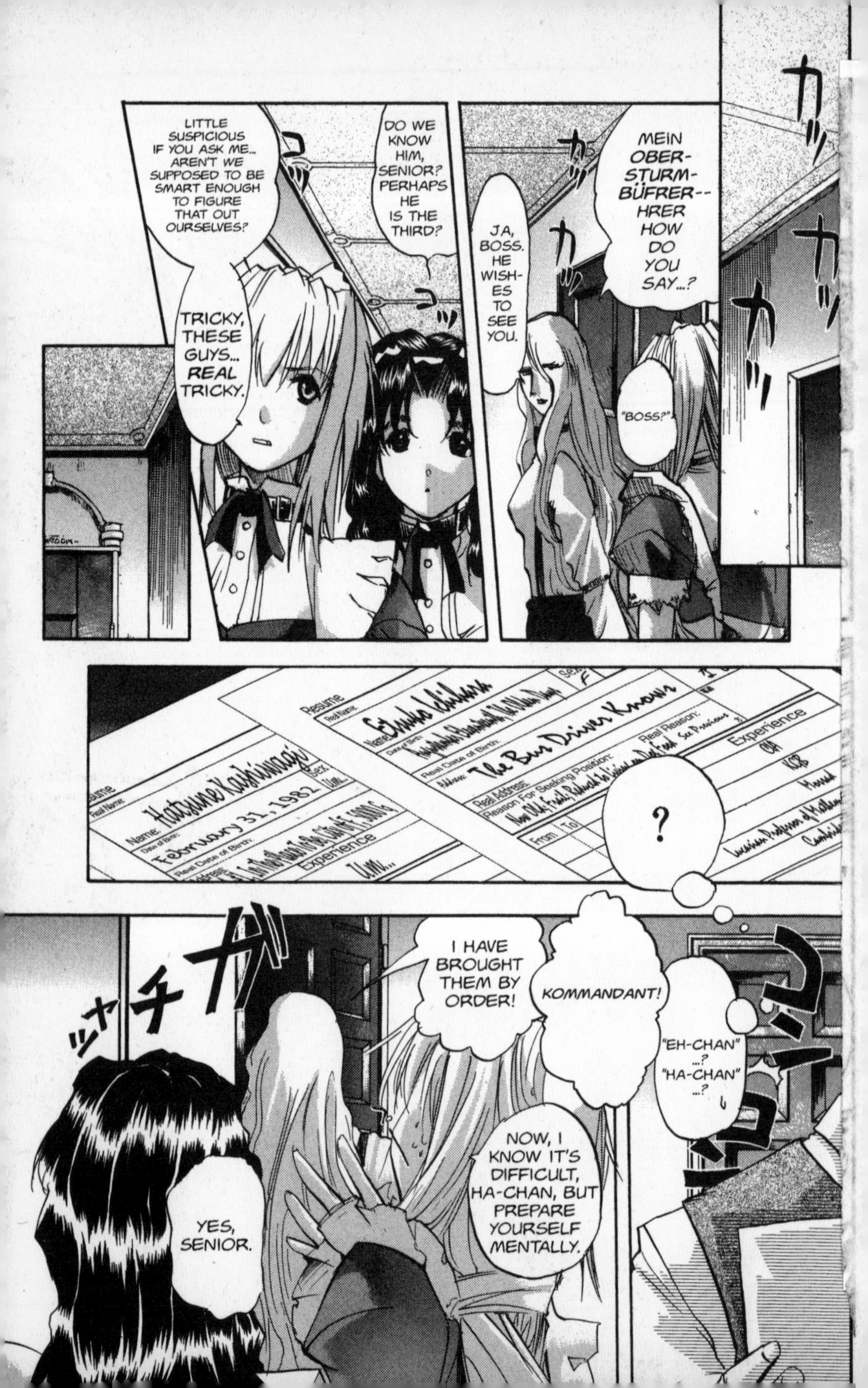
MEIN OBER-STURM-BÜFRER-- HRER HOW DO YOU SAY...?
JA, BOSS. HE WISH-ES TO SEE YOU.
"BOSS?"
DO WE KNOW HIM, SENIOR? PERHAPS HE IS THE THIRD?
LITTLE SUSPICIOUS IF YOU ASK ME... AREN'T WE SUPPOSED TO BE SMART ENOUGH TO FIGURE THAT OUT OURSELVES?
TRICKY, THESE GUYS... REAL TRICKY.
?
The Bus Driver Knows
Experience
Hatsune Kashiwagi
February 31, 1982
Experience
Um...
"EH-CHAN" ...? "HA-CHAN" ...?
KOMMANDANT!
I HAVE BROUGHT THEM BY ORDER!
NOW, I KNOW IT'S DIFFICULT, HA-CHAN, BUT PREPARE YOURSELF MENTALLY.
YES, SENIOR.

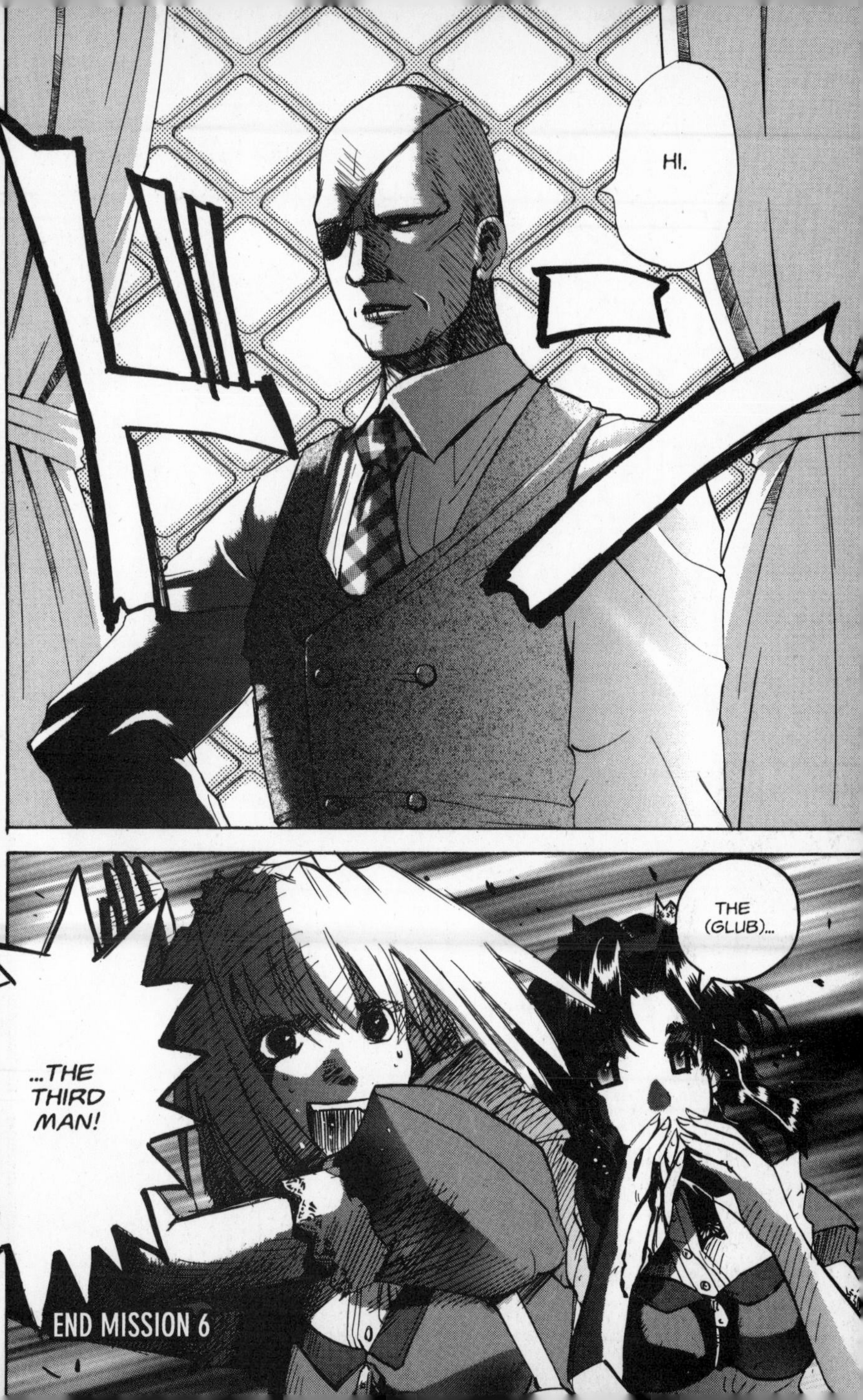
HI.
THE (GLUB)...
...THE THIRD MAN!
END MISSION 6

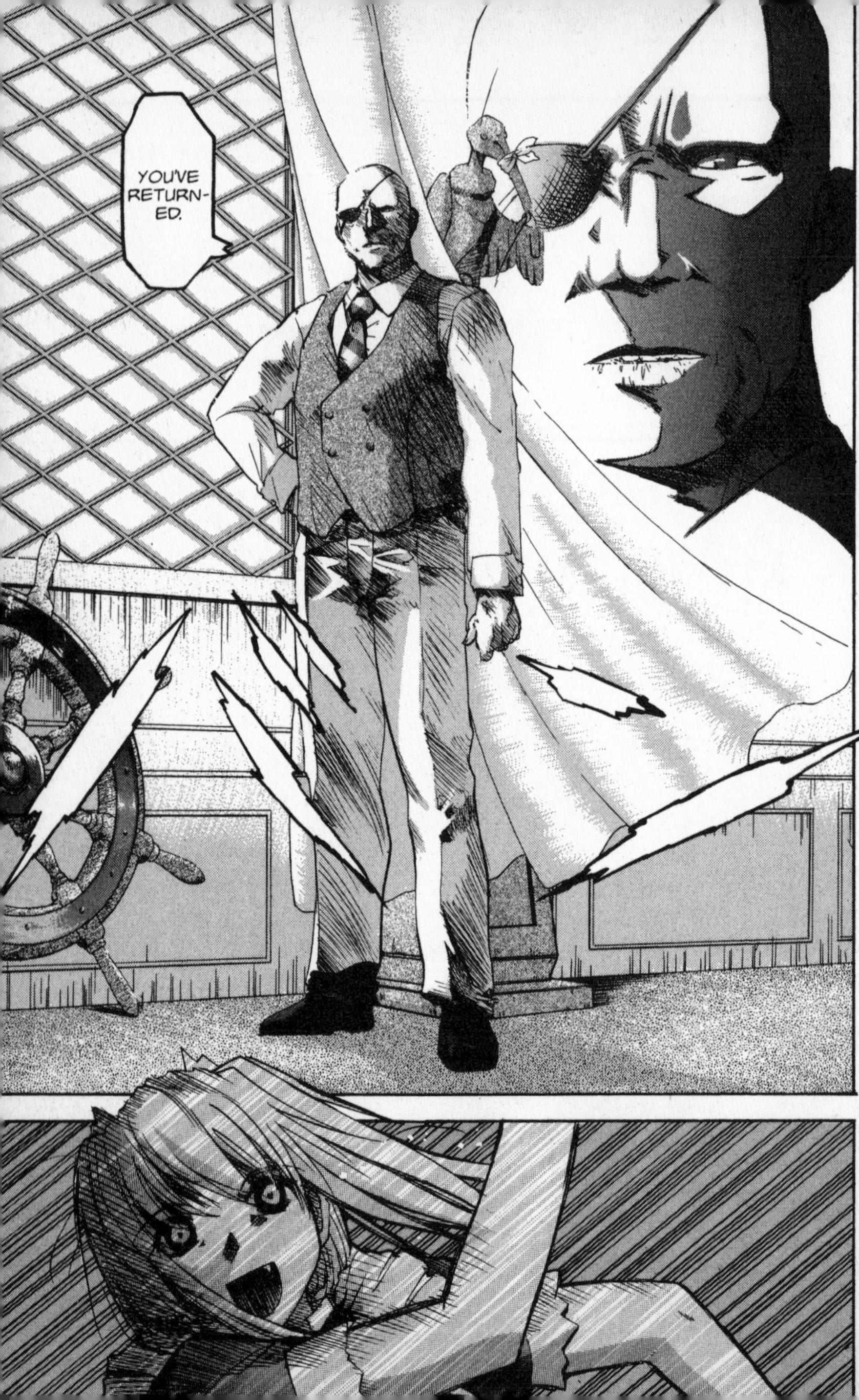
YOU'VE RETURN-ED.

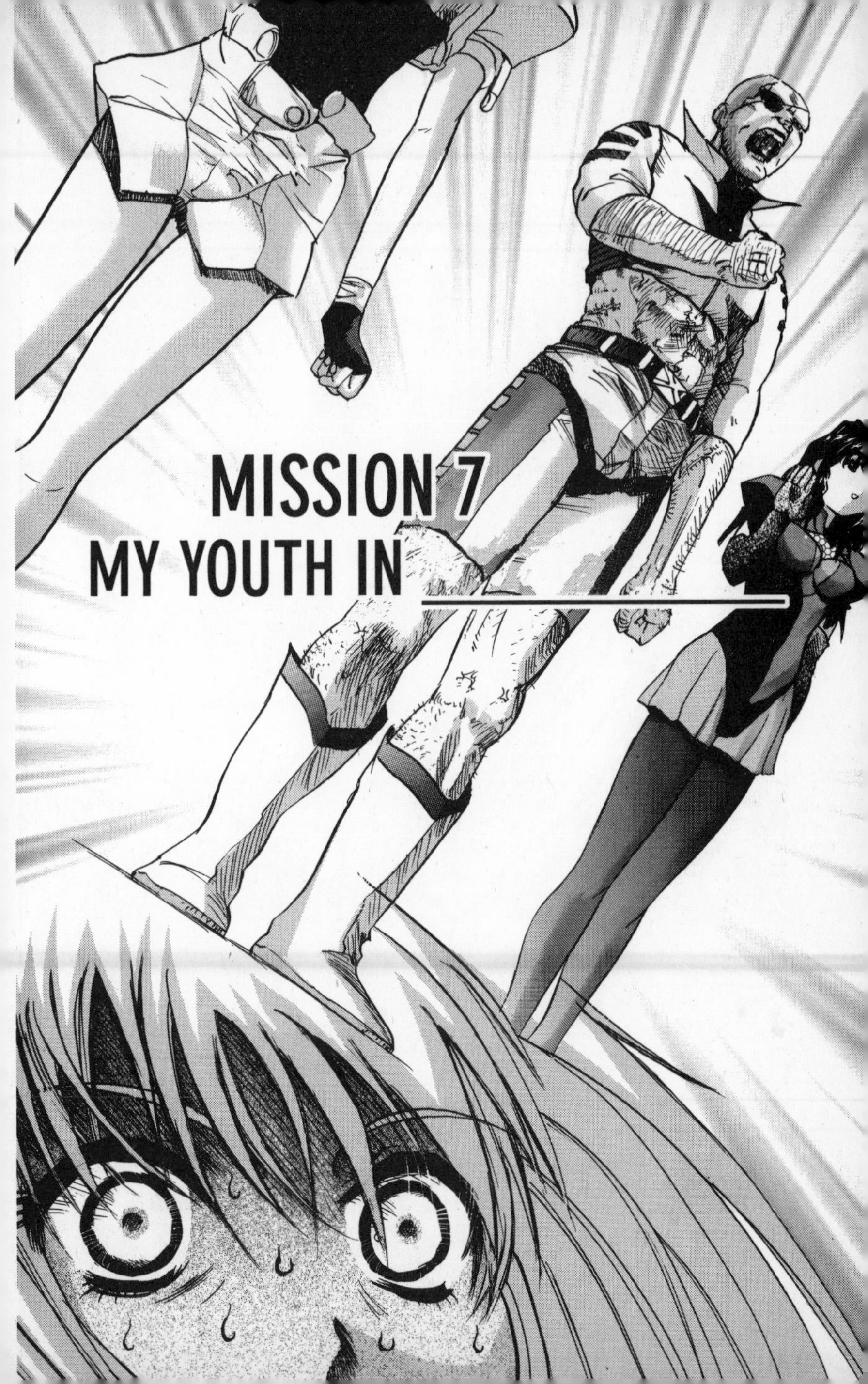
MISSION 7
MY YOUTH IN ______

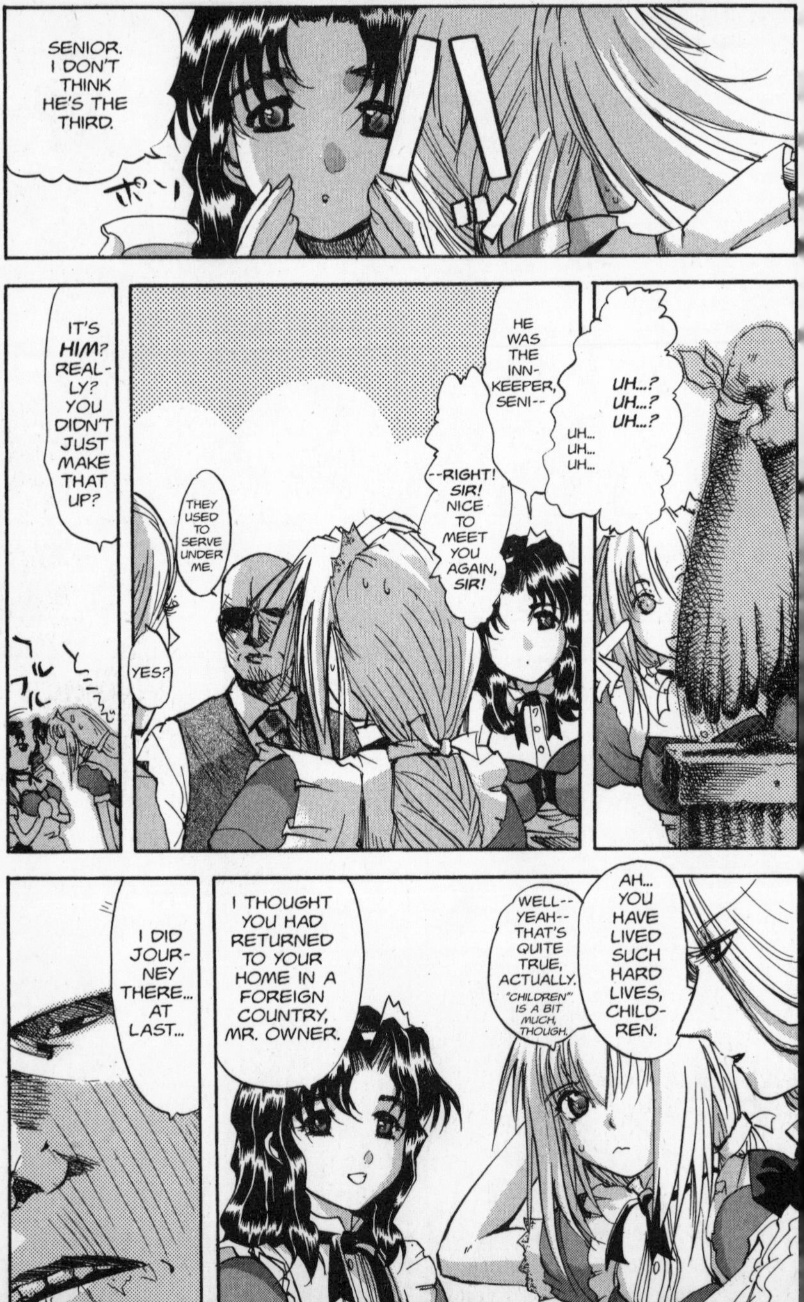
SENIOR. I DON'T THINK HE'S THE THIRD.
UH...? UH...? UH...?
UH... UH... UH...
HE WAS THE INN-KEEPER, SENI--
--RIGHT! SIR! NICE TO MEET YOU AGAIN, SIR!
THEY USED TO SERVE UNDER ME.
YES?
IT'S HIM? REALLY? YOU DIDN'T JUST MAKE THAT UP?
AH... YOU HAVE LIVED SUCH HARD LIVES, CHILDREN.
WELL--YEAH--THAT'S QUITE TRUE, ACTUALLY.
"CHILDREN" IS A BIT MUCH, THOUGH.
I THOUGHT YOU HAD RETURNED TO YOUR HOME IN A FOREIGN COUNTRY, MR. OWNER.
I DID JOURNEY THERE... AT LAST...

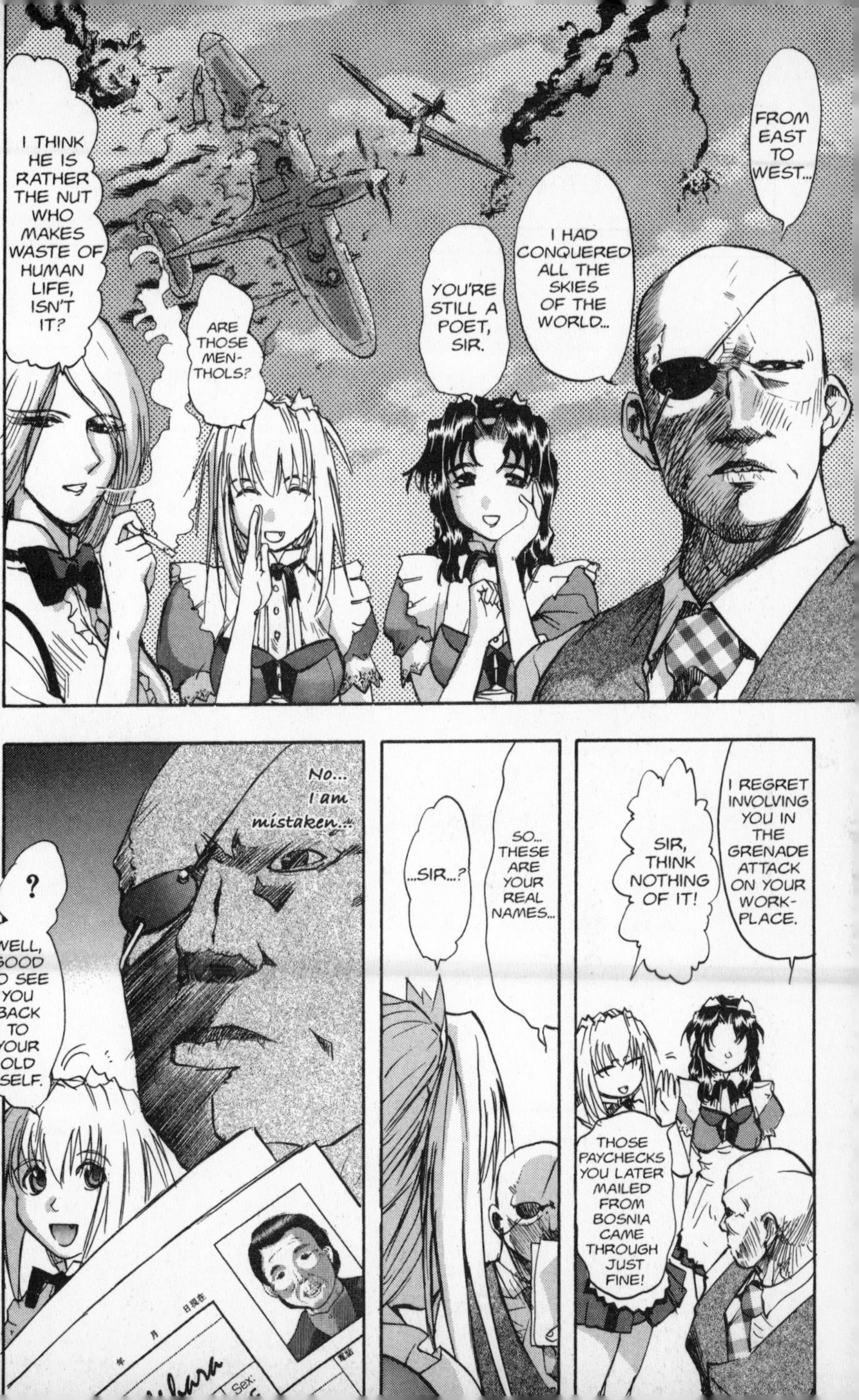
FROM EAST TO WEST...
I HAD CONQUERED ALL THE SKIES OF THE WORLD...
YOU'RE STILL A POET, SIR.
ARE THOSE MEN-THOLS?
I THINK HE IS RATHER THE NUT WHO MAKES WASTE OF HUMAN LIFE, ISN'T IT?
I REGRET INVOLVING YOU IN THE GRENADE ATTACK ON YOUR WORK-PLACE.
SIR, THINK NOTHING OF IT!
THOSE PAYCHECKS YOU LATER MAILED FROM BOSNIA CAME THROUGH JUST FINE!
SO... THESE ARE YOUR REAL NAMES...
...SIR...?
No... I am mistaken...
?
WELL, GOOD TO SEE YOU BACK TO YOUR OLD SELF.
Sex:

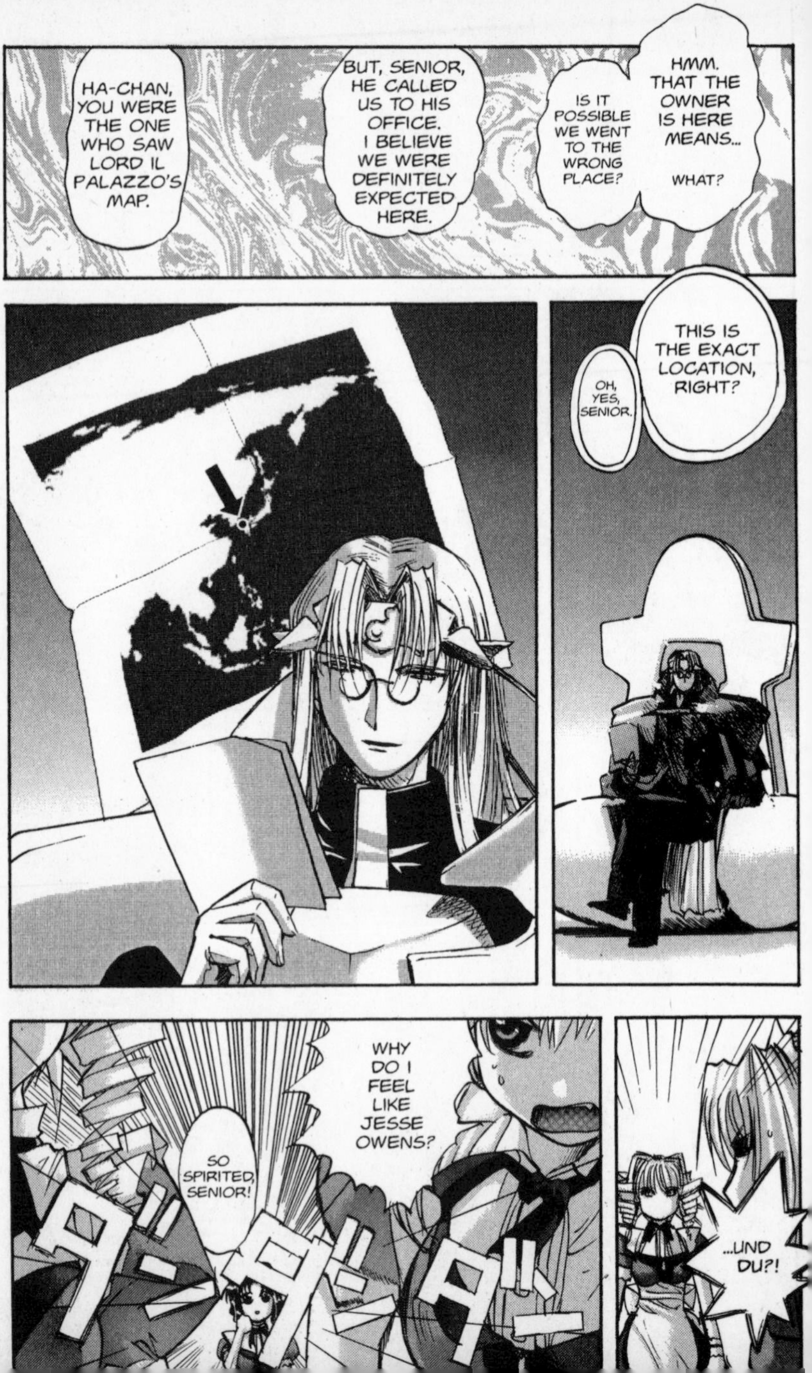
HMM. THAT THE OWNER IS HERE MEANS...
WHAT?
IS IT POSSIBLE WE WENT TO THE WRONG PLACE?
BUT, SENIOR, HE CALLED US TO HIS OFFICE. I BELIEVE WE WERE DEFINITELY EXPECTED HERE.
HA-CHAN, YOU WERE THE ONE WHO SAW LORD IL PALAZZO'S MAP.
THIS IS THE EXACT LOCATION, RIGHT?
OH, YES, SENIOR.
...UND DU?!
WHY DO I FEEL LIKE JESSE OWENS?
SO SPIRITED, SENIOR!

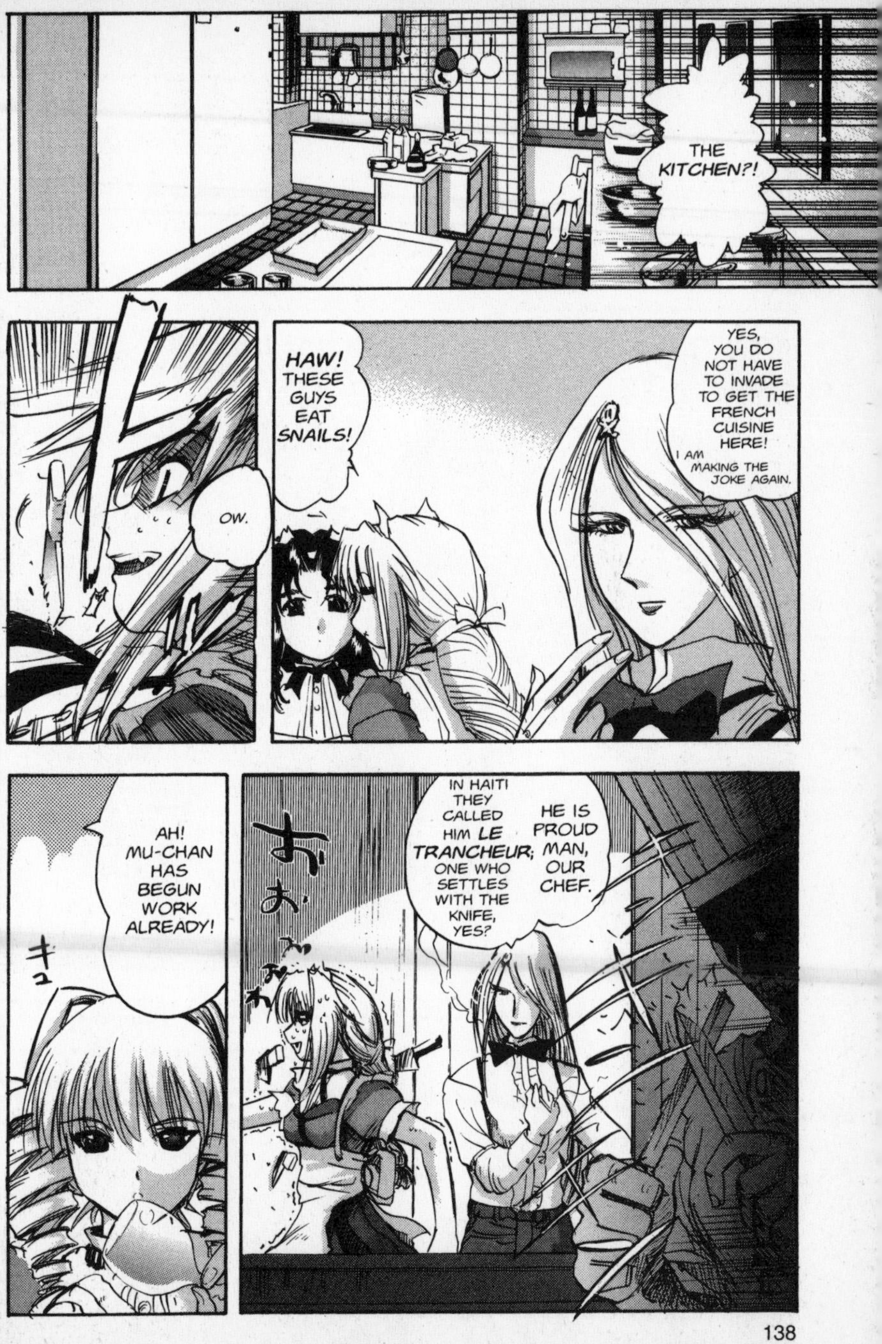
THE KITCHEN?!
YES, YOU DO NOT HAVE TO INVADE TO GET THE FRENCH CUISINE HERE!
I AM MAKING THE JOKE AGAIN.
HAW! THESE GUYS EAT SNAILS!
OW.
HE IS PROUD MAN, OUR CHEF.
IN HAITI THEY CALLED HIM LE TRANCHEUR; ONE WHO SETTLES WITH THE KNIFE, YES?
AH! MU-CHAN HAS BEGUN WORK ALREADY!
キュ

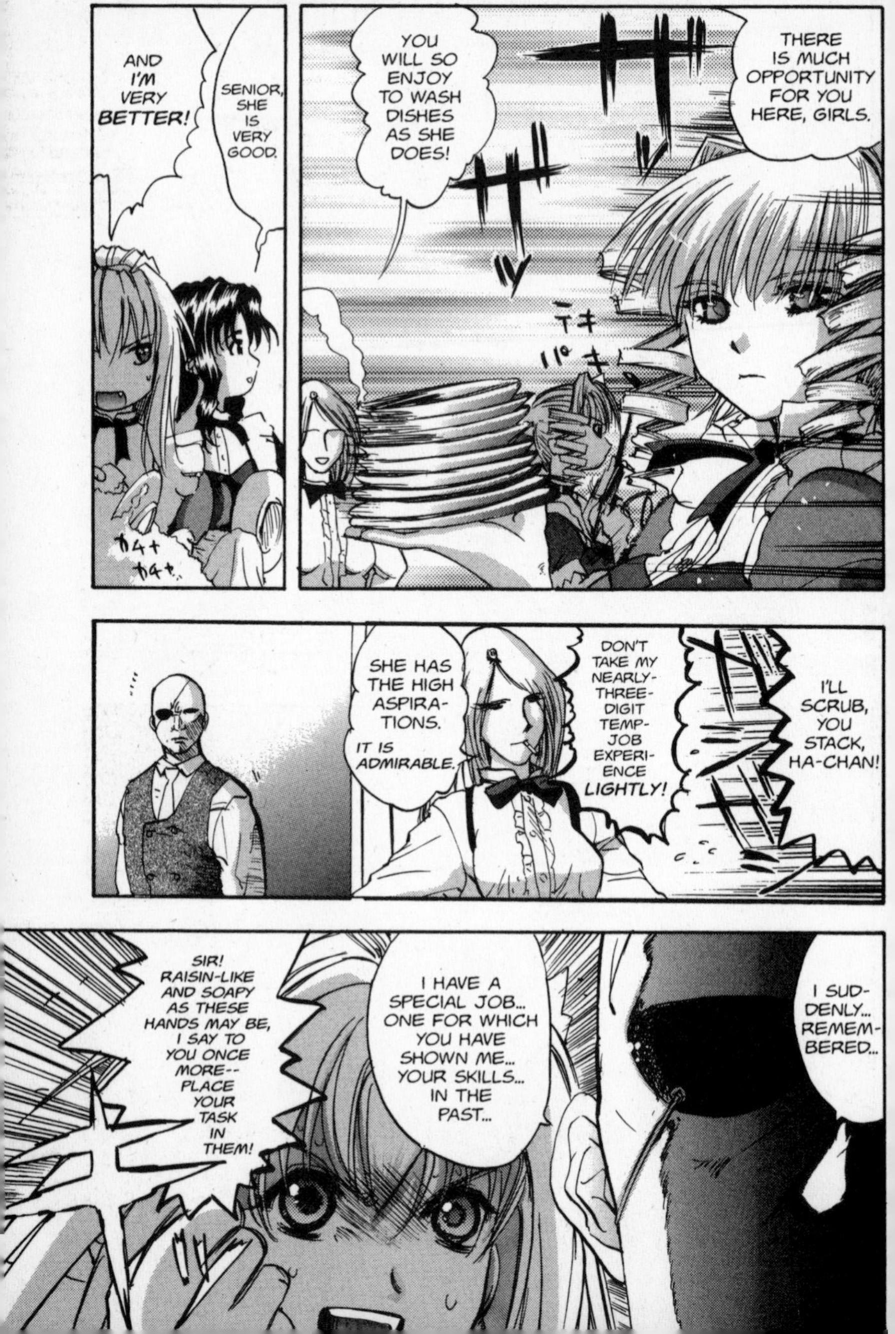
THERE IS MUCH OPPORTUNITY FOR YOU HERE, GIRLS.
YOU WILL SO ENJOY TO WASH DISHES AS SHE DOES!
テキ パキ
SENIOR, SHE IS VERY GOOD.
AND I'M VERY BETTER!
I'LL SCRUB, YOU STACK, HA-CHAN!
DON'T TAKE MY NEARLY-THREE-DIGIT TEMP-JOB EXPERIENCE LIGHTLY!
SHE HAS THE HIGH ASPIRATIONS.
IT IS ADMIRABLE.
I SUDDENLY... REMEMBERED...
I HAVE A SPECIAL JOB... ONE FOR WHICH YOU HAVE SHOWN ME... YOUR SKILLS... IN THE PAST...
SIR! RAISIN-LIKE AND SOAPY AS THESE HANDS MAY BE, I SAY TO YOU ONCE MORE-- PLACE YOUR TASK IN THEM!

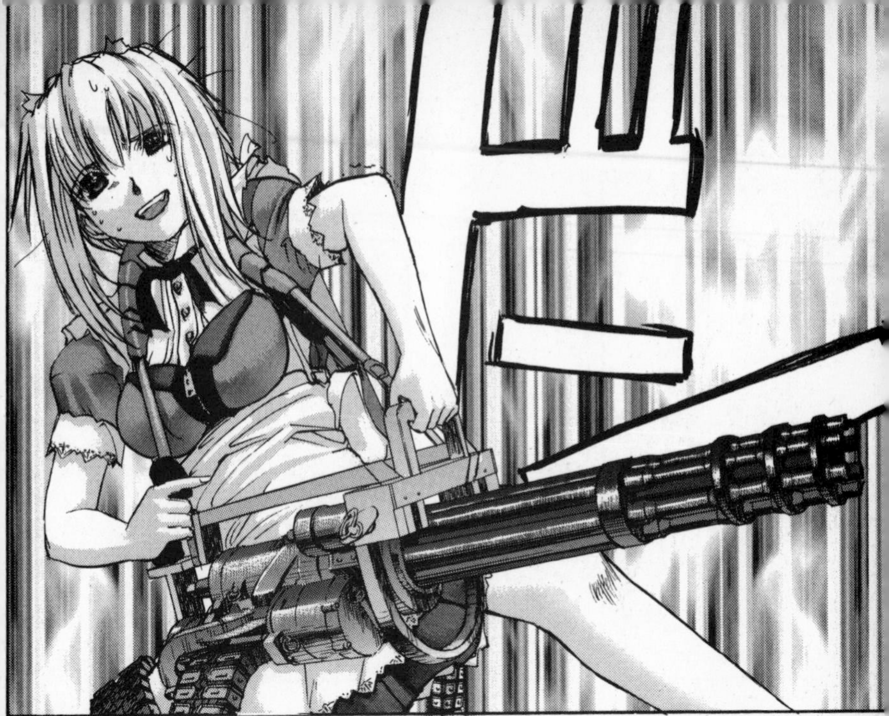

The author wishes to offer up his deepest gratitude to Akihiro Ito-sensei.

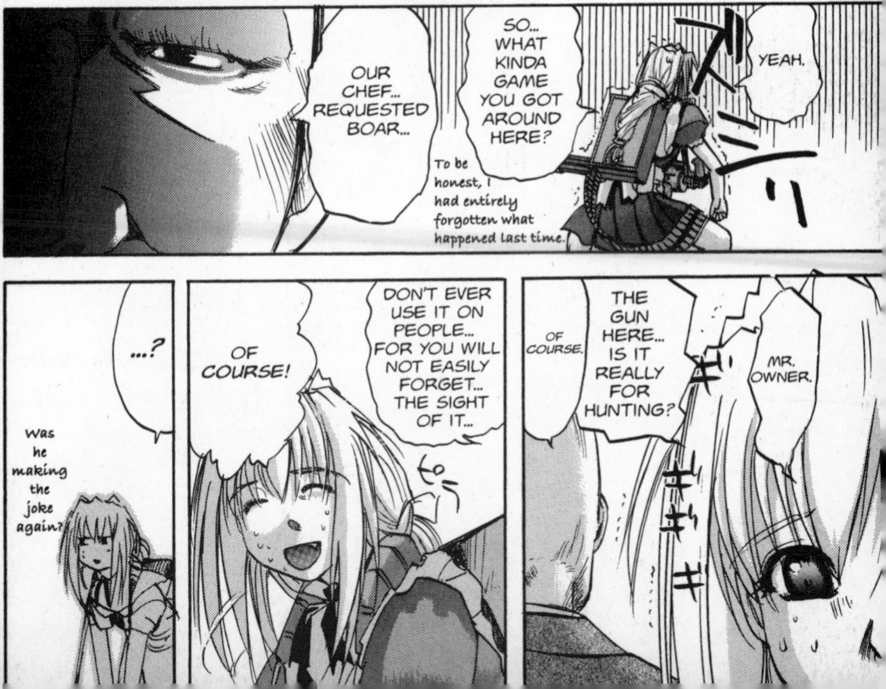
YEAH.
SO... WHAT KINDA GAME YOU GOT AROUND HERE?
OUR CHEF... REQUESTED BOAR...
To be honest, I had entirely forgotten what happened last time.
MR. OWNER.
THE GUN HERE... IS IT REALLY FOR HUNTING?
OF COURSE.
DON'T EVER USE IT ON PEOPLE... FOR YOU WILL NOT EASILY FORGET... THE SIGHT OF IT...
OF COURSE!
...?
Was he making the joke again?

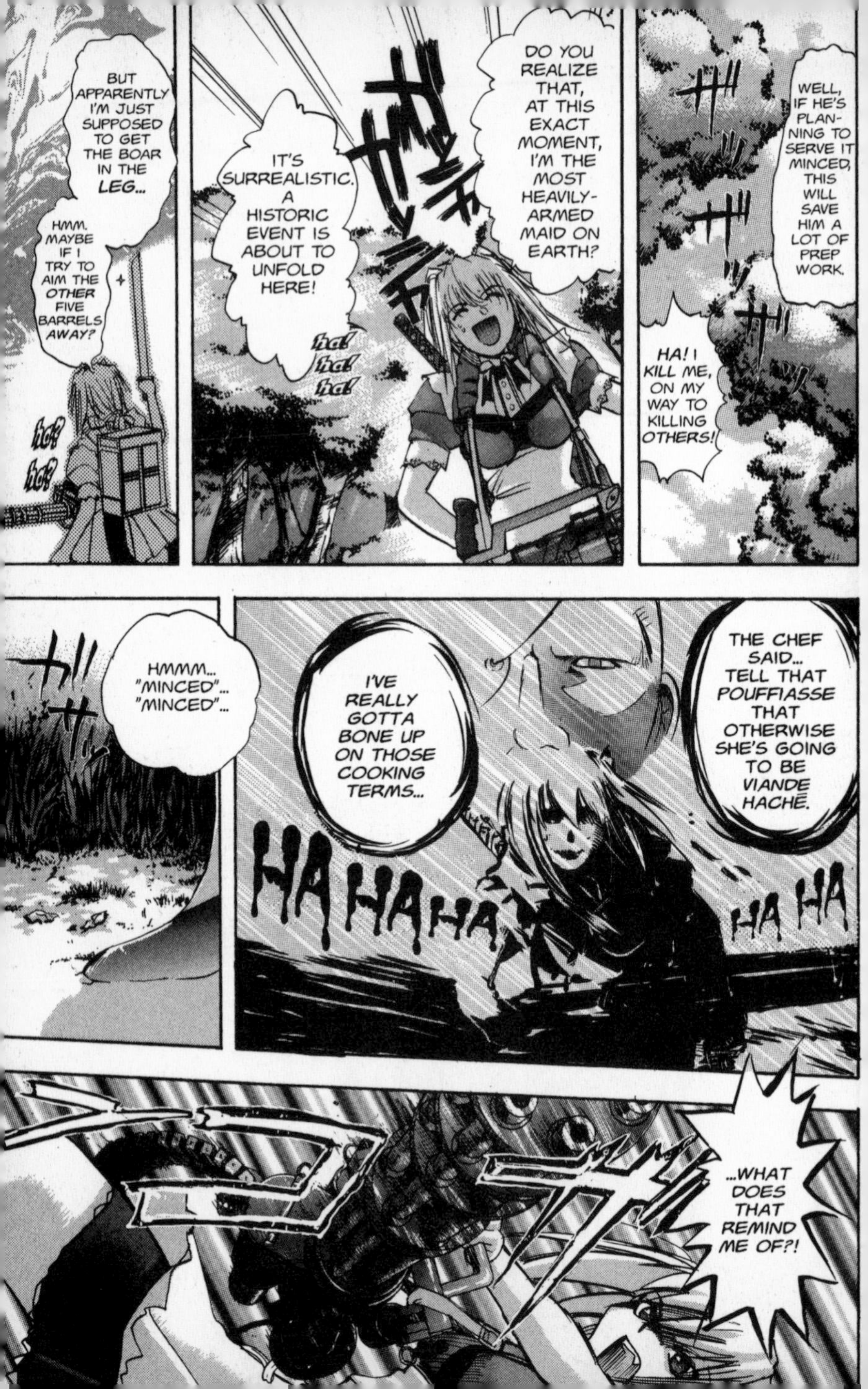
WELL, IF HE'S PLAN-NING TO SERVE IT MINCED, THIS WILL SAVE HIM A LOT OF PREP WORK.
HA! I KILL ME, ON MY WAY TO KILLING OTHERS!
DO YOU REALIZE THAT, AT THIS EXACT MOMENT, I'M THE MOST HEAVILY-ARMED MAID ON EARTH?
IT'S SURREALISTIC. A HISTORIC EVENT IS ABOUT TO UNFOLD HERE!
ha! ha! ha!
BUT APPARENTLY I'M JUST SUPPOSED TO GET THE BOAR IN THE LEG...
HMM. MAYBE IF I TRY TO AIM THE OTHER FIVE BARRELS AWAY?
THE CHEF SAID... TELL THAT POUFFIASSE THAT OTHERWISE SHE'S GOING TO BE VIANDE HACHÉ.
I'VE REALLY GOTTA BONE UP ON THOSE COOKING TERMS...
HA HA HA HA
HA HA
HMMM... "MINCED"... "MINCED"...
...WHAT DOES THAT REMIND ME OF?!

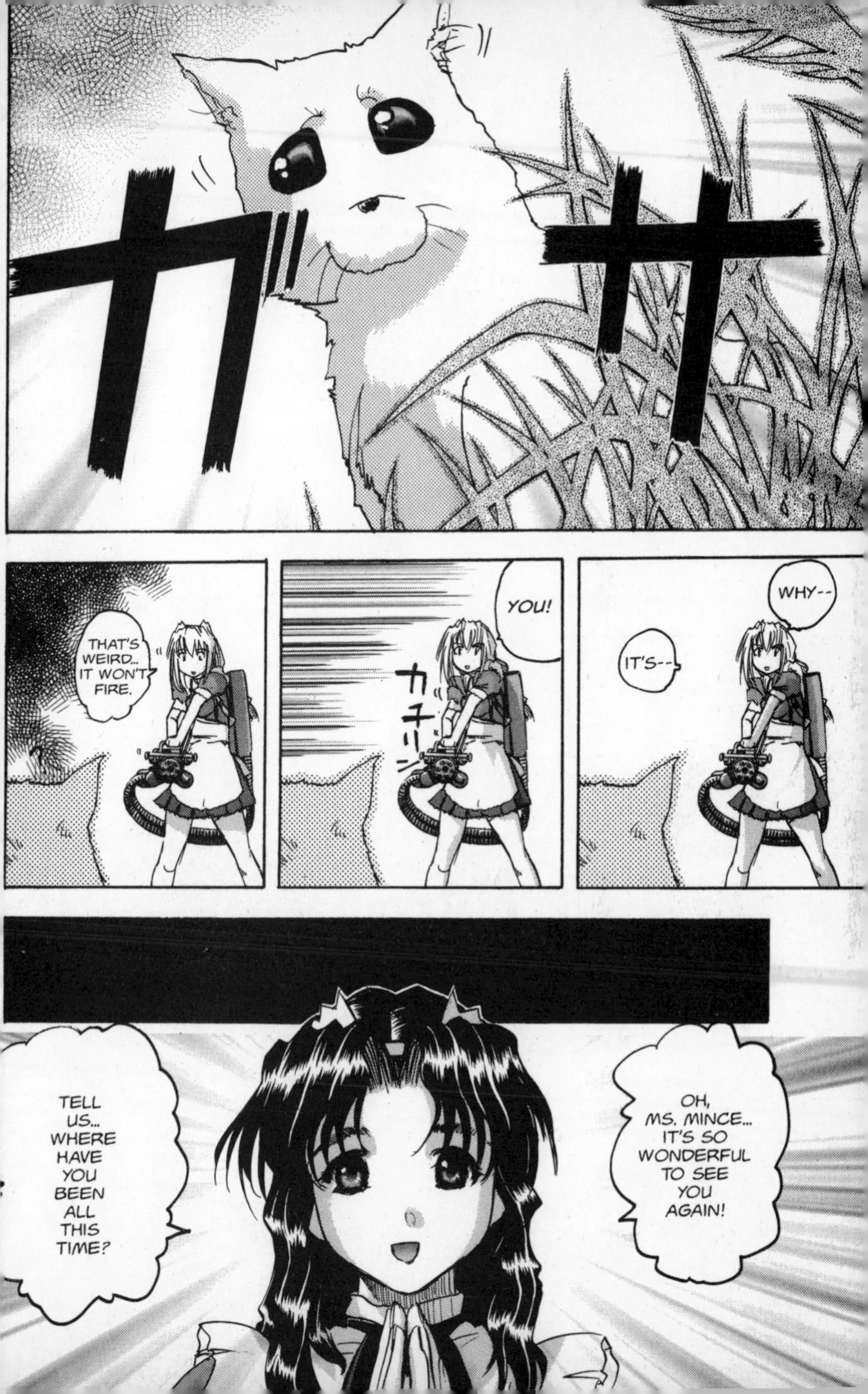
ガサ
WHY--
IT'S--
YOU!
カチリン
THAT'S WEIRD... IT WON'T FIRE.
OH, MS. MINCE... IT'S SO WONDERFUL TO SEE YOU AGAIN!
TELL US... WHERE HAVE YOU BEEN ALL THIS TIME?

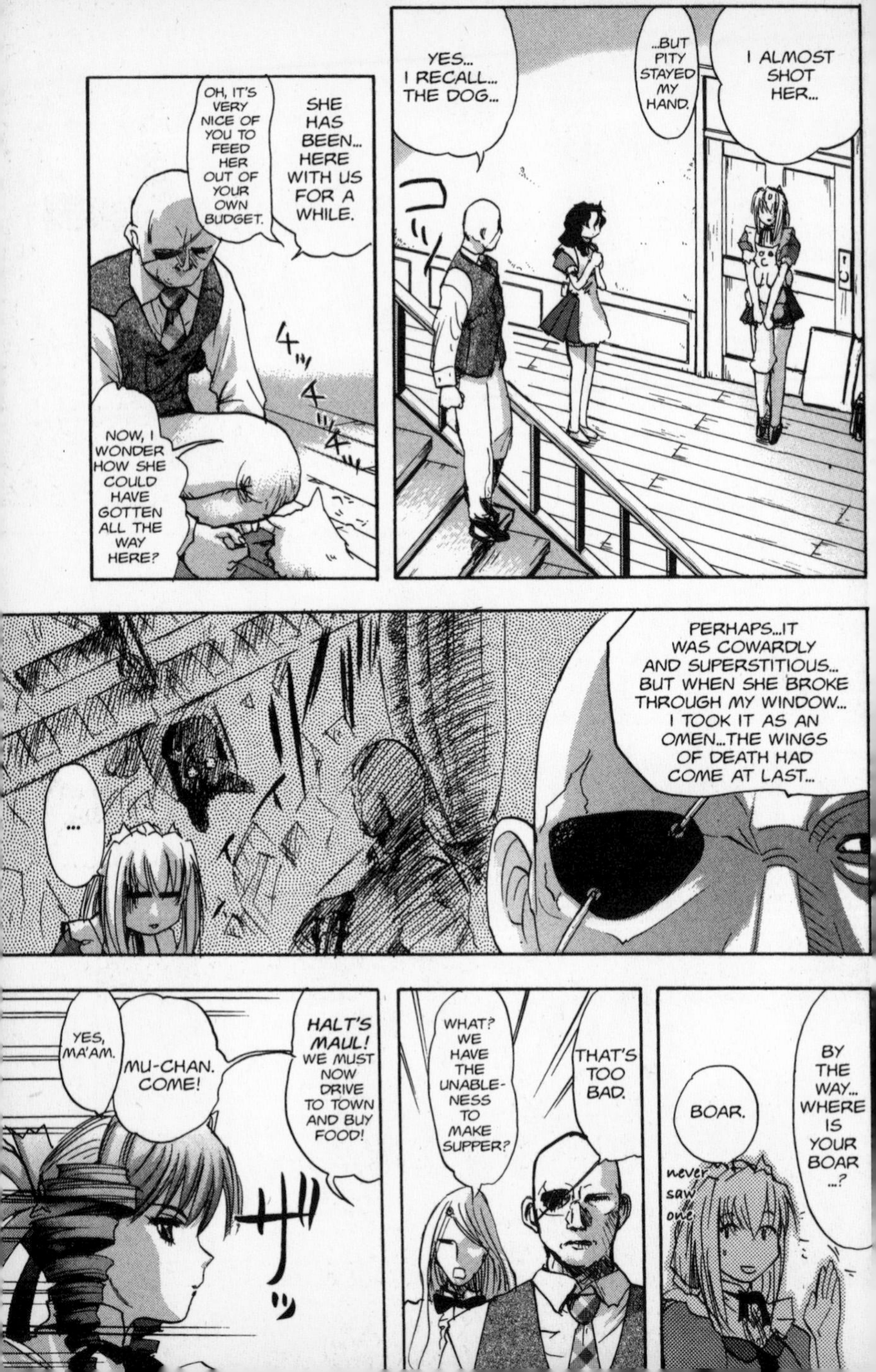
I ALMOST SHOT HER...
...BUT PITY STAYED MY HAND.
YES... I RECALL... THE DOG...
SHE HAS BEEN... HERE WITH US FOR A WHILE.
OH, IT'S VERY NICE OF YOU TO FEED HER OUT OF YOUR OWN BUDGET.
NOW, I WONDER HOW SHE COULD HAVE GOTTEN ALL THE WAY HERE?
PERHAPS...IT WAS COWARDLY AND SUPERSTITIOUS... BUT WHEN SHE BROKE THROUGH MY WINDOW... I TOOK IT AS AN OMEN...THE WINGS OF DEATH HAD COME AT LAST...
...
BY THE WAY... WHERE IS YOUR BOAR ...?
BOAR.
never saw one
THAT'S TOO BAD.
WHAT? WE HAVE THE UNABLE-NESS TO MAKE SUPPER?
HALT'S MAUL! WE MUST NOW DRIVE TO TOWN AND BUY FOOD!
MU-CHAN. COME!
YES, MA'AM.

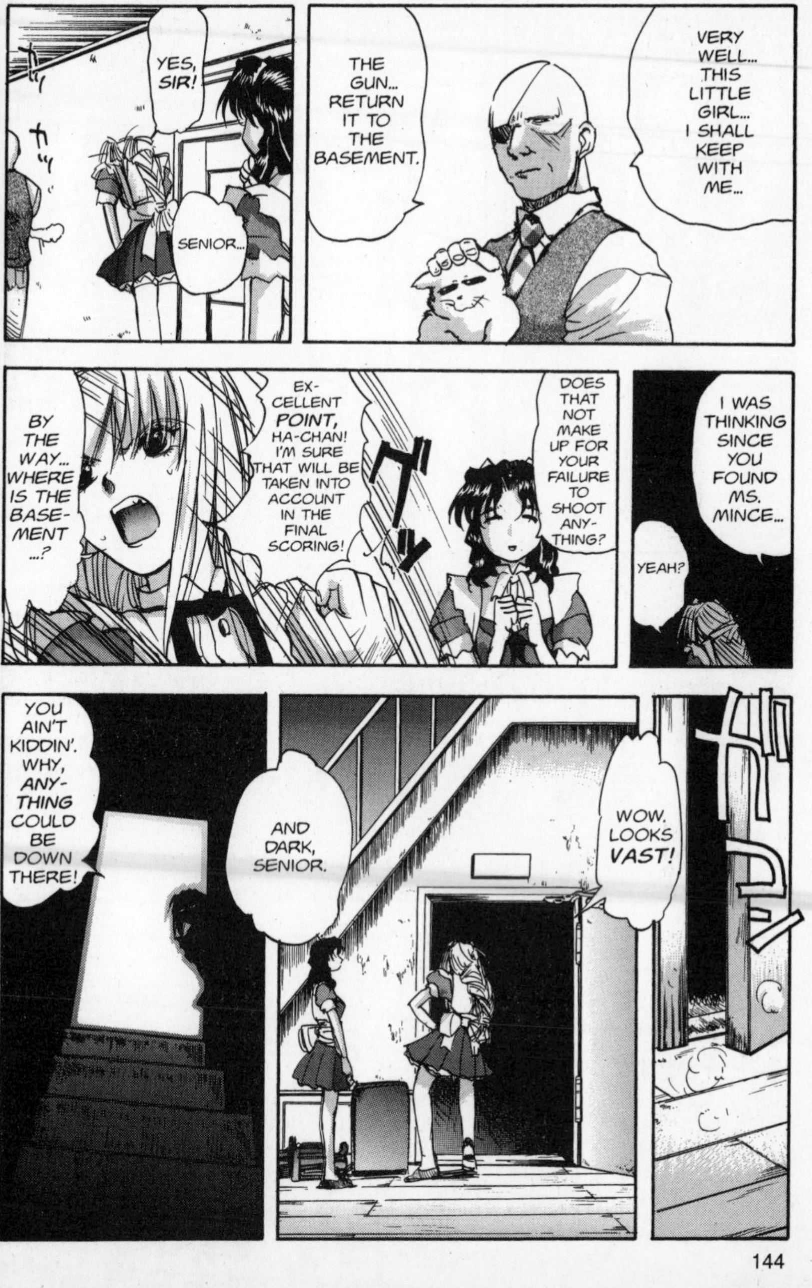
VERY WELL... THIS LITTLE GIRL... I SHALL KEEP WITH ME...
THE GUN... RETURN IT TO THE BASEMENT.
YES, SIR!
SENIOR...
I WAS THINKING SINCE YOU FOUND MS. MINCE...
YEAH?
DOES THAT NOT MAKE UP FOR YOUR FAILURE TO SHOOT ANYTHING?
EX-CELLENT POINT, HA-CHAN! I'M SURE THAT WILL BE TAKEN INTO ACCOUNT IN THE FINAL SCORING!
BY THE WAY... WHERE IS THE BASE-MENT ...?
WOW. LOOKS VAST!
AND DARK, SENIOR.
YOU AIN'T KIDDIN'. WHY, ANY-THING COULD BE DOWN THERE!

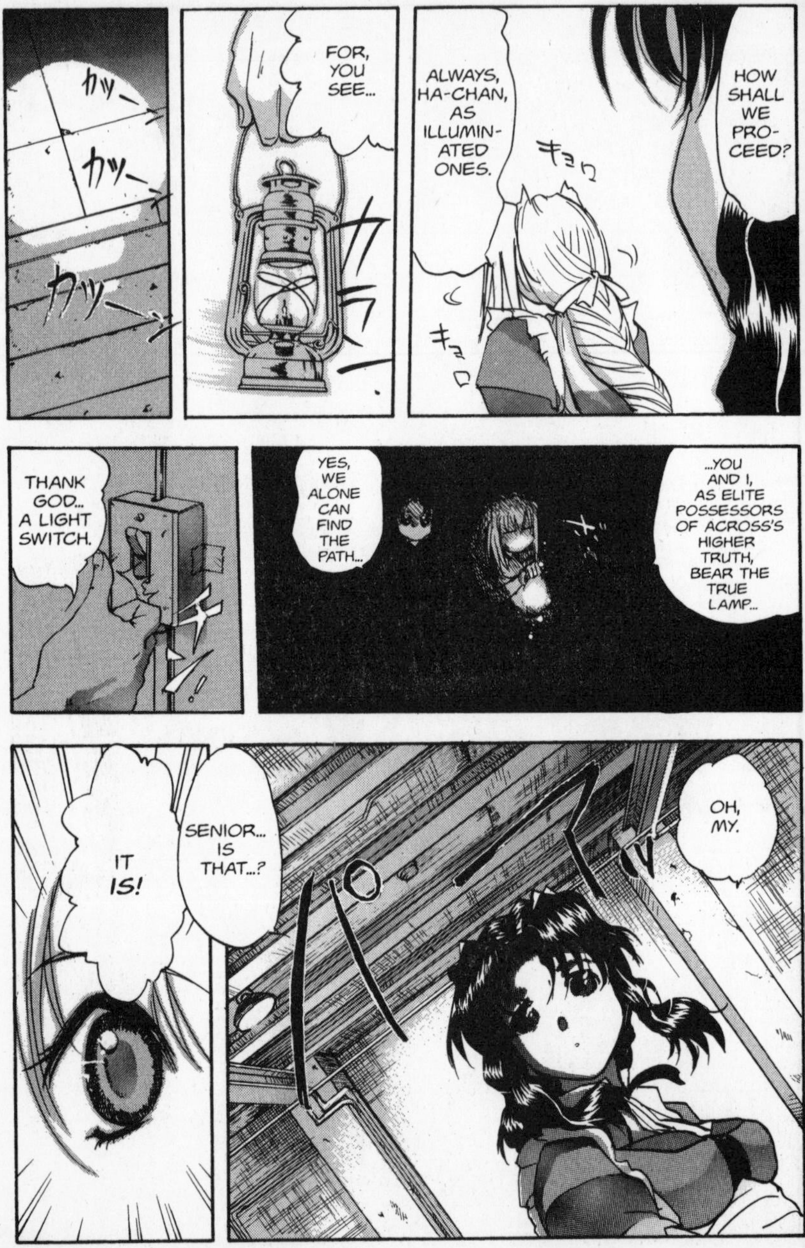
HOW SHALL WE PRO-CEED?
ALWAYS, HA-CHAN, AS ILLUMIN-ATED ONES.
キョロ
キョロ
FOR, YOU SEE...
カッー
カッー
カッー
...YOU AND I, AS ELITE POSSESSORS OF ACROSS'S HIGHER TRUTH, BEAR THE TRUE LAMP...
YES, WE ALONE CAN FIND THE PATH...
THANK GOD... A LIGHT SWITCH.
OH, MY.
SENIOR... IS THAT...?
IT IS!

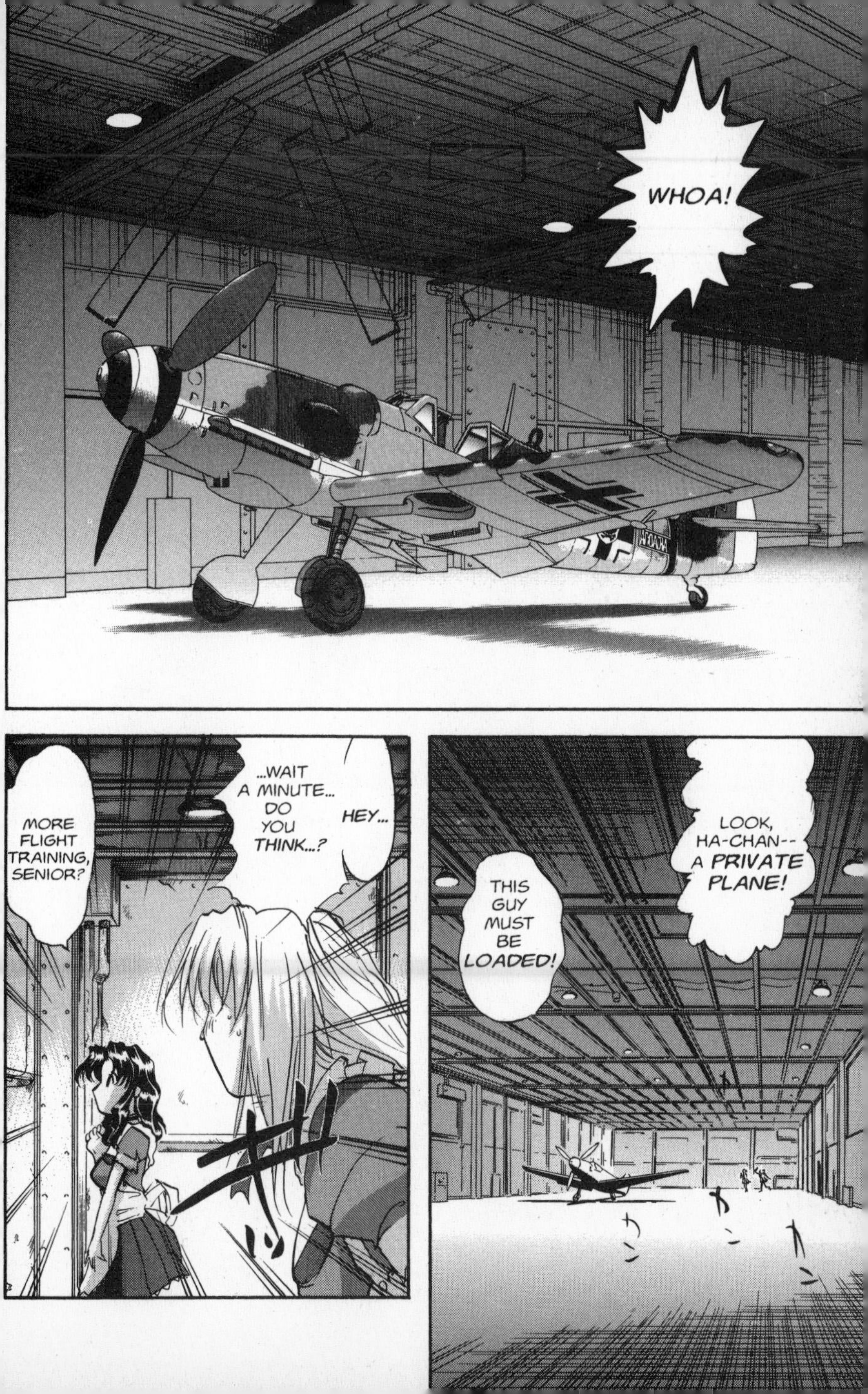
WHOA!
LOOK, HA-CHAN-- A PRIVATE PLANE!
THIS GUY MUST BE LOADED!
HEY...
...WAIT A MINUTE... DO YOU THINK...?
MORE FLIGHT TRAINING, SENIOR?

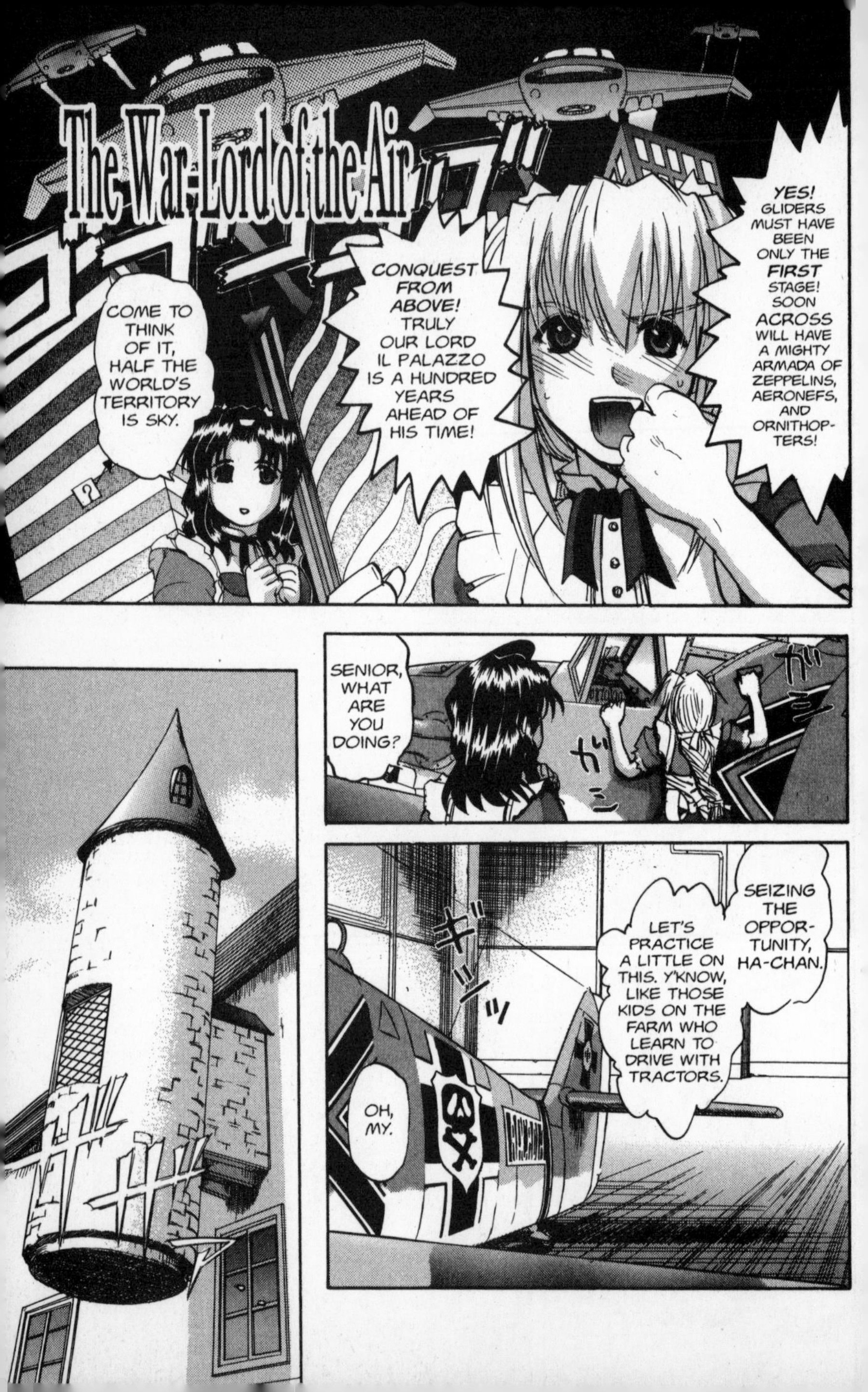
The War-Lord of the Air
YES! GLIDERS MUST HAVE BEEN ONLY THE FIRST STAGE! SOON ACROSS WILL HAVE A MIGHTY ARMADA OF ZEPPELINS, AERONEFS, AND ORNITHOPTERS!
CONQUEST FROM ABOVE! TRULY OUR LORD IL PALAZZO IS A HUNDRED YEARS AHEAD OF HIS TIME!
COME TO THINK OF IT, HALF THE WORLD'S TERRITORY IS SKY.
SENIOR, WHAT ARE YOU DOING?
SEIZING THE OPPORTUNITY, HA-CHAN.
LET'S PRACTICE A LITTLE ON THIS. Y'KNOW, LIKE THOSE KIDS ON THE FARM WHO LEARN TO DRIVE WITH TRACTORS.
OH, MY.

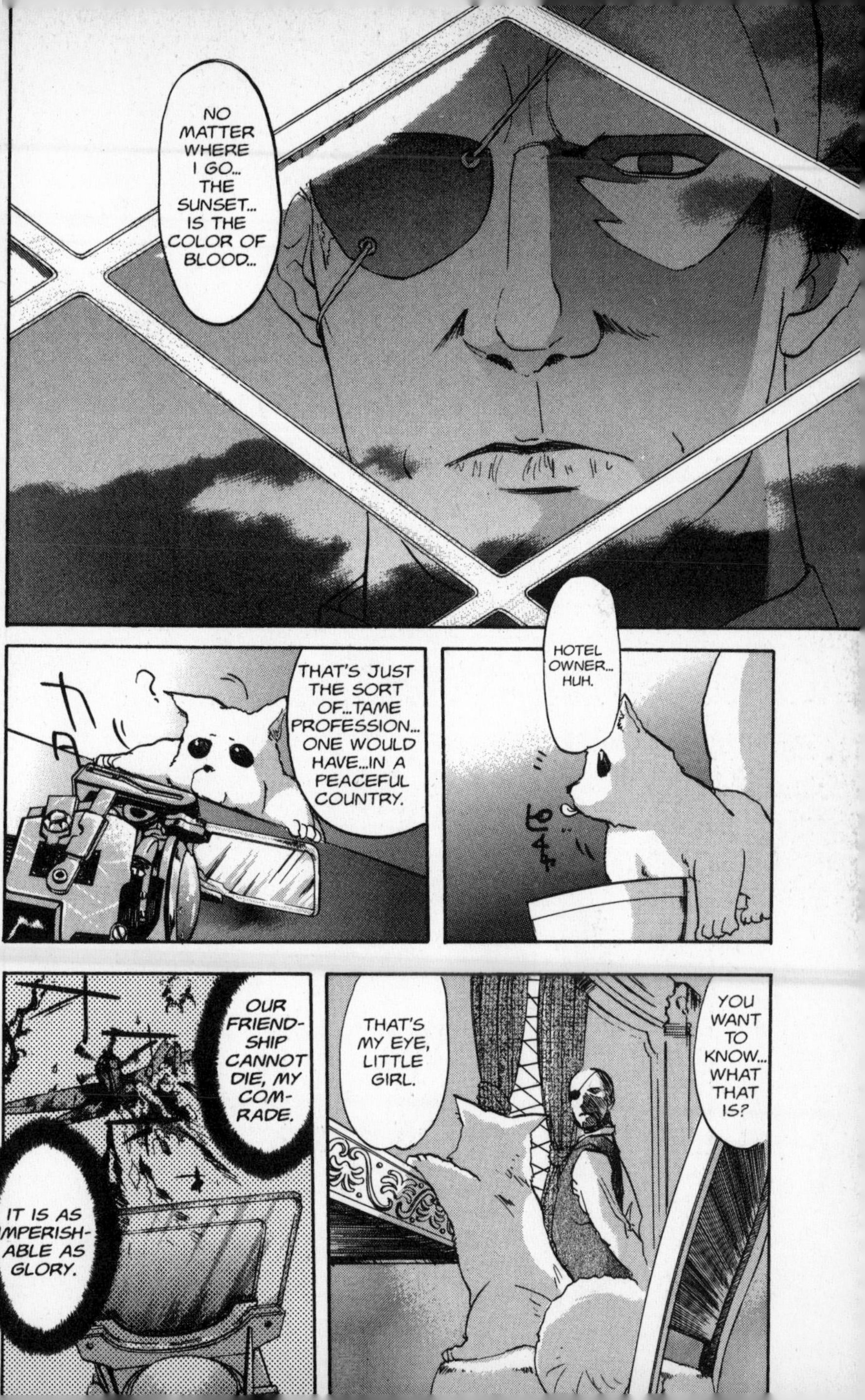
NO MATTER WHERE I GO... THE SUNSET... IS THE COLOR OF BLOOD...
HOTEL OWNER... HUH.
THAT'S JUST THE SORT OF...TAME PROFESSION... ONE WOULD HAVE...IN A PEACEFUL COUNTRY.
YOU WANT TO KNOW... WHAT THAT IS?
THAT'S MY EYE, LITTLE GIRL.
OUR FRIENDSHIP CANNOT DIE, MY COMRADE.
IT IS AS IMPERISHABLE AS GLORY.

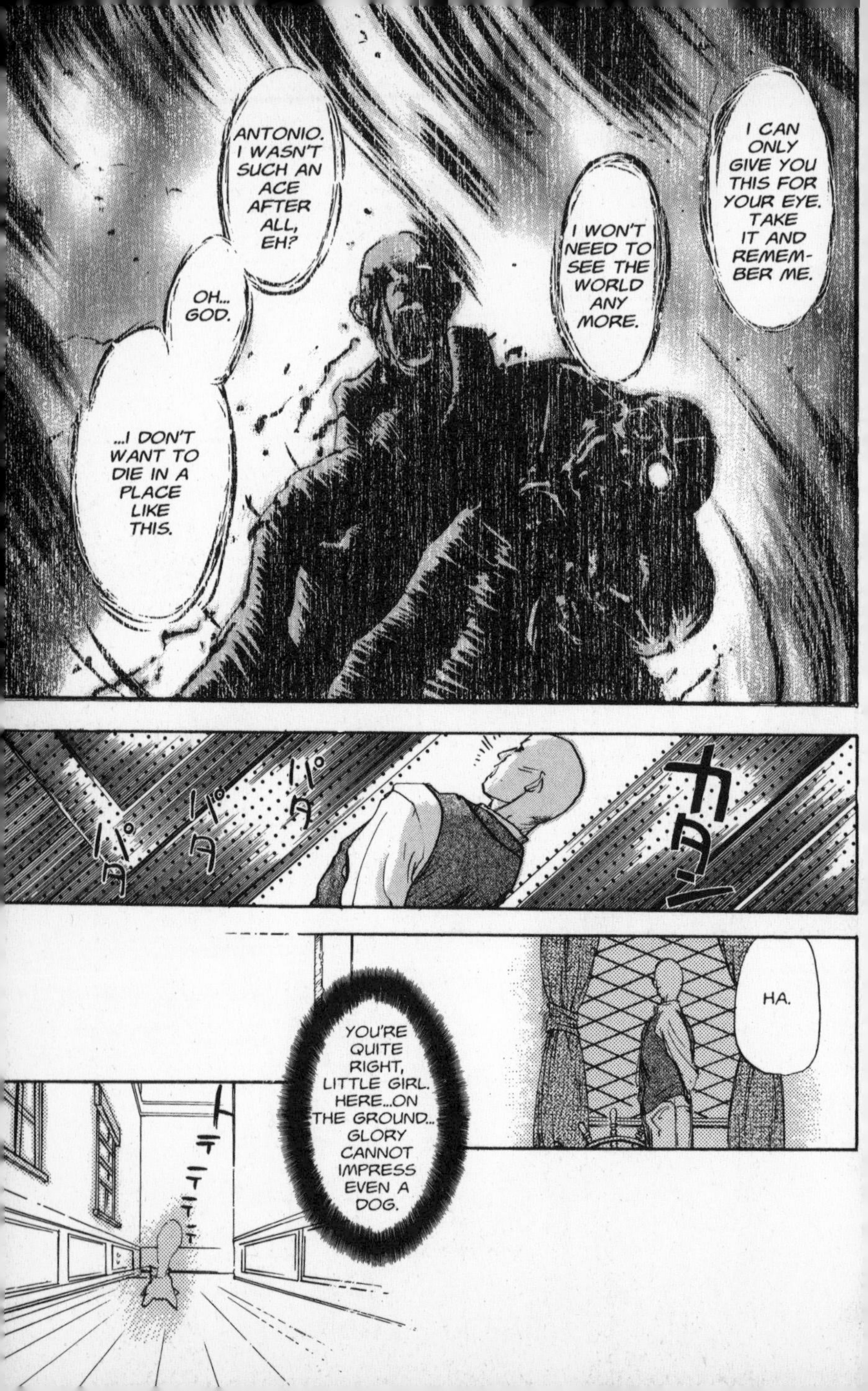
I CAN ONLY GIVE YOU THIS FOR YOUR EYE. TAKE IT AND REMEMBER ME.
I WON'T NEED TO SEE THE WORLD ANY MORE.
ANTONIO. I WASN'T SUCH AN ACE AFTER ALL, EH?
OH... GOD.
...I DON'T WANT TO DIE IN A PLACE LIKE THIS.
カタン
パタパタパタ
HA.
YOU'RE QUITE RIGHT, LITTLE GIRL. HERE...ON THE GROUND... GLORY CANNOT IMPRESS EVEN A DOG.
トテテテテ

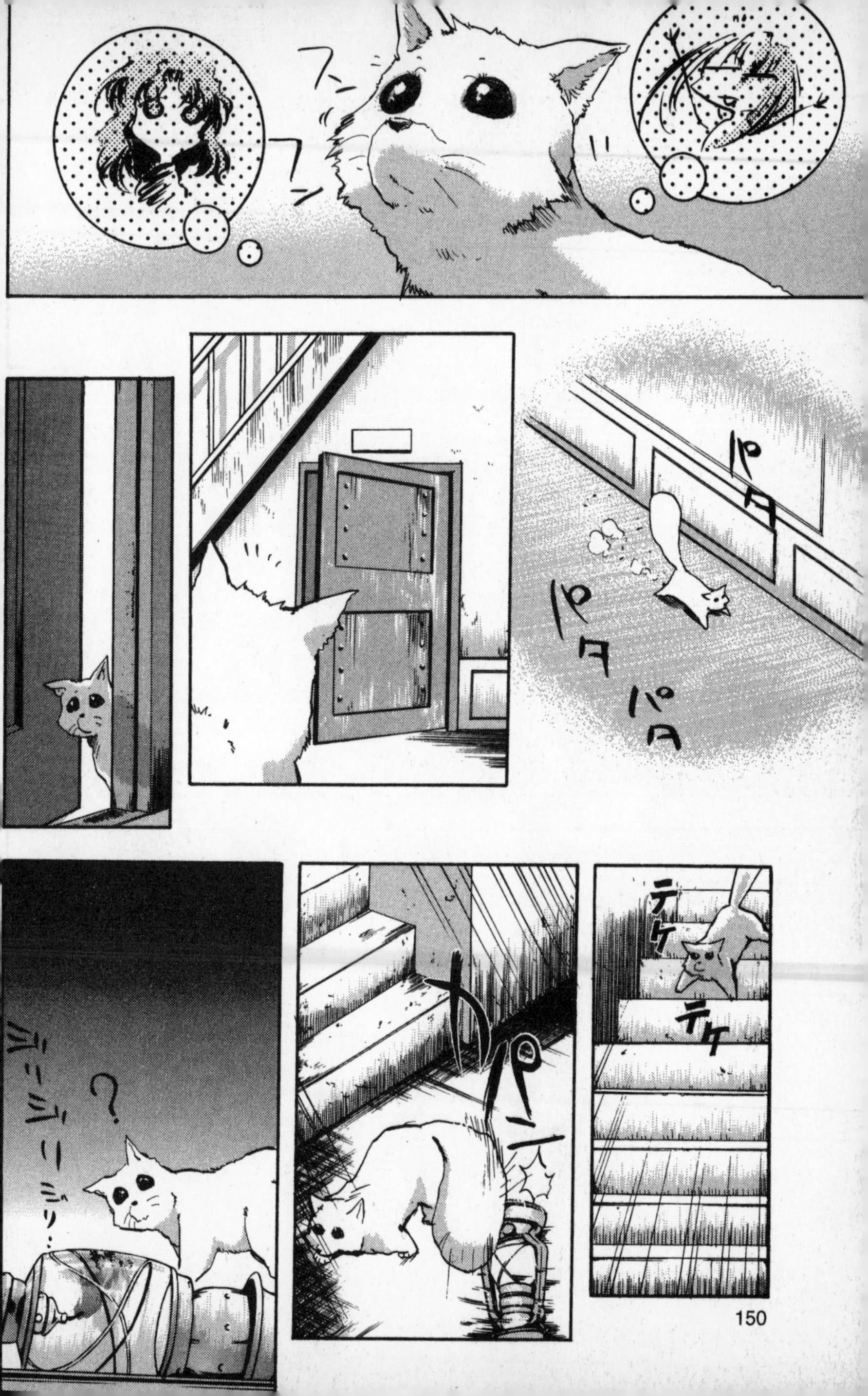
フン
フン
パタ
パタ
パタ
テケ
テケ
カパーン
?
ジリ
ジリ
ジリ…

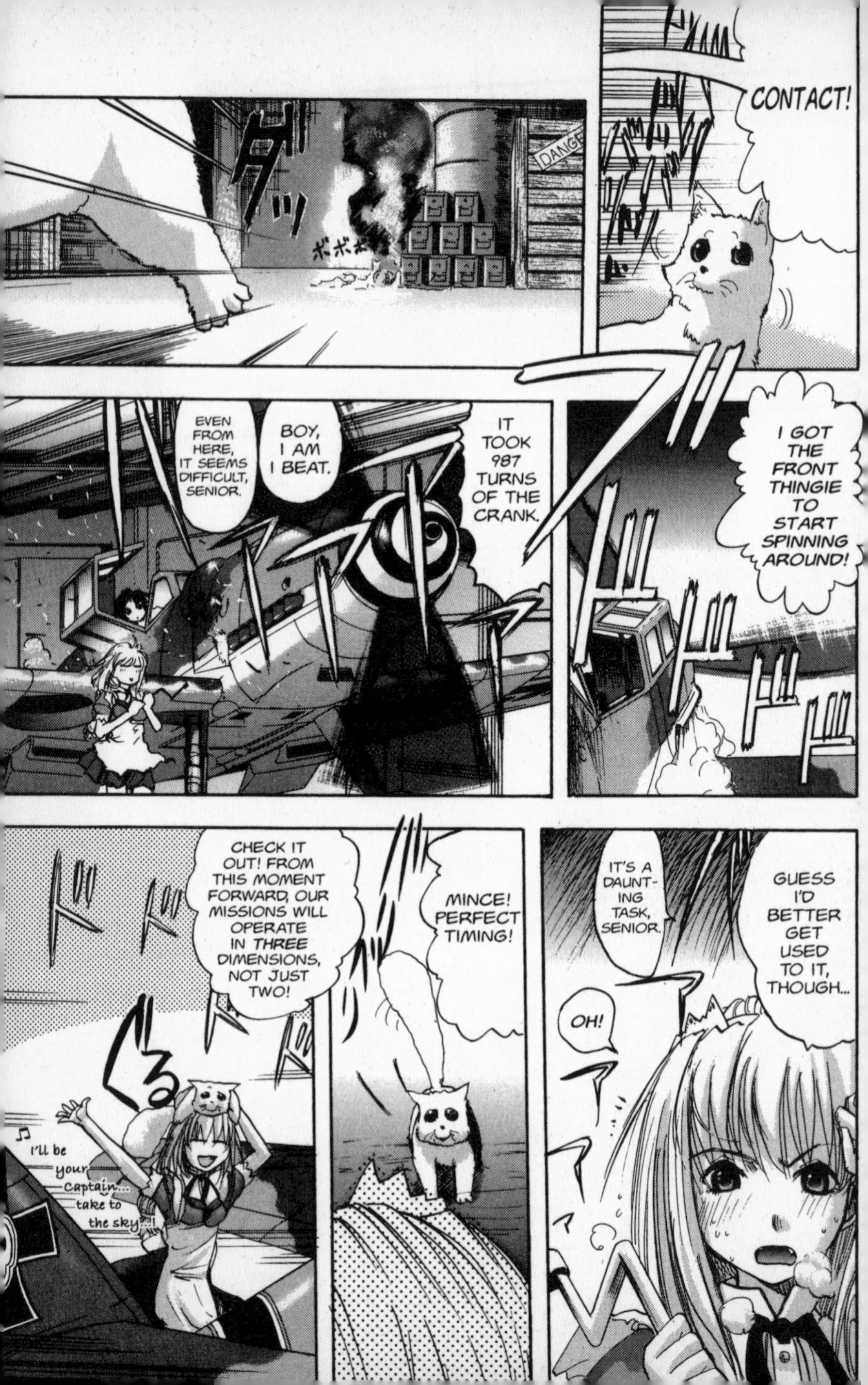
CONTACT!
I GOT THE FRONT THINGIE TO START SPINNING AROUND!
IT TOOK 987 TURNS OF THE CRANK.
BOY, I AM I BEAT.
EVEN FROM HERE, IT SEEMS DIFFICULT, SENIOR.
GUESS I'D BETTER GET USED TO IT, THOUGH...
IT'S A DAUNTING TASK, SENIOR.
OH!
MINCE! PERFECT TIMING!
CHECK IT OUT! FROM THIS MOMENT FORWARD, OUR MISSIONS WILL OPERATE IN *THREE* DIMENSIONS, NOT JUST TWO!
♫ I'll be your Captain... take to the sky...!

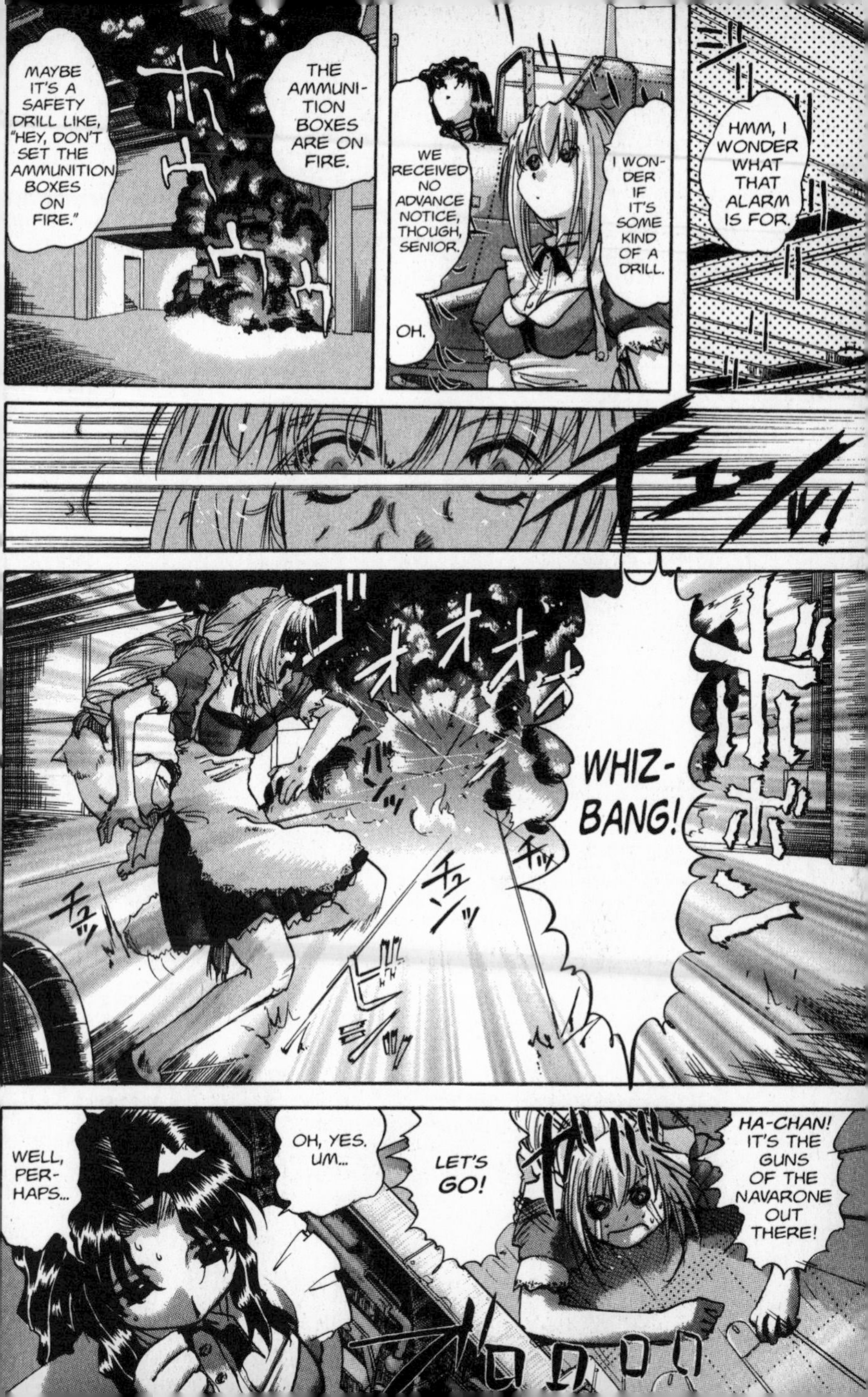
HMM, I WONDER WHAT THAT ALARM IS FOR.
I WONDER IF IT'S SOME KIND OF A DRILL.
WE RECEIVED NO ADVANCE NOTICE, THOUGH, SENIOR.
OH.
THE AMMUNITION BOXES ARE ON FIRE.
MAYBE IT'S A SAFETY DRILL LIKE, "HEY, DON'T SET THE AMMUNITION BOXES ON FIRE."
WHIZ-BANG!
HA-CHAN! IT'S THE GUNS OF THE NAVARONE OUT THERE!
LET'S GO!
OH, YES. UM...
WELL, PERHAPS...

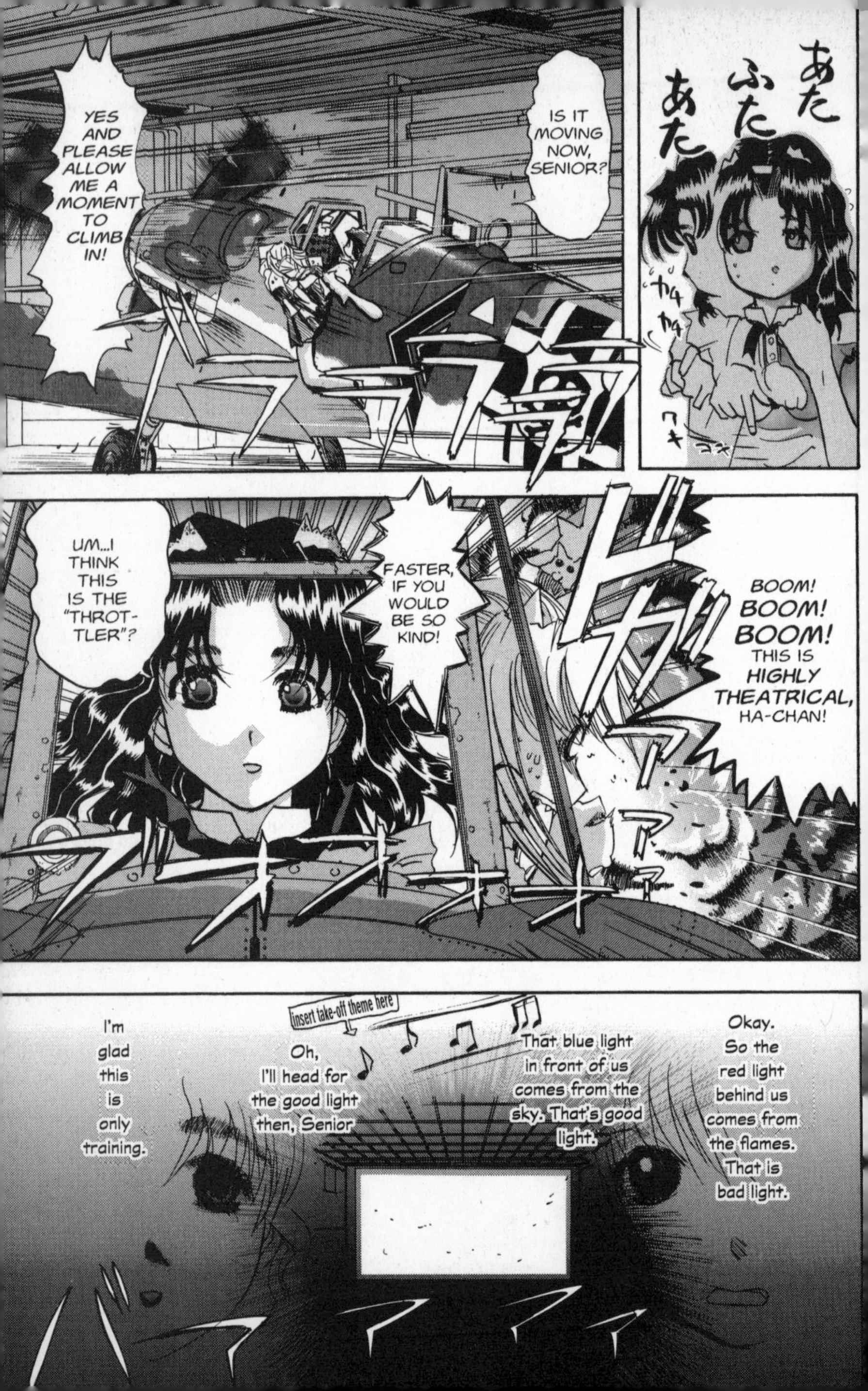
あた ふた あた
IS IT MOVING NOW, SENIOR?
YES AND PLEASE ALLOW ME A MOMENT TO CLIMB IN!
BOOM! BOOM! BOOM! THIS IS HIGHLY THEATRICAL, HA-CHAN!
FASTER, IF YOU WOULD BE SO KIND!
UM...I THINK THIS IS THE "THROT-TLER"?
Okay. So the red light behind us comes from the flames. That is bad light.
That blue light in front of us comes from the sky. That's good light.
insert take-off theme here
Oh, I'll head for the good light then, Senior
I'm glad this is only training.

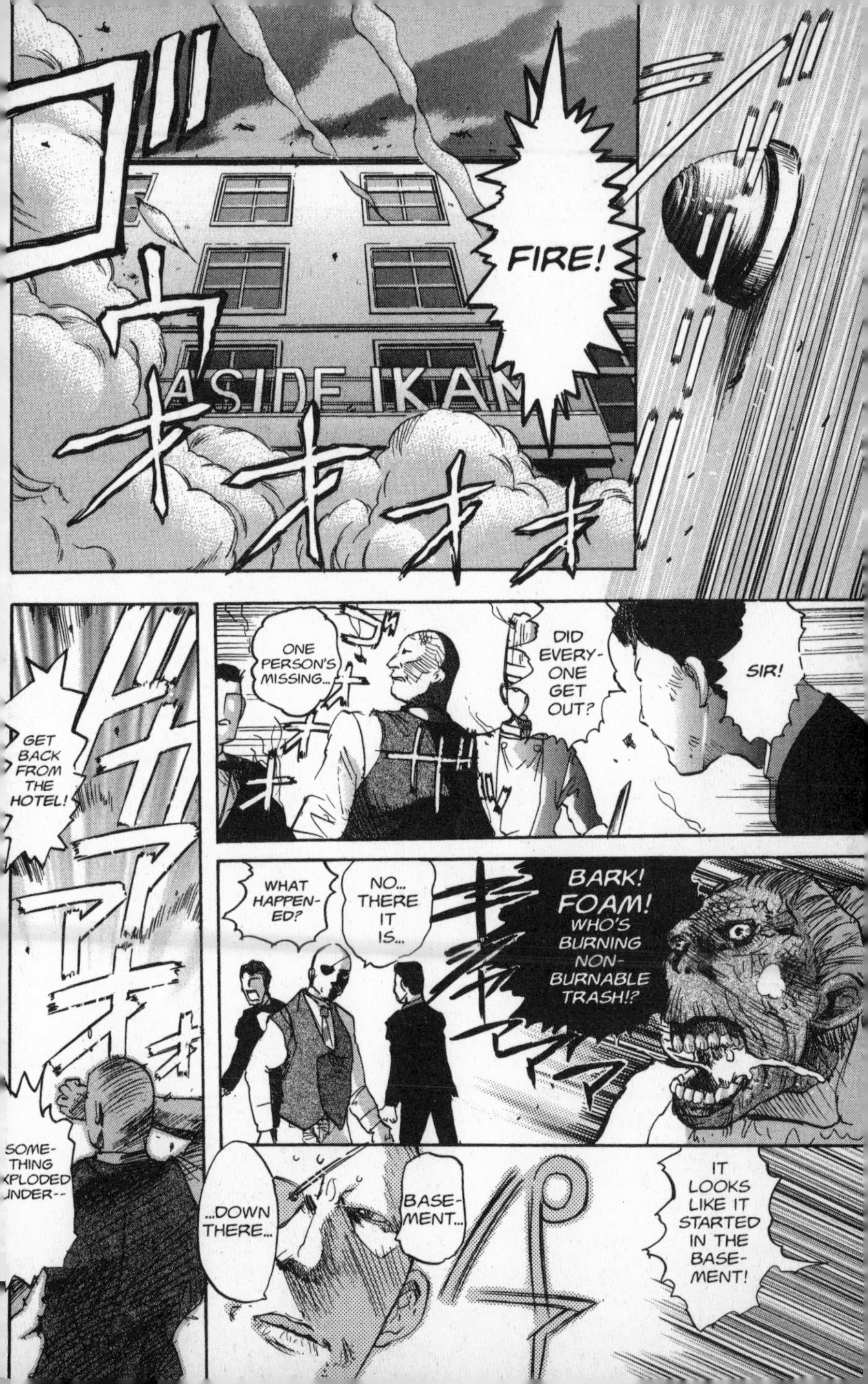
FIRE!
ASIDE IKA
SIR!
DID EVERY-ONE GET OUT?
ONE PERSON'S MISSING...
GET BACK FROM THE HOTEL!
BARK! FOAM! WHO'S BURNING NON-BURNABLE TRASH!?
NO... THERE IT IS...
WHAT HAPPEN-ED?
IT LOOKS LIKE IT STARTED IN THE BASE-MENT!
BASE-MENT...
...DOWN THERE...
SOME-THING XPLODED UNDER--

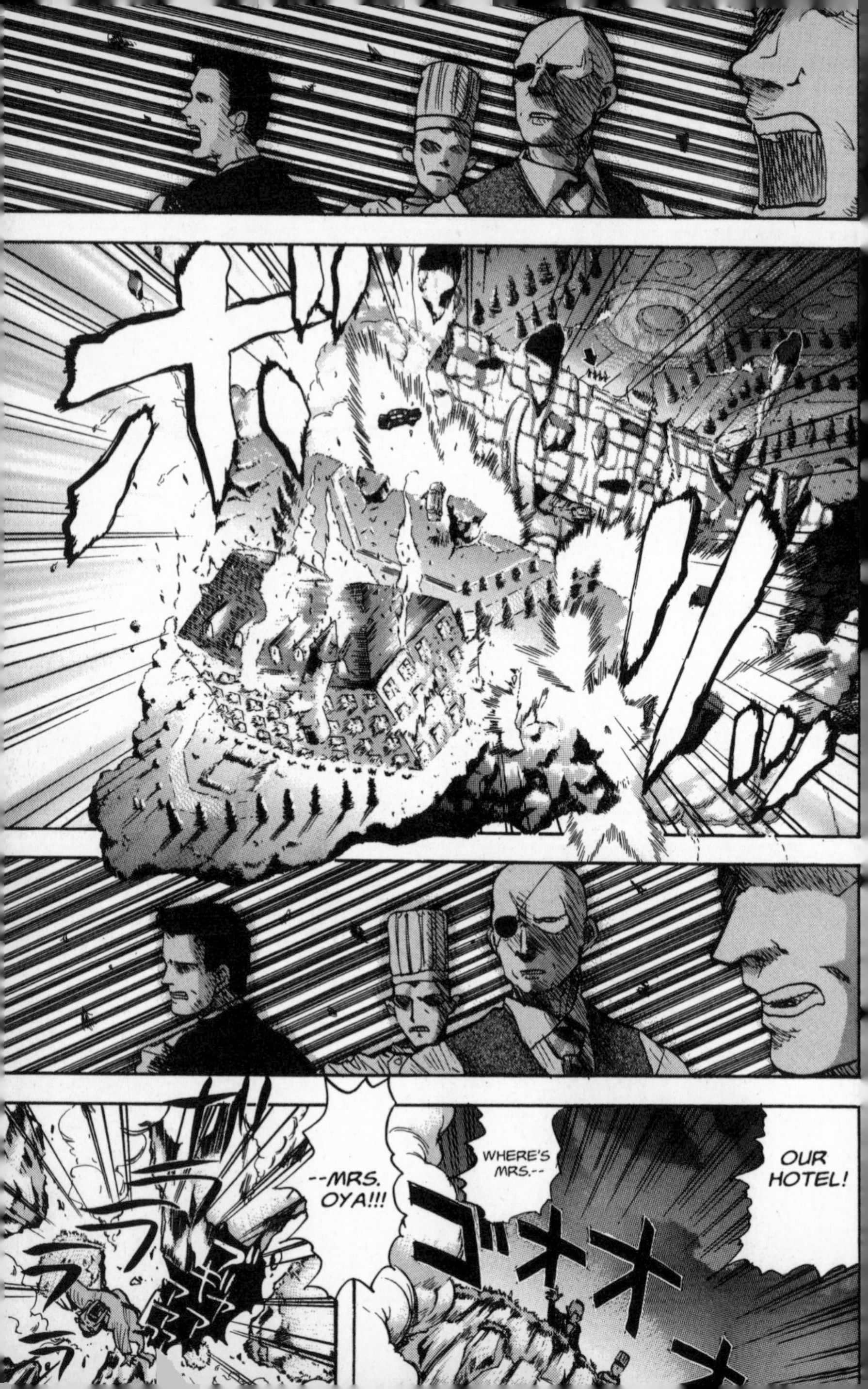
OUR HOTEL!
WHERE'S MRS.--
--MRS. OYA!!!

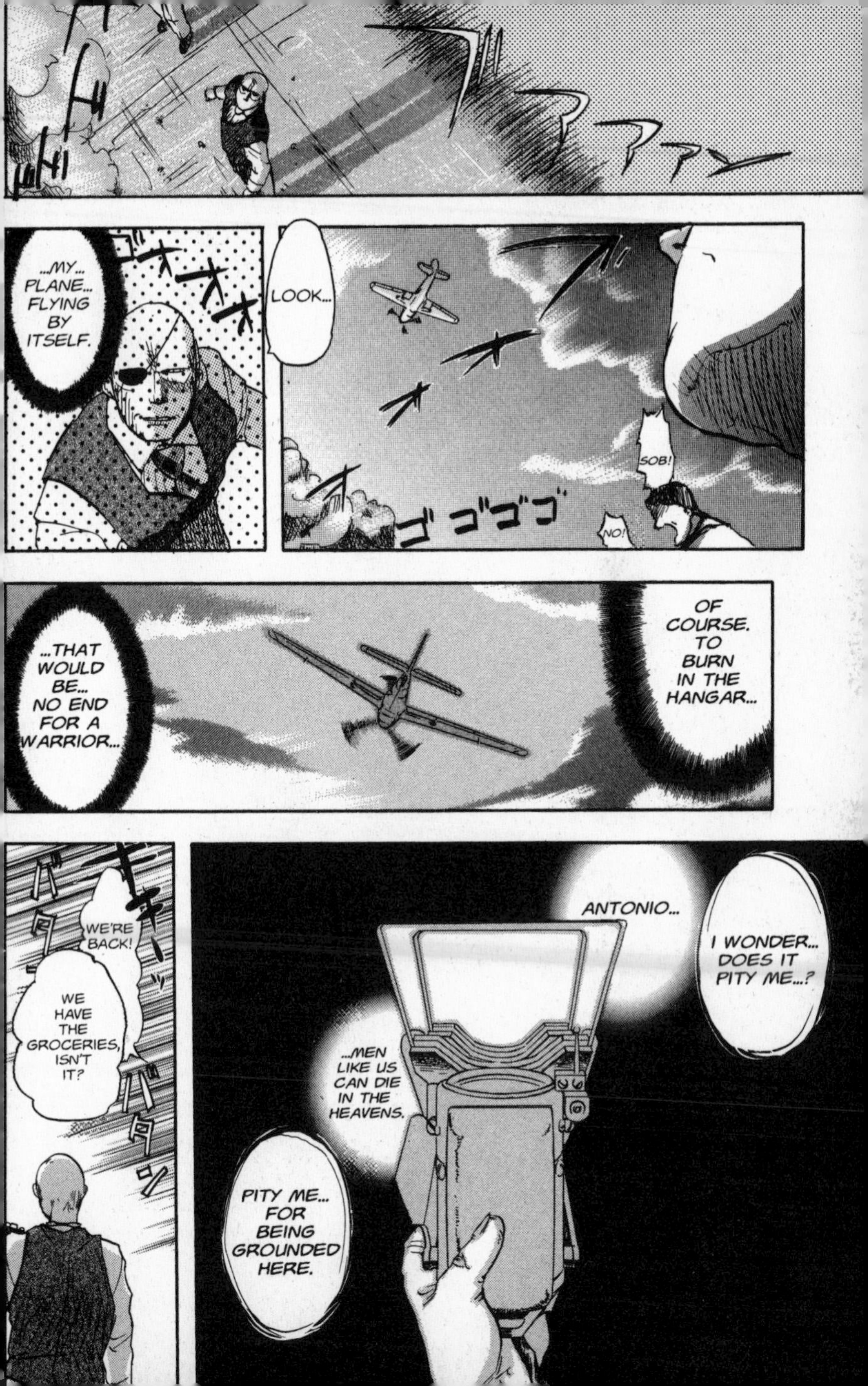
LOOK...
SOB!
NO!
ゴゴゴゴ
...MY... PLANE... FLYING BY ITSELF.
OF COURSE. TO BURN IN THE HANGAR...
...THAT WOULD BE... NO END FOR A WARRIOR...
ANTONIO...
I WONDER... DOES IT PITY ME...?
...MEN LIKE US CAN DIE IN THE HEAVENS.
PITY ME... FOR BEING GROUNDED HERE.
WE'RE BACK!
WE HAVE THE GROCERIES, ISN'T IT?

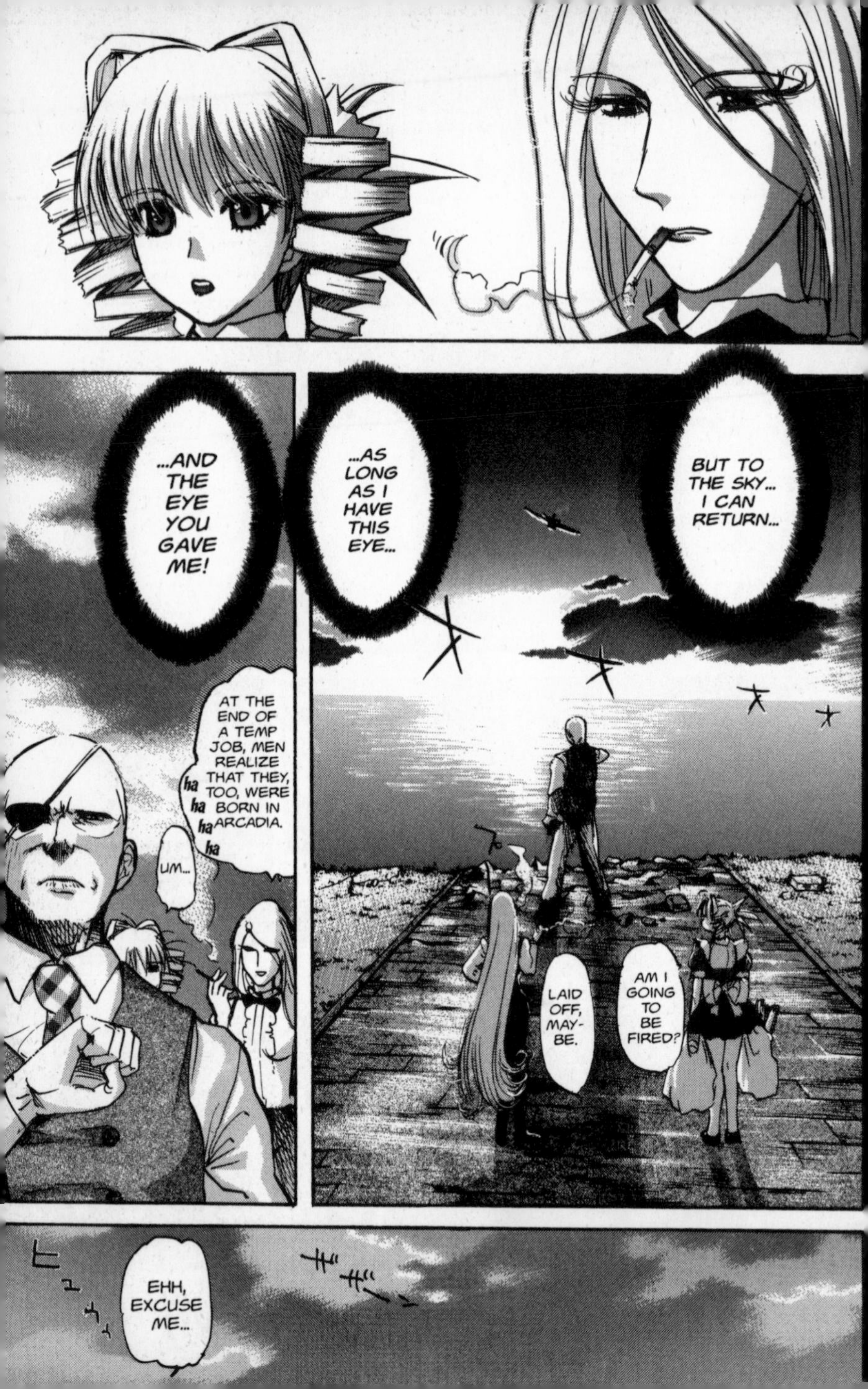
BUT TO THE SKY... I CAN RETURN...
...AS LONG AS I HAVE THIS EYE...
AM I GOING TO BE FIRED?
LAID OFF, MAY-BE.
...AND THE EYE YOU GAVE ME!
AT THE END OF A TEMP JOB, MEN REALIZE THAT THEY, TOO, WERE BORN IN ARCADIA.
ha ha ha ha ha
UM...
EHH, EXCUSE ME...

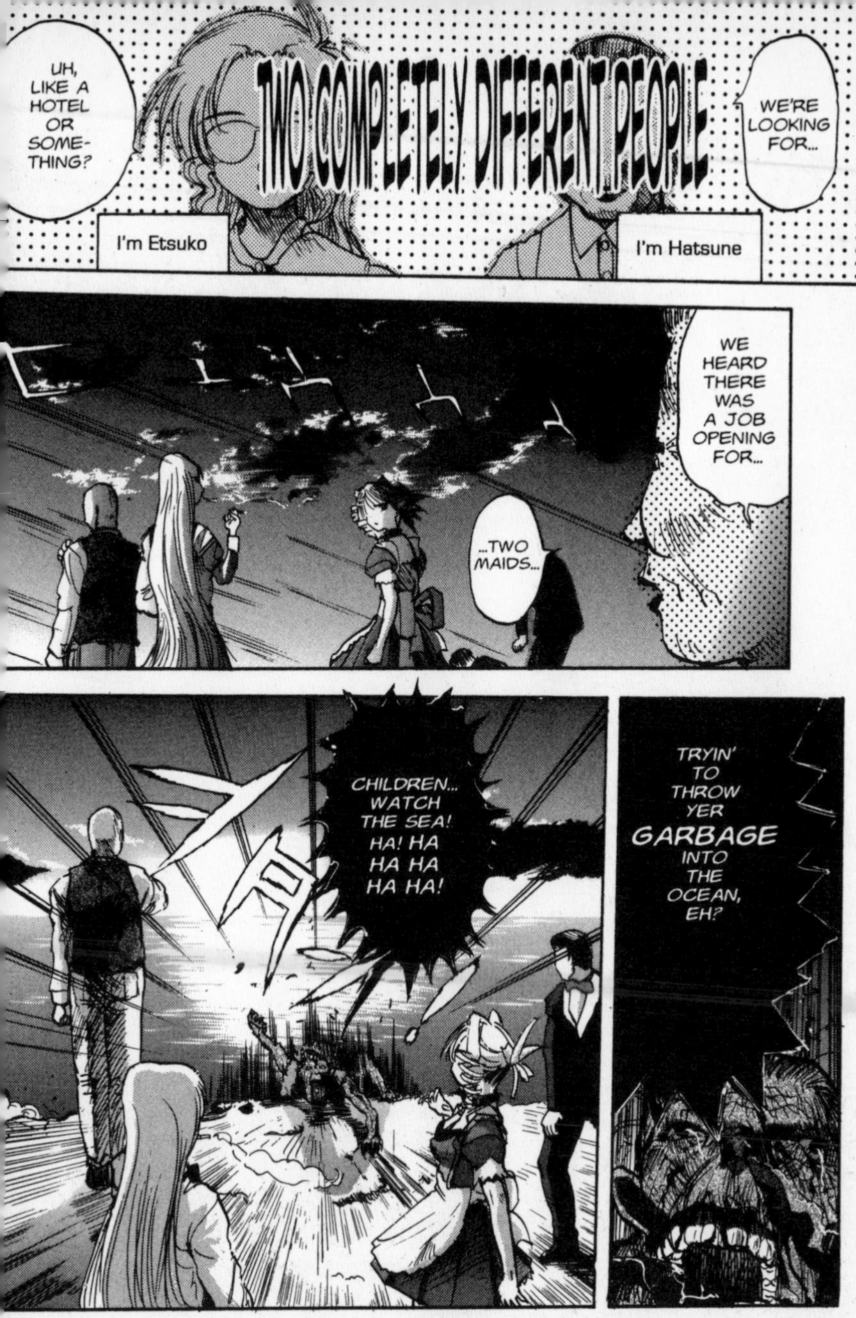
WE'RE LOOKING FOR...
TWO COMPLETELY DIFFERENT PEOPLE
I'm Hatsune
UH, LIKE A HOTEL OR SOME-THING?
I'm Etsuko
WE HEARD THERE WAS A JOB OPENING FOR...
...TWO MAIDS...
TRYIN' TO THROW YER GARBAGE INTO THE OCEAN, EH?
CHILDREN... WATCH THE SEA! HA! HA HA HA HA HA!

END MISSION 7 (It's over, Johnny!)

EXCEL SAGA

Everything she owned was in the hotel
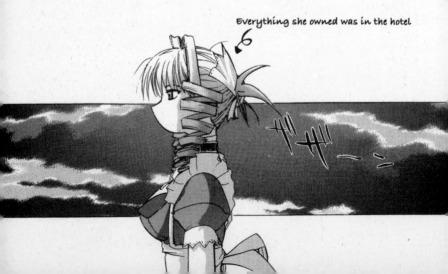

EXCEL SAGA

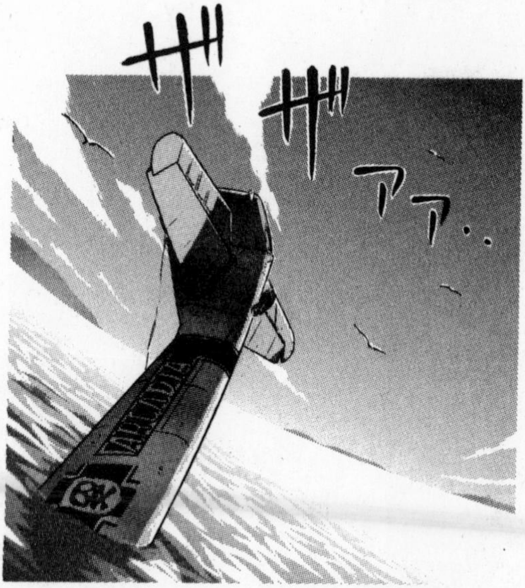
ザ
ザ
アア‥

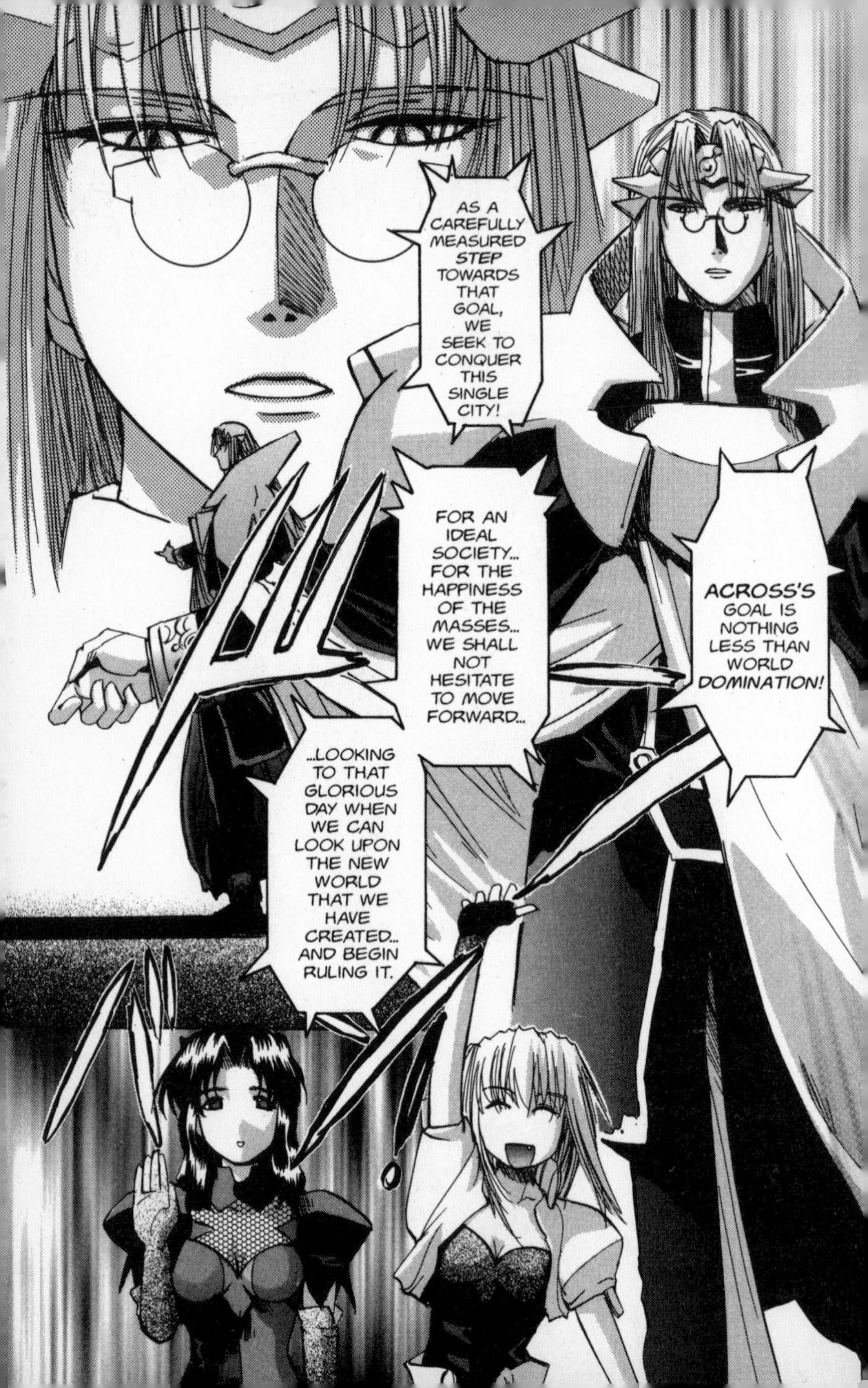
ACROSS'S GOAL IS NOTHING LESS THAN WORLD DOMINATION!
AS A CAREFULLY MEASURED STEP TOWARDS THAT GOAL, WE SEEK TO CONQUER THIS SINGLE CITY!
FOR AN IDEAL SOCIETY... FOR THE HAPPINESS OF THE MASSES... WE SHALL NOT HESITATE TO MOVE FORWARD...
...LOOKING TO THAT GLORIOUS DAY WHEN WE CAN LOOK UPON THE NEW WORLD THAT WE HAVE CREATED... AND BEGIN RULING IT.

MISSION 8
WHEN JAA, NE COMES MARCHING HOME

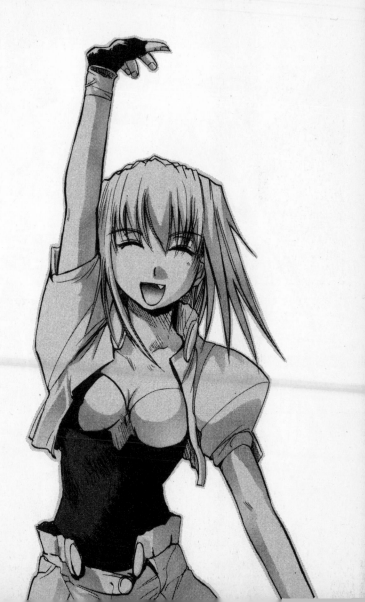

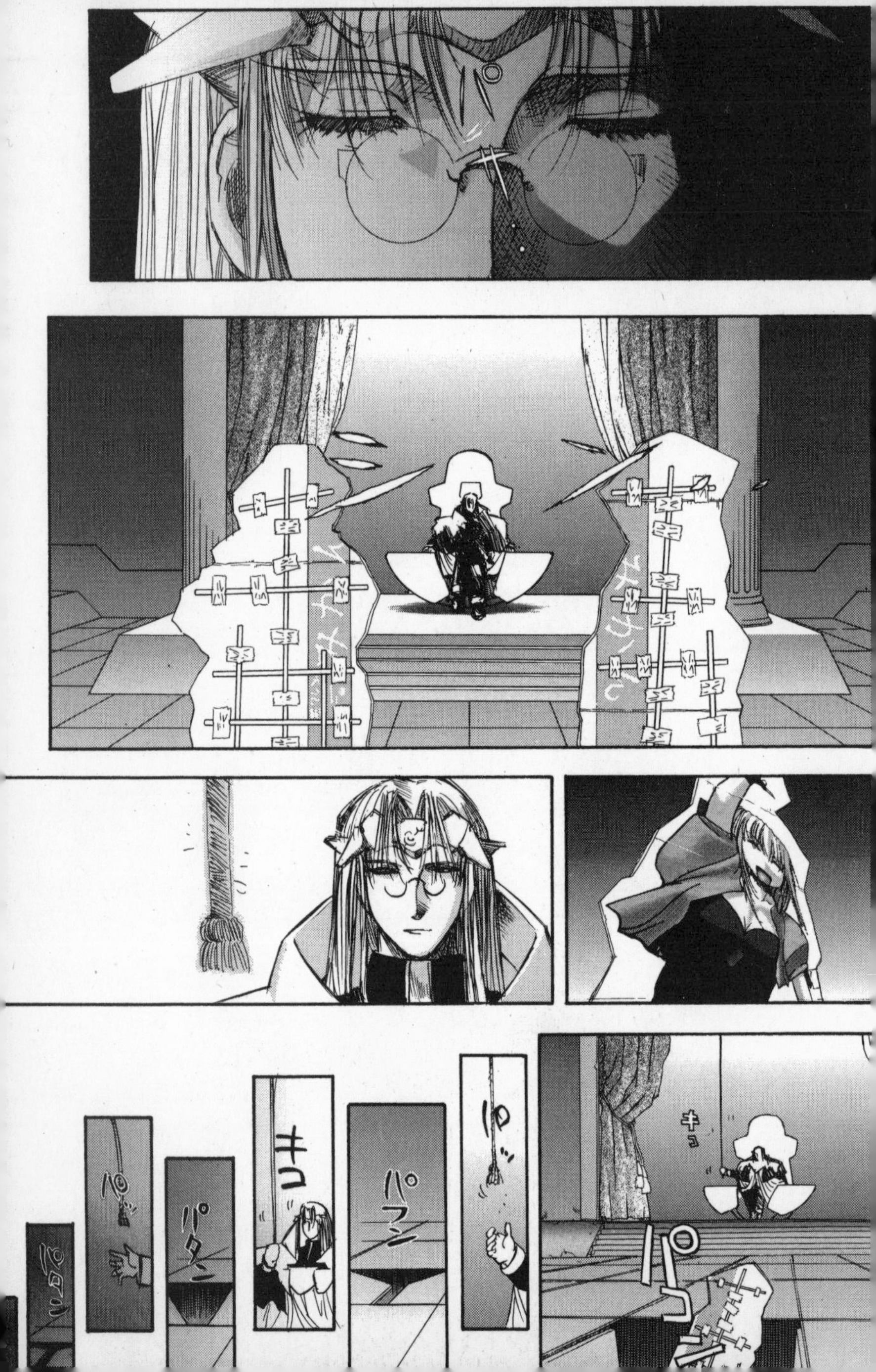
キュ
パコ
パフン
キュ
パタン

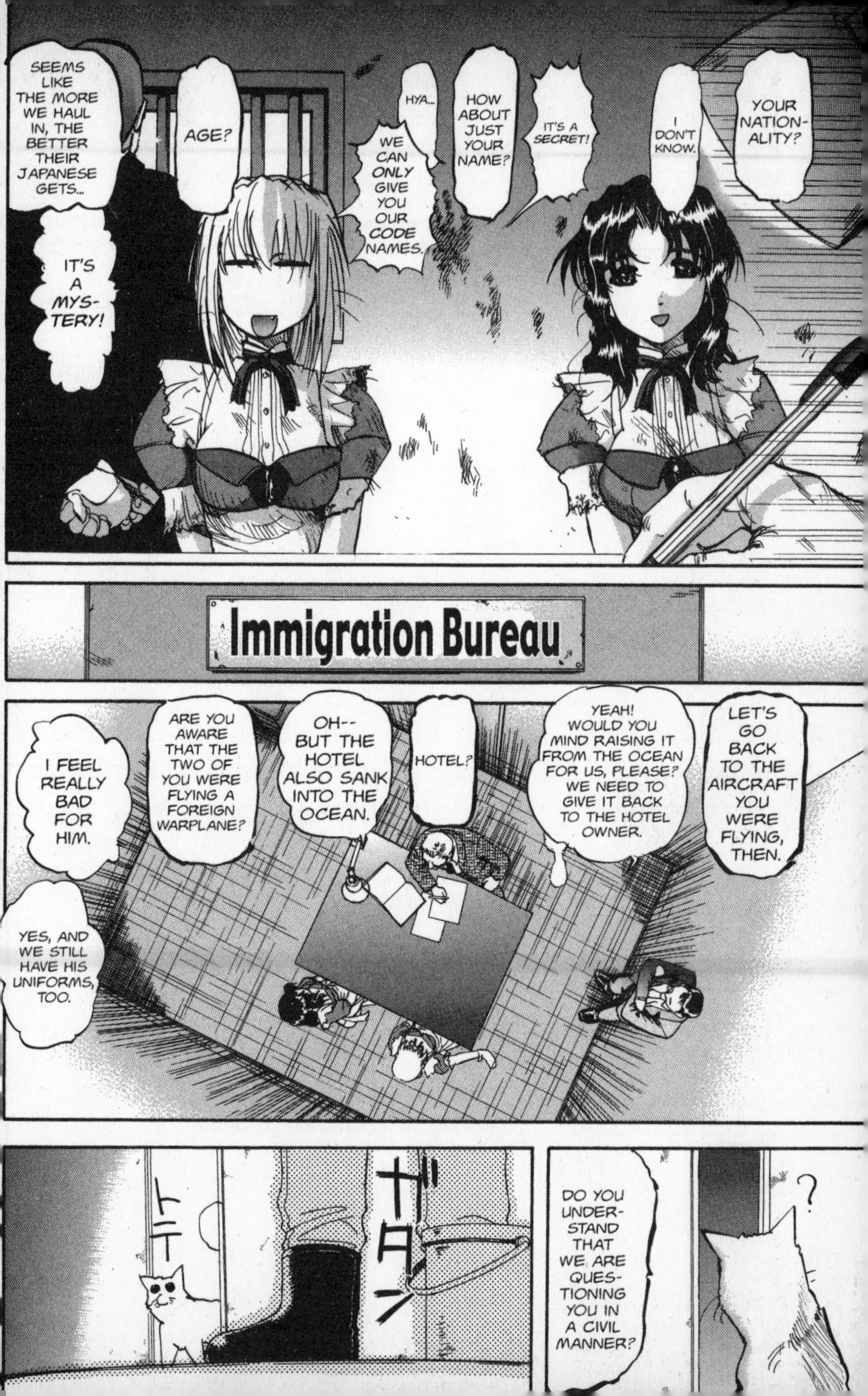
YOUR NATIONALITY?
I DON'T KNOW.
IT'S A SECRET!
HOW ABOUT JUST YOUR NAME?
HYA...
WE CAN ONLY GIVE YOU OUR CODE NAMES.
AGE?
IT'S A MYSTERY!
SEEMS LIKE THE MORE WE HAUL IN, THE BETTER THEIR JAPANESE GETS...
Immigration Bureau
LET'S GO BACK TO THE AIRCRAFT YOU WERE FLYING, THEN.
YEAH! WOULD YOU MIND RAISING IT FROM THE OCEAN FOR US, PLEASE? WE NEED TO GIVE IT BACK TO THE HOTEL OWNER.
HOTEL?
OH-- BUT THE HOTEL ALSO SANK INTO THE OCEAN.
ARE YOU AWARE THAT THE TWO OF YOU WERE FLYING A FOREIGN WARPLANE?
I FEEL REALLY BAD FOR HIM.
YES, AND WE STILL HAVE HIS UNIFORMS, TOO.
DO YOU UNDERSTAND THAT WE ARE QUESTIONING YOU IN A CIVIL MANNER?
?
ガタン
トテ

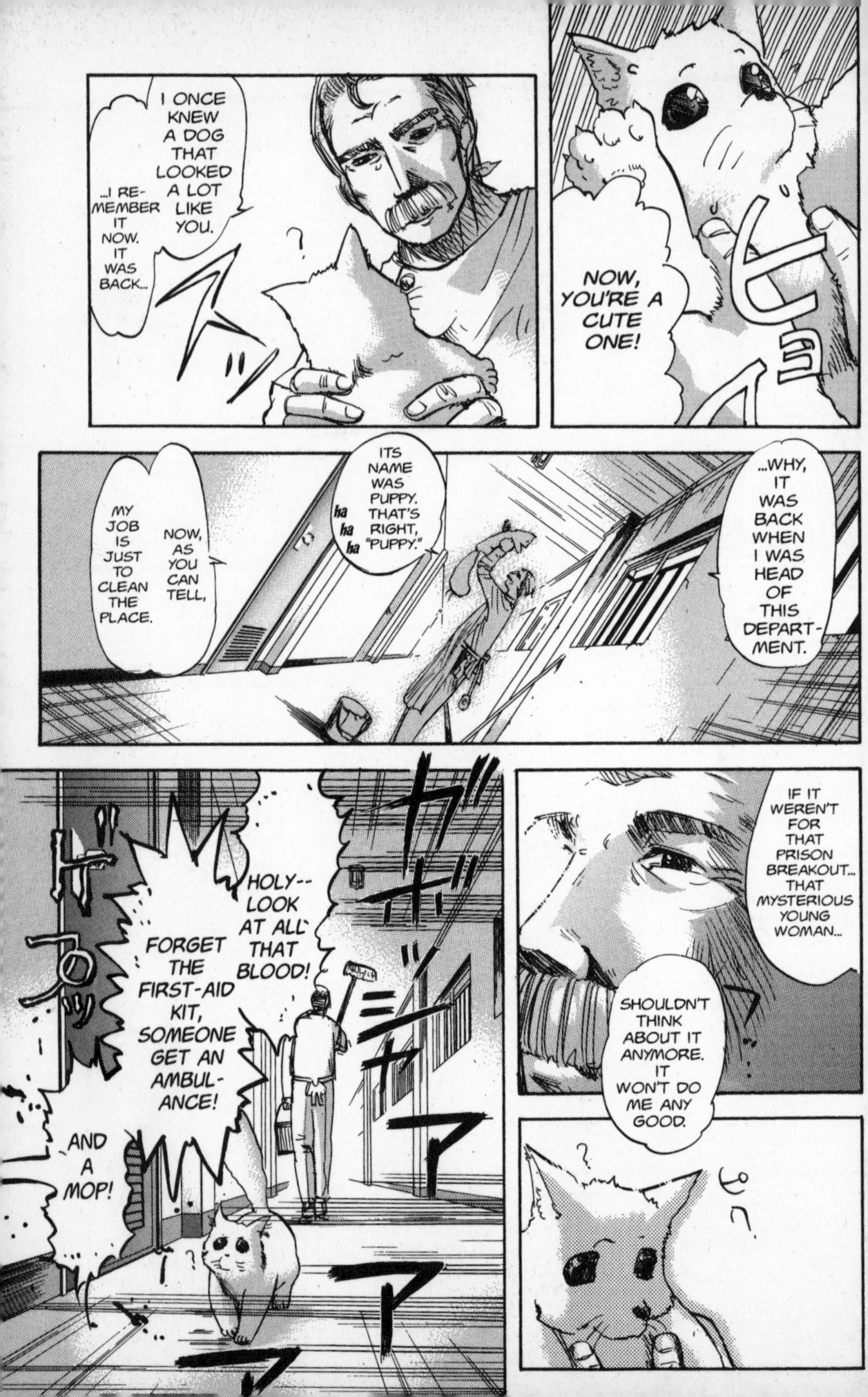
NOW, YOU'RE A CUTE ONE!
I ONCE KNEW A DOG THAT LOOKED A LOT LIKE YOU.
...I RE-MEMBER IT NOW. IT WAS BACK...
...WHY, IT WAS BACK WHEN I WAS HEAD OF THIS DEPART-MENT.
ITS NAME WAS PUPPY. THAT'S RIGHT, "PUPPY."
ha ha ha
NOW, AS YOU CAN TELL,
MY JOB IS JUST TO CLEAN THE PLACE.
IF IT WEREN'T FOR THAT PRISON BREAKOUT... THAT MYSTERIOUS YOUNG WOMAN...
SHOULDN'T THINK ABOUT IT ANYMORE. IT WON'T DO ME ANY GOOD.
HOLY-- LOOK AT ALL THAT BLOOD!
FORGET THE FIRST-AID KIT, SOMEONE GET AN AMBUL-ANCE!
AND A MOP!

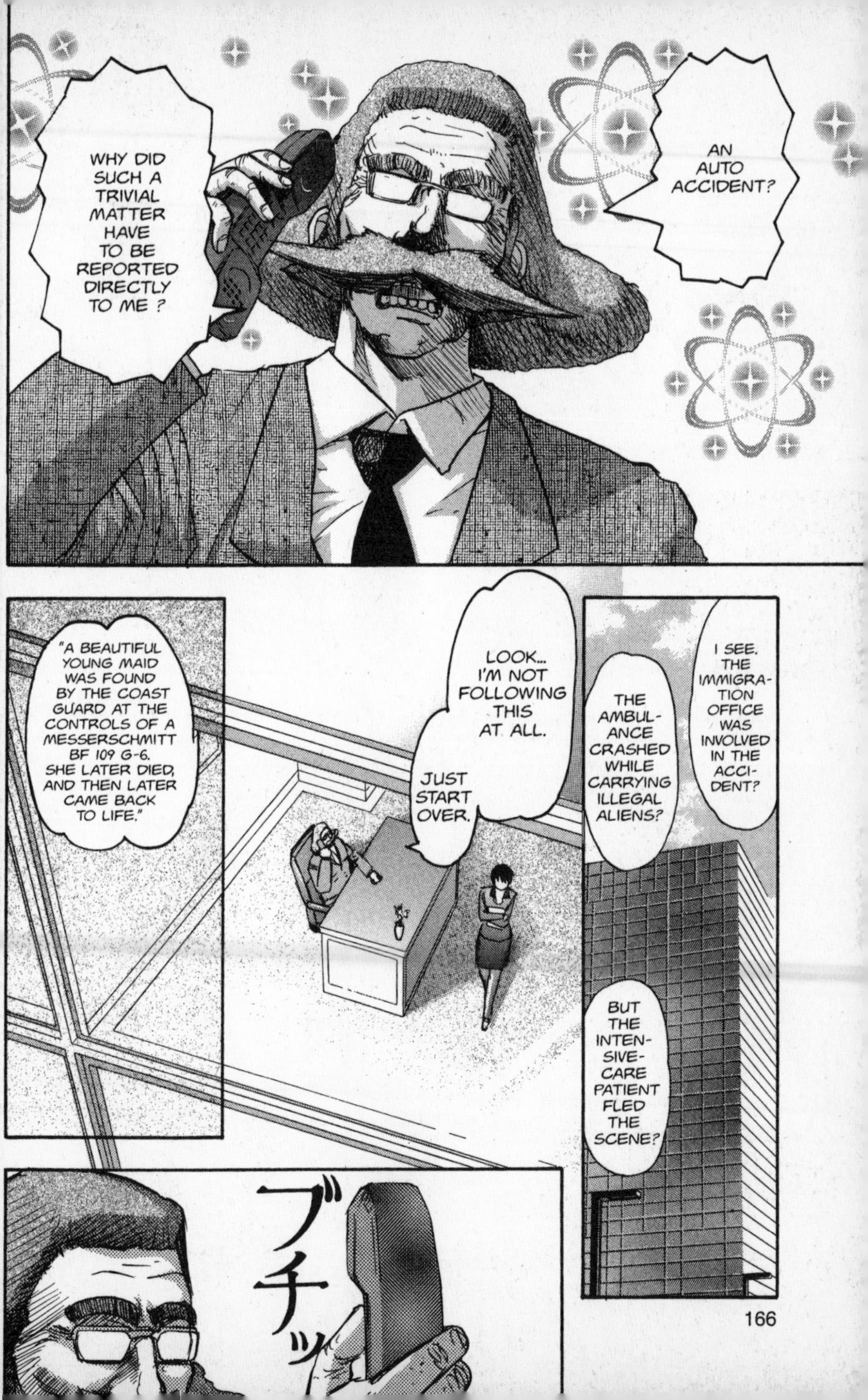
AN AUTO ACCIDENT?
WHY DID SUCH A TRIVIAL MATTER HAVE TO BE REPORTED DIRECTLY TO ME ?
I SEE. THE IMMIGRATION OFFICE WAS INVOLVED IN THE ACCIDENT?
THE AMBULANCE CRASHED WHILE CARRYING ILLEGAL ALIENS?
BUT THE INTENSIVE-CARE PATIENT FLED THE SCENE?
LOOK... I'M NOT FOLLOWING THIS AT ALL.
JUST START OVER.
"A BEAUTIFUL YOUNG MAID WAS FOUND BY THE COAST GUARD AT THE CONTROLS OF A MESSERSCHMITT BF 109 G-6. SHE LATER DIED, AND THEN LATER CAME BACK TO LIFE."
ブチッ

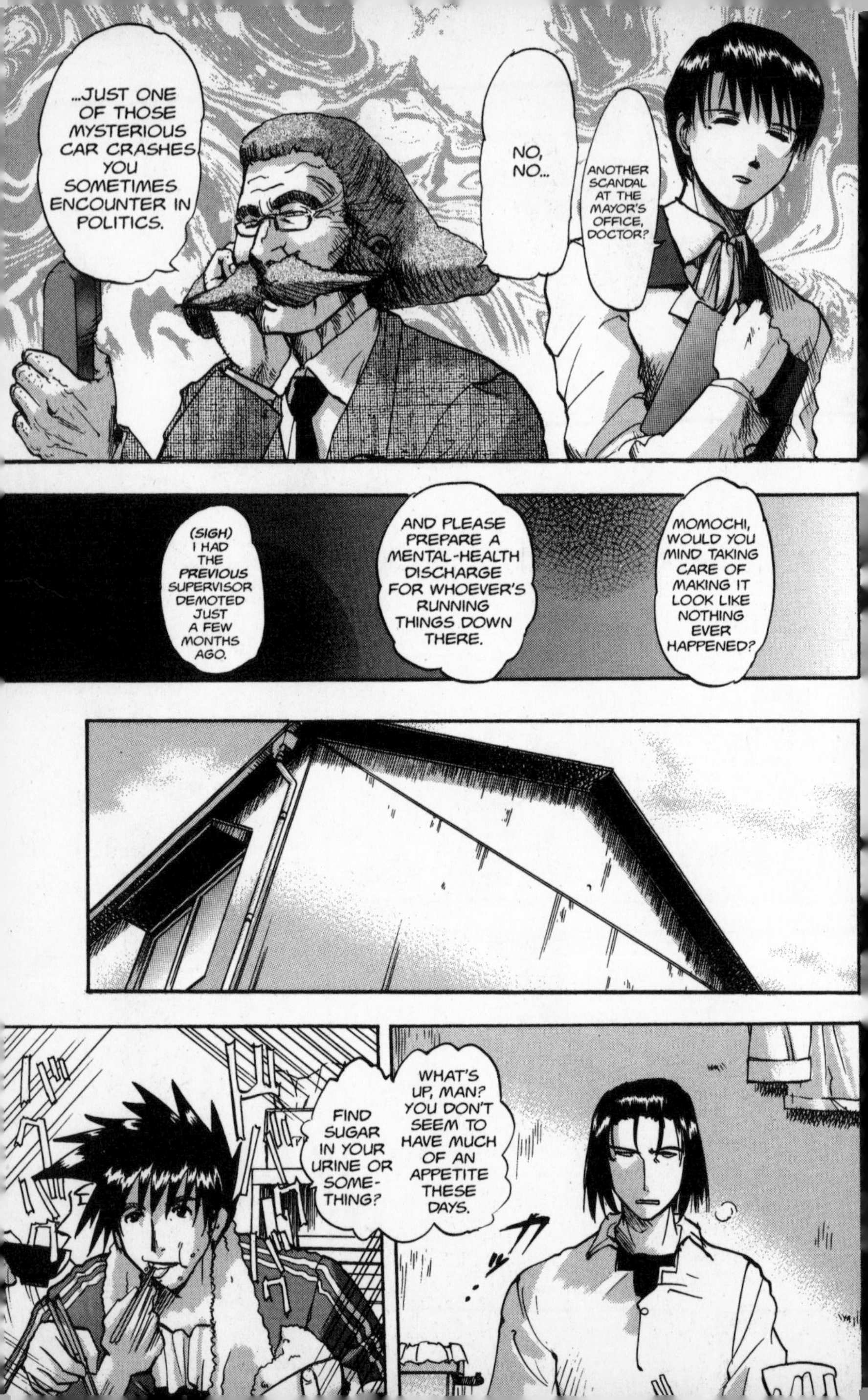
ANOTHER SCANDAL AT THE MAYOR'S OFFICE, DOCTOR?
NO, NO...
...JUST ONE OF THOSE MYSTERIOUS CAR CRASHES YOU SOMETIMES ENCOUNTER IN POLITICS.
MOMOCHI, WOULD YOU MIND TAKING CARE OF MAKING IT LOOK LIKE NOTHING EVER HAPPENED?
AND PLEASE PREPARE A MENTAL-HEALTH DISCHARGE FOR WHOEVER'S RUNNING THINGS DOWN THERE.
(SIGH) I HAD THE *PREVIOUS* SUPERVISOR DEMOTED JUST A FEW MONTHS AGO.
WHAT'S UP, MAN? YOU DON'T SEEM TO HAVE MUCH OF AN APPETITE THESE DAYS.
FIND SUGAR IN YOUR URINE OR SOME-THING?

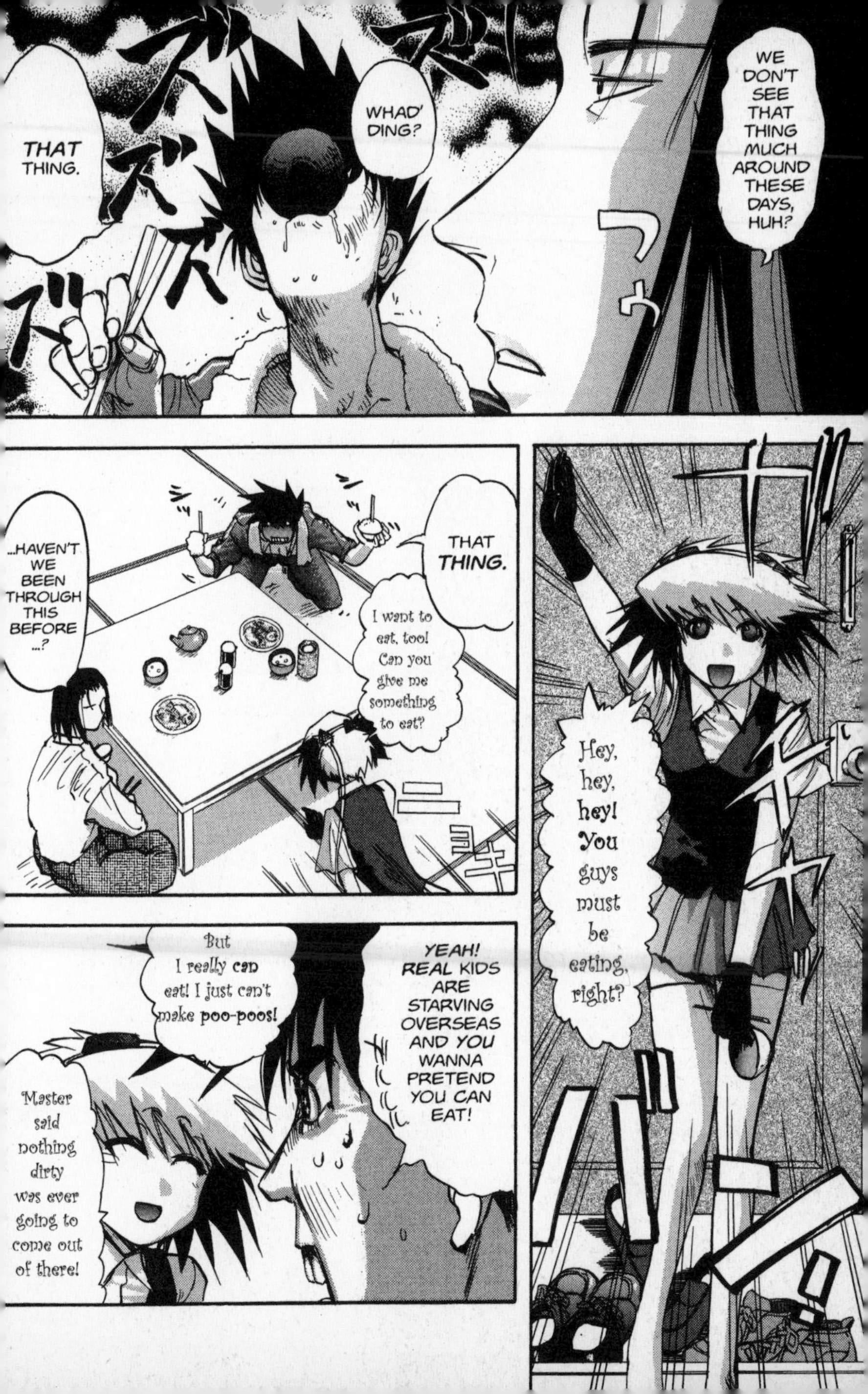
WE DON'T SEE THAT THING MUCH AROUND THESE DAYS, HUH?
WHAD' DING?
THAT THING.
Hey, hey, hey! You guys must be eating, right?
THAT THING.
I want to eat, too! Can you give me something to eat?
...HAVEN'T WE BEEN THROUGH THIS BEFORE ...?
YEAH! REAL KIDS ARE STARVING OVERSEAS AND YOU WANNA PRETEND YOU CAN EAT!
But I really can eat! I just can't make poo-poos!
Master said nothing dirty was ever going to come out of there!

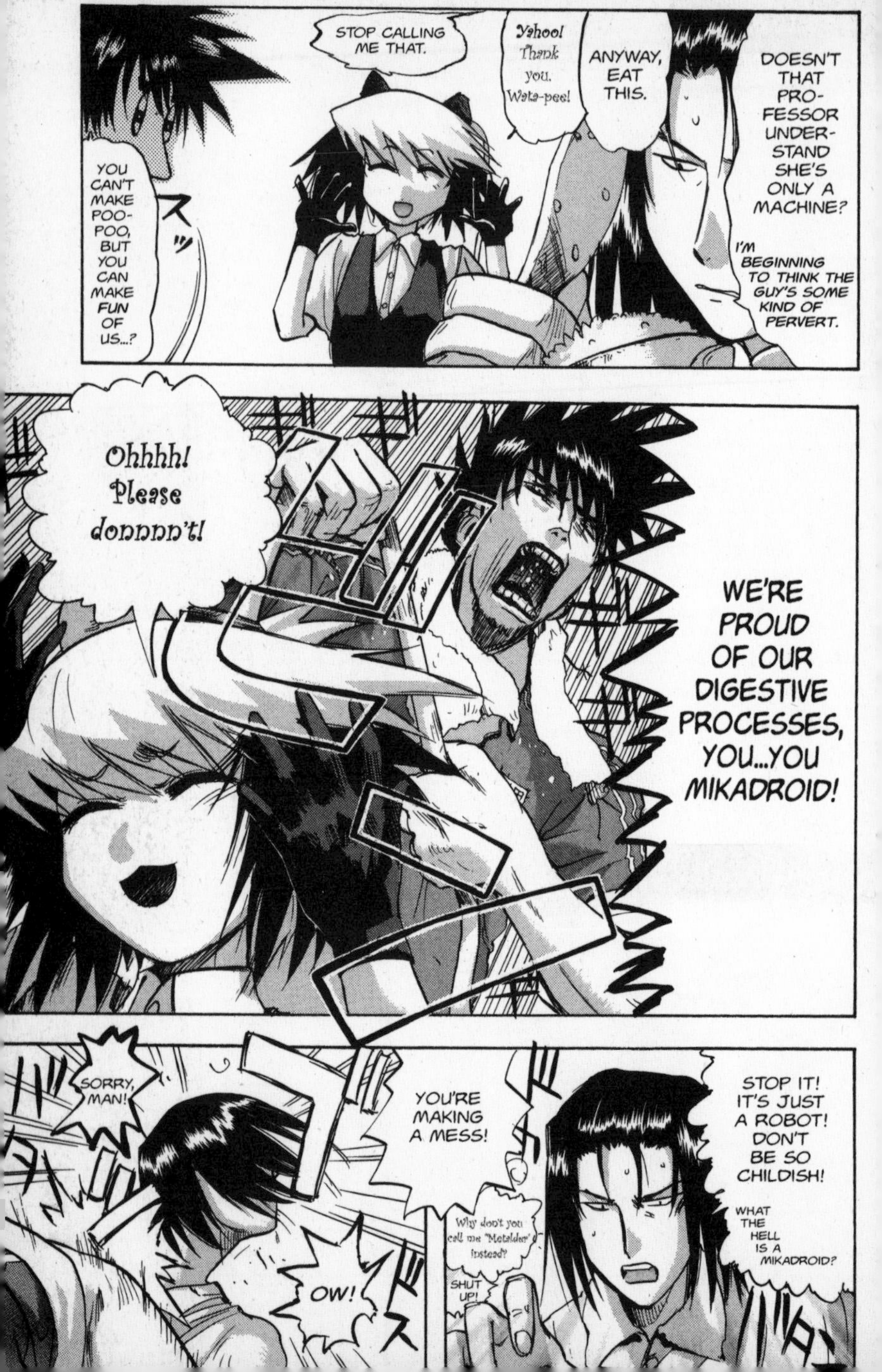
DOESN'T THAT PROFESSOR UNDERSTAND SHE'S ONLY A MACHINE?
I'M BEGINNING TO THINK THE GUY'S SOME KIND OF PERVERT.
ANYWAY, EAT THIS.
Yahoo! Thank you. Wata-pee!
STOP CALLING ME THAT.
YOU CAN'T MAKE POO-POO, BUT YOU CAN MAKE FUN OF US...?
WE'RE PROUD OF OUR DIGESTIVE PROCESSES, YOU...YOU MIKADROID!
Ohhhh! Please donnnn't!
STOP IT! IT'S JUST A ROBOT! DON'T BE SO CHILDISH!
WHAT THE HELL IS A MIKADROID?
Why don't you call me "Metalder" instead?
SHUT UP!
YOU'RE MAKING A MESS!
SORRY, MAN!
OW!

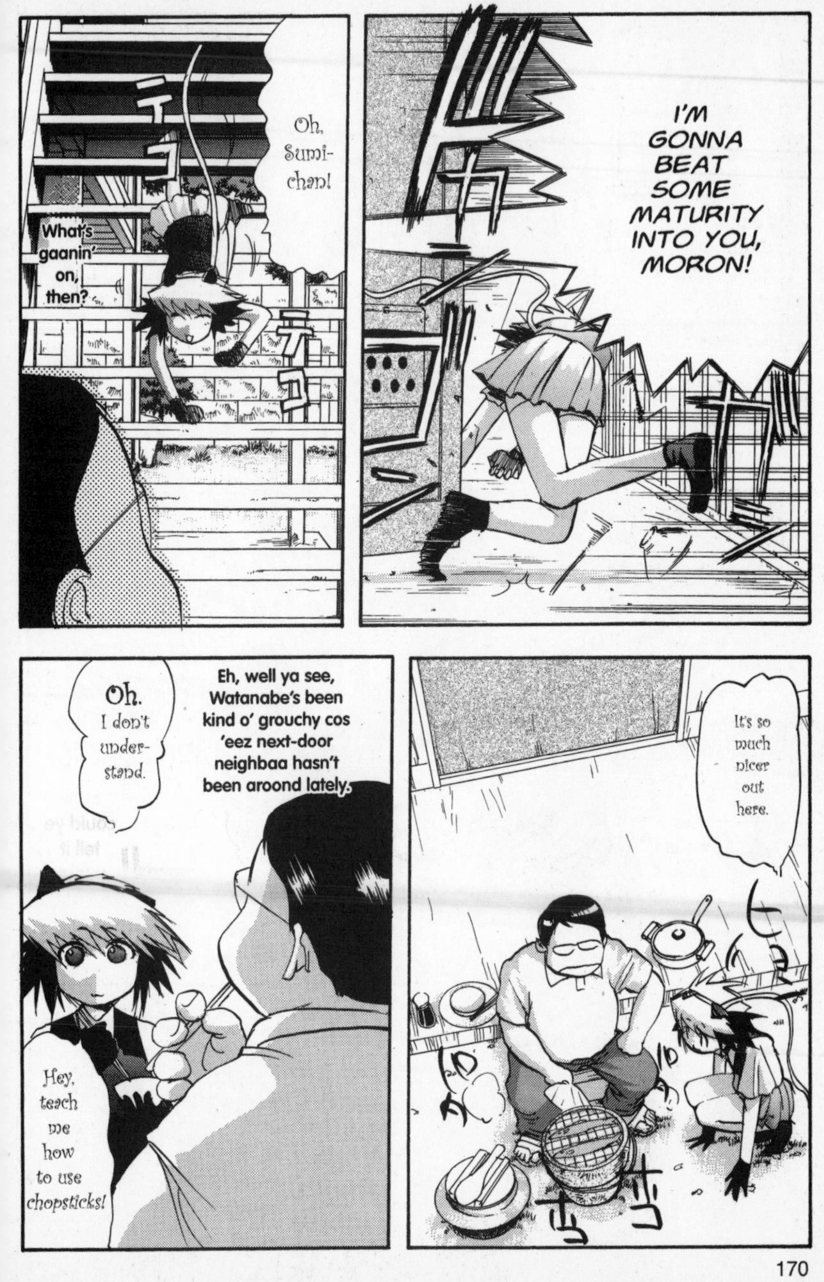
I'M GONNA BEAT SOME MATURITY INTO YOU, MORON!
Oh, Sumi-chan!
What's gaanin' on, then?
It's so much nicer out here.
Eh, well ya see, Watanabe's been kind o' grouchy cos 'eez next-door neighbaa hasn't been aroond lately.
Oh. I don't understand.
Hey, teach me how to use chopsticks!

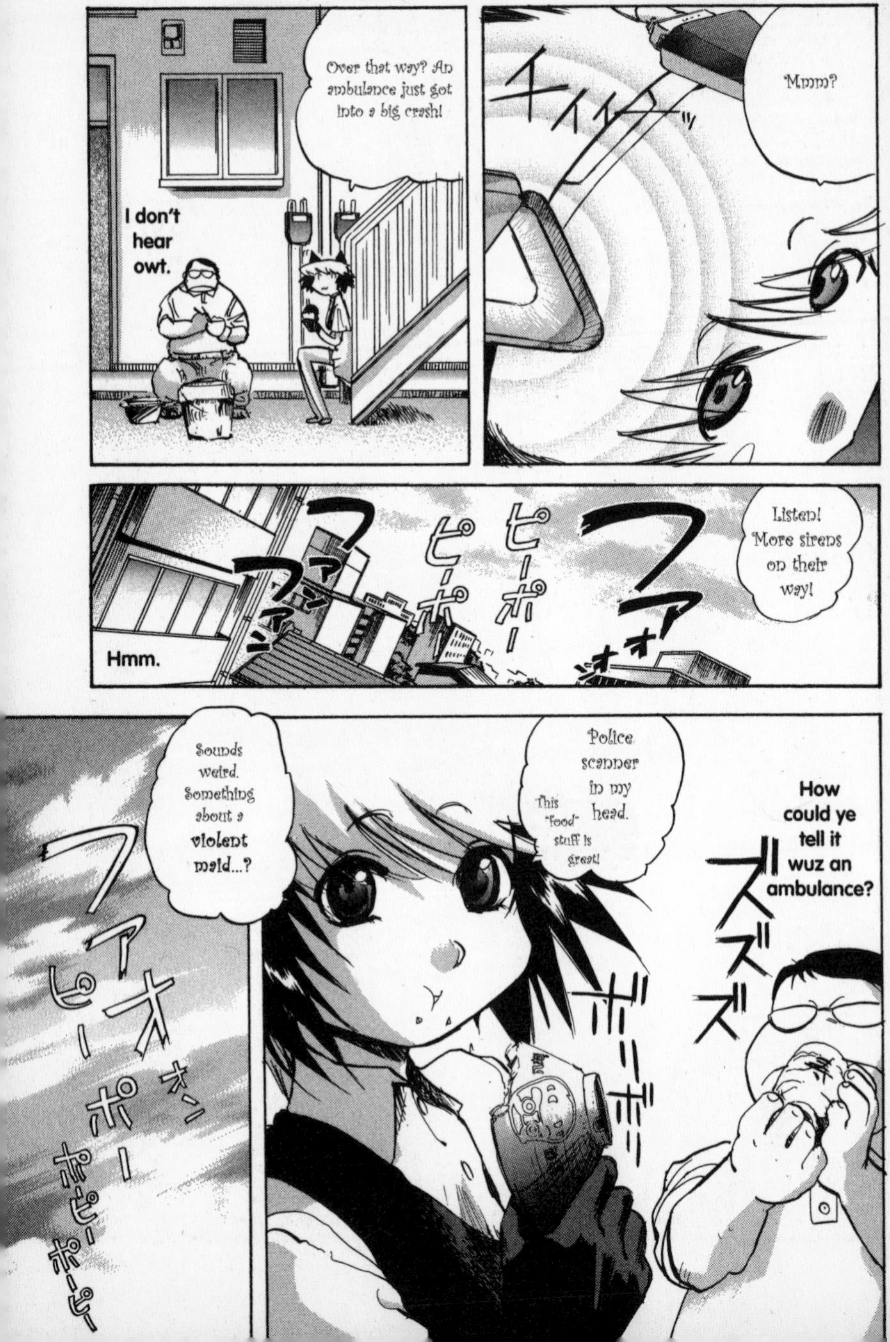
Mmm?
Over that way? An ambulance just got into a big crash!
I don't hear owt.
Listen! More sirens on their way!
ピーポーピーポ
ファンファン
Hmm.
How could ye tell it wuz an ambulance?
ズズズ
ボリボリ
Police scanner in my head.
This "food" stuff is great!
Sounds weird. Something about a violent maid...?
ファオーン
ピーポーポピーポーピー

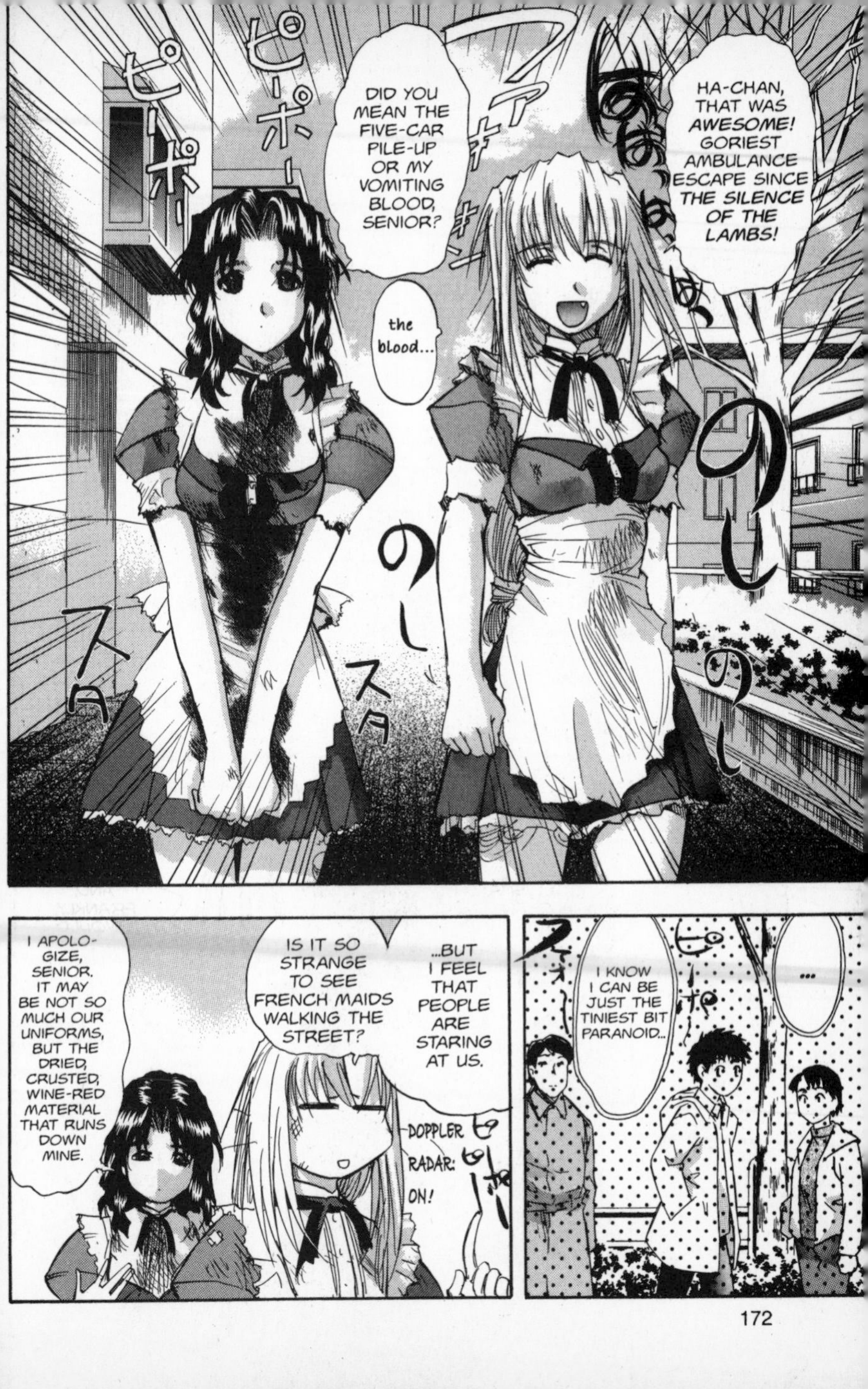
HA-CHAN, THAT WAS AWESOME! GORIEST AMBULANCE ESCAPE SINCE THE SILENCE OF THE LAMBS!
DID YOU MEAN THE FIVE-CAR PILE-UP OR MY VOMITING BLOOD, SENIOR?
the blood...
のしのし
のし
I KNOW I CAN BE JUST THE TINIEST BIT PARANOID...
...
...BUT I FEEL THAT PEOPLE ARE STARING AT US.
IS IT SO STRANGE TO SEE FRENCH MAIDS WALKING THE STREET?
DOPPLER RADAR: ON!
I APOLOGIZE, SENIOR. IT MAY BE NOT SO MUCH OUR UNIFORMS, BUT THE DRIED, CRUSTED, WINE-RED MATERIAL THAT RUNS DOWN MINE.

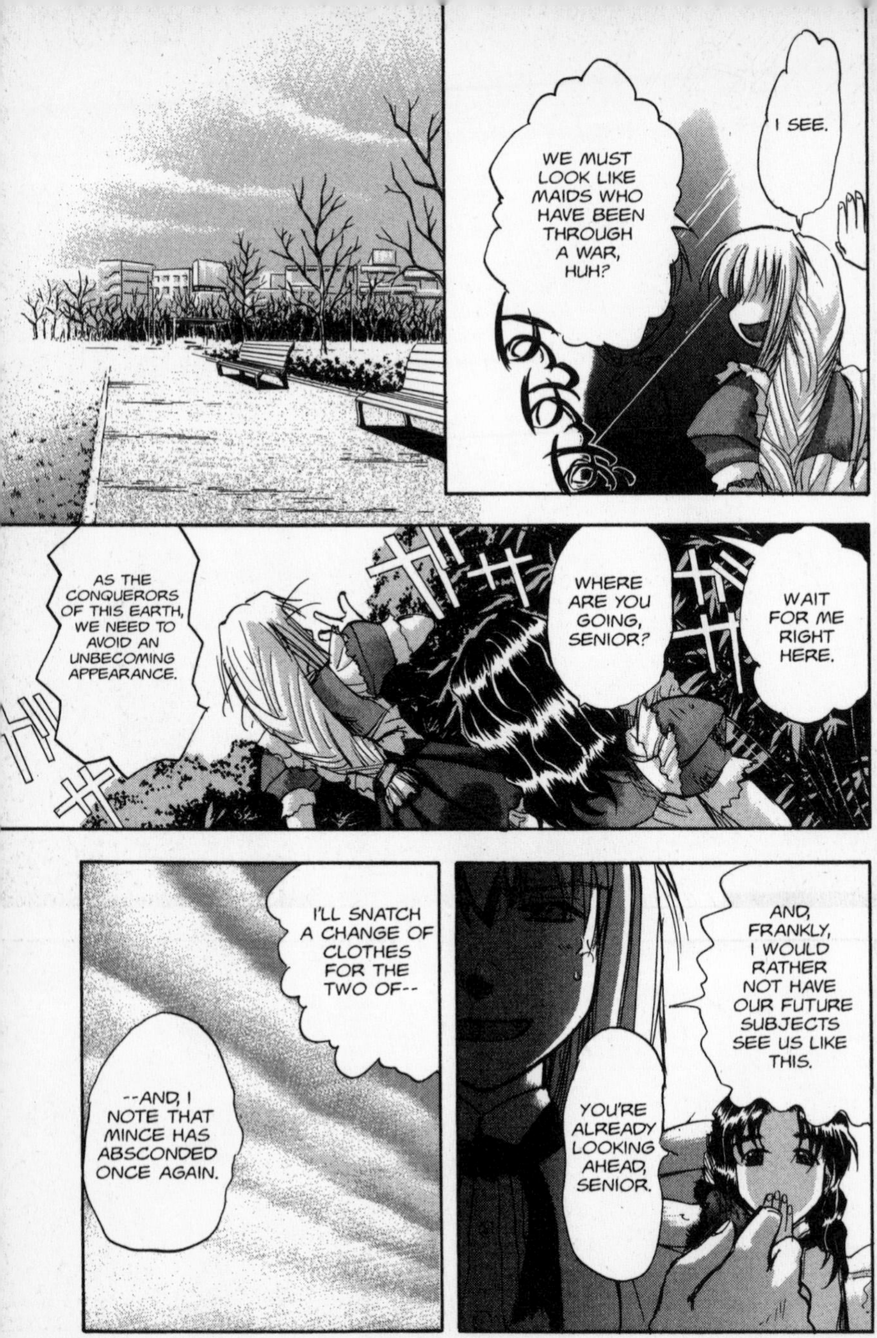
I SEE.
WE MUST LOOK LIKE MAIDS WHO HAVE BEEN THROUGH A WAR, HUH?
WAIT FOR ME RIGHT HERE.
WHERE ARE YOU GOING, SENIOR?
AS THE CONQUERORS OF THIS EARTH, WE NEED TO AVOID AN UNBECOMING APPEARANCE.
AND, FRANKLY, I WOULD RATHER NOT HAVE OUR FUTURE SUBJECTS SEE US LIKE THIS.
YOU'RE ALREADY LOOKING AHEAD, SENIOR.
I'LL SNATCH A CHANGE OF CLOTHES FOR THE TWO OF--
--AND, I NOTE THAT MINCE HAS ABSCONDED ONCE AGAIN.

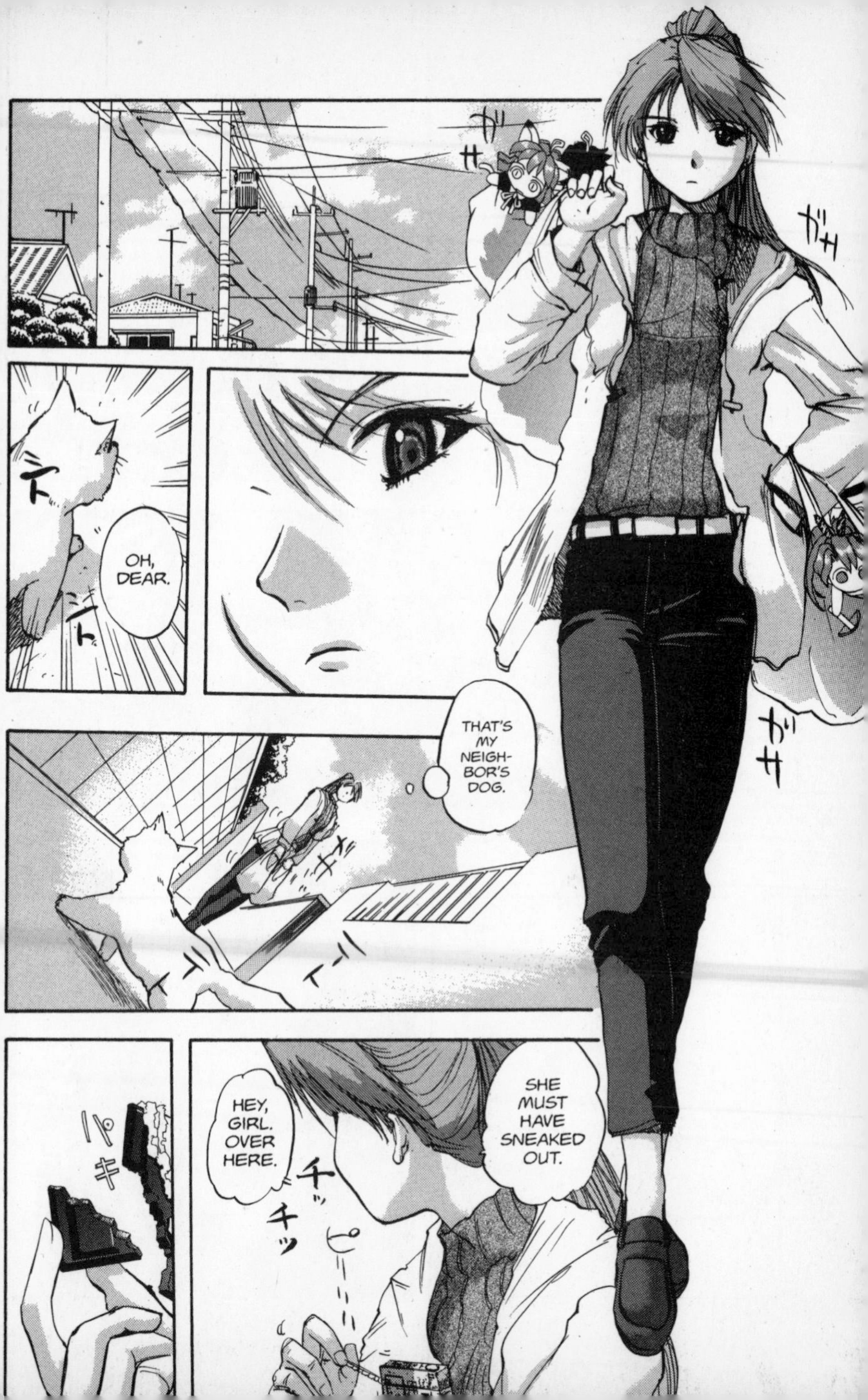
ガサ
ガサ
ガサ
THAT'S MY NEIGHBOR'S DOG.
SHE MUST HAVE SNEAKED OUT.
OH, DEAR.
HEY, GIRL. OVER HERE.
チッ
チッ
ピー
パキ

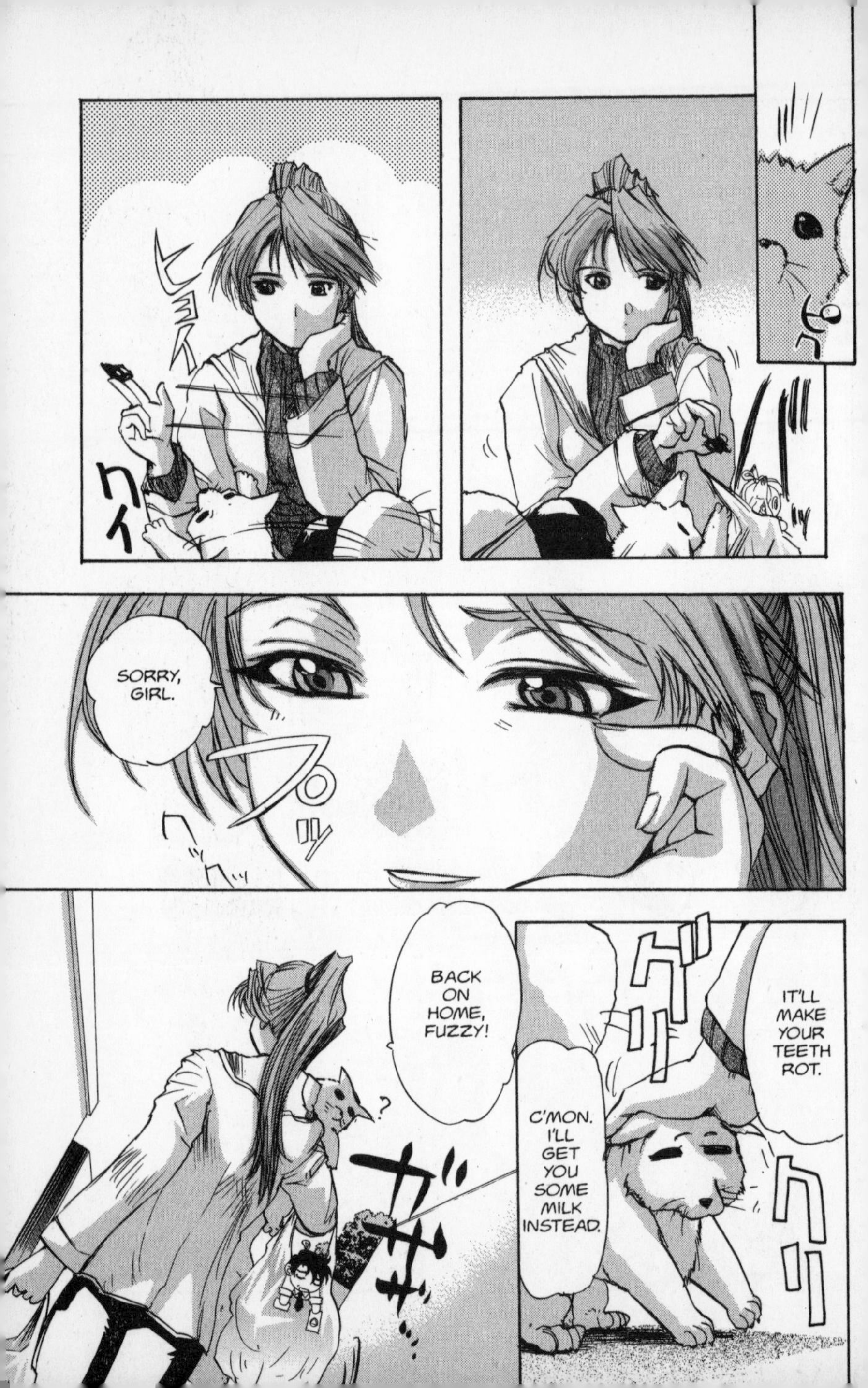
ヒョイ
クイ
SORRY, GIRL.
IT'LL MAKE YOUR TEETH ROT.
C'MON. I'LL GET YOU SOME MILK INSTEAD.
BACK ON HOME, FUZZY!
?

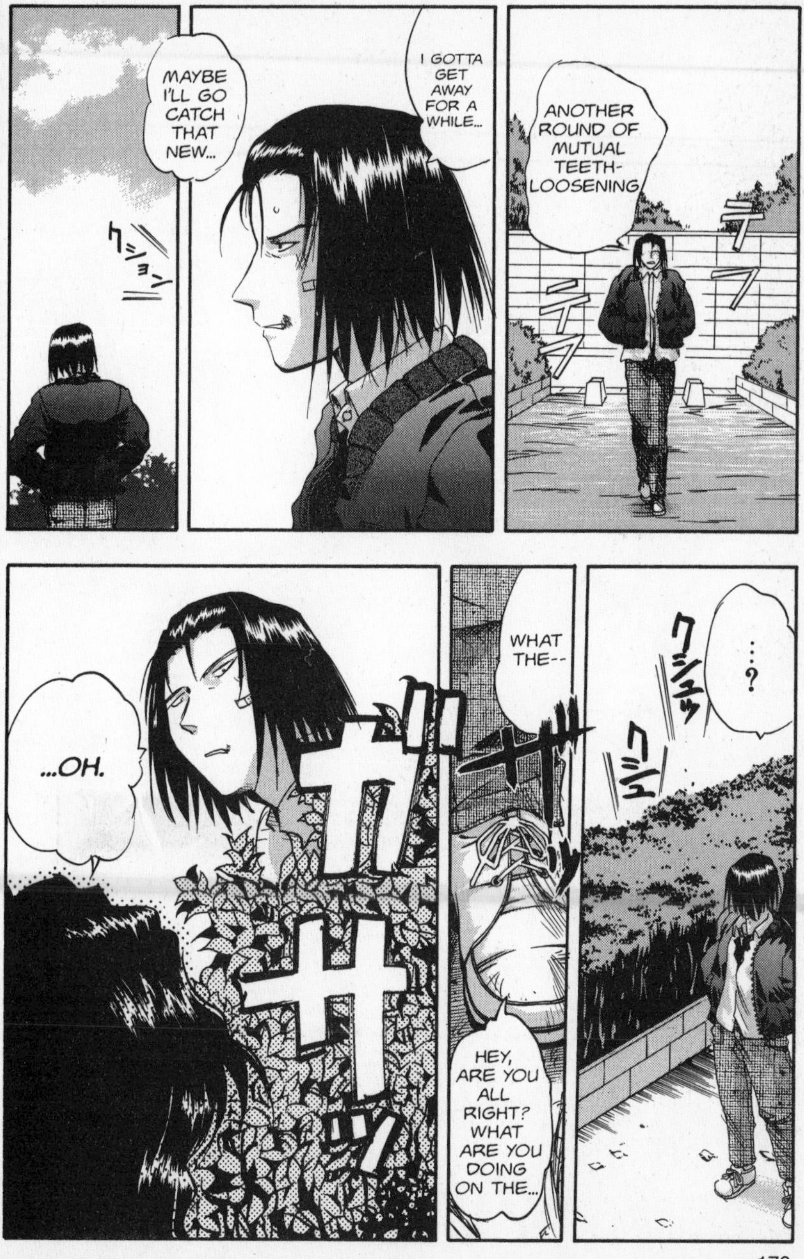
ANOTHER ROUND OF MUTUAL TEETH-LOOSENING
I GOTTA GET AWAY FOR A WHILE...
MAYBE I'LL GO CATCH THAT NEW...
...?
WHAT THE--
HEY, ARE YOU ALL RIGHT? WHAT ARE YOU DOING ON THE...
...OH.

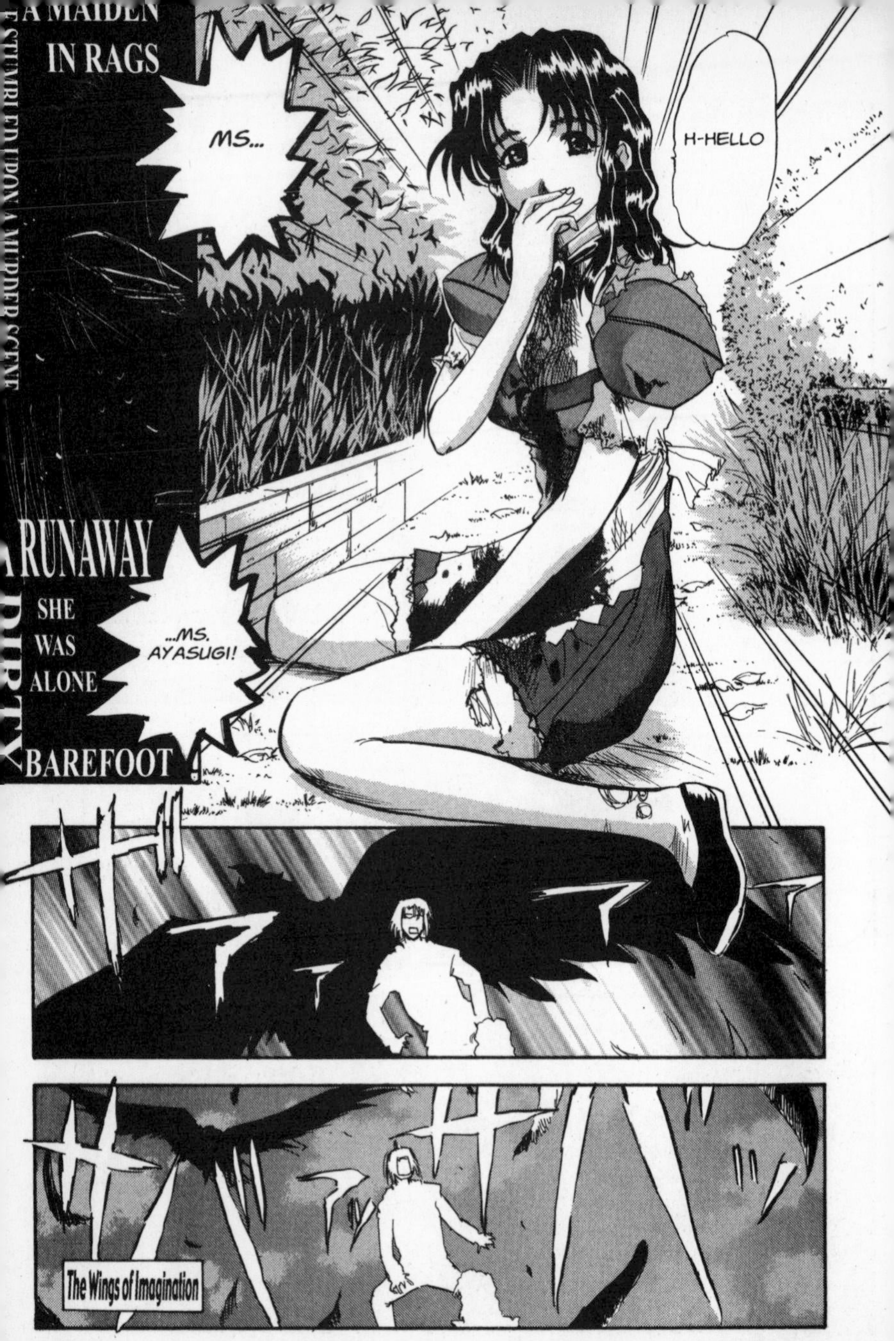
H-HELLO
MS...
A MAIDEN IN RAGS
E STUMBLED UPON A MURDER SCENE
...MS. AYASUGI!
A RUNAWAY
DIRTY
SHE WAS ALONE
BAREFOOT
The Wings of Imagination

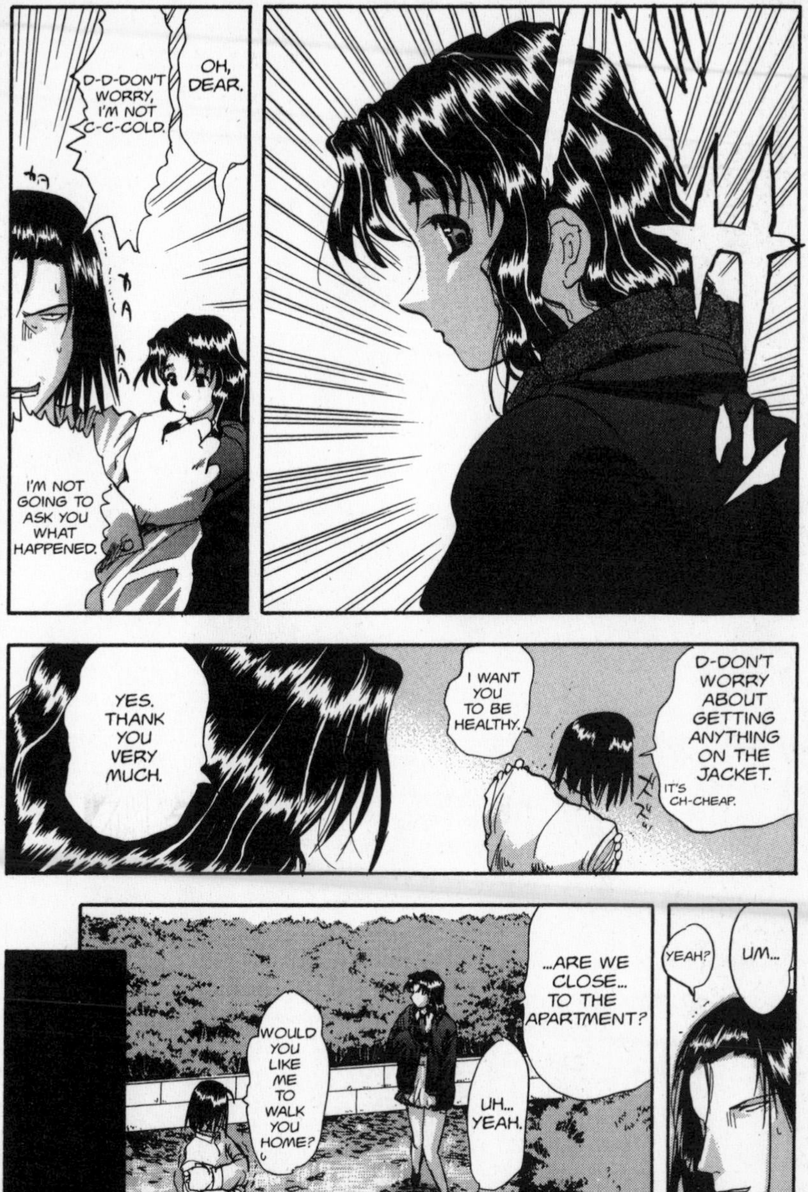
OH, DEAR.
D-D-DON'T WORRY, I'M NOT C-C-COLD.
I'M NOT GOING TO ASK YOU WHAT HAPPENED.
D-DON'T WORRY ABOUT GETTING ANYTHING ON THE JACKET.
IT'S CH-CHEAP.
I WANT YOU TO BE HEALTHY.
YES. THANK YOU VERY MUCH.
UM...
YEAH?
...ARE WE CLOSE... TO THE APARTMENT?
UH... YEAH.
WOULD YOU LIKE ME TO WALK YOU HOME?

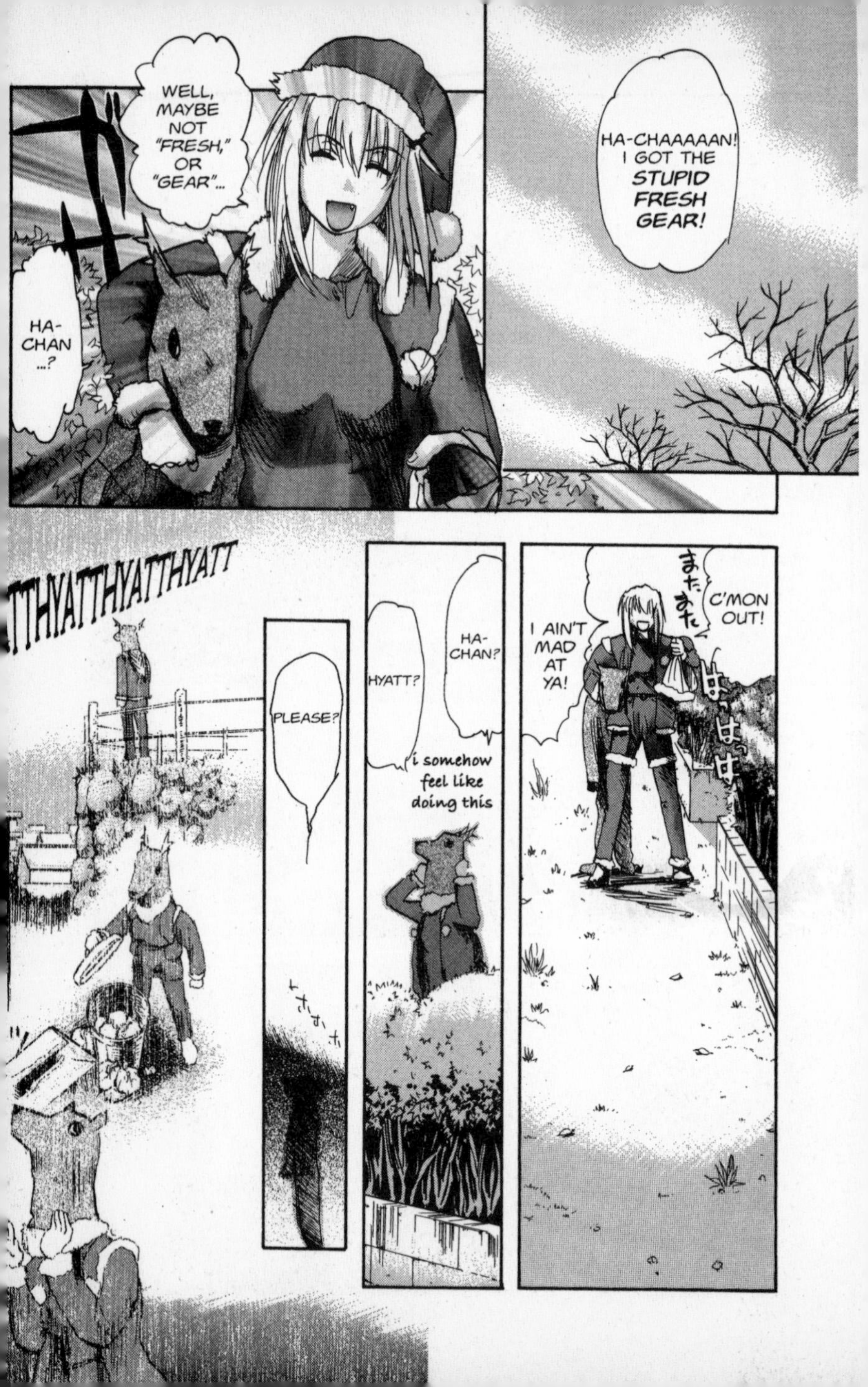
HA-CHAAAAAN! I GOT THE STUPID FRESH GEAR!
WELL, MAYBE NOT "FRESH," OR "GEAR"...
HA-CHAN ...?
またまた
C'MON OUT!
I AIN'T MAD AT YA!
はっはっはっ
HA-CHAN?
HYATT?
i somehow feel like doing this
PLEASE?
ATTHYATTHYATTHYATT

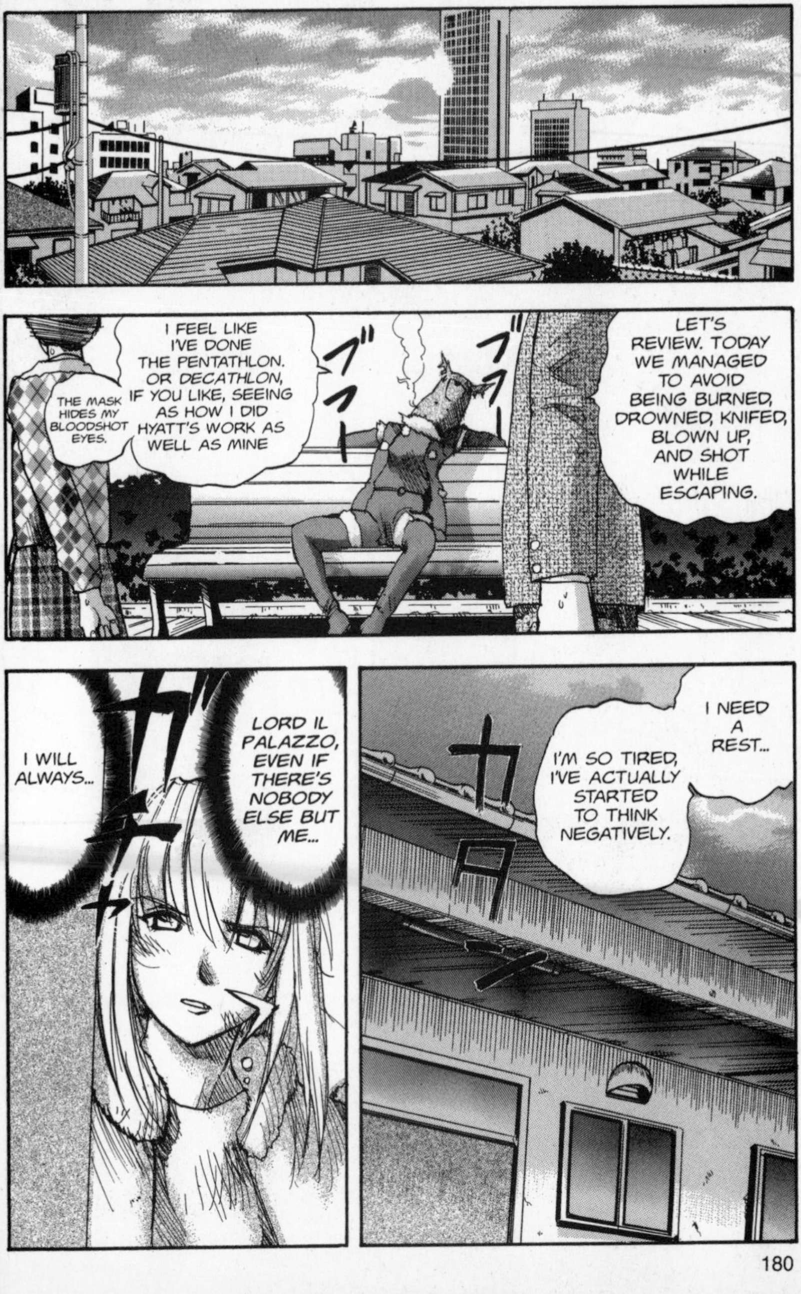
LET'S REVIEW. TODAY WE MANAGED TO AVOID BEING BURNED, DROWNED, KNIFED, BLOWN UP, AND SHOT WHILE ESCAPING.
I FEEL LIKE I'VE DONE THE PENTATHLON. OR DECATHLON, IF YOU LIKE, SEEING AS HOW I DID HYATT'S WORK AS WELL AS MINE
THE MASK HIDES MY BLOODSHOT EYES.
I NEED A REST...
I'M SO TIRED, I'VE ACTUALLY STARTED TO THINK NEGATIVELY.
LORD IL PALAZZO, EVEN IF THERE'S NOBODY ELSE BUT ME...
I WILL ALWAYS...

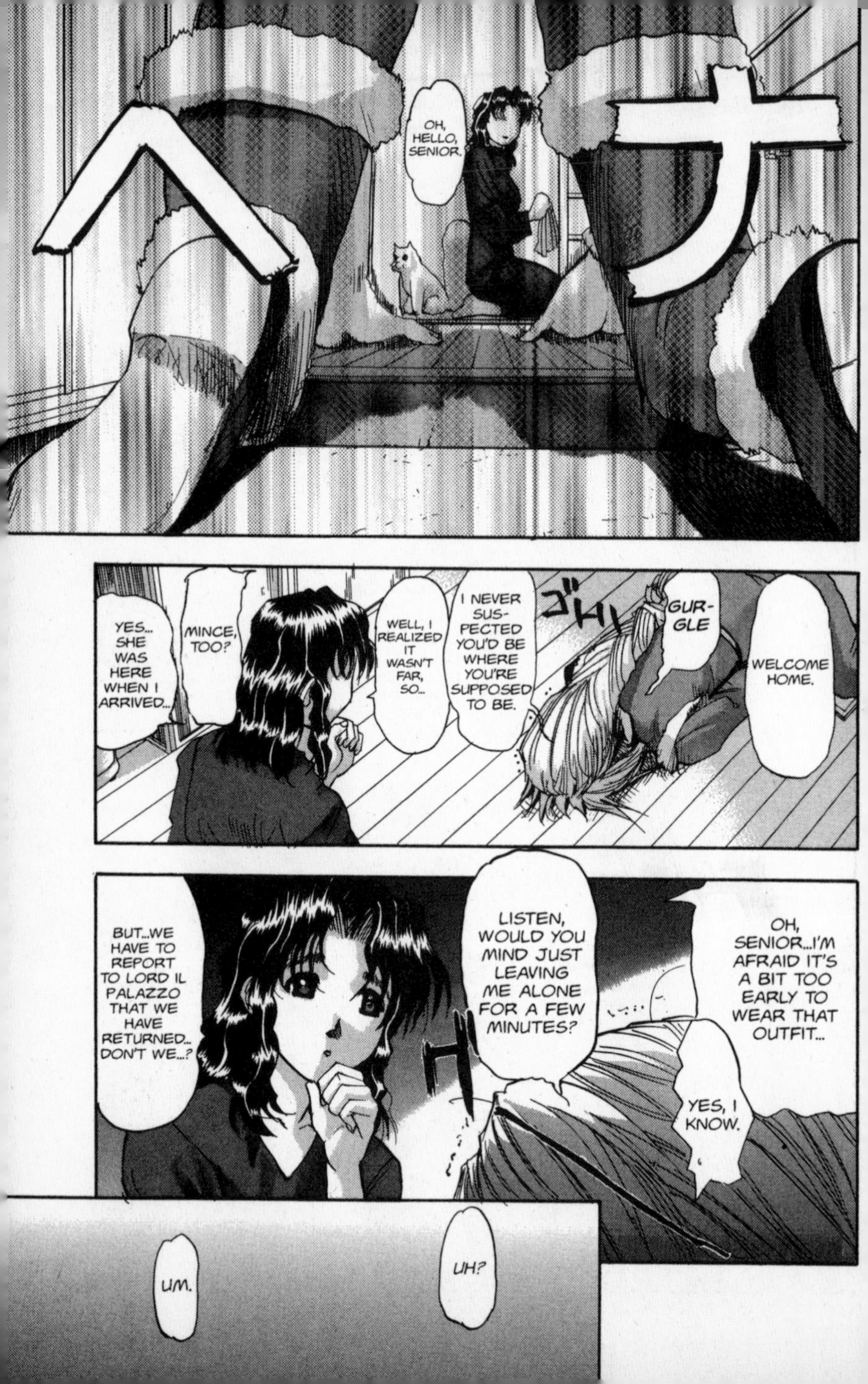
OH, HELLO, SENIOR.
WELCOME HOME.
GURGLE
I NEVER SUSPECTED YOU'D BE WHERE YOU'RE SUPPOSED TO BE.
WELL, I REALIZED IT WASN'T FAR, SO...
MINCE, TOO?
YES... SHE WAS HERE WHEN I ARRIVED...
OH, SENIOR...I'M AFRAID IT'S A BIT TOO EARLY TO WEAR THAT OUTFIT...
YES, I KNOW.
LISTEN, WOULD YOU MIND JUST LEAVING ME ALONE FOR A FEW MINUTES?
BUT...WE HAVE TO REPORT TO LORD IL PALAZZO THAT WE HAVE RETURNED... DON'T WE...?
UH?
UM.

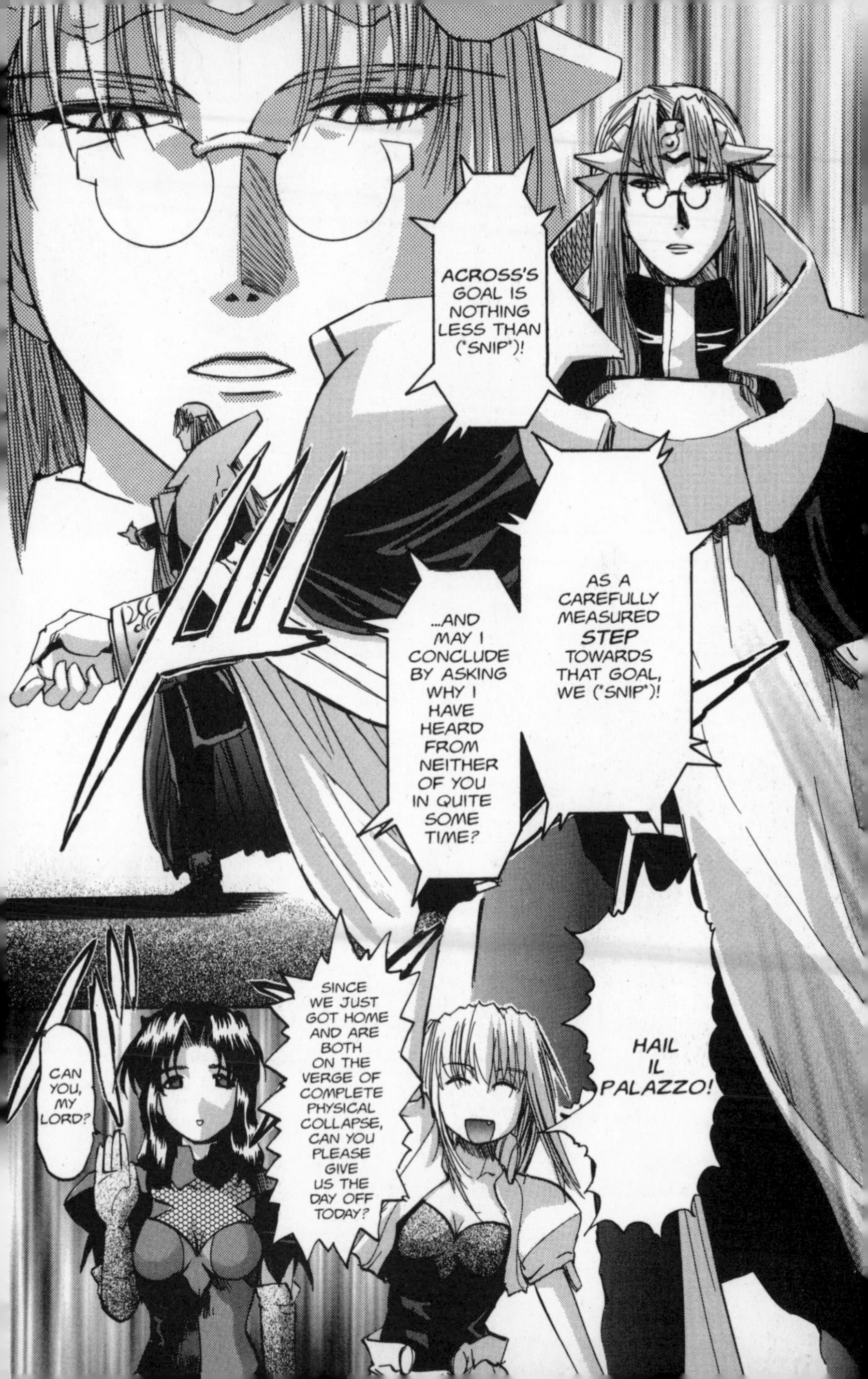
ACROSS'S GOAL IS NOTHING LESS THAN (*SNIP*)!
AS A CAREFULLY MEASURED STEP TOWARDS THAT GOAL, WE (*SNIP*)!
...AND MAY I CONCLUDE BY ASKING WHY I HAVE HEARD FROM NEITHER OF YOU IN QUITE SOME TIME?
HAIL IL PALAZZO!
SINCE WE JUST GOT HOME AND ARE BOTH ON THE VERGE OF COMPLETE PHYSICAL COLLAPSE, CAN YOU PLEASE GIVE US THE DAY OFF TODAY?
CAN YOU, MY LORD?

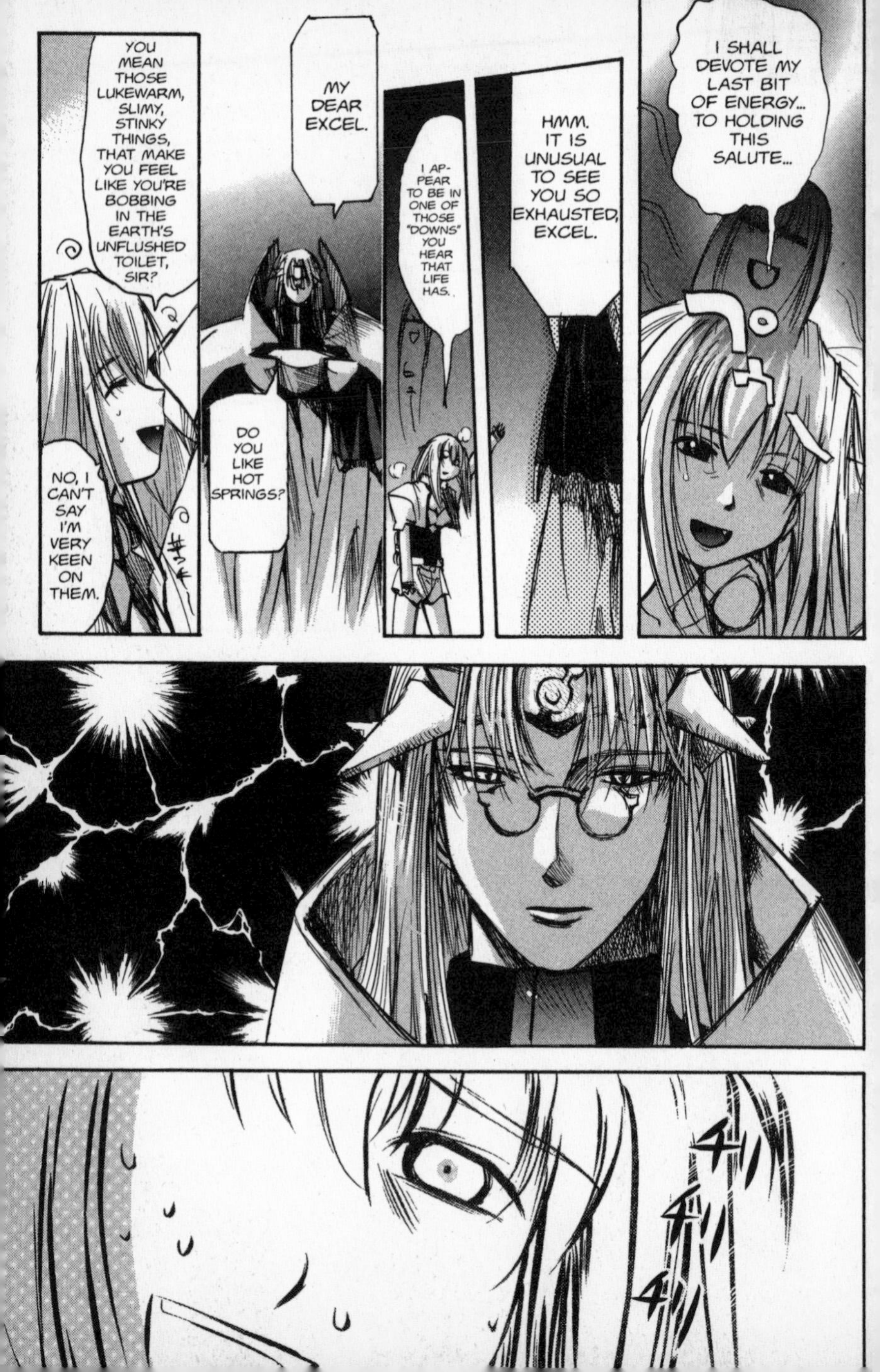
I SHALL DEVOTE MY LAST BIT OF ENERGY... TO HOLDING THIS SALUTE...
HMM. IT IS UNUSUAL TO SEE YOU SO EXHAUSTED, EXCEL.
I APPEAR TO BE IN ONE OF THOSE "DOWNS" YOU HEAR THAT LIFE HAS.
MY DEAR EXCEL.
DO YOU LIKE HOT SPRINGS?
YOU MEAN THOSE LUKEWARM, SLIMY, STINKY THINGS, THAT MAKE YOU FEEL LIKE YOU'RE BOBBING IN THE EARTH'S UNFLUSHED TOILET, SIR?
NO, I CAN'T SAY I'M VERY KEEN ON THEM.

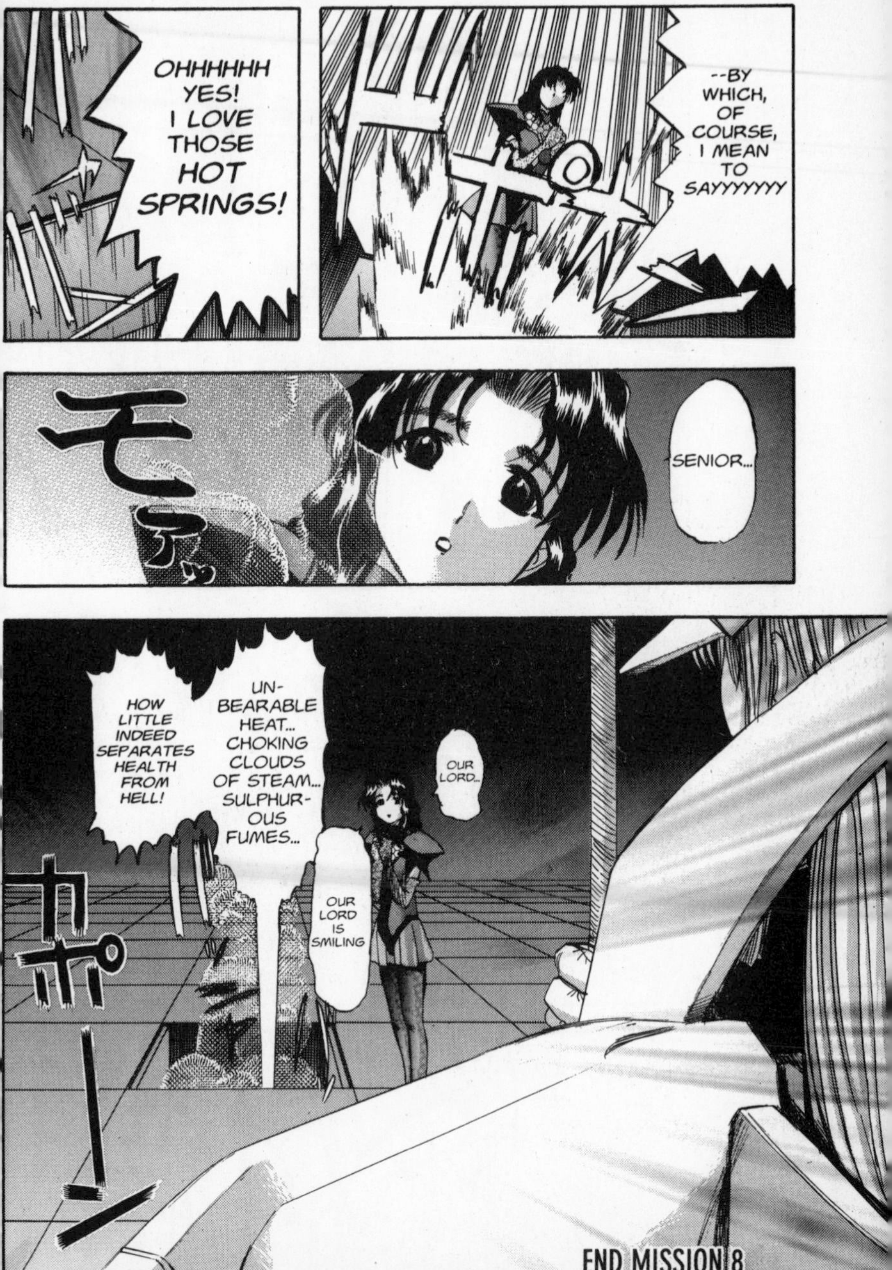
--BY WHICH, OF COURSE, I MEAN TO SAYYYYYYY
OHHHHHH YES! I LOVE THOSE HOT SPRINGS!
SENIOR...
OUR LORD...
UN-BEARABLE HEAT... CHOKING CLOUDS OF STEAM... SULPHUR-OUS FUMES...
HOW LITTLE INDEED SEPARATES HEALTH FROM HELL!
OUR LORD IS SMILING
END MISSION 8

EXCEL SAGA

WILL RETURN IN VOL. 08

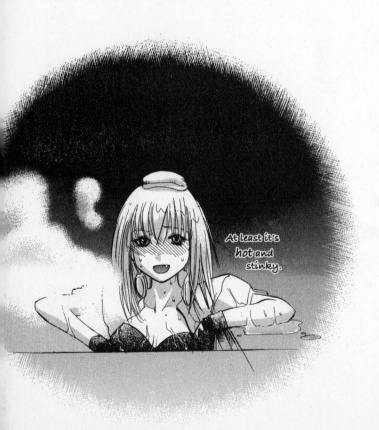

At least it's hot and stinky.

We In The New Millennium

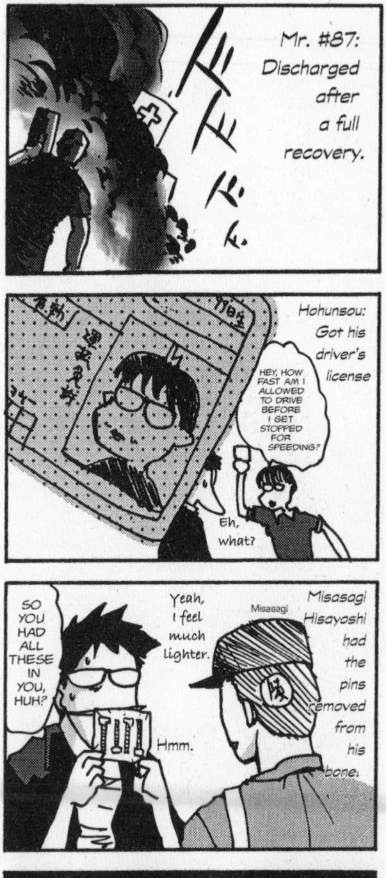
Mr. #87: Discharged after a full recovery.
Hohunsou: Got his driver's license
HEY, HOW FAST AM I ALLOWED TO DRIVE BEFORE I GET STOPPED FOR SPEEDING?
Eh, what?
Misasagi Hisayoshi had the pins removed from his bone.
Misasagi
Yeah, I feel much lighter.
SO YOU HAD ALL THESE IN YOU, HUH?
Hmm.
Tameniso's graduation from university...
WHAT? YOU HAVEN'T "ATTENDED ENOUGH DAYS" TO GRADUATE?
THEY GAVE YOU A BUNCH OF PENALTY HOMEWORK TO COMPLETE BEFORE YOU CAN GRADUATE? WHAT THE HELL ARE YOU DOING?
...remained in the balance.
You were summoned to the office?

You're lucky they offered you the chance.

We Who Communicate By Eye Contact

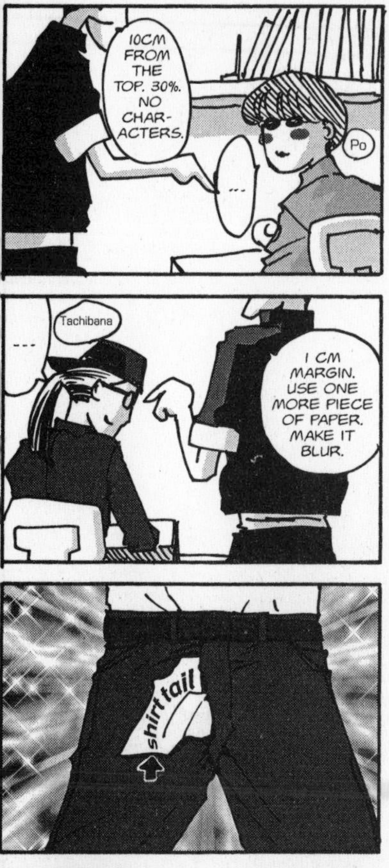
10CM FROM THE TOP. 30%. NO CHAR-ACTERS.
Po
...
I CM MARGIN. USE ONE MORE PIECE OF PAPER. MAKE IT BLUR.
Tachibana
---
shirt tail
HEY!
WHAT'S UP? YOU HAD YOUR HAIR CUT?
HEY!
I really don't know what to say...

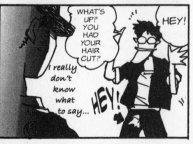

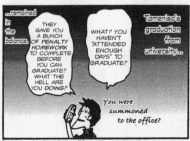

We Who Are Sound In Mind And Body

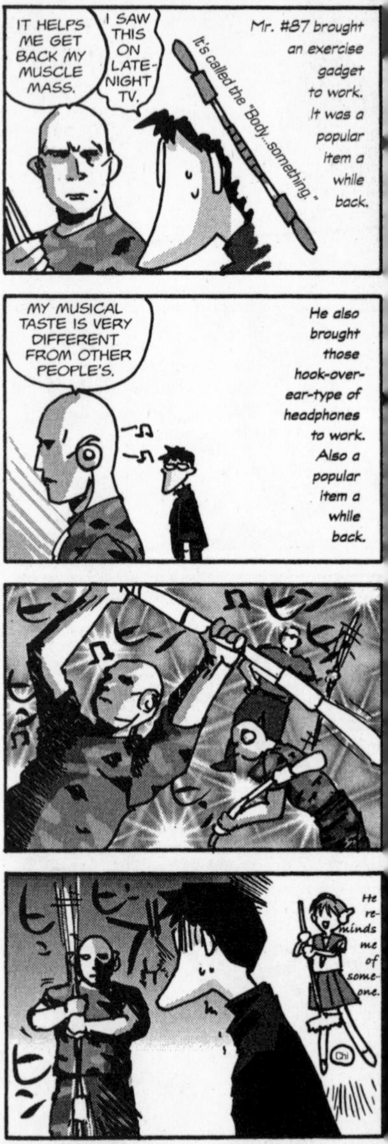
Mr. #87 brought an exercise gadget to work. It was a popular item a while back.
It's called the "Body...something."
I SAW THIS ON LATE-NIGHT TV.
IT HELPS ME GET BACK MY MUSCLE MASS.
He also brought those hook-over-ear-type of headphones to work. Also a popular item a while back.
MY MUSICAL TASTE IS VERY DIFFERENT FROM OTHER PEOPLE'S.
He reminds me of someone.
Chi

We Who Are Shambles of Men

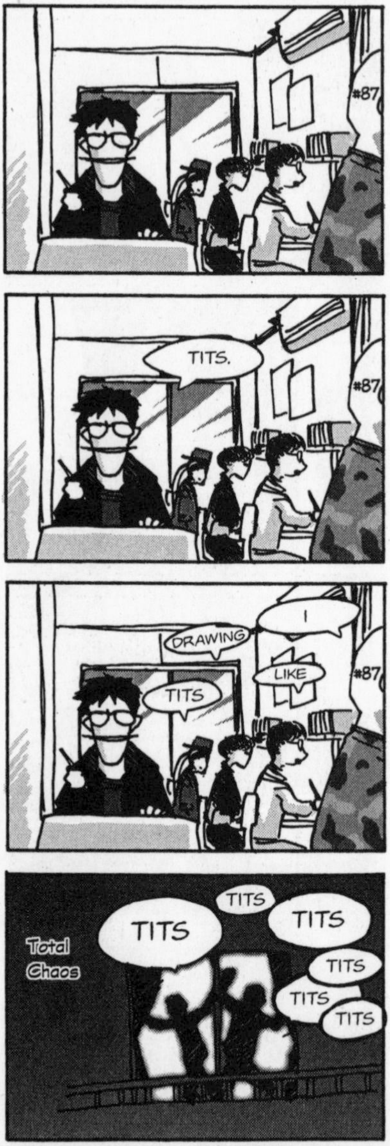
#87
TITS.
#87
I
LIKE
DRAWING
TITS
#87
TITS
TITS
TITS
TITS
TITS
TITS
Total Chaos

For these men there is no cure.

IN TWO MONTHS!

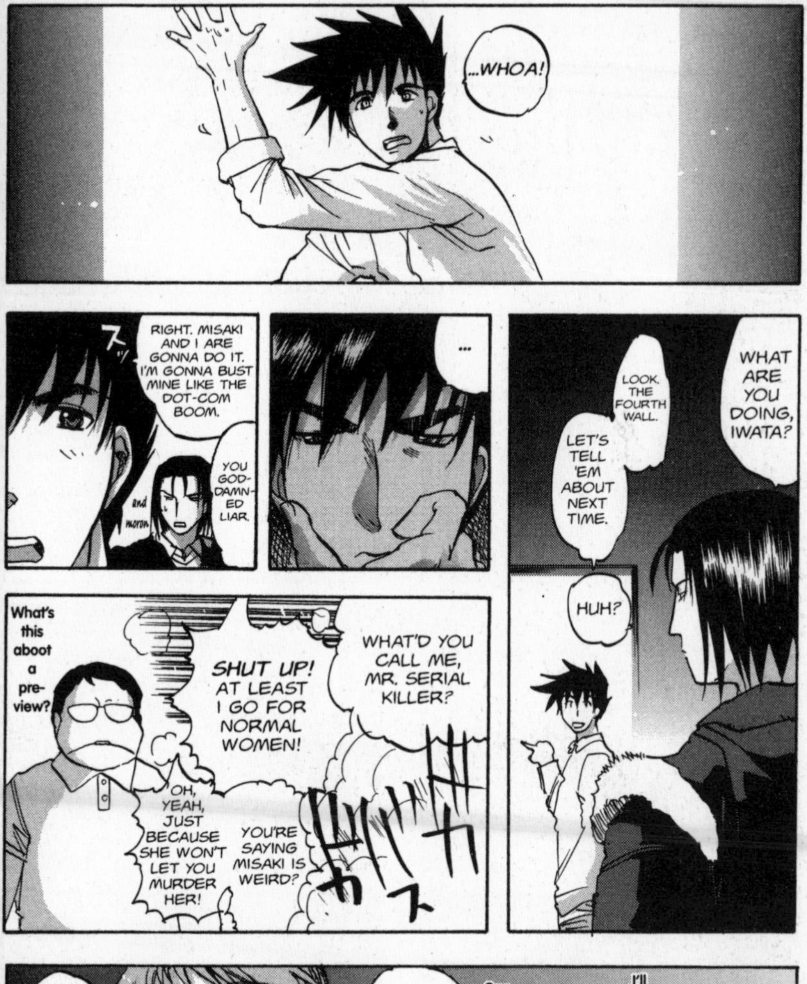

...WHOA!
WHAT ARE YOU DOING, IWATA?
LOOK. THE FOURTH WALL.
LET'S TELL 'EM ABOUT NEXT TIME.
HUH?
...
RIGHT. MISAKI AND I ARE GONNA DO IT. I'M GONNA BUST MINE LIKE THE DOT-COM BOOM.
YOU GOD-DAMN-ED LIAR.
and moron
WHAT'D YOU CALL ME, MR. SERIAL KILLER?
SHUT UP! AT LEAST I GO FOR NORMAL WOMEN!
YOU'RE SAYING MISAKI IS WEIRD?
OH, YEAH, JUST BECAUSE SHE WON'T LET YOU MURDER HER!
What's this aboot a pre-view?
I'll giz ye both three seconds.
One... two...
VOLUME 8?
FRANKLY, YOU'LL SLEEP BETTER NOT KNOWING.

...Whoa!

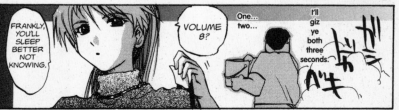

Guide to *Excel Saga* 07's Sound Effects!

5-1	FX	ban [bang]
5-4	FX	gu' [clench]
5-8	FX	bi' [halt]
5-11	FX	paku [swish]
7-1-1	FX	wai wai [wha-haha]
7-1-2	FX	wahahaha [ha ha ha]
7-1-3	FX	kyahaha [teeheehee]
7-1-4	FX	bu [chortle]
7-2	FX	zan [loom]
7-3-1	FX	dosa´[wobble]
7-3-2	FX	wheeeew
7-3-3	FX	zurin´ [ka-bump]
8-1	FX	kikikin [clink clink]
8-2-1	FX	kokyu kokyu [gulp gulp]
8-2-2	FX	mori mori [munch munch]
8-4-1	FX	gashi´ [pssht]
8-4-2	FX	gobu gobu gobu gobu [gulp gulp gulp gulp]
8-5-1	FX	boo boo, [booing]
8-5-2	FX	gashu´ [pssht]
9-3	FX	doka´ [thud]
10-1-1	FX	puaaah [whoo whoo]
10-1-2	FX	goton goton goton [chugga chugga chugga]
10-2	FX	zuzuzuzu [sluurrp]
10-4	FX	gu' [clench]
10-5	FX	haaaa [ahhhh]
11-1	FX	zoka ka ka ka [kling klang klang]
11-2	FX	don don [bang, bang]
11-3-1	FX	zubababa zuzuzu [gulp slurp]
11-3-2	FX	zurururu [sluurrp]
11-3-3	FX	hafu hafu [whoosh whoosh]
11-4-1	FX	zuzu [slurp]
11-5	FX	tsuu [drip]

Most of Rikdo Koshi's original sound FX are left in their original Japanese in the Viz edition of Excel Saga; exceptions being handwritten dialogue and "drawn" notes that have the character of captions. Although these sounds are all listed as "FX," they are of two types: onomatopoeia (in Japanese, *giseigo*) where the writing is used in an attempt to imitate the actual sound of something happening, and mimesis (in Japanese, *gitaigo*) where the writing is used to attempt to convey rhetorically a state, mood, or condition. Whereas the first type of FX will invariably be portrayed with kana, the second may use kana and/or kanji. One should note that there is often overlap between these two types. As always, the numbers are given in the original Japanese reading order: right-to-left.

You are still allowed, however, to write your letters left-to-right to:

Oubliette c/o Excel Saga

VIZ, LLC

P.O. Box 77064

San Francisco, CA 94107

23-5-1	FX	yura [stagger]
23-5-2	FX	chiri [shiver]
24-1	FX	dosa [plonk]
24-2-1	FX	zei zei zei zei [wheeze wheeze wheeze wheeze]
24-2-2	FX	za [klunk]
24-5	FX	zei zei zei [wheeze wheeze]
24-6	FX	peepoh peepoh peepoh [wheeooowheeooo (siren)]
24-7	FX	jara [clink]
35-1	FX	paaai [shortened form of "Kanpai!" (Cheers!)]
35-2-1	FX	goku goku [gulp gulp]
35-2-2	FX	kacha kacha [stirring]
35-2-3	FX	gutsu gutsu [boil bubble]
35-3	FX	mori mori [mumbling]
35-4-1	FX	hagu hagu [munching]
35-5-1	FX	goku goku [gulp gulp]
37-2	FX	mossa mossa [mumbling]
38-1-1	FX	booo [choooo]
38-1-2	FX	shu shu shu [whoosh whoosh]
38-4	FX	boooh [sigh]
39-1-1	FX	gokokokoo [gulping]
39-1-2	FX	mori mori [mumbling]
39-2	FX	gutsu gutsu gutsu [boil bubble boil]
39-3-1	FX	fu [sigh]
39-3-2	FX	mogu [munch]
11-6	FX	zu [slurp]
12-2	FX	jara [rattle]
13-1	FX	chapu [plop]
13-2	FX	keto keto [glance glance]
13-4	FX	gobogobo [flushhh]
13-5-1	Fx	kya kya [hee hee]
13-5-2	FX	gahahahaha [oh ho ho ho]
13-6	FX	gusu [sob]
13-7-1	FX	kiiii [whee]
13-7-2	FX	hoh reh [ah-ha]
13-8-1	FX	yaaan [noooo]
13-8-2	FX	ahahahaha [ha-ha hee-hee]
14-2	FX	papikoon [whoohoo]
15-2	FX	beshi [crack]
15-3	FX	piku [gasp]
15-4-1	FX	gubi [gulp]
15-4-2	FX	kuru [swish]
15-5-1	FX	gefu gopu gopu gopu [gack burble burble burble]
15-5-2	FX	mogomu mogomu [munch munch]
16-1	FX	mogu mogu mogu [munch munch munch]
16-3	FX	kui [point]
17-1	FX	koku [nod]
17-2	FX	pan pan [clatter clatter]
17-5	FX	ba [slam]

53-5 ——FX   gatan [rustle]

54-1-1 ——FX   kaa´ [shine]

54-1-2 ——FX   su´ [pop]

54-2 ——FX   buwa´ [sob]

54-4 ——FX   doka doka [thud thud]

55-1-1 ——FX   pan pan [clap clap]

55-1-2 ——FX   mishi mishi [creak creak]

55-2 ——FX   shuuuu [sizzle]

55-5 ——FX   ki´ [glare]

55-6 ——FX   tsuu´ [stream (of tears)]

56-2 ——FX   doku doku doku [plip plip plip (teardrops)]

56-3-1 ——FX   kyu [turn]

56-3-2 ——FX   hou [sigh]

56-5 ——FX   Oooo [ooooooh]

57-1 ——FX   doka doka [stomp stomp]

58-1 ——FX   kakiiiin [shake]

58-2 ——FX   fuu [sigh]

59-2 ——FX   doya doya doya [rustle bustle]

59-4 ——FX   zuka doka doka [stomp stomp]

59-5 ——FX   wahahahaha [hahaha]

59-6-1 ——FX   zuka zuka [krackle krackle]

59-6-2 ——FX   haran [fwish]

59-7 ——FX   kura´ [dizzy]

62-1 ——FX   ooon [wooo]

62-5 ——FX   gasha [fidget]

63-4-1 ——FX   kan kan [klack klack]

63-4-2 ——FX   kan´ [klack]

64-4 ——FX   su [pop]

65-1 ——FX   goshi goshi [scrub scrubb]

65-5-1 ——FX   palala palala palala palala palala [tadadaadaa (trumpet)]

65-5-2 ——FX   poff popoff [pow kapow]

66-1 ——FX   zawa zawa zawa [hustle-bustle]

66-4 ——FX   zawa zawa [hustle-bustle]

67-2 ——FX   wai wai [hustle-bustle]

41-5-4 ——FX   bun´ [pop]

42-1 ——FX   fuiiiin [whirrrr]

44-4 ——FX   pon [tum]

44-5 ——FX   za´ [fwish]

44-7-1 ——FX   gasa [flip]

44-7-2 ——FX   pimpooon [ding-dong]

44-7-3 ——FX   gishi [squeak]

44-8 ——FX   batan [bam]

45-4 ——FX   fu [sigh]

45-5 ——FX   gi´ [kreek]

46-1 ——FX   gishi [kakreek]

46-3 ——FX   gatan [skweak]

46-4 ——FX   doga doga doga [pound pound pound]

46-5 ——FX   dan´ [ta-da]

47-4 ——FX   zah [ha]

48-1-1 ——FX   mishi´ [creak]

48-1-2 ——FX   biku´ [gasp]

48-3 ——FX   giggi [creeeak]

48-5 ——FX   don don [bang bang]

49-1 ——FX   mishi [creak]

49-2 ——FX   hyuiiiii [bzzzt]

49-3-1 ——FX   bua [pop]

49-3-2 ——FX   zudon [thud]

50-1 ——FX   baba´ [scrunch]

50-2 ——FX   ban bafu [ba-bang]

50-3 ——FX   za´ [bsshht]

50-4 ——FX   pou [pow]

50-7 ——FX   ha´ [gasp]

51-1 ——FX   gata´ [thud]

53-1 ——FX   gogogogogo [seethe]

53-2 ——FX   gakkuri [doom]

53-3 ——FX   kura kura [wobble wobble]

53-4-1 ——FX   ooooo [swoon]

53-4-2 ——FX   wana wana [shiver shiver]

74-1-2	FX	do´ [thud]
74-1-3	FX	paooo [fweeoo (falling)]
74-1-4	FX	zawa [ripple]
74-2	FX	zah zah [kersplash]
75-1	FX	waa waa [rooaar (crowd cheering)]
75-2	FX	waa ooo [roooar]
75-3	FX	waa waa [rooaar (crowd cheering)]
75-4	FX	waa waa [rooaar (crowd cheering)]
76-1	FX	goso goso [fumble fumble]
76-2	FX	don [thud]
76-3	FX	fun fun [sniff sniff]
76-4	FX	pon [tum]
77-3	FX	wa˜ wa˜ zawa [rooaar (crowd cheering)]
77-4-1	FX	wa˜ wa˜ [rooaar (crowd cheering)]
77-5	FX	zawa zawa [buzz buzz]
78-2	Fx	doya doya doya [stomp stomp stomp]
78-3-1	FX	gachikon [kareeek (coming from the costume)]
78-3-2	FX	gachikon [kareeek (coming from the costume)]
78-3-3	FX	furun furun [flop flop]
78-3-4	FX	mucchi [flex]
78-3-5	FX	mucchi [flex]
78-3-6	FX	juushii [ripple (referring to muscular body)]
78-5	FX	ki´ [glare]
79-1	FX	orororooo [boo hoo hoo]
79-5	FX	doro doro doro [drip drip drip]
80-1	FX	soiya soiya soiya [hurray hurray hurray]
80-3-1	FX	waaaa [roar]
80-3-2	FX	ooooo [oooh]
80-4	FX	go´ [bang]
80-5	FX	waaa waaa [rooaar (crowd cheering)]
80-6	FX	fu´ [crinkle]
81-1	FX	petta petta [flip-flop]
81-3	FX	pi-yo [peep peep]
82-1	FX	waaa [rooaar (crowd cheering)]
67-3	FX	waya gaya gaya [hustle-bustle]
68-1-1	FX	kata kata [klak klak]
68-1-2	FX	zawa zawa [hustle-bustle]
68-2	FX	wai wai [hustle-bustle]
68-4-1	FX	biribiri [brringbrring]
68-4-2	FX	karan [klink]
68-6	FX	fufufufu [chuckle chuckle]
68-7-1	FX	kiiin [whiiine]
68-7-2	FX	zawa zawa [murmur murmur]
69-1-1	FX	gu´ [clench]
69-1-2	FX	uiiiiin [bweeen]
69-2	FX	basa [flap]
69-3	FX	ban´ [bam!]
69-4-1	FX	zawa zawa [murmur murmur]
69-4-2	FX	bi´ [twirl]
69-4-3	FX	ja´ [bam]
70-1	FX	dan dan dan dan [bang bang]
70-2	FX	kishaaaa [creee cree]
70-3	FX	zawa zawa zawa [buzz buzz buzz]
70-4	FX	za za za za [stomp stomp stomp stomp]
71-1	FX	zuru zuru zuru [slurp slurp slurp]
71-2	FX	tat tat tat [chomp chomp chomp]
71-3	FX	zawa zawa [hustle bustle]
72-1	FX	ya´ [yaa!]
72-3	FX	do´ [haaa]
72-4	FX	jaki [kalink]
73-1-1	FX	waaa [rooaar (crowd cheering)]
73-1-2	FX	kyuiiii [creak]
73-1-3	FX	dadadadada [thud thud]
73-1-4	FX	waaa [rooaar (crowd cheering)]
73-2	FX	waaaa [rooaar (crowd cheering)]
73-3	FX	hahaha [ahhhh]
73-4	FX	dan´ [bang]
74-1-1	FX	kaku [crack!]

OUBLIETTE
Your *EXCEL SAGA* bonus section!

95-2	FX	waa waa [rooaar (crowd cheering)]
95-3	FX	oraa' ["blast-off!"]
95-4	FX	dodadada [thud thud thud]
95-6	FX	bun [blam]
96-2	FX	oooo [oooooh]
96-5	FX	waa waa [roar]
97-1	FX	buaa [yaay]
97-2	FX	waa waa [roar]
97-3	FX	waa waa [roar]
97-5	FX	kira [sheen]
98-1	FX	da' [stomp]
98-7	FX	zawa zawa [buzz buzz]
99-1	FX	goron goron [rolling]
99-2-1	FX	waa' [wow]
99-2-2	FX	ban' [zzoop]
100-2	FX	lalalalalala [yaaaaa]
100-3	FX	zaaaa [zap]
100-4-1	FX	bua' [take-off]
100-4-2	FX	hyu [glide]
101-1	FX	baaa [wheee]
101-2	FX	gagagaga [chuggachugga]
101-3	FX	bibi [creek]
101-4	FX	buaa [gliiide]
101-5	FX	kun' [description of aircraft going down]
102-1	FX	waa [rooaar (crowd cheering)]
102-2	FX	baaaa [falll]
102-3	FX	hyuu [whew]
103-1	FX	katata [klatter]
103-2	FX	bochi' [push]
103-3	FX	kiiin [crriiik]
103-5	FX	baran [bomp]
104-1	FX	zan' [zzoop]
104-3	FX	babababa [flapflapflap]
104-4	FX	zabooo [slam]
82-2	FX	su' [look]
82-3	FX	za' [stomp]
83-5	FX	pii poo pii poo [wheeooo wheeooo (siren)]
86-6	FX	pupi [spew]
87-2	FX	zawa zawa [buzz buzz]
87-3	FX	kata kata [bzzzt]
88-3-1	FX	waa waa [buzz]
88-3-2	FX	kyaa [screaming]
89-1	FX	hyu [glide]
89-2	FX	fuwa [float]
89-3	FX	pachi' [snap (eyes opening)]
89-4	FX	zawa zawa [buzz buzz]
91-1	FX	bio' [whoosh]
91-2-1	FX	biooooo [whooooosh]
91-2-2	FX	buo' [bwoosh]
91-3	FX	gashi [grab]
91-4	FX	buaaaa [bwooaash]
91-5	FX	aaa [aaarrg]
92-1	FX	piii [phweeet]
92-2	FX	dogabooon [kablam]
92-3	FX	dan' [bang]
92-5	FX	jiiiin [nuummb]
92-6	FX	poro [doom]
92-7	FX	kiii [squeak]
93-1	FX	gasa [rustle]
93-2-1	FX	gogogogo [chugga chugga]
93-2-2	FX	gogogogo [chugga chugga]
93-3	FX	ooooo [whooo]
93-4	FX	ki' [glare]
93-5	FX	ki' [glare]
94-1	FX	gata [clink]
94-4-1	FX	poki poki [klink klink]
94-4-2	FX	awawawa [lost]
94-6	FX	waa waa [rooaar (crowd cheering)]

123-1——FX dosa dosa [hustle bustle]
123-2-1——FX sassa [rush]
123-2-2——FX pasa [flap]
123-4-1——FX doka doka [tromp tromp]
123-4-2——FX zuru zuru [draaagg]
125-1——FX dodododo [stomp stomp stomp]
125-2——FX gikyakyakyakya [zip zip zip zip]
125-3——FX dadada [whirl whirl]
125-4——FX zajaaaaa [mop mop]
125-5——FX dadadada [whirling]
126-1-1——FX dosa dosa [dump]
126-1-2——FX dan' [bam]
126-2——FX dodo doka [bam bang]
126-3——FX gyooo [eeek]
126-4——FX gi' [glare]
126-5——FX sha' [shhhh]
127-1-1——FX gasa [rustle]
127-1-2——FX gasa goso [rustle rustle]
127-2——FX gogogogo [grrrrr]
127-5——FX zaku zaku [chop chop]
128-2-1——FX zako zako [choppity chop]
128-2-2——FX zako zako zako [chop chop chop]
128-3——FX zaku zaku [chop chop]
129-1——FX za [ta-da]
129-2——FX za [ta-da]
129-4——FX mukka [arrrgh]
130-1-1——FX taaan [dash]
130-1-2——FX zuzaaaa [climb]
130-2——FX kyu kyu [scraping]
130-4-1——FX gatsu [clank]
130-4-2——FX piyo piyo piyo [beep beep beep]
130-4-3——FX pi' [blip]
130-4-5——FX ja' [hello?]
131-1——FX katsu katsu [clank clank]

104-6——FX pahpapa pahpapa [tadaa tadaa (trumpet)]
105-1-1——FX zawa zawa zawa zawa [buzz buzz buzz buzz]
105-1-2——FX pachi pachi pachi [clap clap clap]
105-1-3——FX panpakapan [tah-dah]
105-1-4——FX waaa [roar]
105-2-1——FX pach pachi [clap clap]
105-2-2——FX dooo [Who-ho-ho]
105-3——FX pachi pachi [clap clap]
105-5——FX wa wa [roar]
105-6——FX wa wa [roar]
106-5——FX ahahaha [ha ha ha]
111-2——FX kuru kuru [glance glance]
111-3——FX gapopan [swish]
112-1——FX su [push]
112-2——FX fuwa [crinkle]
112-4-1——FX katsu katsu [tap tap]
112-4-2——FX katsu katsu [tap tap]
113-3——FX goku [gulp]
114-5——FX tee' [yiiii]
115-2——FX gasa gasa [rustle rustle]
116-1——FX zappaan [lashing]
116-2——FX zazaaa [lashing]
116-3——FX oooo [wow]
117-4——FX ban' [bang]
118-3——FX piko piko [point point]
118-5——FX gata gata [rustle-bustle]
119-2——FX buu [boo]
121-1——FX tsuka tsuka tsuka [stomp stomp stomp]
121-2-1——FX bo' [bam]
121-2-2——FX gogogogo [sizzle]
121-5——FX ki' [glare]
122-2——FX tsuka tsuka tsuka [stomp stomp stomp]
122-3——FX teki paki teki paki [snapitty snap]
122-4——FX pan' [pull]

144-2——FX	katsu katsu [clack clack]	
144-4——FX	gu' [clench]	
144-5——FX	gakon [kalank]	
145-1——FX	kyoro kyoro [glance glance]	
145-2——FX	karan [klank]	
145-3——FX	katsuun katsuun katsuun [clack clack]	
145-4——FX	bou [darkness]	
145-6——FX	chin [click]	
145-7——FX	paa' [tada]	
146-2——FX	kan kan kan [clack clack clack]	
147-1——FX	go go go go go [rumble rumble]	
147-2——FX	gashi gashi [grab grab]	
147-3——FX	gishi [squeak]	
147-4——FX	zazaa [woosh]	
148-2——FX	picha [lick]	
148-3——FX	kata [clank]	
149-2-1——FX	katan [clank]	
149-2-2——FX	pata pata pata [flap flap flap]	
149-4——FX	totetetetete [flappity flap]	
150-1——FX	fun fun [sniff sniff]	
150-2——FX	pata pata pata [flap flap flap]	
150-5——FX	teke teke [clop clop]	
150-6——FX	kapan [clank]	
150-7——FX	jiri jiri [scorch scorch]	
151-1——FX	bari bari bari [rumble rumble]	
151-2-1——FX	bobobo [flash]	
151-2-2——FX	da' [dash]	
151-3——FX	budododo [rummmble]	
151-4——FX	baaaa [throb]	
151-5——FX	baaaa [throb]	
151-6——FX	bari bari [rumble rumble]	
151-7-1——FX	do do do do [throb throb throb]	
151-7-2——FX	guru [swish]	
152-1——FX	jiriririri [beepbeepbeep]	

131-2——FX	katsu katsu [clank clank]	
131-3——FX	kotsu kotsu [clank clank]	
131-6——FX	kon kon [knock knock]	
131-8——FX	gacha [click]	
132-1——FX	don' [bam]	
133-1——FX	ban [doom]	
135-1-1——FX	poso [whisper]	
135-1-2——FX	ha' [wha]	
135-4——FX	furu furu [tremble tremble]	
137-5——FX	dan dan dan [stamp stamp stamp]	
138-3——FX	to' [boiingg]	
138-4-1——FX	kin kin kin [wssht wssht wssht(sharpening knives)]	
138-4-2——FX	dosa dosa [wobble wobble]	
138-5——FX	kyu [creak]	
139-1-1——FX	za' za' [wsht wsht]	
139-1-2——FX	teki paki [snap crackle (moving deftly)]	
139-2——FX	kacha kacha [click click]	
139-3——FX	gashi gashi [scrub scrub]	
139-4——FX	ki' [clench]	
140-1——FX	don [thud]	
140-2——FX	zushi' [weigh]	
140-3——FX	gi gi gi gi [squeak squeak squeak]	
140-4——FX	pira [plop]	
141-1——FX	za' za' za' za' [thump thump thump]	
141-2——FX	gassha gassha [clink clink]	
141-5——FX	gasa' [rustle]	
141-6——FX	zakon [swoosh]	
142-1——FX	gasa [rustle]	
142-3——FX	kachirin [clickety]	
143-1——FX	kotsu [clacking]	
143-2-1——FX	chi' chi' chi' chi' [tsk tsk tsk tsk]	
143-2-2——FX	fun fun [sniff sniff]	
143-3——FX	bariiii [babang]	
143-6——FX	za' [swish]	

152-3——FX bouuu [crackle]

152-4——FX chun' [zing]

152-5-1——FX bobon [bam]

152-5-2——FX gooooo [flash]

152-5-3——FX chun chu' [zing]

152-5-4——FX bishi' [ping]

152-6-1——FX gaba' [bang]

152-6-2——FX burorororo [throbbb]

153-1-1——FX ata futa ata [flutter flutter]

153-1-2——FX kacha kacha [clink clink]

153-1-3——FX kuki koki [clank clank]

153-2——FX burararara [throb throb]

153-3-1——FX dogaaaa [blast]

153-3-2——FX buooooo [throbbb]

153-4——FX baaaaa [rumble]

154-1——FX jiririririri [beepbeepbeep]

154-2——FX guoooo [fwoosh]

154-3-1——FX za' [rustle]

154-3-2——FX goooo [crackle]

154-4——FX kishaaaaa [aaaaaah]

154-5——FX paa [flash]

154-6——FX dokaaooo [kablam]

155-2——FX bori' [bam]

155-4——FX gooooo [crumble]

155-5-1——FX bugyaaaa [wahhhhh]

155-5-2——FX garararara [rumble]

156-1-1——FX buaaan [thunder]

156-1-2——FX dododo [bambambam]

156-2-1——FX buooo [rumble]

156-2-2——FX gogogo [crumble]

156-3——FX goooo [crumble]

156-6-1——FX kikiii [squeak]

156-6-2——FX batan batan [bang bang]

157-4-1——FX zaza [whoosh]

157-4-2——FX hyuuu [whooo]

158-2——FX hyuuu [whoo]

158-3——FX sitan' [bang]

159——FX zazaan [whooosh]

160——FX zazaaaa [whsssssh]

161-1——FX don' [bam]

161-2——FX ban' [bang]

163-2——FX shin [silence]

163-5-1——FX kyu [pull]

163-5-2——FX pakon [ka-cha]

163-6——FX pa' [bump]

163-7——FX pafun [ka-chunk]

163-8——FX kiko [pull]

163-9——FX patan [click]

163-10——FX pa' [bump]

163-11——FX patan [click]

163-12——FX kiko [pull]

164-5-1——FX gatan [clank]

164-5-2——FX tote [trot]

165-1——FX hyoi [fwish]

165-4——FX fu' [sigh]

165-5——FX piku [flinch]

165-6-1——FX gabo [puke]

165-6-2——FX dopu' [splash]

165-6-3——FX shaaaa [speewww]

166-6——FX buchi' [click]

167-4——FX ka' [wha]

167-5——FX doba baku baku baku [munch munch munch]

168-1-1——FX fuu [sigh]

168-1-2——FX zuzuzuzu [slurpslurp]

168-2-1——FX gacha' [click]

168-2-2——FX ban [bang]

169-1——FX su [wha-]

169-2-1——FX bin' [yank]

174-4-1	FX	gasa [rustle]
174-4-2	FX	teto teto [stomp stomp]
174-5-1	FX	chi´ chi´ [tsk tsk]
174-5-2	FX	piriri [peel peel]
174-6	FX	paki [snap]
175-1	FX	piku [flinch]
175-2	FX	ba´ [pounce]
175-3-1	FX	hyoi [dodge]
175-3-2	FX	kui [flick]
175-4-1	FX	pu´ [chuckle]
175-4-2	FX	ku´ ku´ [chuckle chuckle]
175-5	FX	guri kuri [pat pat]
175-6	FX	gasasa [rustle]
176-1	FX	tefu tefu [stomp step]
176-3-1	FX	kushon [ah-choo]
176-3-2	FX	kushu´ kushu´ [achoo achoo]
176-5-1	FX	za´ [rustle]
176-5-2	FX	gasa [rustle]
177-3	FX	zaaa [flap]
177-4	FX	zaba´ zaba´ [flap flap]
178-1	FX	basa [thud]
178-2	FX	kata kata [shiver shiver]
178-3	FX	zuzu [sniff sniff]
179-2	FX	gasa [rustle]
180-2	FX	bufuu bufuu [siiiighh]
180-3	FX	katan [clack]
180-4-1	FX	gacha [clink]
180-4-2	FX	fu´ [puff]
181-1	FX	hena [slump]
181-2	FX	gotori [plank]
181-3	FX	gu´ [frazzle]
182-1	FX	doba [bang]
183-1	FX	puu [frazzling]
183-7	FX	chiri chiri chiri [tingling]

169-2-2	FX	gigigi [squeeek]
169-3-1	FX	don´ [bang]
169-3-2	FX	batan [bam]
169-4-1	Fx	bu´ [bam]
169-4-2	FX	bata [bong]
169-4-3	FX	dosu [bam]
170-1-1	FX	dokan [bang]
170-1-2	FX	gashi [clank]
170-1-3	FX	gon [bong]
170-2	FX	teko teko [clink clank]
170-3-1	FX	hyon [crouch]
170-3-2	FX	hoko hook [crackle glow]
170-3-3	FX	pata [flop]
171-1	FX	chii [eeep]
171-3-1	FX	faoo [waaooo]
171-3-2	FX	pi po pi po [siren]
171-4-1	FX	zuzuzu [slurpslurp]
171-4-2	FX	bori bori [crunch crunch]
171-5-1	FX	faooon [siren]
171-5-2	FXP	pi po popi popi [siren]
172-1-1	FX	ha ha ha [ha ha ha]
172-1-2	FX	faooon [siren]
172-1-3	FX	pipo pipo [siren]
172-1-4	FX	noshi noshi noshi [stomp stomp]
172-1-5	FX	suta suta [stride stride]
172-2-1	FX	pi´ po [siren]
172-2-2	FX	fooo [siren]
172-3	FX	pi´po´ pi [siren]
173-1	FX	ha ha ha [ha ha ha]
173-3-1	FX	gasa [rustle]
173-3-2	FX	gasa [rustle]
173-3-3	FX	gasa [rustle]
174-1-1	FX	gasa gasa gasa [rustle rustle]
174-1-2	FX	shito shito [trudge trudge]

30-1 The phrase in Romanized Japanese just above "NEWS 23" logo says, somewhat cryptically, "If you like me, please don't tell me to eat sashimi."

35-2 *Motsunabe* is a one-pot dish, the type of which sukiyaki is best-known in the west. Motsunabe is made with a light broth base, soy, garlic, paprika, leeks, garlic, *hakusai* (bok choi), and cow guts, which is what *motsu* means. As Lisa would say, "They can't honestly expect us to swallow that tripe." Fukuoka is known for this dish as well, as well as (being the part of Japan closest to Korea) the related *kimuchinabe*, cooked with kimchi and sliced pork.

46-5 Watanabe originally compared Sumiyoshi to Don Matsugoro, the eponymous talking dog of Hisashi Inoue's novel, later adapted into anime by Toei in the 1980s.

54-5 The kanji on the far left of this panel indicated *dosoku*, that Professor Shiouji is committing the so-named act, of entering into a house with one's shoes on, contrary to Japanese etiquette. And to quote my favorite line from *The Producers*, "White, white, white is the color of our carpet!"

73 Although we must admit the possibility that Ropponmatsu II has merely been *programmed* to be an otaku, she is headed up the runway to a medley of anime references: the first line of the theme to the classic 1978-1981 anime series *Galaxy Express 999* (in an age of 13-episode anime on premium cable, it was popular enough to run *114* episodes on broadcast television), the very series on which Viz's two *Galaxy Express* films are based. The crack about the pig is of course a bit of self-deprecation from the eponymous hero of Hayao Miyazaki's *Porco Rosso*, the 1992 anime feature from the director of *Spirited Away*—look for it later this year on DVD in English from Buena Vista. Amuro is most likely Amuro Rei, or Ray, or however the hell they spell his last name in the official release of the 1978-79 TV series *Mobile Suit Gundam*. You might have caught it on Cartoon Network a few years back, and as always bears repeating, this show was the probably the biggest single influence on the founders of Studio Gainax, and there's a lot of Amuro in Shinji, but not his hair—Shinji has better hair. The contemporary manga remake (by its original co-creator, Yoshikazu Yasuhiko) *Gundam: The Origin* is also a title published by Viz. The co-English adapter of *Excel Saga* (or however his involvement with the title may now best be properly stated) notes that when he was the gay Ropponmatsu II appears to be, he lived in a place without A/C and employed cold showers for the wholesome purpose of cooling down enough to get to sleep during summer evenings.
Equally wholesomely, he endured the cold showers by singing the theme to *Star Blazers* at the top of his little lungs.

75-1 No doubt making mock of *Kyushu* University in Fukuoka. They accept foreign students, so base your choice to apply there carefully on what you are about to witness.

78 The students are speaking in heavy Fukuoka dialect. The original for "yo" here was "ossu," an expression popular among students, especially athletic types. Of almost limitless utility, it can mean "hello," "yes," "sorry," etc., etc. The students also employ the loan-word borrowed from English *juushiii*, "juicy," by which they mean a muscular body. Being students, they probably borrowed it without asking.

184-1	FX	dopo [splash]	
184-2	FX	baban [bang]	
184-3	FX	moa' [steam]	
184-4-1	FX	bassha ba [kerplash]	
184-4-2	FX	kapo [plunk]	
186-1	FX	dododo [throbbing]	
187-3	FX	Hin hin hin [whirrrr]	
187-4	FX	Hin hin hin [whirrrr]	
188-4	FX	su' [but-]	
188-5	FX	doka basu doka [bang bam bang]	
188-6	FX	gashi doka beki [bang bam thud]	

7 Japan has the springtime tradition of cherry-blossom viewing parties. One sets out a tarp, blanket or mat beneath the trees and then drinks until the world dissolves into a pink and white whirl of floating petals; fading gradually into the charcoal greys and carbon blacks of oblivion. If it is to be an office cherry-blossom viewing party, it is equally traditional for the lo-jack on the totem pole to be assigned the task of staking out a choice space in the park for their brethren. In ye olde days, and even ye today, it has been known for dandies to practice the elegant vagrancy of following the cherry blossoms north: to enjoy a long season of viewing parties by starting in southern Japan with the very earliest blossomings, and moving slow up the length of the islands with each warming day. Poor Excel and Hyatt have to work, however.

9-2 The particular drunks stumbling around Excel and Hyatt's workplace are surprised because ramen stalls are usually (see 10-1 for exact details) clustered around business and entertainment districts where people belly up to the counter and eat a bowl of ramen. By contrast, cherry-blossom-viewing parties take place at parks, and people are more likely to picnic, bringing their own food and drink. A park stall might be more likely to sell finger food such as yakitori or *takoyaki* (not often seen in U.S. Japanese restaurants, this is Osaka's immortal contribution to world cuisine—bits o' octopus in a fried chewy ball covered in dark brown material. Very good, and if the stall outside the Benihana in SF's Japantown is selling, you best be buying). The idea, again, for a blossom-viewing festival is that you would want to take your grub back to the trees rather than consume it at the stall. Excel and Hyatt, being relatively new to this business, don't know why people are taking the bowls with them, nor do they quite fathom why this is bound to cut into their bottom line a little.

17-1 Kyushu, the southernmost of Japan's four major islands—and Fukuoka, its largest city, in particular—is famous for its noodles in pork bouillon (*tonkotsu ramen*). As Homer Simpson would say in Japan, "Mmmmm…*tonkotsu ramen*."

23-5 In the original Japanese, Matsuya vaguely directs at Iwata the command "You must sit on your heels," an uncomfortable position and therefore a form of punishment.

a 70s childhood, seems to have survived a bit more in Japan; it was not until 1989 that Takara Shuzo, one of Japan's largest manufacturers of *shochu* (raw spirits—if you think efforts are made to enjoy sake, try shochu) introduced the aptly-named SOT (stay-on tab) to the Japanese market. To be fair, the tabs never created quite as big a problem over there because the Japanese were always more likely to dispose of the tab inside the empty can as you were supposed to.

132-1 Antonio, the haunted soldier/nut (albeit a nut considerably kinder to Mince than her owner) takes inspiration for his latest incarnation here from the lineage of Captain Harlock, perhaps anime's greatest *hero* (as opposed to just "good guy"). An entertaining and well-informed introduction to the character can be found at http://www.cor po flicks.org/harlock/ harlockmain.html; it's worth reading for its history of the many bizarre English dubbed versions of *Harlock* alone.

169-3-1 What, indeed. *Mikadroid* was also released in the enlightened West under the title *Robokill Beneath Disco Club Layla*. This 1991 film by Tomo Haraguchi (the director credited with reviving *Gamera* over the past decade) involved that hoary favorite, the forgotten Japanese secret weapon of WWII brought back to life, except this time the weapon was an android, and it is brought back to life in a modern dance club. *Mikadroid* was the first time former Gainax (and now Studio Gonzo) animator Shinji Higuchi demonstrated his remarkable ability to make interesting live-action special effects out of no budget; he would later work with Haraguchi on his *Gamera* films.

169-3-2 As in *Chôjinki Metalder*, or "Super-Machine Metalder," as in, yet another not-conceptual-art-performance-but-straight-faced-live-action-Japanese superhero-show, this one from 1987–88. In "Oubliette"'s never-ending quest to render you the in-joke behind the in-joke *behind* the in-joke, the point here is that Metalder, like the Mikadroid, was *also* a forgotten android weapon from World War II. Like Bob Dole.

187-4 Rikdo-san is disturbingly reminded of Mr. #87's physical antipode but sister in dedication, "Multi" (spelled with a *chi* in Japanese), the adorable, hard-sweeping robot maid of the H-game turned multimedia phenomenon *To Heart.*

By Carl Gustav Horn with assistance from Yuko Sawada

80 The hooded society is shouting *soiya, soiya, soiya*—a chant traditionally heard in those Japanese festivals where a portable Shinto shrine is borne through the streets. Their name is an amalgam of several notorious cults of recent Japanese experience, including "Life Space," "The Laws of the Sun," (who recently commissioned their own anime promotional film— *Tokyoscope*'s Patrick Macias has seen it, but I haven't yet read his review) and of course, those zany zealots over at "Supreme Truth," better known by their Japanese name *Aum Shinri Kyo.* Just this March, Aum's leader, Chizuo Matsumoto, a.k.a. Shoko Asahara, a.k.a. Johnny Blaze, the "subway sarin-gassing, face-fried-chicken-stuffing, hairy-face-head-and-body-having" messiah to whom Il Palazzo referred back in *Excel Saga* Vol. 01, was finally sentenced to death by hanging. Unless prison thinned him out sufficiently, it occurs to one that they're gonna need a pretty stout rope. If not, we may end up having one of those EC-horror comic cover scenes, where we see the appalled/pleased/nauseated reactions from witnesses as Asahara's Jesus-like head and Buddha-like body part ways after a long and fruitful partnership. Actually, since Shoko Asahara *did* in fact maintain he could levitate, this will be an excellent opportunity for everyone to verify the claim under scientific conditions.

81-83 About the fans by which poor Hyatt endeavors to "be the hokey fly," as Patrick would put it: the fan in 82.3 says *H-zaki Gu* on top and *Hojo-e* on bottom. Hojo-e is an autumn festival held at a Shinto shrine, and its literal meaning is "a ritual for releasing living beings." Its intended purpose is to express one's thanks to all living things for their sacrifice during the year; Excel's assignation of the fan to Hyatt admits a multi-layered gesture of complicated ambiguity. *H-zaki Gu* is an apparent reference to *Hakozaki Gu* (*gu* means "shrine") which is located in the eastern part of Fukuoka; this is where the Hojo-e festival is held locally each year, although, like many Shinto festivals, it has acquired the feeling more of a street fair in recent times. For more information on the Hojo-e rituals, the translator suggests the comments to be found at http://rossbender.org/HOJOINTRO.html. Note that the fans seen in 81.3 and 83.1 say "Defense Agency" on top and "Warrior Spirit" on bottom; perhaps another in Rikdo's ongoing series of respectful gestures towards the Japanese Self-Defense Force.

108 The original form of Mrs. Oya (Old Lady)'s phrase is *waruigohainega?* which is literally "Aren't there any bad kids here?" spoken in a northern Japanese dialect. The phrase is associated with the *Namahage* festival in Akita Prefecture, Japan; men disguised as a demon go door-to-door shouting it—another parental invention designed to terrify youngsters into behaving themselves ("Why, yes, we *do* have two children who won't eat their vegetables . . ."). The translator has suggested the site http://bama.ua.edu/~mlc/japanese/celebra-tions/namahagepg.html for more on Namahage.

113-2 In the original Japanese, Excel invokes *fukokukyohei*, "rich country, strong military," the slogan by which the Japanese government promoted modernization during the early years of the Meiji era, as so dishonenly portrayed in *The Last Samurai*. 127-1 The foot-slicing aluminum pull-tab, beach bane of many

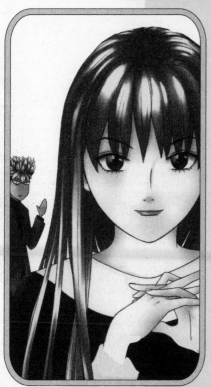

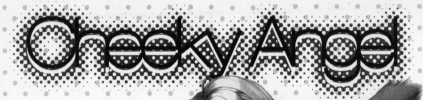
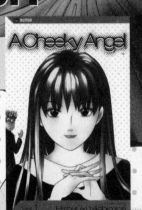

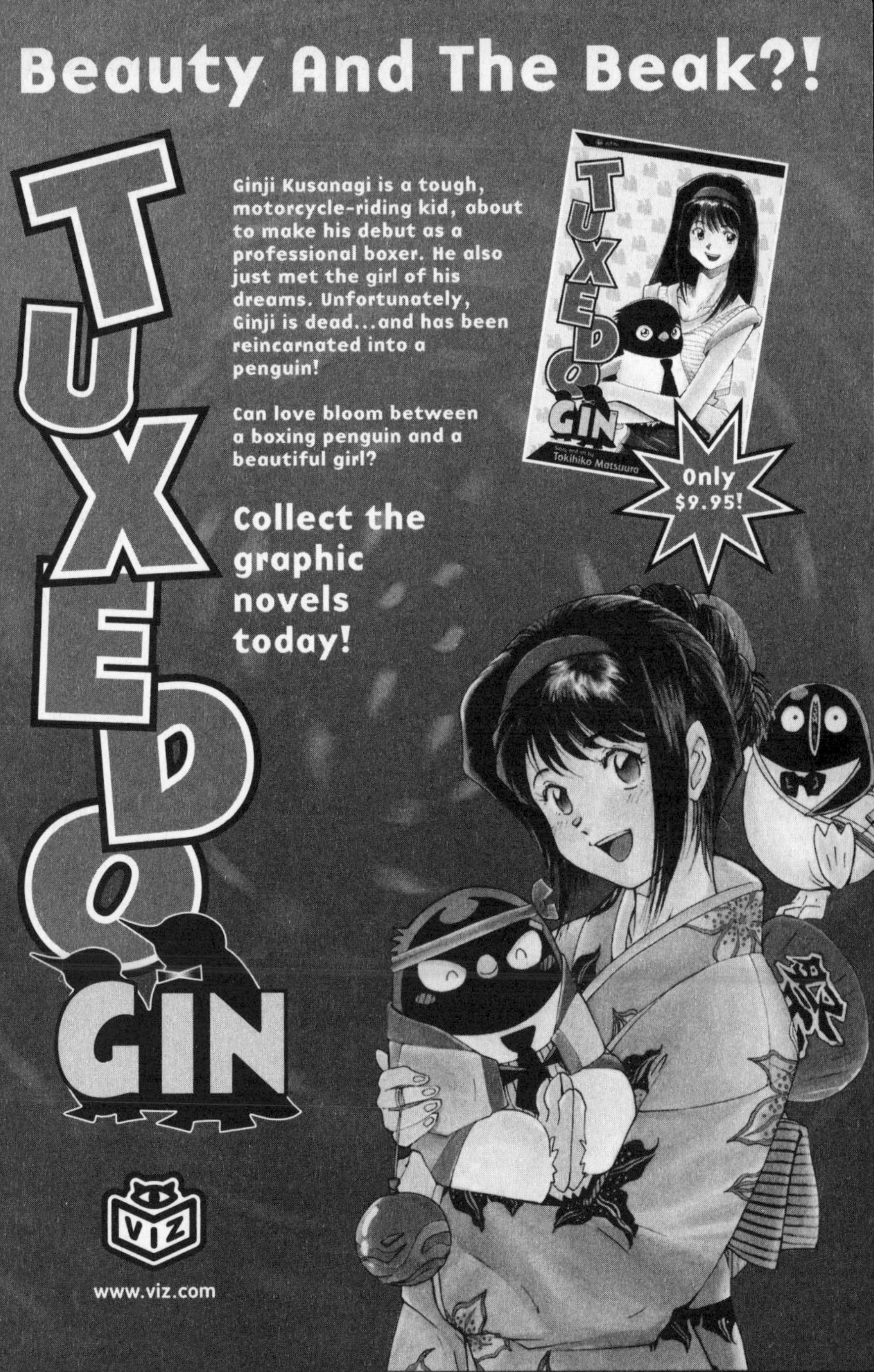
Beauty And The Beak?!
TUXEDO GIN
Ginji Kusanagi is a tough, motorcycle-riding kid, about to make his debut as a professional boxer. He also just met the girl of his dreams. Unfortunately, Ginji is dead...and has been reincarnated into a penguin!
Can love bloom between a boxing penguin and a beautiful girl?
TUXEDO GIN
Tokihiko Matsuura
Only $9.95!
Collect the graphic novels today!
VIZ
www.viz.com

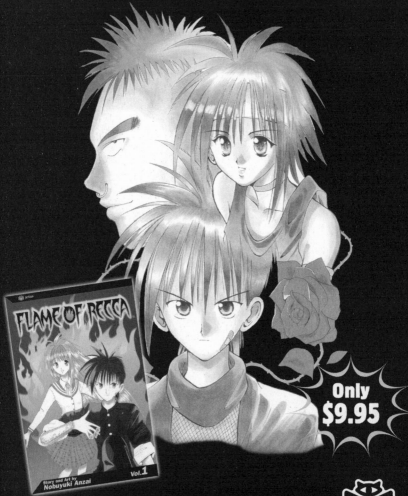

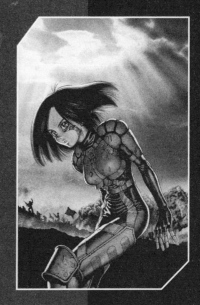
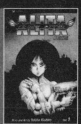

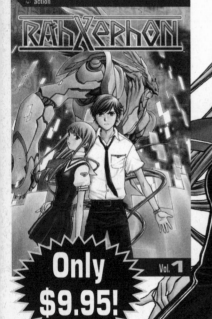

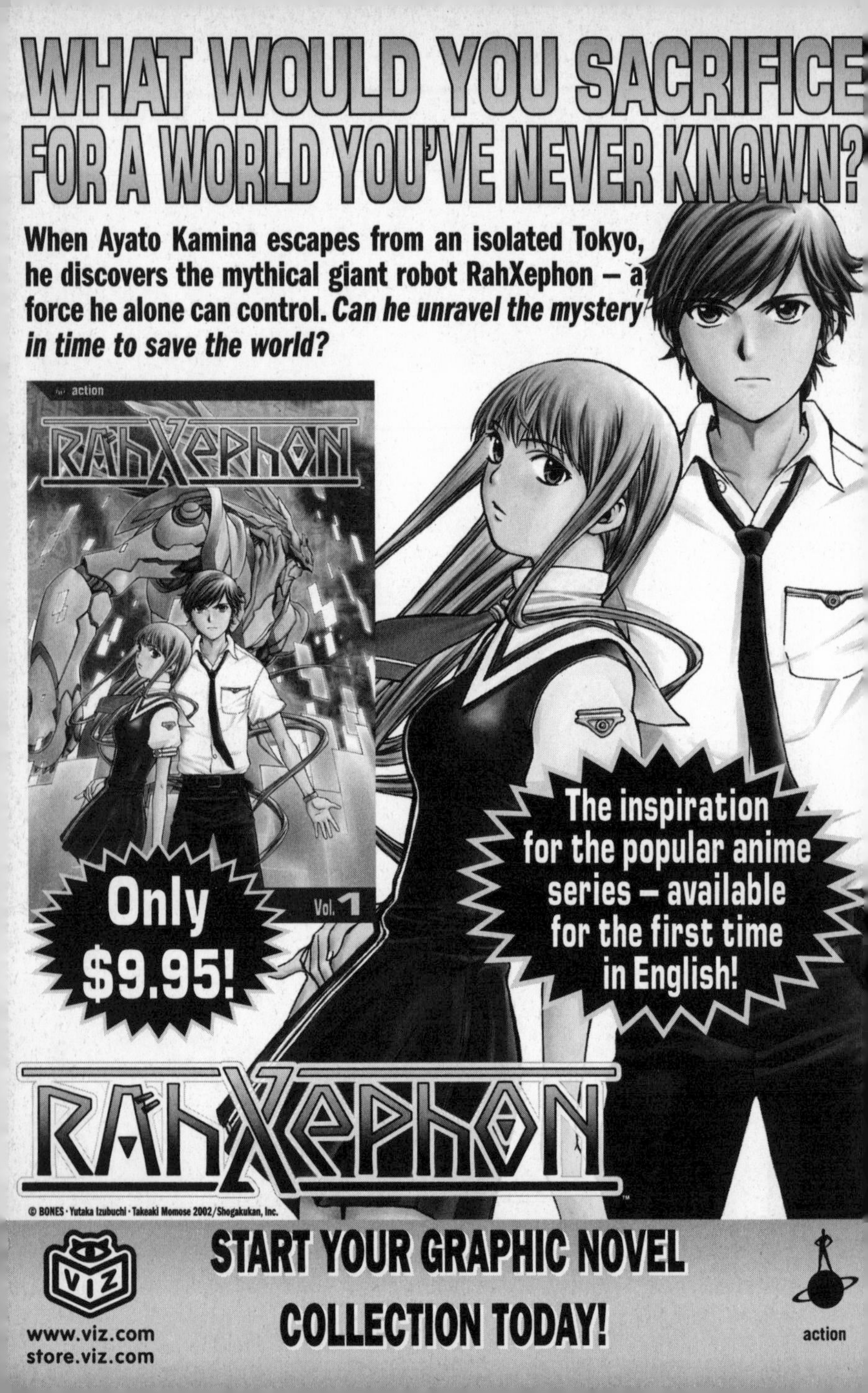

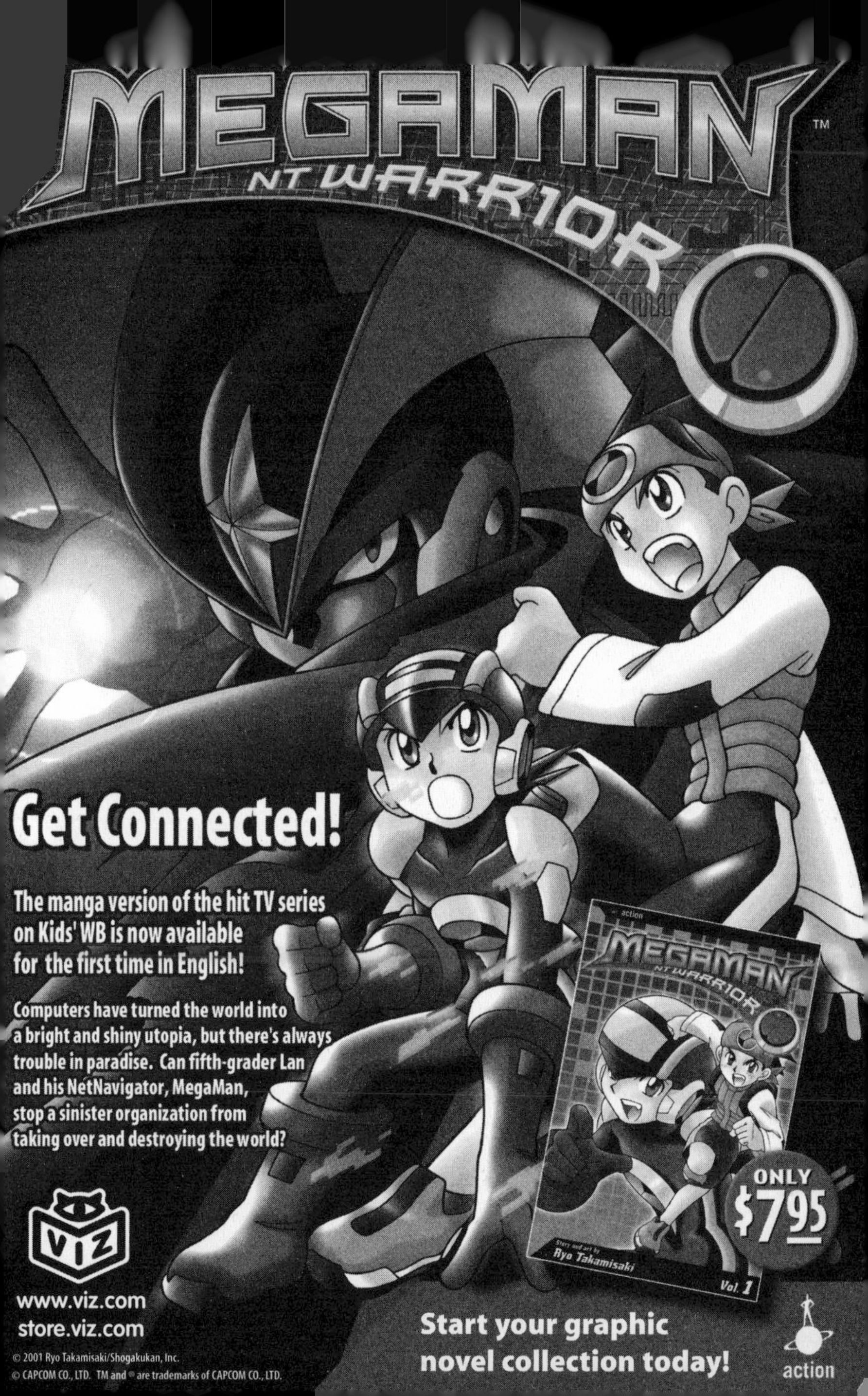
MEGAMAN™
NT WARRIOR
Get Connected!
The manga version of the hit TV series on Kids' WB is now available for the first time in English!
Computers have turned the world into a bright and shiny utopia, but there's always trouble in paradise. Can fifth-grader Lan and his NetNavigator, MegaMan, stop a sinister organization from taking over and destroying the world?
action
MEGAMAN
NT WARRIOR
Story and art by
Ryo Takamisaki
Vol. 1
ONLY
$7.95
VIZ
www.viz.com
store.viz.com
Start your graphic novel collection today!
action
© 2001 Ryo Takamisaki/Shogakukan, Inc.
© CAPCOM CO., LTD. TM and ® are trademarks of CAPCOM CO., LTD.

COMPLETE OUR SURVEY AND LET US KNOW WHAT YOU THINK!

☐ Please do NOT send me information about VIZ products, news and events, special offers, or other information.

☐ Please do NOT send me information from VIZ's trusted business partners.

Name: _____

Address: _____

City: _____ State: _____ Zip: _____

E-mail: _____

☐ Male ☐ Female Date of Birth (mm/dd/yyyy): ___/___/___ (Under 13? Parental consent required)

What race/ethnicity do you consider yourself? (please check one)

☐ Asian/Pacific Islander ☐ Black/African American ☐ Hispanic/Latino

☐ Native American/Alaskan Native ☐ White/Caucasian ☐ Other: _____

What VIZ product did you purchase? (check all that apply and indicate title purchased)

☐ DVD/VHS _____

☐ Graphic Novel _____

☐ Magazines _____

☐ Merchandise _____

Reason for purchase: (check all that apply)

☐ Special offer ☐ Favorite title ☐ Gift

☐ Recommendation ☐ Other_____

Where did you make your purchase? (please check one)

☐ Comic store ☐ Bookstore ☐ Mass/Grocery Store

☐ Newsstand ☐ Video/Video Game Store ☐ Other:_____

☐ Online (site: _____)

What other VIZ properties have you purchased/own? _____

How many anime and/or manga titles have you purchased in the last year? How many were VIZ titles? **(please check one from each column)**

ANIME	MANGA	
☐ None	☐ None	
☐ 1-4	☐ 1-4	
☐ 5-10	☐ 5-10	☐ 5-10
☐ 11+	☐ 11+	☐ 11+

I find the pricing of VIZ products to be: **(please check one)**

☐ Cheap ☐ Reasonable ☐ Expensive

What genre of manga and anime would you like to see from VIZ? **(please check two)**

☐ Adventure ☐ Comic Strip ☐ Science Fiction ☐ Fighting

☐ Horror ☐ Romance ☐ Fantasy ☐ Sports

What do you think of VIZ's new look?

☐ Love It ☐ It's OK ☐ Hate It ☐ Didn't Notice ☐ No Opinion

Which do you prefer? **(please check one)**

☐ Reading right-to-left

☐ Reading left-to-right

Which do you prefer? **(please check one)**

☐ Sound effects in English

☐ Sound effects in Japanese with English captions

☐ Sound effects in Japanese only with a glossary at the back

THANK YOU! Please send the completed form to:

NJW Research
42 Catharine St.
Poughkeepsie, NY 12601

All information provided will be used for internal purposes only. We promise not to sell or otherwise divulge your information.